Hydropolitics in the Third World

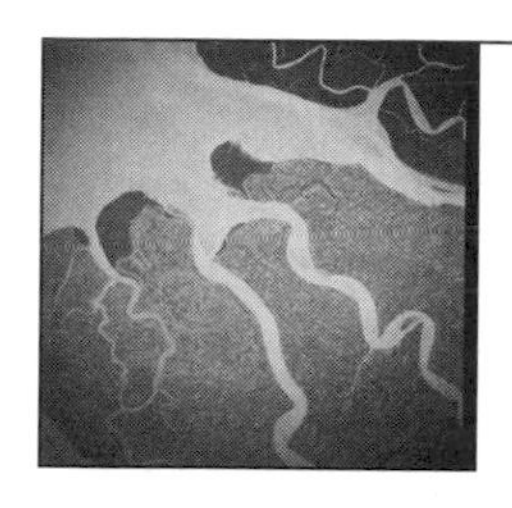

Hydropolitics in the Third World

Conflict and Cooperation in International River Basins

Arun P. Elhance

UNITED STATES INSTITUTE OF PEACE PRESS
Washington, D.C.

The views expressed in this book are those of the author alone. They do not necessarily reflect views of the United States Institute of Peace.

United States Institute of Peace
1200 17th Street NW
Washington, DC 20036

First published 1999

Printed in the United States of America

The paper used in this publication meets the minimum requirements of American National Standards for Information Sciences—Permanence of Paper for Printed Library Materials, ANSI Z39.48-1984.

Library of Congress Cataloging-in-Publication Data
Elhance, Arun P.
Hydropolitics in the Third World : conflict and cooperation in international river basins / Arun P. Elhance.
p. cm.
Includes bibliographical references and index.
ISBN 1-878379-91-7 (hardback). — ISBN 1-878379-90-9 (pbk.)
1. Water resources development. 2. Water resources development—Economic aspects. 3. Water resources development—Government policy—International cooperation. 4. Water-supply—Political aspects. 5. Water rights (International law). I. Title.
HD1691.E43 1999
333.91—dc21 99-30901
CIP

Rivers have a perverse habit of wandering across borders . . . and nation states have a perverse habit of treating whatever portion of them flows within their borders as a national resource at their sovereign disposal.

— *John Waterbury,* Hydropolitics of the Nile Valley *(1979)*

It is space, not time, that hides consequences from us.

— *John Berger,* The Look of Things *(1972)*

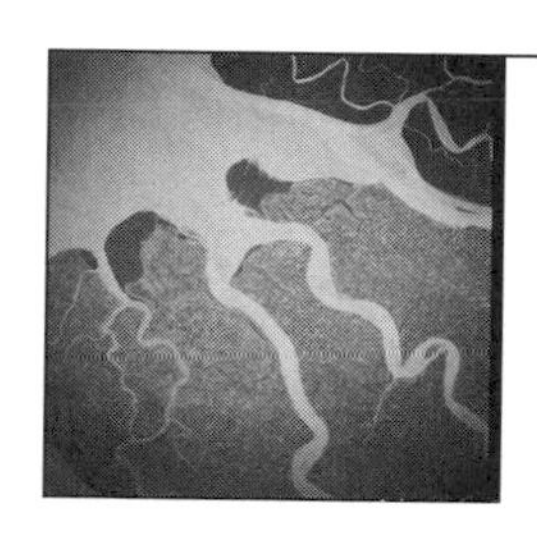

Contents

Maps

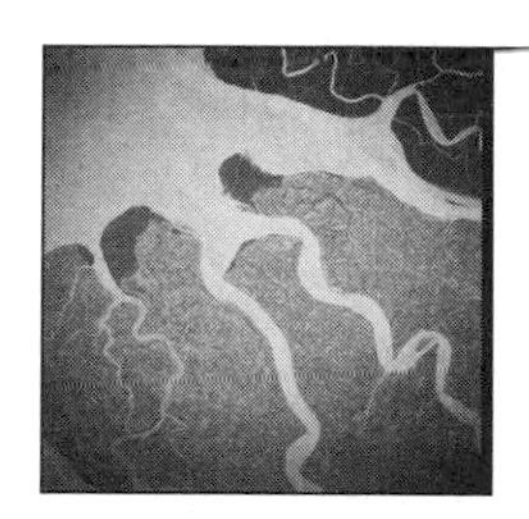

FOREWORD

As nature's fundamental environmental resource, water tends to attract attention—when there's too much of it, or too little. Accustomed as we are in the urbanized Western world to a more or less reliable and plentiful supply, we pay scant regard to the quantity of water available to us. And although water sometimes figures as an important issue in local or regional politics, in the developed world it rarely plays a significant role in international politics.

Such inattention to water is unthinkable in large parts of the world. Especially in many developing countries, obtaining a safe and sufficient supply of water is a daily necessity for vast numbers of people and an abiding ambition for their governments. Sufficiency of supply is, moreover, a growing concern, for as the size of populations increases and the pace of industrialization quickens in the developing world, so the demand for freshwater intensifies and the already scare supplies become all the more valuable. Acutely conscious of the manifold dangers that water shortages pose to their countries and peoples, governments jealously guard their existing freshwater supplies while trying to find new sources to exploit.

Like governments everywhere, the first instinct of Third World governments is to act unilaterally: to decide for themselves how, when, and where they will exploit their freshwater resources. But, as *Hydropolitics in the Third World* makes abundantly clear, unilateralism and water don't mix—especially when "most remaining major exploitable sources of freshwater are now in river basins that are shared by two or more sovereign states."

Foreword

International river basins cover between 60 and 65 percent of the continents of Asia, Africa, and South America. Africa alone has more than fifty basins that are shared by two or more states. Consequently, when a developing country looks to alleviate its present or prospective water shortages by making more or better use of the water in its rivers, the chances are that those rivers also pass through a number of other countries. And those countries will almost certainly be concerned about actions by an upstream riparian neighbor that reduce the quantity or quality of the water in the shared rivers.

Thus, according to many observers, the stage is set in the Third World for impending "water wars"—for violent conflicts driven by the search for secure and sufficient supplies of freshwater. Some commentators, indeed, go so far as to suggest that such conflicts have already occurred, as in the case of Israel's wars with its neighbors, or tensions between Turkey and Syria. There is no doubt that water figures prominently as a strategic concern for virtually all the states of the Middle East, and that long-term peace in the region will remain a chimera until agreement has been reached on the allocation of its scarce water resources.

Predicting the political consequences of environmental changes—for example, global warming—or of changing demands on the environment—as in the case of water resources—is an activity that seems to invite alarmism. It is not uncommon for worst-case scenarios to be presented as though they were most-likely scenarios, with the paradoxical result that interest in the problem tends to quickly dissipate as publics and politicians soon weary of predictions of imminent catastrophes that fail to materialize. One of the great virtues of *Hydropolitics in the Third World* is that it avoids alarmism in favor of a balanced, thoughtful consideration of the risks of hydropolitical conflicts escalating into violence. That said, Arun Elhance certainly does not make light of the dangers. The conclusion to this book—drawing on case studies of the Párana–La Plata, Nile, Jordan, Eurphrates-Tigris, Ganges-Brahmaputra-Barak, and Mekong basins—lays out a daunting array of "grounds for despair," reasons why acute conflict may occur.

Yet Elhance does not exaggerate the dangers. And the conclusion also presents a set of "reasons for hope"—a number of factors that can justly inspire hydropolitical optimism. Among these is perhaps this study's most remarkable, and certainly its most encouraging, finding: "Although sovereign states are inherently inclined to exploit 'their' water resources unilaterally, in the end even the strongest riparian states sharing international basins are compelled to seek some form of cooperation with their weaker neighbors." Sooner or later, argues Elhance, the inescapable interdependencies among riparian states and the costs of noncooperation make cooperation inevitable. The shortcomings of unilateral action spur bilateral cooperation, which then tends to expand into multilateral efforts to make more productive and equitable use of the waters of shared rivers.

This embrace of multilateralism is by no means the end of the story, however. Numerous political, geographic, technical, and other obstacles must be overcome if a readiness to cooperate is actually to yield positive, tangible rewards. Here, the author notes, is where third parties can play critical roles, applying political pressure and supplying economic and technical support to help developing countries cooperate effectively. One of the stated aims of this book is to help in this process by enabling the international community to gain a more sophisticated understanding of the highly complex field of hydropolitics. It is an aim that, by dint of the breadth, depth, and even-handedness of the author's study, he has plainly achieved.

Arun Elhance was a fellow in the Jennings Randolph Program at the United States Institute of Peace in 1991–92, and his concern to provide a balanced perspective, reliable information, and analyses that are stimulating for scholars and useful for policymakers harmonizes perfectly with the broad aims of the Institute. In funding and publishing the results of research into the sources of international conflicts and the means by which they may be peacefully managed or resolved, the Institute seeks to help equip the academic and policymaking communities, and the interested public, with the informational and analytical tools with which to construct a more peaceful world. With its emphasis on geography and natural resources, *Hydropolitics in the Third World* adds a new facet to the Institute's published works, along with a variety of other projects examining the relationship between environmental issues and conflict management supported by our Grant Program.

One hopes that the "guarded optimism" for hydropolitical cooperation with which the author concludes this book is well placed. To facilitate such a future, the Institute will continue to support and disseminate wide-ranging, balanced, and policy-relevant research into the possibilities for international cooperation—hydropolitical and otherwise—to overcome the dangers of violent conflict.

Richard H. Solomon, President
United States Institute of Peace

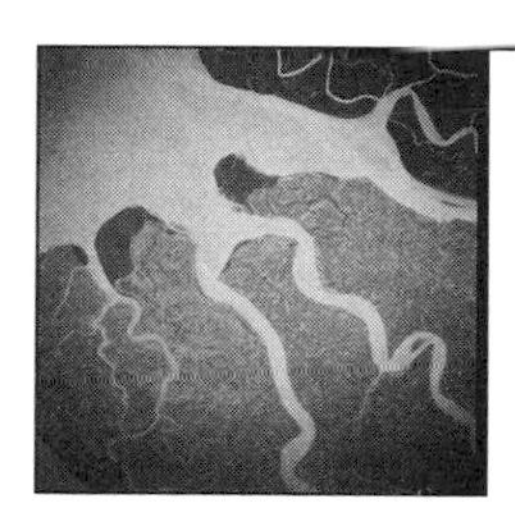

Preface

Hydropolitics in international river basins is a very complex, multidimensional, and multidisciplinary subject. If the international community is to help prevent the emergence of acute conflicts among the states and peoples sharing transboundary water resources, it needs to acquire a much more sophisticated understanding of hydropolitics. I hope that this book will help to enhance such understanding. The book reflects a growing conviction that the attainment of sustainable economic development, environmental well-being, human security, and human rights in large parts of the world is not possible without cooperation among states and peoples that share major river basins.

I am grateful to the United States Institute of Peace for the award of a 1991–92 Jennings Randolph Peace Fellowship. The fellowship enabled me to spend a year at the Institute, away from the academic environment but in the company of some of the most distinguished international scholars and thinkers. I am very fortunate to have had the opportunity to interact with and learn from the Distinguished Fellows and Peace Fellows who were at the Institute during the tenure of my fellowship. In alphabetical order they are Muhammad Faour, Alexander George, David Little, Don Peretz, Indar Jit Rikhye, Walt Rostow, Robert Rothstein, Shimon Shamir, and Louis Sohn. I am thankful for their critical but highly constructive observations and comments.

In writing this book I have relied heavily on the works of numerous scholars and journalists. The notes to this book indicate my indebtedness; however, there may be occasions on which I have not fully referenced works on which I have drawn, and in these instances I wish to apologize to the authors involved for my oversight. In a very real sense, this book is a collective endeavor.

The project could not have been completed without the oversight and encouragement of several individuals associated with the Institute; in particular, I would like to thank Ambassador Samuel Lewis, Charles Nelson, Michael Lund, Joseph Klaits, Barbara Cullicott, David Smock, Otto Koester, Scott Thompson, and Hrach Gregorian. The book would not have seen the light of day without the editorial guidance and support of Nigel Quinney and Dan Snodderly, who have seen me through many dark patches. Research assistance provided by Tim McInnis during the fellowship was invaluable. I hope that the library and administrative staff at the Institute, whom I do not mention individually, will also recognize the contributions that they have made to this endeavor. I am indebted to my wife, Yunae Yi, for her unwavering faith and patience, and to my son, Ajit Yi Elhance, for his delightful companionship. The book is dedicated to my parents, Sri Gyan Prakash and Shrimati Malati Devi, and to the memory of my uncle, Professor D. N. Elhance.

Hydropolitics in the Third World

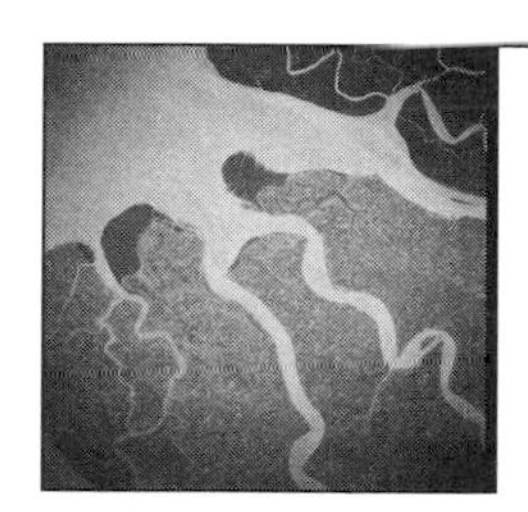

Introduction

Nature does not respect national borders; human beings seem incapable of managing their affairs without them. Nature has also not endowed every place or nation on earth with the same type and amount of resources. Herein lie the roots of likely interstate conflict and cooperation over essential and scarce natural resources. Hydropolitics is the systematic study of conflict and cooperation between states over water resources that transcend international borders.

This book focuses on hydropolitics in river basins that are shared by two or more sovereign states in the so-called Third World.[1] This thematic and spatial focus reflects two crucial facts: scarcity of freshwater for multiple societal needs is rapidly escalating in many parts of the Third World, and most remaining major exploitable sources of freshwater are now in river basins that are shared by two or more sovereign states.[2] If these states are not willing or able to develop and use their common water resources in a cooperative, sustainable, and equitable manner, the potential for acute (violent) conflict over water in the Third World will keep growing.

Water is first and foremost an essential biological need. Without an adequate input of potable water, the human body cannot survive or grow. Large amounts of water are also needed for personal hygiene, sanitation, and other household activities, including cooking, cleaning, and laundry. Furthermore, huge quantities of freshwater are needed for agriculture, fisheries, mining, industrial production, generation of electricity, riverine navigation, maintenance of ecological assets and biodiversity, promotion of tourism, and many other societal demands. This multiple-use potential of freshwater, especially transboundary water resources, combined with the certainty of growing water scarcities in many arid and semiarid regions of the Third World, makes hydropolitics between riparian states that share international river basins one of the most urgent, complex, and contentious issues that the developing countries and the international community will have to face and resolve in the next century.

Water scarcity—understood here as a lack of secure, uninterrupted, and long-term availability of adequate amounts of freshwater, of required quality, on a regular basis, and for multiple needs—has already reached alarming proportions and is fast accelerating in many arid and semiarid regions of the Third World.[3] High population growth rates, accompanied by urbanization, industrialization, agricultural development, and environmental degradation, are greatly intensifying pressures on the scarce and degraded domestic freshwater resources in many developing countries. As the demand for water increases and the currently available water supplies are exhausted, pressures on the transboundary water resources are multiplying.[4]

By itself, the unequal distribution or scarcity of natural resources does not necessarily lead to acute interstate conflict, because human beings have historically shown an ingenious capability to survive by adjusting their lifestyles to even the most resource-deficient environments on earth, and by engaging in trade in scarce resources as well as commodities produced from such resources. It is when severe scarcities of an *essential, nonsubstitutable, and shared resource*, such as freshwater, are experienced or anticipated by one or more states, or when such a resource is rightly or wrongly perceived as being overexploited or degraded by others at a cost to oneself, that states may become prone to conflict. Even in the absence of debilitating scarcities, conflict among states may arise from the belligerent, resource-expansionist claims of one or more states.[5] Interstate conflict may also arise from the established, but increasingly challenged, notion of "national sovereignty," which has traditionally been understood as bestowing inalienable and exclusive rights of ownership and use over all natural resources contained within or flowing through a state's territory.

More than two hundred river basins in the world are currently shared by two or more sovereign states.[6] Of these, fifty-seven are in Africa, thirty-five each in North and South America, forty in Asia, and forty-eight in Europe. All together, these basins cover about 47 percent of the total landmass on earth, including 65 percent of continental Asia, 60 percent of Africa, and 60 percent of South America. The entire territory of some developing countries, such as Paraguay in South America and Uganda in Africa, is covered by international river basins. If, as has happened in Eastern Europe and the erstwhile Soviet Union, some of the existing states in Africa and Asia break up into smaller states in the future, the number of international river basins and the sovereign states sharing them will also increase. What is also important for this study is that although more than three hundred treaties have been signed worldwide by states to deal with specific concerns about international water resources and more than three thousand treaties have provisions relating to water, coordinated and integrated management of international river basins is still extremely rare. This is especially so for almost all international basins in the Third World.[7]

Within a recently accumulating body of literature, broadly grouped under the title "environmental changes and acute conflict,"[8] some scholars have identified growing scarcity of freshwater as one of the primary causes of impending interstate conflict.[9] The potential for conflict over water is predicted to be specially high in the arid and semiarid regions of the Third World, where rapidly growing water needs of individuals and societies are expected to put increasing pressures on the already scarce, overexploited, and degraded freshwater supplies.[10] Others have warned that growing pressures on scarce domestic water supplies, combined with the fact that most remaining exploitable freshwater resources in the Third World are now in international basins, are bound to accentuate the potential for acute interstate conflict.[11] Some scholars assert that, in a geopolitical sense, water is likely to become the "oil of the next century."[12]

Some ongoing and anticipated global environmental changes may further accentuate the potential for interstate conflict over water. For example, a rise of only a few feet in the sea level from global warming would ruin the inland water supplies in many low-lying developing countries, such as Egypt and Bangladesh, which already depend heavily on freshwater supplies originating outside their borders.[13] Millions of "environmental refugees," forced out of their habitats by water scarcity and other environmental disasters are expected to crisscross international borders in parts of Africa and Asia. Consequently, the territorial integrity and the stability of many states are likely to come under severe strain.[14] At the very least, many developing countries may soon find water scarcity to be the most severe constraint for economic development and societal well-being.[15] Thus, the literature on environmental changes and acute conflict suggests that, if not through outright wars between states then certainly through great domestic upheaval, the growing scarcity of freshwater is likely to lead to large-scale dislocation and violence in the Third World.[16]

What is often not recognized is that many so-called ethnic conflicts and separatist movements currently raging in the Third World are already closely tied to water resources, and some are bound to further intensify the potential for acute interstate conflict. For example, the movements for independence and separatism launched by Palestinians, Kurds, and Kashmiris in the Middle (Near) East and South Asia, if successful, may some day create new states on the headwaters of some large rivers and aquifers that are already shared by two or more hostile states. The new states will very likely claim sovereignty over the waters flowing through or lying underneath their territories, in the process further complicating the already contentious hydropolitics in several international basins.[17]

However, despite this gloomy prognosis, there is nothing inevitable about water scarcity necessarily leading to acute conflict in the Third World. There are many intervening variables—geographic, political, economic, cultural, and so forth—that mediate any resource scarcity–acute conflict relationship. As we shall see in the case studies presented in the following chapters, the hydrology and the geography of an international river basin tie all the riparian states sharing it into a highly complex web of economic, political, environmental, and security interdependencies, leaving them no choice but to interact with one another indefinitely. These interdependencies grow with time as the demand for water for multiple needs grows in all the riparian states. Although states are inherently inclined to unilaterally exploit the rivers flowing across or along their borders, the hydrologically induced interdependencies in international basins gradually compel states to entertain at least the possibility of cooperation with their neighbors. An important fact to remember about the behavior of states in the "anarchic" international system is that, despite all the nationalistic posturing and confrontational rhetoric, even states otherwise openly hostile to each other do often cooperate in many overt and covert ways on a variety of issues and problems of mutual concern;[18] hydropolitics has historically not been immune to this aspect of international relations.[19]

Thus it may be that an awareness of growing water scarcity and of the prospects for large-scale violence if conflicts over water are not resolved may impel Third World states to seek collective solutions for the water-related problems they currently face and are likely to face in the future. The hope is that in the arena of hydropolitics, at least, interstate cooperation rather than conflict will become the norm in the Third World. However, cooperation between states that share international basins is never easy to achieve, especially when such cooperation challenges some core concerns of the states such as sovereignty, territorial integrity, and security. There are other political, economic, technical, and strategic impediments that can also stand in the way of interstate cooperation in specific basins, as we will see.

What the case studies also will show is that sustained international initiatives and support are often needed to overcome the many barriers to interstate cooperation in hydropolitics and to persuade and enable the respective riparian states to see cooperation as a "win-win" situation for all concerned. Consequently, as water scarcity for multiple needs grows in the Third World, more and more international efforts will be required to bring about peaceful resolution of conflicts over transboundary water resources and to help forge interstate cooperation for the development and sharing of their full multiple-use potential. It should be obvious that such efforts will need to be informed by systematic knowledge about the factors, circumstances, and strategies that can help to overcome the many barriers to interstate cooperation. Such knowledge can be best developed by undertaking systematic and comparative case studies of hydropolitics in a select set of international basins in the Third World. Based on the specific and generalizable findings from such case studies, a whole host of complicated policy-related questions will need to be addressed, including: How can sovereign states, pursuing their national self-interest, be persuaded to cooperate for the development and sharing of transboundary water resources? What global, regional, and domestic conditions and factors enhance or frustrate the possibility of interstate cooperation for the collective ownership and use of transboundary water resources? What role can actors and agencies from outside the region play in facilitating and sustaining basinwide cooperation? How can domestic and international nongovernmental organizations (NGOs), "epistemic communities,"[20] and professional networks facilitate such cooperation? What kind of cooperative "regimes" can be designed to ensure long-term and sustainable cooperation in the international basins?[21]

These are some of the questions and issues this comparative study of hydropolitics in the post–World War II era, in six major international river basins—the Paraná–La Plata, Nile, Jordan, Euphrates-Tigris, Ganges-Brahmaputra-Barak, and Mekong basins—addresses from a geography-centered yet multidisciplinary and policy-oriented perspective.[22] The hope is that the specific and generalizable findings from a systematic analysis of hydropolitics in these basins will inform local, national, regional, and international efforts to ensure that the full potential of transboundary water resources in all the international basins in the Third World is developed and used in a cooperative, sustainable, and equitable manner for the benefit of all concerned.

WATER SCARCITY IN THE THIRD WORLD

Unlike oil, which is a finite and nonrenewable resource, water is a finite but renewable resource.[23] The total amount of water in the earth's ecosphere has remained the same over millennia, despite all the transformations and recycling it has gone through. This amount is estimated to be about 1.4 billion cubic kilometers;[24] the generally accepted figure for the average annual freshwater requirements of a human being is a mere 1,000 cubic meters—the so-called water barrier.[25] Thus, if all the water in the earth's ecosphere were freshwater, and if it were available for human use in its entirety and in an equitable manner, there would be no problem of water scarcity on earth for a long time to come. However, about 95 to 97 percent of the total volume of water on earth is in the oceans. "Of the remaining, about 77 percent is stored in ice caps and glaciers, 22.4 percent is in groundwater and soil moisture, and 0.35 percent is in lakes and marshes. Allowing for 0.04 percent in the atmosphere, there is a bare 0.01 percent of the world's freshwater supplies in streams."[26] In particular, although they currently provide human beings about 80 percent of their freshwater needs, rivers carry a mere 0.000003 percent of all the water on the planet.

Although minuscule in comparison to the saline ocean waters, the world's renewable freshwater supplies are still capable of supporting a much larger population than exists today.[27] The problem is that whereas some states and peoples in the world enjoy and even suffer from time to time from water surpluses, for a large portion of the world's population, especially in the Third World, serious water shortages have become an everyday fact of life.

Some eighty countries, supporting 40 percent of the world's population, currently suffer from serious freshwater shortages for personal and household needs. As many as 1.2 billion people, mostly in the Third World, are suffering physically from shortages of potable water and 1.8 billion people lack adequate water for sanitation. About 80 percent of all illnesses and 30 percent of all unnatural deaths in the Third World are due to waterborne diseases and consumption of highly polluted water.[28] By the year 2025, thirty-seven countries are likely to be without enough water for household and agricultural needs, let alone water for industries, energy production, navigation, recreation, and other societal needs.[29]

The worst affected by water scarcities are often the poorest strata of society. In the rural areas of many developing countries, scarce water supplies are usually monopolized by the ruling elites. Access to water resources is often limited to a select few by a whole host of historical, political, economic, and sociocultural "entitlements."[30] Women and children in the poor rural families often suffer the most since typically they are responsible for fetching water, in some cases from sources as far away as two or three hours of walking time. This activity can burn off up to 600 calories per day, about one-third of their average daily food intake.[31] Even then the available water may not be usable without extensive treatment. In addition, many contaminated sources carry waterborne diseases that, if not treated adequately and in time, lead to very high mortality and morbidity rates among the poor. The water resources of the rural poor are also often the worst affected by floods, droughts, and other natural calamities, such as earthquakes and cyclones. The "urban biases" inherent in most developing countries' economic development programs also lead to a severe deprivation of basic needs, including water, among the rural poor.[32] Even in the urban areas, scarce water of potable quality is likely to be provided disproportionately to the upper strata of society. Either the urban poor have to buy water of questionable quality from private vendors, at prices estimated to be four to one hundred times higher than piped city water, or they have to make do with free but highly contaminated water from other sources.[33]

Estimates prepared by the World Bank in 1980 showed that a complete coverage of rural and urban populations in the Third World, with varying levels of service for just household water needs, would require an investment of at least $82.2 million (1978 dollars) *per day* for at least ten years.[34] More recent estimates show a need for an investment of $600 to $700 billion over the course of a decade for irrigation, hydropower, and water supply and sanitation.[35] Already, about $10 billion per year is invested by the developing countries in water and sanitation systems.[36] But most developing countries are currently heavily in debt and likely to remain so for the foreseeable future.[37] As their populations continue to rise, more and more water-related investment will be needed just to maintain even the currently dismal standard of living and quality of life for hundreds of millions of people in the developing countries. Whether the international community will be able or willing to make the needed financial resources available to such countries remains highly doubtful.

Agriculture is still the primary economic activity for a very large portion of the growing populations in many developing countries; in some countries, as much as 85 percent of the population derives sustenance from agriculture and related activities. Overall, the agriculture sector currently accounts for about 80 percent of all water consumption. The Food and Agriculture Organization (FAO) has estimated that for the Third World to simply maintain its presently inadequate food supply will require the extension of irrigation to an additional 22 million hectares (54 million acres) of farmland and delivery of an additional 440 billion cubic meters of freshwater by the year 2000.[38] This is because modern agriculture has become increasingly dependent on higher and higher inputs of water, as demonstrated by the so-called green revolution in India and some other developing countries. Urban encroachment on productive farmlands and the growing need to open up more and more marginal lands to irrigated agriculture will further intensify pressures on the available water supplies in the Third World.

In some developing countries, a large portion of the population relies heavily on freshwater marine catch as a major source of protein. As ecosystems, freshwater marine environments tend to be very fragile and vulnerable to human activities as well as to nature's vagaries. Degradation or contamination of these ecosystems can have devastating consequences for the health and well-being of millions of people. Survival of all domesticated livestock and wild animal species on which millions in the developing world rely for sustenance depends largely on the availability of adequate and uncontaminated freshwater supplies. Moreover, biodiversity in the Third World—a great concern of international environmentalists recently—cannot be maintained without preserving the Third World's dwindling and deteriorating freshwater sources.[39]

The success of many ongoing economic development programs in the arid and semiarid regions of the Third World is also contingent upon the availability of adequate amounts of water for industries and other economic activities. Every form of commercial energy production, whether petroleum based, thermal, nuclear, or hydroelectric, also requires huge quantities of water. The water intensities of some industrial products are shown in table I.1.

Many developing countries are still at the preindustrial stage or the beginning stages of industrialization. As table I.1 shows, they are likely to face severe water constraints as they attempt to industrialize and modernize their economies. It is very likely that growing water scarcities will actually lead to substantial deterioration and, perhaps, the demise of many existing and nebulous industries in some countries.

Table I.1. Water Intensities of Selected Industrial Products[40]

Quantity and product	Quantity of water consumed
1 liter of petroleum	10 liters of water
1 can of vegetables	40 liters of water
1 kilogram of paper	100 liters of water
1 ton of woolen cloth	600 liters of water
1 ton of dry cement	4,500 liters of water
1 ton of steel	20,000 liters of water
1 ton of dacron	4,200 cubic meters (140,000 cubic feet) of water
1 ton of rayon	2,000 cubic meters (70,000 cubic feet) of water
1 ton of kapron fiber	5,600 cubic meters (200,000 cubic feet) of water

What is also often not recognized is that international tourism, including the rapidly growing business of "eco-tourism," now plays a very important role in the local and national economies of many developing countries. Not only does this sector generate substantial income and employment for a sizable portion of the population in some countries, but it also generates substantial tax revenues for the cash-starved local and national governments.[41] Tourism is also now one of the main sources of foreign investment and foreign exchange earnings for many developing countries. Clearly, international tourism cannot be initiated or sustained either in the short or long run by any country without adequate and assured supplies of freshwater for drinking and sanitation, for maintaining the nation's ecological assets and biodiversity, and for satisfying other recreational needs of the tourists.

Historically, rivers have provided humankind one of the most cost-effective and ecologically sound means of transporting people and goods. Inland riverine navigation is especially important for many developing countries that lack other forms of transportation infrastructure, such as roads and railways, and/or face severe scarcities of energy to operate the transportation systems. For some landlocked countries, riverine navigation may be their only means of conducting international trade. Water deficits in navigable rivers can seriously impact the economies and well-being of landlocked countries by paralyzing their transportation arteries.

To make matters worse, the more easily accessible water resources in many Third World regions are already being overexploited. At the same time, the cost of discovering new supplies and constructing large water projects is fast escalating. According to an international water expert, Asit

K. Biswas, "Many countries do not have any major additional sources of water to develop economically," and "even for those countries that may have additional sources of water, time periods required to implement water projects are likely to be much longer than expected at present."[42] Typically, even under the best of circumstances—that is, when the needed interstate cooperation, financial resources, and technical expertise are all in place—large water projects such as dams and irrigation systems take fifteen to twenty years to develop and implement.

Many developing countries worst affected by water scarcities currently lack the financial, technical, material, organizational, and human resources to unilaterally design and implement large water projects. Without substantial external aid and technical/managerial expertise, it will be very difficult for these countries to maintain even their few existing water projects. At the same time, the developed countries and international organizations that can provide such assistance have become very reluctant to support large water-related projects, especially those that may create environmental problems and may, consequently, encounter opposition from the growing and increasingly more powerful domestic and international environmental movements and lobbies. The international donors and creditors have also become reluctant to invest in water projects in those international river basins where interstate conflict over the shared water resources have not been resolved.

Clearly, there is an urgent need for concerted efforts at all levels—local, national, regional, and global—to enable and support the Third World states sharing international basins in cooperatively developing the full potential of their common water resources. This need for interstate cooperation is mandated also by the hydrologically induced interdependencies in international river basins.

HYDROLOGICAL INTERDEPENDENCE

Hydrological cycles—linking the stocks and flows of water in the atmosphere, on the surface of the earth, and below the ground—are primary examples of natural phenomena and processes that transcend national borders. Rivers, in particular, are indifferent to the national borders that run across or along their banks; some rivers have the habit of meandering from their established courses, violating and distorting international borders in the process. Underground aquifers and other water bodies, such as marshes and lakes, also often transgress national borders and territories. Thus, transboundary water resources, especially rivers, raise three major concerns for the riparian states—sovereignty, territorial integrity, and national security.

The hydrology of an international river basin also links all the riparian states sharing it in a complex network of environmental, economic, political, and security interdependencies, in the process creating the potential for interstate conflict as well as opportunities for cooperation among the neighbors. This is because any unilateral action by one riparian state that may affect the quantity and/or quality of water flowing down a shared river can have serious consequences in some or all of the other riparian states. Withdrawal of water for household and agricultural needs, cutting of forests, construction of large hydroelectric and irrigation projects, use of chemical fertilizers and insecticides in agriculture to enhance productivity, overexploitation of marine life, and discharges of toxic industrial wastes into the shared water bodies are but a few of the ways one riparian state can alter the quantity and quality of water available to other riparian states. Thus, states sharing a river basin naturally form a highly interdependent unit, whose economic, political, and security dynamics are intimately tied to hydropolitics, especially in a situation of growing water scarcity.[43]

Periodic floods and droughts already play havoc with the political, socioeconomic, and environmental stability of several Third World countries sharing international basins, one of the most dramatic examples being Bangladesh in South Asia.[44] In some cases, these problems can be best addressed by constructing large dams and reservoirs on the headwaters of the shared rivers. The stored floodwaters can then be released downstream during droughts.[45] Many developing countries also suffer from severe shortages of electricity for household, agricultural, and industrial needs. In some basins, hydroelectric power plants built on the shared rivers can provide a substantial portion of these needs as well as help prevent severe deforestation for fuelwood. However, because of hydrological interdependencies, such projects necessarily require cooperation among some or all of the riparian states in an international basin.

Historically, rivers had provided the means for the colonization of hinterlands in Africa, Asia, and Latin America by the European powers. The navigational needs of the competing colonizers had often led to wars over navigational rights on many rivers in these continents.[46] Today, for many developing countries, especially those lacking adequate surface transportation infrastructure and/or facing huge energy costs for the transportation of people and goods, river navigation is becoming increasingly important. For some landlocked countries, such as Bolivia, Laos, Nepal, and

Paraguay, unrestricted navigational access to the sea for bringing in essential supplies and for conducting international trade has become a matter of economic viability and survival. These growing needs for unrestricted freedom of navigation on the shared rivers both reflect and create hydrologically induced interdependencies among the riparian states.

Unfortunately, a recognition of the hydrological interdependence of states sharing a river basin, of the growing water scarcities for multiple societal needs, and of the urgent need for interstate cooperation does not guarantee that such cooperation can be easily arrived at, implemented, or sustained, even when it can be shown to be in the best interests of all the parties concerned.[47] There are many political, economic, strategic, and technical impediments to interstate cooperation in the arena of hydropolitics, as we shall see in the case studies. But the case studies will also show that growing scarcities of freshwater for multiple needs create the imperatives for cooperation among the riparian states that share international river basins.

STUDY PERSPECTIVE AND ORGANIZATION

The analysis of hydropolitics in this book is based on a state-centric view; that is, riparian states are seen here as the main actors who engage in hydropolitics in international river basins. Whatever their specific nature and constituents, these entities are ultimately responsible for engaging in conflict or cooperation with other riparian states, and for entering into negotiations and agreements for the control and sharing of transboundary water resources. While both impelled and constrained by a myriad of domestic and external factors and circumstances, the riparian states in an international river basin also have the primary responsibility for developing and maintaining domestic support for both conflict and cooperation with other riparian states. In the arena of hydropolitics, international organizations and nonbasin states also interact primarily with the riparian states. This is not to imply that individuals, political parties, domestic and international NGOs, epistemic communities, and other stakeholders do not exercise considerable influence on the stands taken and strategies adopted by different riparian states, or that a consensus has always or necessarily to exist on water-related issues among the different organs and agencies of a state, as the case studies will demonstrate.

In our view, equitable sharing of the waters of international river basins to fulfill multiple societal needs is one of the most complex issues that many Third World countries and the international community will have to resolve in the next century. Consequently, in each case study we will examine the role played in hydropolitics by geography and hydrology; the riparian structure of the basin; international and domestic politics; the history of interstate relations; the power resources of the riparian states; the personal authority and political clout of national leaders; the nature and timing of changes in regimes; the severity of the needs for water for multiple uses; the role of NGOs and regional and international organizations; and the successes and failures of attempts at developing bilateral and multilateral agreements relating to the transboundary water resources.

A substantial body of literature is now available that documents and analyzes different aspects of interstate conflict and cooperation over transboundary water resources in international basins. Several comprehensive case studies on hydropolitics in specific international river basins have also been written.[48] Although this study makes use of many theoretical and empirical insights developed in the available literature, it is distinguished by its comparative approach, by its balanced perspective between "water wars" doomsaying and starry-eyed optimism about international cooperation, and by its emphasis on the central role that geography—broadly defined here as the physical, economic, and political geography of states and peoples—plays in defining or circumscribing hydropolitics in international river basins.[49]

Geography and Hydropolitics

The physical geography of a river basin comprises its morphology, hydrology, climatology, and ecology, which together determine the physical parameters of its catchment and drainage area; the periodicity, amount, and rate of flow of precipitation, sedimentation, nutrients, and pollution along the channels; and the rates of water evaporation aboveground and seepage underground. These parameters, in turn, define the spatio-temporal aspects (the where and the when) of water availability in the basin as well as the potential uses of water for household needs, agriculture, industry, hydroelectricity generation, navigation, recreation, and so forth in the riparian states. Consequently, the physical geography of a basin defines the possibility for where, how, and when the multiple-use potential of its waters can be developed and utilized by which of the riparian states. To a large extent, the physical geography also determines the nature and degree of dependence of each riparian state on the shared waters as well as the urgency of its need for cooperation with other riparian states. The fact that many of the physical parameters of a shared basin can be substantially altered by intentional or unintentional human activity sets the stage for both conflict and cooperation among hydrologically interdependent riparian states.

Whereas the riparian structure of a basin—that is, which state is the uppermost, middle, or lowermost riparian, and which state is co-riparian with which other state—is determined primarily by the way international borders have been demarcated in the basin, physical geography plays a substantial role in defining the relative bargaining powers of the riparian states in hydropolitics. For example, it is generally accepted that the uppermost riparian position in a basin is potentially the strongest since the quantity and the quality of water flowing down a river may be substantially altered by the uppermost riparian state. Such a position may not only allow the uppermost riparian to dictate terms to the lower riparians in any negotiations over the shared waters, but it may also make the uppermost riparian state oblivious to any manipulation of the downstream hydrological regime of the river.

What is often not recognized, however, is that some unique features of a basin's physical geography may substantially curtail the degree of freedom and clout of even the uppermost riparian state. For example, the terrain through which the river flows within the territory of the uppermost riparian may be such that it may not be able to exploit fully or even partially the potential of these waters: a low gradient of the river may not allow substantial production of hydroelectric power whereas a very high gradient may make any navigational use of the river very difficult, if not impossible.[50] In addition, marine catch and fisheries in the uppermost riparian's territory may be highly dependent on upstream migration of fish through the territories of the lower riparians. The pattern of precipitation in a basin may be such as to deprive the uppermost riparian state of large flows whereas the lower riparian(s) may enjoy substantial water surpluses. Thus, the presumably strong bargaining position of the uppermost riparian state in hydropolitics may be substantially moderated by the unique physical geography of a river basin. As we shall see, this can have substantial implications for developing international laws for the nonnavigational uses of international rivers since the guiding principle in international law has often been the protection of the interests of lower riparian states.[51]

In some basins, physical geography, in combination with the national borders, may also create a very complex riparian structure such that an upper riparian on some portions of a river may also be a co-riparian and/or a lower riparian on different stretches of the same river, as is the case of Brazil in the Paraná–La Plata basin (chapter 1). This can complicate the stand(s) the upper riparian state may be able to take in hydropolitics, as the gains from taking one riparian position may be negated by losses from its other riparian position(s). In other cases, a state may share one river basin with one set of states and another basin with a very different set of states. For example, in South Asia, India shares the Indus basin with Pakistan and the Ganges-Brahmaputra-Barak basin with Bangladesh, Bhutan, Nepal, and Tibet-China (chapter 5); the same is the case for Brazil in the Paraná–La Plata and the Amazon basins (chapter 1). In such a situation, the state sharing different river basins from different riparian positions may have to weigh carefully the stands it may want to take in hydropolitics. Of course, a powerful state, whatever its riparian position in a basin, or a strategically located riparian state may still manage to have its way in hydropolitics, but the strong influence of physical geography on hydropolitics cannot be underestimated.

The physical geography of a river basin also forms, to a large extent, the material basis for its economic geography, especially in the resource-oriented, primary production economies of most developing countries. And economic geography, in turn, impacts hydropolitics in a variety of ways, as we shall see in the case studies.

The economic geography of a river basin encompasses the locations of all natural resources, human settlements, economic activities, and infrastructure—roads, railways, power grids, and so forth—as well as the spatial organization of all related activities in the basin as a whole and within the territory of each riparian state. Other economic geographic variables include size, rate of growth, demographic composition, and migration patterns of populations. Historically, availability of water has played an important role in the evolution of the economic geography of states and regions. Because all human activities require direct and indirect inputs of water, the economic geographic variables together determine the magnitude, location, and timing of the demand for freshwater. Conversely, changes in the availability of water can substantially alter the magnitude and rate of change of nearly all the demographic and economic variables. Thus, alone and in combination with its physical geography, the specific economic geography of a river basin has substantial impacts on hydropolitics.

On the one hand, the physical geography and the economic geography of a river basin can work together in such a way as to negate or at least moderate the potential advantages of an otherwise strong riparian position. For example, whereas a basin's physical geography may have endowed a riparian state with a huge potential for generating hydroelectricity on a stretch of the shared river within its own territory or on its borders, the agribusinesses and other industries within the country, which could consume the electricity to produce substantial economic returns, may be located so far away as to make the transmission losses and costs prohibitive. Such is the case of Paraguay in the Paraná–La Plata basin, where the construction of the Itaipu hydroelectric project has made the country one of the largest producers of hydroelectricity in the world (chapter 1). However, most of its industries and agribusinesses are located far away from the project site, making very costly the transmission of electricity to potential users. Further, the current level of development of its economy is such that Paraguay cannot hope to consume even a fraction of its huge surplus of electricity anytime in the foreseeable future. Thus, Paraguay currently has no choice but to sell its surplus electricity to its neighbor Brazil in a "one buyer–one seller" market. The same is true of Ethiopia, Bhutan, and Nepal, in other international basins (chapters 2 and 5).

On the other hand, the physical and the economic geography of a river basin and of its riparian states may also create the possibility of substantial trade-offs in hydropolitics. For example, in some basins it may be possible to trade the hydroelectric potential of one riparian state for navigational rights through another state's territory. In other basins, where more than one river is shared by two or more states, the economic potential of one river at one location may be traded for the economic potential of another river at another location. Thus, physical and economic geography may also dictate the nature and extent of possible cooperation between and among the riparian states sharing an international basin.

In addition to the physical and economic geography of a basin, its political geography is likely to impact hydropolitics in substantial ways. The domain of political geography covers the sources, dynamics, and spatial manifestations of political power at different levels of geographical aggregation within and among states. In the arena of hydropolitics, a geography-centered analysis requires linking the political geography of individual riparian states as well as the whole basin to the nature and conduct of interstate conflict and cooperation. By pointing out not only the individuals and the groups that hold power within the different riparian states, but also where exactly their power bases are located, and which activities and places the individual states are likely to favor with patronage and for what reasons, political geographers can greatly enhance the understanding of hydropolitics. Clearly, the political geography of different regime types (for example, democracies and dictatorships) differs greatly, with different implications for hydropolitics.

Earlier it was suggested that concerns for national sovereignty, especially as they relate to the control and use of scarce natural resources located within or flowing through a state's territory, may make it difficult for the riparian states in an international basin to cooperatively develop and share their transboundary water resources. In the Third World especially, where, with very few exceptions, nearly all states have emerged as sovereigns in the post–World War II era after long periods of colonial rule, there is likely to be great resistance to any dilution of sovereignty that cooperation with other states necessarily requires. The symbolic value of large water projects for such emergent states; the highly politicized nature of water allocations; the vagaries of domestic politics; the problem of reconciling diverse water-related interests within the riparian states; and so forth may make it difficult for them to collectively develop and share the multiple-use potential of common water resources. As we shall see, even the long-established Third World states, such as those sharing the Paraná–La Plata basin in South America, have not been immune to the symbolic value of large water projects. And they too have taken a very long time to overcome the impediments to basinwide cooperation created by their particular political geography (chapter 1).

An often ignored fact in the literature on the genesis, conduct, management, and resolution of interstate conflict is that ultimately all international accords have to be implemented in concrete geographical spaces (places) within the territories of the signatory states. All international agreements and accords, when implemented, benefit some places and people more than others; the costs of reaching and implementing international accords are also distributed unequally across places and peoples. This spatial mismatch in the costs and the benefits of interstate cooperation may engender severe domestic conflict in one or more states. Rapid changes in the ruling regimes may also make it problematic for a state to honor its obligations under an international water agreement. Ignorance or neglect of these facts on the part of negotiators and mediators attempting to resolve interstate water disputes may thus lead to even an excellent international water accord being rendered ineffective or problematic, because it may not be subsequently ratified or may have to be renegotiated.

Thus, overall, although geography may not strictly be "national destiny" in the modern world, if it ever was in the past, clearly geography can and does play a substantial role in defining and shaping hydropolitics in international river basins. Of course, each basin is geographically unique, making it necessary to examine how specific geographical features, alone and in combination with one another, and with other factors and circumstances, may play different roles in defining and shaping hydropolitics in different international basins.

Choice of Cases

There are more than 165 international river basins in the Third World that are shared by two or more sovereign states.[52] Ideally, a comprehensive study of hydropolitics would examine a representative sample of comparable cases from this large set to identify the conditions, factors, actors, and strategies that have engendered interstate conflict and facilitated or impeded interstate cooperation in international basins. This is clearly beyond the scope and resources of the present project. The six cases examined in this study have been selected for the primary reason that they exhibit some important similarities as well as differences, making it possible to carry out a smaller comparative study that will still allow us to derive some generalizable conclusions from the findings.[53] The other reason is the availability of extensive secondary source materials, in English, on each of the six basins.

The similarities the six international basins share include the following: These basins are among the largest river basins, in terms of their catchment and drainage areas, in the respective continents and subcontinents. All the basins are shared by more than two riparian states, and a substantial portion of the respective region's population currently lives in these basins. On the whole, these populations are growing at rates faster than the world average. Rates of urbanization and rural-to-urban migration are also higher in these basins than in other regions. With very few exceptions, all the riparian states sharing the six basins are currently characterized as low to middle income by the World Bank and all are currently heavily in debt, making it very difficult for them to unilaterally undertake large water projects. Most of the states also lack the material, technological, organizational, and human resources required for unilaterally implementing and maintaining such projects.[54]

In each basin at least one country is already a dominant regional power or has the potential to become one—Brazil in the Paraná–La Plata basin, Egypt in the Nile basin, Israel in the Jordan basin, Turkey in the Euphrates-Tigris basin, India in the Ganges-Brahmaputra-Barak basin, and Thailand (or Vietnam) in the Mekong basin. These states place great strategic and economic value on the transboundary water resources they share with their neighbors, and they have the power to veto or delay any multilateral water accords in their respective basins.[55]

In all the basins the boundaries of two or more riparian states were demarcated by the colonizing powers, often without much regard for the hydrological/geographical integrity of the respective river basins. There are also unresolved conflicts over the international borders, ethnic conflicts of different degrees of severity, and, in many cases, violent movements for autonomy or separation, all of which have substantial effects on hydropolitics. This should enable us to examine the role of contestations and conflicts about identity, territory, and ethnicity in hydropolitics.

Nearly all the states sharing the six basins are now members of the United Nations, the World Bank, and the International Monetary Fund, as well as several other regional and international organizations that, given the opportunity, may be able to facilitate and support interstate cooperation over the shared water resources.[56] Further, for each river basin, integrated plans for the development of transboundary water resources have been proposed from time to time; however, to date, none has been implemented in its entirety.

All the basins studied here have experienced colonial rule, albeit over different time periods and of varying severity, by one European power or another. This has made the riparian states especially susceptible and sensitive to issues of sovereignty, territorial integrity, and national self-interest.

But these "macro-level" similarities notwithstanding, each international river basin is unique in its physical, economic, and political geography, and the nature and dynamics of its political, economic, and security structures. Many historical, social, cultural, and behavioral factors also condition differently the way the riparian states in each basin perceive themselves and the world, and their position and evolving role in it. The particular historical experiences of specific states with their respective neighbors and with the rest of the world also color their perceptions of, and interactions with, one another in different ways. This uniqueness of each basin and of the states sharing it, as well as the similarities they share, should enable us to identify the set of factors that, individually and in combination with other factors, shape hydropolitics in international basins in the Third World.

Choice of Time Period

This study is limited to the period following World War II, for a number of reasons outlined below. Earlier historical information is analyzed for each case only when it pertains directly to the nature and conduct of hydropolitics in the particular basin during the past five decades.

Among the primary reasons for the limited time frame of the study are the following: The end of World War II created a radically new geopolitical context for interstate conflict and cooperation in the Third World. The defeat of some erstwhile colonizers—Germany, Italy, and Japan—and the substantially reduced geopolitical clout of others—Belguim, Great Britain, France, Portugal, Spain, and The Netherlands — created the conditions for the emergence of two superpowers, the United States and the Soviet Union, that then engaged in the long Cold War whose impacts in the Third World, especially on the nature, longevity, and severity of interstate conflict, have been and continue to be considerable.

Many sovereign states now sharing international river basins in the Third World achieved independence as a result of the post–World War II wave of decolonization; in some cases, new states were created by partitioning the erstwhile colonies. Boundaries of these states were often demarcated without much regard for the integrity of large river basins. Decolonization thus left the Third World states with legacies of unresolved territorial conflict, and transboundary resource claims and counterclaims continue to fuel such conflict among the states to this day.

The end of World War II also created the need and conditions for the establishment of new international organizations, such as the United Nations, the World Bank, and the International Monetary Fund, among many others. Many regional organizations for military and economic cooperation were also created in the post–World War II era. These organizations have provided new forums and resources for dealing with interstate conflict and, in some cases, for achieving interstate cooperation over a range of issues, including water, in the Third World.

There has also been a growing awareness over the past five decades of the importance of water for multiple uses other than navigation, which often was the primary concern of the erstwhile colonizers. In many Third World states, large-scale economic development programs have been undertaken only in the past few decades. Many large dams, irrigation systems, and other water-related infrastructure projects have been implemented, often with the assistance of the United Nations and the World Bank. These projects—both implemented and planned for the future—have created new imperatives for conflict as well as cooperation among the respective riparian states.

The post–World War II era has also witnessed substantial militarization of some states in the Third World. This has, in some cases, changed the historical regional balance of power, leading to new insecurities and conflict. At the same time there has been a growing recognition of environmental and economic interdependence among states. Many global and regional "initiatives" (e.g., the 1992 Earth Summit in Rio de Janeiro, Brazil, and the Rio-plus-Five in 1997 in New York) have been and are being launched that would have been inconceivable in the past. The large number of international and regional accords the states have signed in the recent decades also show that there has been a growing acceptance of some dilution of state sovereignty for the larger purpose of dealing with global problems as well as avoiding interstate conflict.

Now another geopolitical context for conflict and cooperation in the Third World is emerging. The demise of the Soviet Union as a superpower and the end of the Cold War have led some to proclaim the "end of history," others to contemplate a "new world order." For the moment, it is not entirely clear whether this new geopolitical context will facilitate or impede the resolution of transboundary resource conflicts in the Third World. This comparative study attempts to throw some informed light on this question, based on the experiences from five regions and six major international river basins over a period of half a century.

A final note is due on the ordering of the cases. Simply put, in the absence of any analytically rigorous criteria for ordering the cases, the strategy adopted here is to begin with the most "western" of the six selected Third World basins—the Paraná–La Plata basin in South America—and to end with the most "eastern" basin—the Mekong basin in Southeast Asia.

Within the comparative and geography-centered focus of this study, each of the six case studies in the following chapters (chapters 1 through 6) begins with a brief description of the physical, economic, and political geography of the particular basin and of the riparian states sharing it. This is followed by a discussion and an analysis of the specifics of interstate conflict and cooperation over the shared waters in each basin, and of the factors, circumstances, and actors that have been and are instrumental in hindering or facilitating interstate cooperation. A summary of findings from each case study is presented at the end of each chapter. Finally, the generalizable findings and conclusions from the six case studies are consolidated and presented in the concluding chapter.

1

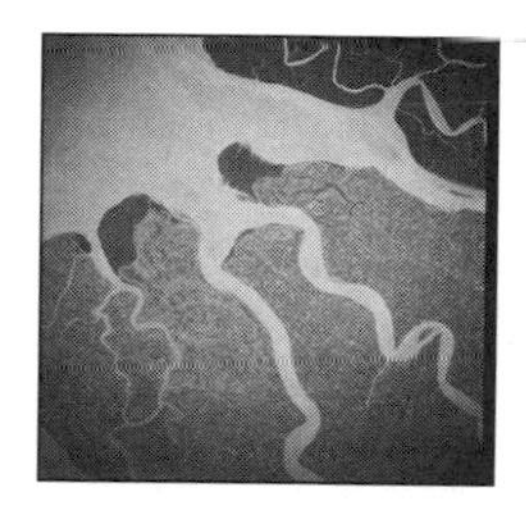

The Paraná–La Plata Basin

On May 6, 1991, President Fernando Collor de Mello of Brazil and President Andrés Rodríguez of Paraguay participated in a ceremony to put into operation the eighteenth generating unit of the world's largest hydroelectric power project, the Itaipu, located on their common border in the Paraná–La Plata basin. Each of the eighteen Itaipu turbines weighs 6,600 tons, equal to the combined weight of a line of Volkswagen cars 30 miles long, and each is capable of supplying enough power for a city four times the size of the Paraguayan capital, Asunción. The total amount of earth excavated for the project—more than eight and a half times the volume excavated for the Channel Tunnel now linking England and France—would have filled a line of trucks as long as *three times* the circumference of the earth. The total amount of concrete poured would have been enough to construct more than two hundred large football stadiums or twelve thousand eight-story buildings. At the height of its construction the project had employed about forty thousand workers; more than 6.5 million visitors from 141 countries have already visited the project site.[1] If the Itaipu Dam were to ever collapse, Buenos Aires, located 870 miles downriver, would be inundated with five feet of water.[2]

The Itaipu project took twenty years to set in motion and another seventeen years to construct, and it cost Brazil and Paraguay more than $15 billion.[3] Its hourly capacity to produce 12.6 million kilowatts of electricity is nearly 2 million kilowatts more than the Grand Coulee Dam in the United States.[4] However, unlike the Grand Coulee, the Itaipu is a joint undertaking of two developing countries: the electricity generated by the project is owned and shared by the two countries on an equal basis. As a result of this collaboration, tiny Paraguay is today the leading exporter of electricity in the world; it now produces more electricity per capita than the United States. And Itaipu is only one of several large collaborative water projects being planned and implemented by the five riparian states sharing the Paraná–La Plata basin.

How did Brazil and Paraguay—two countries with a history of acrimonious relations—arrive at an agreement to construct the giant project on their historically contested border? How could two developing countries, with immense disparities in size and population, as well as economic strength and military capabilities, fashion a bilateral agreement that established the principle of equality between them in the conduct of hydropolitics? What roles—individually and in combination—have historical, geographic, strategic, and other factors played in hydropolitics in the Paraná–La Plata basin? What generalizations can be derived from an analysis of interstate conflict and cooperation over the shared waters in this basin? Can these generalizations be useful in understanding hydropolitics in other international river basins in the Third World? These are some of the questions this case study will address from a geography-centered perspective.

GEOGRAPHY

Physical Geography

With an area of nearly 3.2 million square kilometers (1.25 million square miles), the Paraná–La Plata basin is among the five largest international river basins in the world, second only in size to the Amazon basin in the Western Hemisphere.[5] It includes parts of territories of five states—Argentina, Brazil, Bolivia, Paraguay, and Uruguay—and it is drained by three large rivers—the Paraná, the Paraguay, and the Uruguay—and by some other rivers and tributaries (see the map facing). Nearly half (45.9 percent) of the basin's area falls within Brazilian territory, followed by Argentina (28.2 percent) and Paraguay (13.1 percent); the remaining (12.8 percent) is shared by Bolivia and Uruguay. All of Paraguay lies within the basin.

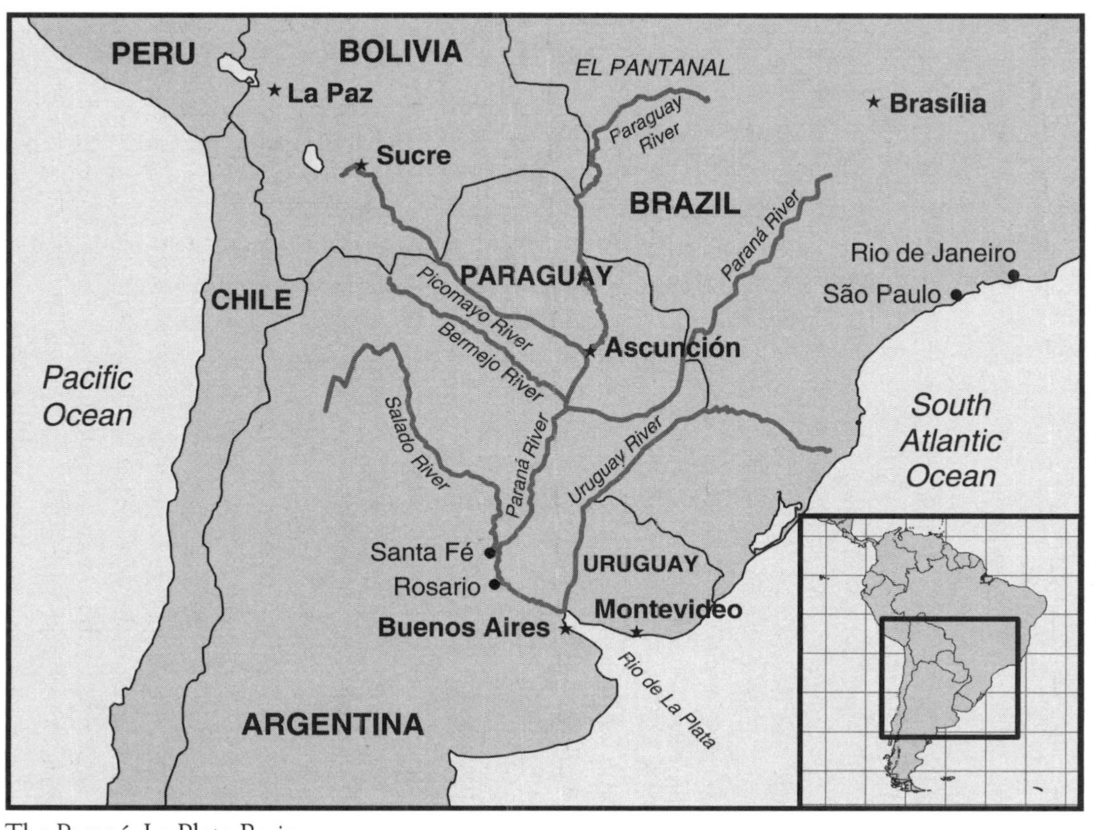

The Paraná–La Plata Basin

The basin runs north-south; the northern 40 percent of the basin is located within the tropical belt, with the remaining 60 percent in the subtropics. Rainfall in the basin makes for a humid climate throughout the year: even in the less-wet winter months of June to August, monthly rainfall averages do not drop below 60 millimeters (2.4 inches) and the average relative humidity hovers around 80 percent.[6]

The Paraguay is the longest of the basin's rivers, draining an area of about 1.1 million square kilometers (430,000 square miles). Rising in the vast wetland plains of the Gran Pantanal in Brazil, this river traverses a course of 2,550 kilometers (1,580 miles) before joining up with the Upper Paraná. When flooded, the Paraguay in the north links up with some southern tributaries of the Amazon, allowing an exchange of fish and other organisms between the two river systems.[7] Near the Paraguayan capital, Asunción, the east-flowing Pilcomayo River and a little downstream another east-flowing river, the Bermejo, join the Paraguay. Both the Pilcomayo and the Bermejo have their origins in Bolivia.

The headwaters of the Paraná, formed mainly by the Paranaíba and Grande Rivers, rise on a plateau in southeastern Brazil. Later, the two rivers join to form the Superior Paraná. Downstream from the Guairá Falls, now submerged under the Itaipu reservoir, the Iguazú River from Brazil joins the Superior Paraná to form the Upper Paraná River. Near the cities of Corrientes and Resistencia in Argentina, the river is joined by the Paraguay flowing down from the north and by the Bermejo flowing east from Bolivia. Together, these rivers are known as the Middle Paraná. Farther downstream, near the cities of Santa Fe and Paraná, yet another east-flowing river from Argentina, the Salado, joins the Middle Paraná. From this point on until the estuary, Río de la Plata, the river is called the Lower Paraná.

The Uruguay River also originates in southeastern Brazil and traverses an east-west and north-south course before joining the Paraná near Tigre. A westward-flowing river from Uruguay, the Negro, joins the Uruguay near the Río de la Plata. Thus, while Brazil is in effect the uppermost riparian state on the three largest rivers in the basin, Bolivia and Argentina are the uppermost riparians on some major tributaries, and the estuary is shared by Argentina and Uruguay.

The combined average flow of the basin's rivers at the outlet to the Atlantic Ocean has been estimated at 22,000 cubic meters per second (cumecs), compared with an average flow of 202,000 cumecs for the Amazon River, and while the main Paraná–La Plata basin rivers maintain relatively constant flows in their lower reaches, there are great variations of flow in their tributaries. Variations in rainfall have a significant impact on stream flows, although these impacts are modified and even reduced in the complex flow regimes of the basin.[8]

Over a long geological period, silts brought down by the rivers have turned large areas in the basin into highly productive land for farming and cattle raising; however, a large number of dams and other waterworks constructed in the basin in recent decades, especially on the Paraná River, now hold back much of the silt, creating serious environmental problems, both upstream and downstream of the man-made obstructions. Clearing of land for farming and cattle grazing has reduced the native forest cover in the upper part of the basin to just 3 percent of its original size.[9] Large-scale deforestation has also led to severe soil erosion in some parts of the basin. These ongoing and detrimental developments have adverse consequences for entire river regimes, in the process tying all the countries sharing the basin into environmental interdependencies and creating common environmental concerns.

The riparian states, especially the downstream riparians, also share an interest in controlling naturally occurring floods. In particular, flooding seriously affects Argentina and Uruguay from time to time. In the upper valley of the Paraguay River, shared by Brazil, Bolivia, and Paraguay, a huge depression known as El Pantanal is responsible for delaying the annual flood of the river. This prevents the Paraguay River from rising simultaneously with the Paraná, thus diminishing the downstream inundation in Argentina. Any future project in El Pantanal will thus have major impacts in the downstream countries.[10] The Paraná–La Plata basin countries also have common interests in developing reservoir capacity to store water for drought relief and in preventing major ecological disasters in the basin.[11]

The Uruguay is now only partly navigable; however, navigation is quite important in the lower 500 kilometers (310 miles) of the Paraná, from the estuary on the Atlantic Ocean to Santa Fe in Argentina. When the river is in full flow, oceangoing vessels can go up to Asunción. For smaller vessels the Paraná is navigable for over a 2,400-kilometer (1,490-mile) stretch, from Buenos Aires to the port of Corumbá in Brazil. Plans also exist for extending navigation by large vessels upstream to Asunción.[12] It is expected that the various lock systems already constructed and planned on the Paraná will also facilitate passage, currently obstructed by the Apipe rapids, upstream from Itaipu.[13]

The Paraná, Paraguay, and Pilcomayo Rivers are the main transportation arteries of landlocked Paraguay.[14] For Bolivia, landlocked since 1884 after a war with Chile, which cut off Bolivia's access to the Pacific Ocean, the Paraná–La Plata basin rivers now provide its only access to the ocean. River navigation also plays an important role in the Brazilian and Argentine economies. These rivers are also the main sources of water for drinking and sanitation, for irrigation and industries, and for recreational activities in a large part of the basin.

In addition to its agricultural and navigational potential, the basin contains large amounts of other exploitable natural resources. Among these, sections of the river shared by Argentina, Brazil, and Paraguay together contain the largest pools of hydroelectric potential in the world. As we shall see, the riparian states sharing the basin view these resources as highly valuable assets, for different reasons. This leads us to a discussion of the economic geography of the basin and how it may impact the nature and conduct of hydropolitics among the riparian states.

Economic Geography

Historically, the rivers and their alluvial valleys in the basin were used for fishing, hunting, cattle rearing, and light industry, based primarily on the abundant supply of timber. Cash crops, such as coffee, soybean, wheat, rice, corn, cotton, sugar cane, and oil-yielding plants, are now grown on the better soils. The economies of Bolivia, Paraguay, and Uruguay are still primarily and predominantly based on agriculture and livestock; both activities also make substantial contributions to the Argentine and Brazilian economies. Large amounts of grain, beef, wool, timber, and some manufactured goods are now exported from the basin to other parts of the world.

In recent years, as Argentina and Brazil, have industrialized, large industrial concentrations have emerged around São Paulo and within a narrow corridor extending for 450 kilometers (279 miles) along the west bank of the Lower Paraná, between Rosario and Buenos Aires. In Brazil some of the most industrialized and developed states (provinces)—Goiás, Mato Grosso, Paraná, Rio Grande do Sul, Santa Catarina, and São Paulo—are situated in the basin; in Argentina the provinces adjacent to the river contain 60 percent of the country's population and support 85 percent of its economic activities.[15] Many Argentine oil refineries, iron and steel plants, paper and pulp-producing industries, and other heavy industries are now located in the basin.[16] All of these industries are heavy consumers of chemicals, electric power, and water; furthermore, they produce a large amount of waste that is mostly discharged into the basin's rivers.

In 1997 the combined population of the five basin countries was estimated at 208.5 million, with annual rates of growth varying from a mere 0.6 percent for Uruguay to 2.8 percent for Paraguay. By the year 2000 total population of the five countries is expected to reach 233 million—an increase in just one decade roughly equal to the current population of Argentina. Overall, whereas the size of the population and its growth rate remain low in the basin compared with the size and growth rate of some other regions in the Third World, the rate of urbanization has been typically very high in all the basin countries.[17]

Four of the five national capitals—Asunción, Brasília, Buenos Aires, and Montevideo—are located on or near the rivers and tributaries comprising the Paraná–La Plata basin. Only La Paz, the Bolivian administrative capital, is located outside the basin.[18] About fifty cities with more than a hundred thousand people are now located within the basin, and the waters of the La Plata system are used heavily in both Argentina and Brazil for domestic, municipal, and industrial purposes. Additionally, many cities in the basin, including Buenos Aires, Corumbá, Rosario, and São Paulo, discharge their sewage and industrial wastes directly into the rivers.[19] Consequently, pollution has become a major problem in the basin. Along the Lower Paraná, industrial pollution, though not very high in absolute terms, has begun to impose limitations on various uses of the river's waters, especially recreation. Poorly regulated and badly managed discharges of industrial contaminants and occasional releases of toxins into the rivers have seriously affected fishing, while sewage effluents have caused local damage.[20]

Nevertheless, as mentioned earlier, the Paraná–La Plata basin is richly endowed with abundant natural resources, including one of the largest pools of hydroelectric potential in the world. Highly dependent as the large and industrializing economies of Brazil and Argentina are on energy supplies, the oil crises of the 1970s clearly underscored for the two countries the critical importance of the vast hydroelectric potential of the basin. In 1981 Brazil's net energy deficit accounted for almost all the energy imported by the whole of South America and for nearly half the energy imports of all the Latin American countries combined. By 1983 offshore oil provided half of Brazil's production and almost two-thirds of its total reserves; however, despite substantial deposits of oil shales and a very active program of producing energy from sugar cane, that is, from ethanol and waste, Brazil currently imports about 60 percent of all its energy needs.[21]

Argentina, on the other hand, is Latin America's third-largest producer of petroleum, after Mexico and Venezuela. However, the per capita energy consumption in Argentina went up from 975 to 1,525 kilogram of oil equivalent (koe) between 1965 and 1995; it currently consumes almost all of the oil and gas it produces. Thus, despite the large indigenous production of energy, Argentina also projects a growing need for electricity for industrial and household consumption, especially as it proceeds to liberalize its economy to attract foreign investment.

Bolivia has a small oil industry, which was nurtured by the Standard Oil Company of the United States and has later continued under a state-owned body, following nationalization in 1973. Although Bolivia's oil production declined in the 1970s and the country ceased to be an exporter in 1978, natural gas production has expanded and major gas finds were made in 1976, 1978, and 1982. Argentina currently imports natural gas and Brazil buys gasoline from Bolivia.

According to a UN report, there was a total of 130 large and small hydroelectric plants in the basin in 1990.[22] Together, these hydroelectric plants have an installed capacity of 42,700 megawatts, with Brazil accounting for nearly 93 percent of the total capacity. The basin also has about 60 thermoelectric plants, many in Argentina, located along the rivers and other bodies of water, with a total generating capacity of 7,622 megawatts.[23] In addition, Argentina has constructed 13 dams and reservoirs in the basin, Uruguay 5, and Brazil 107, including some dikes. Cumulatively, these reservoirs can store up to 273 billion cubic meters of water. Brazil's share is more than 90 percent of this total storage capacity; however, only a few of the reservoirs are reported to be used for flood control, irrigation, navigation, water supply, or recreational purposes.

In light of the seemingly abundant water resources of the basin, one would expect the people sharing it to be well supplied with drinking water and sanitation facilities; however, in 1995 Brazil was supplying safe drinking water to only 86 percent of its population. Safe drinking water coverage varied from 75 percent of the population in Bolivia to 73 percent in Argentina and to 79 percent in Paraguay. In particular, the supply of safe drinking water to rural areas ranged from 5 to 17 percent coverage. Whereas all of Argentina's urban population had access to sanitation services, only 13 percent of the Bolivians in the rural areas were claimed by their government to be receiving safe drinking water.[24]

In 1997, per capita incomes among the basin countries varied from $950 in Bolivia to $8,570 in Argentina. Brazil—the largest country and economy in South America—had a 1997 per capita income of about $4,720. At the same time, all the basin countries were heavily in debt, with external debt in 1996 ranging from $2 billion for Paraguay to $179 billion for Brazil. Brazil's external debt was the largest of all developing countries in the world.[25] All together, in 1996 the five Paraná–La Plata riparian states owed about $280 billion to their international creditors. The reluctance of international financial institutions to help relieve the heavy debt burden of the developing countries by making additional large loans means that none of the riparian states in the Paraná–La Plata basin currently is, or is likely in the foreseeable future to be, capable of unilaterally implementing very large hydroelectric or water supply projects.[26] In fact, the region acquired much of its past external debt from implementing large hydroelectric projects and from developing water-related infrastructure in the Paraná–La Plata basin.[27] Very high inflation rates in these countries have, in the past, only worsened the problem of funding large water projects from domestic or external sources; however, major strides have been made in recent years to control inflation. But without basinwide cooperation in developing and sharing the multiple-use potential of the shared waters, the riparian states will not be able to secure further funding for large water-related projects from the international community.

Thus, overall, a particular combination of physical and economic geographic features implies that the riparian states in the Paraná–La Plata basin now share many common economic and environmental interests, which include ensuring the freedom and the development of riverine navigation, developing and sharing the hydroelectric potential of the basin's rivers, building reservoir capacity for multiple uses, and addressing the environmental concerns and problems raised by large water-related projects. It may thus seem that the riparian states do not have much choice but to develop the multiple-use potential of the basin's shared water resources in a cooperative and sustainable manner. However, as we are likely to find in the other case studies, such cooperation necessarily requires, among other things, political will and ability at the highest echelons of power in all the riparian states to resolve interstate conflicts and to reconcile diverse domestic interests. This is where political geography comes in.

Political Geography

One political geographic feature that distinguishes the Paraná–La Plata basin from other international river basins in the Third World is the length of time the countries sharing it have existed as sovereign states. Whereas most states in Asia and Africa achieved independence from colonial rule only in the post–World War II era, Paraguay had become independent from Spain as early as 1811, followed by Argentina (1816, from Spain), Brazil (1822, from Portugal), Bolivia (1825, from Spain), and Uruguay (1828, from Brazil). Thus, about 175 years ago and within just two decades five sovereign states came to share the Paraná–La Plata basin, setting the stage for both interstate conflict and cooperation over the different rivers.

From the viewpoint of hydropolitics, what distinguishes this region from some other regions studied here is also the long period of time it was under colonial rule: from as early as the sixteenth century until the early nineteenth century. Among other things, this long history of domination by distant colonizers gave rise to the idea of Latin American unity, an idea whose chief proponent was the much-celebrated Simón Bolívar. Latin American unity is generally understood to mean presenting a common front—politically, economically, and strategically—against possible aggression and coercion from outside the region. The attempts at unity have intensified since the end of World War II for a number of reasons, among them the unrivaled emergence of their northern neighbor, the United States, as a superpower and a regional hegemon. However, this quest for unity and autonomy has yielded very mixed results. In particular, to retain independence and achieve economic growth, the Latin American countries have often had to first become dependent on the United States and Western Europe, a condition commonly known as the "Latin American Dilemma."[28] What this condition meant for hydropolitics in the Paraná–La Plata basin in the past were intermittent conflicts among the riparian states based on historical rivalries and suspicions, as well as several attempts at bilateral and multilateral cooperation.

Decolonization left behind many legacies of unresolved territorial and boundary conflicts and interstate rivalries among the different riparian states, especially between Argentina, controlled earlier by Spain, and Brazil, by Portugal. From 1825 to 1828, and from 1839 to 1852, Argentina and Brazil fought two wars which resulted in the creation of a "buffer country" between them, the Oriental Republic of Uruguay, with the help of British pressure and mediation. This was followed, from 1864 to 1870, by the Paraguayan War, or the War of Triple Alliance, with Paraguay on one side and Argentina, Brazil, and Uruguay on the other side. Although the genesis of the war was complex, one of the key issues was control over the Upper Paraná basin, which formed a vital transport link into southwest Brazil. When the Paraguayan dictator Francisco Solano López sought to counteract

Brazilian domination of Uruguay, by marching his troops toward Brazil through Argentine territory, Argentina, Brazil, and Uruguay formed a triple alliance to defeat López. After a long and very costly advance up the Paraguay River, the Triple Alliance forces captured Asunción in January 1869. Paraguay was occupied from 1870 to 1876 and lost a large portion of its territory, mostly to Argentina.

The last major interstate armed conflict among the countries in the Paraná–La Plata basin was the Gran Chaco War between Paraguay and Bolivia. The war broke out in mid-1932 after a series of armed clashes in the northern Chaco area, whose ownership had long been disputed by the two countries. After nearly a hundred thousand deaths (mostly Bolivian), the war ended in 1935, after considerable international pressure and with some territorial gains for Paraguay. A peace treaty was subsequently signed by the two countries in 1938.[29]

Among the as-yet-unresolved boundary disputes in the basin are several short sections of the boundary between Argentina and Uruguay, one short boundary section between Brazil and Paraguay just west of Guairá Falls on the Paraná River, and two short boundary sections between Brazil and Uruguay.[30] However, none of these boundary disputes poses a serious threat of armed conflict in the near future, given the earnest attempts made by these countries in recent years to resolve their differences peacefully, within the context of the changing geopolitical situation and a new spirit of regional cooperation in the basin.[31]

All of the Paraná–La Plata riparian states are currently governed by democratically elected administrations, but all have experienced a checkered history of authoritarian rule throughout this century.[32] Although episodes of military intervention in the domestic politics of these countries have proved difficult to maintain for long periods (exclusive military rule has tended to be accompanied by great economic and political stability), it would appear that the military still remains a type of "state within a state." Thus, the long-term sustainability of the democratically inclined administrations in the basin remains to be proved. Military rule has also left behind tendencies toward strong, authoritarian leadership in the riparian states, with considerable impact on hydropolitics in the basin, as we shall see.

Typically, military governments in the basin were more concerned with internal matters than with external matters.[33] Only recently, as the basin states have demonstrated varying degrees of democratization, has there been a willingness shown toward expanding relations with the neighbors. Indeed, in recent years Argentina, Brazil, and Uruguay have been working closely on integrating their economic systems and improving relations across the political spectrum. These three countries, along with Bolivia and Paraguay, have furthermore designed an economic integration plan whose centerpiece is the development of the Paraná–La Plata basin rivers as major shipping and transportation links.[34] Thus, overall, it can generally be said that relations among the riparian states are now guided by principles of pragmatism, nonintervention, respect for national sovereignty, regional integration, and reliance on the rule of law to settle disputes.

Nonetheless, in the domestic sphere all the riparian states have historically been characterized by large disparities in the ownership of land and other natural resources, and by great disparities in the distribution of income and wealth across the different strata of society.[35] The native peoples of the region, in particular, have been largely deprived of the gains from economic development. Consequently, the recent moves toward democratization have brought with them a growing awareness of the past harm done to the native peoples as well as their right to a fair share of the basin's natural resources, including its water resources. It is also being recognized that these people have suffered considerably from some large water projects implemented in the basin in the past. Environmental damage caused by such projects has further politicized the native peoples, making it more and more difficult to implement large developmental projects in the basin without their consent and participation. Thus, the evolving political geography of the basin as a whole and of the individual riparian states is likely to have growing impacts on the nature and conduct of hydropolitics in the basin.

HYDROPOLITICS

Because of the Paraná–La Plata basin's peculiar physical geography and the way national borders were historically demarcated by the colonizers in South America, the riparian structure of the basin is a highly complex one; not only do the many rivers and tributaries in the basin flow through more than one country successively, but they also form substantial stretches of borders between different sets of riparian states.

Brazil is the uppermost riparian on the three major rivers, the Paraguay, the Paraná, and the Uruguay, which mark Brazil's borders with every other country in the basin, making Brazil a co-riparian with all other riparian states. Similarly, Paraguay is an upper riparian with respect to Argentina on the Paraguay and Paraná Rivers, making the two countries co-riparians on both rivers. Among the major tributaries, the Pilcomayo and the Bermejo originate in Bolivia, making it an upper riparian; however, a little downstream the Pilcomayo becomes a border between Paraguay and Argentina. Thus, although Argentina is certainly the lowermost riparian in the basin, it is also a co-riparian on different rivers with all the other basin countries. Uruguay, in turn, is both a lower riparian and a co-riparian with Brazil, and an upper riparian and a co-riparian with Argentina.

This highly complex riparian structure has substantial implications for hydropolitics in the Paraná–La Plata basin. In essence, what it does is to make each riparian state cautious about the position it may want to take and the postures it may want to adopt in the conduct of hydropolitics with its neighbors, since the benefits of claiming one type of riparian status (e.g., upper riparian status) may be negated by another riparian status (e.g., middle or co-riparian status) the country may have with other riparian states in the basin. All the riparian states except Paraguay also share other international river and lake basins with different sets of countries in South America, which also influences hydropolitics in the Paraná–La Plata basin.[36]

Historically, hydropolitics in the Paraná–La Plata basin has been circumscribed by the legacies of territorial conflict and mutual suspicions inherited from the colonial era and by the long and checkered history of authoritarian rule in the postindependence era. The historical rivalry between Brazil and Argentina for regional and continental domination, and for international recognition and influence, combined with the smaller countries' attempts to maintain their sovereignty and territorial integrity while seeking to derive sizable economic benefits from cooperation with their powerful neighbors, explains, to a very large extent, the nature and conduct of past conflict and cooperation over the shared water resources. Since the end of World War II, and especially over the past two decades, new economic, political, and strategic developments within the region and internationally seem to be impelling a more encompassing attempt at regional cooperation, including cooperation in respect of the transboundary water resources of the Paraná–La Plata basin.[37]

Conflict and Cooperation

Although the history of armed territorial conflicts and boundary disputes in the Paraná–La Plata basin may seem relatively benign compared with that in other regions in the Third World, some acrimonious legacies did color the perceptions of the neighbors toward one another, especially when it came to issues that impinged on the territorial integrity and sovereignty of the nation-state. To take one example, a dispute has existed since the nineteenth century between Argentina and Paraguay over the demarcation of the northeastern part of their border, which is theoretically constituted by the Pilcomayo River originating in Bolivia. The dispute has centered on the fact that the course of the river has from time to time changed by up to 1.5 kilometers on either side.[38] After a 1974 agreement between the two countries to jointly explore how the floodwaters of the river could be best exploited, Argentina carried out some projects to control the movement of the river and to lessen flood damage, claiming that this did not change the border. In 1980, however, Paraguay alleged that the Argentines were unilaterally using water from a portion of the Pilcomayo River shared by the two countries and, by altering the river's course in violation of established international law and of some earlier agreements signed by the two governments, impinging on the territorial integrity of Paraguay. Although Argentina denied these allegations, its fears that the dispute might jeopardize the joint construction of the Yacyreta project with Paraguay on the Paraná River (discussed later) finally led to an agreement in August 1985 whereby the two countries and Bolivia agreed to expedite boundary demarcation on the Pilcomayo River. Argentina also proposed clear demarcation of boundaries on the Paraná and Paraguay Rivers and determination of sovereignty over some islands that would be permanently above water as a result of the planned hydroelectric projects.[39]

The historical suspicions of the three small countries, Bolivia, Paraguay, and Uruguay, regarding the geopolitical ambitions and designs of their two large neighbors have resurfaced many times, as demonstrated by their stands and postures on cooperatively developing the navigational and hydroelectric potential of the basin's rivers.

Attempts at basinwide cooperation over the shared waters date back to 1932 when Brazil—the uppermost riparian state on all the major rivers—accepted the principles of international rivers law and prior consultation with co-riparians. A report outlining these principles was then produced by the Permanent Commission of International Public Law of Rio de Janeiro.[40] In Montevideo in December 1933, the Seventh Inter-American Conference adopted, with the votes of all the riparian states, the LXXII Declaration on Industrial and Agricultural Use of International Rivers. This declaration emphasized the principle of previous consultation among the riparian states before building any hydraulic works on the basin's rivers.

In 1941, at the Regional Conference of the Paraná–La Plata Basin States in Montevideo, an attempt was made to form a customs union among the basin countries. However, the attempt failed primarily because of the conflicting needs and desires of the participants: "The two land-locked states, Paraguay and Bolivia, desired an amelioration of their infrastructure and transport facilities, while Argentina was interested in an improvement of her inferior position as a downstream state. Brazil continued to rely on her favorable upstream position."[41]

Following the Montevideo declaration, many other bilateral and multilateral agreements and declarations were signed in the 1960s by the basin countries, all of which restated the principles outlined in the 1933 declaration. However, shortly thereafter, the Brazilian foreign ministry, Itamaraty, drastically changed its position on multilateral cooperation in the basin. Brazil now began to assert the so-called Harmon Doctrine, on the basis of which it claimed exclusive rights to develop and use the basin's waters on its own territory in the manner it saw fit and without prior consultation. Brazil sought to develop unilaterally and speedily the hydroelectric potential in the Brazilian stretches of the basin rivers, and to construct the Itaipu Dam with Paraguay, without informing or consulting the lower riparian, Argentina (discussed later).

In 1966, at the initiative of Argentina, the foreign ministers of the five states met in Buenos Aires and, in February 1967, issued a joint declaration in which they proposed a balanced and harmonious development of the region as well as the creation of an Intergovernmental Coordination Committee (CIC). Finally, after much preparatory work in the interim, the five states signed the La Plata Basin Treaty in 1969 in Brasília. The treaty came into force in 1970, the CIC was formally installed in Buenos Aires in 1973, and the institutional structure for implementing the treaty was finally completed in 1974 with the foundation of the Development Fund of the La Plata Basin (FONPLATA).

The conceptual framework of the treaty was, however, heavily debated. Thus,

> Whereas the proposals of the three minor basin States argued for the creation of an international organization with its own organs and international legal personality, Argentina and Brazil strictly opposed such a high degree of integration. Their opinion finally prevailed and the treaty adopted an intermediate position. The "system" . . . itself has no international legal personality, but one of its organs (the CIC) does.[42]

Overall, the La Plata Basin Treaty tends to foster regional cooperation within the basin rather than economic integration, especially cooperation in navigation, utilization of water and natural resources, conservation, transport and telecommunications, industrial development, economic complementation in frontier areas, education, health, and acquisition of knowledge about the basin.[43]

Aside from the multilateral activities incorporated within its regime, the La Plata Basin Treaty allowed restricted multilateral treaties among some of the signatories (e.g., the Statute of the URUPABOL of 1981 among Bolivia, Paraguay, and Uruguay), bilateral agreements (e.g., the Itaipu and Yacyreta Treaties), and agreements on mere river regimes (e.g., agreements over the Uruguay river between Argentina and Uruguay, and among Argentina, Brazil, and Uruguay).

However, despite these well-intentioned efforts toward efficient and equitable development and use of the basin's water resources, a 1983 evaluation of the performance of the La Plata Basin Treaty showed that it has not been very successful: "of the 167 resolutions issued by the Meetings of the Foreign Ministers up to 1980, only 28 had been duly implemented."[44] Another evaluator of the performance of the institutional structure created by the treaty has blamed the "Kafkaian" nature of the organizational machinery, as well as "the initial mistake of including in the Treaty and allocating to CIC a range of subjects unrelated to water resources development, such as education, flora and fauna, railroads, and communications."[45] Many other shortcomings of the treaty and of the organizations it created have meant that as yet there are no truly multilateral projects in the basin, though some are planned. Nonetheless, while multilateralism as envisaged in the treaty still remains to be fully realized, bilateralism has had some notable but controversial successes, as demonstrated by the Itaipu and Yacyreta projects.

The Itaipu Accord

Facing large energy deficits at the time, Brazil by the mid-1950s had already constructed a series of hydroelectric power projects within its own territory on the Paraná River as well as on some tributaries in the nearby basin, yet the projected electricity demand for future industrial development made the construction of a large hydroelectric project at the very attractive Itaipu site a high priority. (Itaipu is an Indian word meaning "Singing Rock"; it is at this location that the Guairá Falls are formed.) The main difficulty in unilaterally undertaking a large project at Itaipu was that the prospective site was on Brazil's border with Paraguay, and the two countries were then engaged in a dispute—dating back to 1872—over where exactly the border dividing them at Guairá Falls ought to be.

A series of negotiations that began in the 1950s between the two countries over demarcation of the common border as well as development of the Paraná River at the Itaipu site was interrupted when the military government in Brazil, frustrated by what it perceived as Paraguayan foot-dragging, opted for a unilateral show of force, invading and occupying some of the contested border area in 1962. After five years of occupation, the Brazilian forces were withdrawn, leading to a series of negotiations that culminated in a 1973 agreement to jointly build the giant Guairá-Itaipu hydroelectric power complex. In addition to producing electricity for the two countries, the proposed project would submerge Guairá Falls, thus making moot the question of demarcating the boundary between them at the project site. Thus, a joint water project was to be instrumental in laying to rest a boundary conflict between the two riparian states.

Political developments within each country heavily influenced the timing and nature of negotiations over Itaipu. Although both countries were under military dictatorship when Brazil started its belligerent posturing, Paraguay under the authoritarian rule of General Stroessner was "languishing under its peculiar political and social structure. . . . Brazil's first strategic moves, which concluded with the development of the Itaipu plant, found Stroessner leading a divided country with most of its intelligentsia excluded from participation in the political process."[46] Consequently, Paraguay entered the negotiations without adequate technical support or expertise. In 1962 Brazil through a diplomatic note reasserted its complete sovereignty over Guairá Falls. Paraguay rejected the note, but agreed in 1964 to establish a joint committee to examine the hydroelectric potential of the falls, as well as the downstream 200-kilometer (125-mile) stretch of the Paraná River up to the Argentine border. In June 1966, Brazil joined Paraguay in declaring through the Acta de Foz de Iguazú (Ata das Catarats) that the two countries recognized their common and indivisible ownership of the hydroelectric potential of the Paraná River, from and including Guairá Falls to the Iguazú River, without renouncing their conflicting claims on the ownership of the falls.[47] After the withdrawal of the Brazilian occupation forces from the contested territory, in 1968 the joint Paraguayan-Brazilian Technical Commission was formed.

Finally, after prolonged negotiations and consultations, in April 1973 the military heads of state of Paraguay and Brazil—General Stroessner and General Castelo Branco—signed the Itaipu Accord to jointly develop the hydroelectric potential of the stretch of the Paraná River shared by the two countries. They agreed to build the largest hydroelectric power complex in the world, with a capacity more than five times that of the Aswân High Dam in Egypt and a quarter that of the already sizable existing hydropower capacity of Brazil. To implement the accord, and to supervise and manage the project, a Council of Administration and an Executive Directorship, each with an equal number of representatives from both countries, were established.[48]

Every feature of the planned Itaipu project could be described only in grandiose terms. Eighteen generators, with a capacity of 700 megawatts each, would produce more electricity every year than any other hydroelectric plant in the world, equal to the combined production of the three largest Soviet hydroelectric power stations of the time, or a good 20 percent of all the electricity to be generated in West Germany by 1980. The reservoir water level would be 220 meters above mean sea level. Moreover, the reservoir would be 170 kilometers (105 miles) long and up to 7 kilometers (4.3 miles) wide and, at high water, would cover an area of 1,460 square kilometers (570 square miles) in Brazil and Paraguay. The total volume of excavation for the project would amount to 40 million cubic meters of rock and 22 million cubic meters of earth. Transportation of the huge turbine units from São Paulo to the dam site would require four years of preparatory logistic work to strengthen bridges, widen roads, and alter road gradients.[49]

According to the Itaipu Accord, both countries agreed to share the electric output of Itaipu equally. Further, each country had to specify what proportion of its share would be needed for its domestic market over a period of twenty years, and each country was granted the exclusive right to buy from the other any electricity the latter did not require or could not use. The selling price for the electricity was to be fixed by the Itaipu Binacional on the basis of a formula combining production costs, partial appropriation of the capital stock, the finance charges and other costs for the loans raised by Itaipu Binacional, royalties for the two countries for the use of the electricity, and administrative costs. According to the original treaty, no changes in the financial arrangements would be permitted until fifty years after signing the treaty, that is, until the year 2023.

The two national electricity companies, ANDE in Paraguay and Electrobras in Brazil, agreed to contribute half of the $100 million capital stock of Itaipu Binacional. However, Brazil had to provide a loan of $50 million to Paraguay to cover the latter's share of the capital stock. Terms of this loan included a 6 percent interest rate, a waiting period of at least eight years until the start of energy production from the project, and a repayment period of fifty years.

For Brazil, critically dependent as it was on imported oil, the 1973 oil price shock was a rude awakening, underscoring the urgent need to develop alternative sources of energy within and near Brazilian territory. For Paraguay, on the other hand, with a very small and underdeveloped domestic market incapable of absorbing large electric power inputs well into the future, the prospect of jointly developing the tremendous hydroelectric potential of the Paraná River provided its only chance to acquire a valuable export commodity. With the completion of Itaipu by the 1990s, Paraguay would become the largest exporter of electricity in the world. However, the results have not been as rosy as were expected at the time of signing of the Itaipu Accord.

In June 1972 the whole project was estimated to cost a total of $2 billion; by 1983 the cumulative costs actually incurred for building and financing the project had gone up by 750 percent to a total of $15.3 billion (not adjusted for inflation). Of this amount, 78 percent was raised by Brazil by borrowing on the national money market, the remaining $3.4 billion had to be borrowed from the international market. The large foreign debt incurred for the Itaipu project and the fantastic cost overruns have also raised the question about when, and if at all, Paraguay would actually be able to derive significant financial benefits from the sale of electricity to Brazil since, according to the terms of the agreement, compensation for the selling of one country's share of electricity to the other has to be paid equally by both partners. Thus, half of the compensation for any surplus electricity sold by Paraguay to Brazil is paid by Paraguay itself.[50]

An associated problem for Paraguay has been the increasing influx of Brazilian migrants into the eastern Paraguayan region. Many Brazilian farmers of European descent, who had earlier settled on the eastern banks of the Paraná in Brazil, have in recent years bought fertile land in Paraguay with loans from Brazilian banks.[51] These farmers have radically transformed the cultural, socioeconomic, and political structure of the region, leading to protests by some Paraguayans that their national sovereignty is being compromised. Some see in this encroachment the workings of the larger Brazilian geopolitical thinking of the past, which had included such ideals as "active, mobile and dynamic frontiers" or "borderland integration."[52]

Further, according to the original agreement, Brazilian and Paraguayan firms were to share equally in the highly lucrative contracts for construction work, supply of equipment, and so on. The project did create an economic boom in Paraguay, but given the tremendous asymmetry in the two countries' economic development and industrialization, more than four-fifths of all equipment—generators, turbines, and the like—have been supplied by Brazil. This has created thousands of new jobs in the industrial, construction, and service sectors in Brazil. Brazil has also acquired considerable expertise in the construction of large hydroelectric projects; however, this has also meant that a significant Brazilian lobby now exists that forcefully advocates the building of more and more hydroelectric power stations.[53]

Land for the Itaipu project was to be compulsorily bought from nearly eight thousand families living in the area that would be flooded by the reservoir and the safety zone around the planned power station. However, scant regard was initially paid to the complexity of land ownership in a chaotic pioneer area, which had begun to be opened and settled only two decades before the project's inception. Later, corruption, favoritism, misinformation, and, in some cases, outright deprivation without compensation led to civil disobedience. The resettlement of the displaced families was also handled haphazardly, without adequate preplanning.[54]

Further, while Brazil had well-established plans for using its share of the electricity produced by Itaipu, Paraguay had no such plans.[55] In Brazil the electricity was to be used for industries located near São Paulo, requiring a transmission system to carry the electricity hundreds of kilometers away from the project site. However, there were no overall development plans for the regions surrounding the project site in either country, nor were there plans for systematically monitoring the short- and long-term ecological impacts and health and other problems the project may create. As it turned out, the very ambitious projections for the growth of the Brazilian economy and for its electricity needs have not materialized. Falling world oil prices have raised further questions about the wisdom of sinking billions of precious borrowed dollars into a scheme of such gigantic proportions.

Finally, a conflictual feature of the negotiations for the Itaipu Accord was the difference in frequencies at which Brazil and Paraguay were producing and consuming electricity at the time. Although it would have been much more economical to produce electricity at Itaipu and to distribute it to the two countries at just one frequency, Paraguay insisted on the production and distribution of its share of the Itaipu electricity at its own 50 cycles/second frequency rather than at Brazil's 60 cycles/second, even though Brazil offered to pay the whole cost of converting the Paraguayan electricity system to 60 cycles/second. In the end, Paraguay's ambivalence over the Brazilian proposal led Brazil to unilaterally decide in 1977 that half of the generators at Itaipu would produce electricity at its own frequency while the other half would produce electricity according to the requirements of the Paraguayan distribution system. This also meant that to be able to buy and use surplus electricity from Paraguay, Brazil first would have to transform and transmit it in high-voltage direct current (HVDC) and then put it into alternating current (AC) form before distribution. Summarizing this episode, a researcher has commented: "On the political side, the solution adopted helped to reduce the fear of many Paraguayans that the change in frequency to sixty cycles. . . . would represent a surrender of Paraguay's political and economic independence."[56] This is an illuminating but hardly the only instance of a water project in an international basin in the Third World that has been substantially modified and made more problematic by the national sovereignty concerns of one or more riparian states.[57]

The Yacyreta Treaty

Negotiations for the Itaipu project had completely excluded Argentina, even though any upstream manipulation of the Paraná River would naturally have serious consequences for Argentina's own plans for developing the hydroelectric and navigational potential of the river. Argentina saw any bilateral accord between the two upstream countries as greatly increasing Brazil's economic and political influence in Paraguay, at a time when the Brazilians were already providing training and arms to the Paraguayan military to deal with internal dissent. Consequently, under the authoritarian Argentine leader Juan Perón's personal instructions to "sign it now and renegotiate it later," the Yacyreta Treaty was hastily signed with Paraguay in December 1973, just seven months after the signing of the Itaipu Accord. Interestingly, the blueprint for the Yacyreta Treaty was none other than the text of the Itaipu Accord! [58]

The Yacyreta project was to be constructed downstream from the Itaipu project, but upstream from the confluence of the Paraná and Paraguay Rivers. Yacyreta would operate with thirty generators, each with a capacity of 135 megawatts. Like the power generated by Itaipu, the power generated by Yacyreta would be shared equally by Argentina and Paraguay, with the provision that any surplus would be sold to the other country on a priority basis. Because of this last provision, the Yacyreta Treaty differed from the Itaipu Accord in that the latter could be interpreted to allow the sale of electricity to a third party, albeit under very restricted circumstances. Finally, similar to the Itaipu Binacional, a binational public corporation, Yacyreta Binacional, would be established, with each country contributing one-half of the corporation's capital stock; however, as Brazil did in the Itaipu project, Argentina had to lend $50 million to Paraguay to cover the latter's share of the capital.

As originally conceived, the Yacyreta reservoir would have flooded a total area of 1,690 square kilometers (660 square miles), of which about 1,000 square kilometers would have been within Paraguayan territory. However, after Paraguay objected to the site suggested by Argentina as well as to the disproportionately larger area of its territory likely to be flooded, a new location was selected which would reduce the Paraguayan territory to be flooded to 815 square kilometers. A new formula for calculating the compensation to be paid for loss of agricultural production on the flooded lands was also evolved, along with a more equitable way of resolving differences in the bilateral Executive Council of Yacyreta.[59]

Like the Itaipu Accord, the Yacyreta Treaty specified a fixed cost at which one country could sell surplus electricity to the other country. However, using the same formula as the Itaipu Treaty to calculate this fixed compensation, the two countries arrived at a figure of $2,998 per gigawatt-hour, nearly three times the amount of compensation per gigawatt-hour for the Itaipu surplus. This fallacy becomes apparent and perhaps understandable when it is observed that the envisaged fixed investment of $1.1 billion for Yacyreta was expected to produce only 18,000 gigawatt-hours per year, compared with the estimated 93,000 gigawatt-hours the Itaipu project would produce with a fixed investment of $1.8 billion. Thus, in effect, the less efficient the project, the larger the compensation for the party selling the surplus electricity![60]

Close to a billion dollars had been spent on the project before dam construction even began; for an additional $3 billion, the work was about two-thirds complete.[61] In the past, most of the money for this ambitious project was lent by the World Bank and the Inter-American Development Bank, which later became weary of lending an additional $3 billion needed to complete the project, not including the high costs for transmission of power to places that could conceivably use it. Argentina does indeed need more electricity; however, crushed under a heavy burden of debt, the country is unlikely to be able to spend more money for the project, even assuming that it would want to. In 1990, the Argentine president, Carlos Menem, described the Yacyreta project as a "monument to corruption" and said that work on the project must stop.[62] Some construction still goes on, but it is not at all clear if the project can be fully implemented any time in the near future.

In hindsight many observers agree that the Yacyreta project should never have been started; indeed, it could not have been were not two authoritarian leaders—Stroessner and Perón—ruling the two countries at a crucial juncture in the early 1970s, without any meaningful participation of their people in the political process or interstate negotiations.[63] The project might not even have been conceived if Argentina, more specifically the Peronist regime, had not seen itself threatened by the Itaipu Treaty and in competition with Brazil for influence over Paraguay.

On the question of whether the Itaipu Accord and Yacyreta Treaty have attempted to implement fair partnerships, one observer has argued that it "depends on the particular way each payment is determined. What remains to be determined is whether the two countries in partnership receive the economic rent for the water they contribute."[64] Thus, on the one hand, it can be argued that Paraguay does not in fact receive the full economic rent for the 50 percent water it contributes to the two projects and, consequently, it subsidizes Brazil's and Argentina's electricity consumption, since the costs of producing equivalent amounts of electricity by oil or nuclear energy within the latter countries would be much higher. Some proponents of renegotiating the compensation scheme for the sale of Yacyreta power have calculated that for Argentina not to purchase power from Paraguay but produce it in a thermal electric plant would cost close to $3,234 per gigawatt-hour.[65] On the other hand, the Brazilian and Argentine opponents of any renegotiation of the respective treaties claim that Paraguay has benefited highly disproportionately from a natural resource that it could not develop on its own, nor make full use of in the foreseeable future.[66]

Whether the Itaipu and Yacyreta treaties (and projects) have been fair to all parties or not will be debated for a long time to come in the three countries; however, what needs to be emphasized is that both treaties did recognize the "common pool nature" of water[67] as well as establish the principle of equality between two co-riparians, despite vast disparities in their levels of economic development, military capabilities, and regional and international clout. The treaties have also created international regimes and enforcing mechanisms for the joint development and sharing of the basin's water resources. Additionally, the two projects have created a huge surplus electricity potential for Paraguay that it can export to the two countries or use to attract large energy-consuming industries from outside the basin. Further, the two projects have tied the three countries together in intricate environmental, economic, and political interdependencies.

Other Hydropower Projects

In addition to the Yacyreta project, Argentina and Paraguay have discussed plans for jointly building yet another hydroelectric project on the Paraná. This project, known as the Corpus project, would be located between the Itaipu and Yacyreta projects on the Paraná River. Although still in the planning stages, Corpus is expected to have a capacity similar to that of Yacyreta. However, whether Corpus can be built to yield any economic benefit depends totally on the height of the Itaipu Dam and on how much water is released downstream of the dam.[68] Construction of the Corpus reservoir will also flood a large area of the nearby Brazilian territory.

Recognizing these hydrologically induced interdependencies, the three countries held a series of negotiations in the 1970s, culminating in 1979 in a trilateral agreement, known as the Itaipu-Corpus Accord. The accord provides solutions for the problem of setting the heights of the three dams, as well as mechanisms for resolving other problems of trilaterally managing the river's waters in an efficient and environmentally sound manner. Argentina and Uruguay have already connected their power grids at Salto Grande; Argentina and Brazil have also agreed to interconnect their electricity networks.[69]

Argentina and Uruguay, under a bilateral treaty signed in 1946, are jointly constructing the Salto Grande hydroelectric project on the Uruguay River, with a capacity to produce 1.6 million kilowatts of electricity. Under a treaty signed in May 1980, Argentina and Brazil are also studying the hydroelectric development of the Pepri-Guazu and Upper Uruguay River where it divides the two countries. This treaty provides for separate but simultaneous operation of the generating stations, but not for the creation of any bilateral agency.[70] There is also an agreement between Brazil and Uruguay on the Jaguarão and Mirim lagoons. Further, there is a trilateral agreement among Argentina, Bolivia, and Paraguay on joint research and development of the Pilcomayo River. However, most of these agreements have been generally limited to exchange of information and to preliminary research and joint studies. Usually a joint or mixed commission is proposed to be created, with equal representation of technical personnel from each nation.[71]

The Hidrovia Project

The Hidrovia project is a large scheme to convert 3,400 kilometers (2,110 miles) of the Paraguay and Paraná system into a shipping canal, navigable year-round for oceangoing vessels, from the Atlantic Ocean to Cáceres in

Brazil, located at the head of the Pantanal depression. The claimed benefits of the waterway include the overall economic development of the region by facilitating exports through cheaper riverine transportation and by providing encouragement for the economic and political integration of the region. Many see the project as the physical manifestation of the Mercosur free trade agreement among Argentina, Brazil, Paraguay, and Uruguay, which was scheduled to be fully implemented by 1995.[72]

Implementation of the Hidrovia project would require major modifications to the river regime to allow for large increases in boat size, amount of shipping traffic, and the volume of exports and imports. Major improvements would also need to be made to existing port facilities, the main channel and existing navigation facilities along the whole length of the river. To design and implement the project an executive agency, the Intergovernmental Committee on Hidrovia (CIH), was formed in 1989 by the ministers of public works and transport from the five La Plata riparian states. Technical feasibility studies are being supported by the Inter-American Development Bank (IDB) and the United Nations Development Programme (UNDP).

Opponents of the project in its present form point to several adverse socioeconomic and environmental consequences for the region. Among these are the very high capital costs of constructing heavy engineering works, especially in a region already heavily debt laden; significant changes in the hydrology of the Pantanal, with the potential of draining 40 to 50 percent of the wetlands in about forty years and increasing the occurrence of floods and droughts in the downstream areas; loss of biodiversity; and significant social dislocation from both direct and induced development in the region. Promotion of monocrop soybean production, greater timber harvesting, increased mining, cattle ranching, and dynamite fishing may also impact the ecology of the basin in irreversible ways.[73] Facing these objections, the riparian governments have called for meetings with UNDP, IDB, nongovernmental organizations from the region, and support groups from the United States and Europe to explore different options and alternatives. Thus, it is not clear what shape the final project will take or when it will be implemented. Nonetheless, the Hidrovia project is certainly a far cry from the manner in which the Itaipu and Yacyreta projects were negotiated, designed, and implemented.

Thus, overall, hydropolitics in the Paraná–La Plata basin has evolved from unilateralism to bilateralism to multilateralism. However, this does not mean that the vast multiple-use potential of the shared waters is yet being developed by the riparian states in the most efficient and sustainable manner possible. But as the deliberations over the Hidrovia project indicate, perhaps a better future for the Paraná–La Plata basin still lies ahead.

SUMMARY AND CONCLUSION

Conflict and cooperation over transboundary water resources among the five riparian states sharing the Paraná–La Plata basin have revolved around four substantive issue areas and national interests. First and foremost have been the concerns of the riparian states about maintaining their national sovereignty and territorial integrity in light of a shared history of colonial domination. An associated issue has been the shared need and desire to prevent extraregional powers from manipulating the geopolitical situation in the basin to the detriment of the riparian states' interests. The third substantive issue has been to ensure freedom of navigation on the basin's rivers as well as access to the Atlantic Ocean. The fourth issue, which has acquired increasing prominence in the basin in the last three decades, is the integrated development of the basin's considerable hydrological and economic resources. More recently, environmental degradation and demands by indigenous peoples for a fair share of the fruits of economic growth have become common concerns among the riparian states. The salience of these issues has varied over time, and from country to country; however, for a variety of economic, political, and strategic reasons, the overall national interests of the five basin states have become increasingly convergent. This applies to the multiple-use potential of the shared transboundary water resources also.

A number of tentative generalizations have emerged from this case study that need to be further examined in other basins. First, conflict and cooperation over shared waters in an international river basin are very likely to be embedded within the larger framework of interstate relations as well as within the specific geopolitical concerns of one or more riparian states in the basin, especially the larger states. Thus, major interstate water disputes may be resolved only within the arena of high politics rather than within the arena of low politics.

Second, states sharing a river basin may seek cooperation over the shared waters only when one or more of them experience or anticipate water scarcity for some crucial need and then only if the option of unilaterally exploiting the shared water resources is no longer available or is likely to lead to an avoidable conflict with the other riparian states. Additionally, the initiative or coercive power of the most advantaged riparian state, in this case Brazil, in terms of its riparian position and its military and economic clout, may be crucial in facilitating cooperation in an international basin.

Third, even the potentially strongest uppermost riparian position of a state in an international basin may be moderated by a host of intervening factors. Thus, although Brazil certainly has the strongest riparian position in the basin, its vulnerabilities in the global economy and its lack of petrochemical resources as well as some geographical features of the basin have gradually turned the country into a benevolent hegemon. Among the geographical features of a basin, a complex riparian structure may play a substantial role in restricting the degrees of freedom that each of the basin states has in the conduct of hydropolitics with its neighbors. Further, a complex riparian structure may also be able to compensate for the lack of strict legal instruments and enforcement mechanisms in the treaties and agreements for cooperation. Additionally, as demonstrated by the Itaipu and the Yacyreta projects, other physical, economic, and political geographic features of a basin may determine whether cooperation will be sought, who will cooperate, what will be the nature of cooperation, and whether cooperation will be long-lasting.

This case study clearly demonstrates that geography—physical, economic, and political—can tie up the riparian states sharing an international river basin into many taut Gordian knots of multifaceted interdependencies, making it difficult for them not to cooperate in the long run over the shared water resources. Such highly interdependent riparian states have no recourse but to interact indefinitely in the arena of hydropolitics. Thus, at some stage, the value of cooperation may outweigh the benefits of unilateral or noncooperative behavior in an international river basin.

Fourth, the need to cooperate in a variety of other substantive issue areas and a long history of attempts at economic and strategic cooperation may provide the backdrop against which bilateral and multilateral cooperation over transboundary water resources can evolve. Thus, a historical predisposition to cooperate in other issue areas may facilitate interstate cooperation over the shared waters also. Further, though bilateralism may be easier to achieve and sustain than multilateralism, the successful implementation and functioning of even bilateral projects in an international basin may finally require multilateral cooperation. In turn, a stage may be reached when a history of cooperation over water may also open up opportunities for cooperation in other arenas, for example, for expanding trade and for reducing military competition.

Fifth, international and regional organizations may be able to or may need to play only a supportive and facilitating role in hydropolitics, especially in regions where, for historical reasons, extraregional influences are viewed with great suspicion. Further, cooperation may be achieved without an active role for epistemic communities, nongovernmental organizations, or interest groups as long as strong authoritarian leaders are in power in the countries seeking to cooperate on water projects. However, whether the treaties and agreements are able to achieve the goals of genuine and equitable cooperation may be highly dependent on the participation of actors other than the state in treaty negotiations and implementation.

Sixth, although great asymmetries in power may exist among the basin states, provided that geography allows it, the weaker riparian states, to ensure that their own interests are not jeopardized by bilateral or multilateral cooperation, may still be able to play a "balancing of powers" game or "pendular diplomacy" with the stronger and rival powers. Facing large asymmetries in power, the smaller or weaker riparian states may focus primarily on concrete and equitable "absolute gains" rather than the more intangible "relative gains." However, they may have to compromise on the timing of the cooperative agreements, and on the nature and extent of cooperation with their stronger neighbors, unless the latter are themselves vulnerable—economically and strategically—in the larger international and regional arenas. Even then, the stronger powers may be able to control the timing of all agreements and shape these to their own liking.

Finally, this case study of hydropolitics in the Paraná–La Plata basin suggests that water accords between riparian states in an international basin may typically take a very long time, in the order of decades, to fashion, and equally long or longer to actually implement. With these tentative generalizations in hand, we now proceed to describing and analyzing the nature and conduct of hydropolitics in the Nile basin.

2

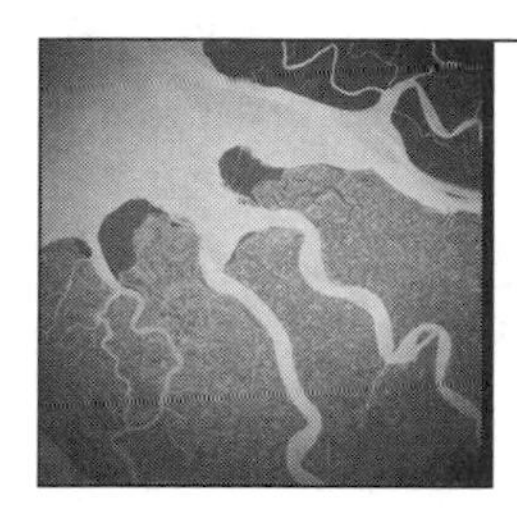

The Nile Basin

Flushed with the anticipation of national water surpluses after the construction of the Aswân High Dam, in 1970 the late Egyptian president Anwar al-Sadat had publicly entertained the idea of supplying the Nile's water to Saudi Arabia and to Israel, by laying down pipelines under the Suez Canal and across the Sinai desert. After signing the historic Camp David peace accords with Israel, in 1979 Sadat is reported to have said that the only reason his country might go to war again with any of its neighbors would be a dispute over water.[1] To date, Egypt has not supplied water to any other country, primarily because the Nile's waters are not for Egypt to give away (or sell) as it chooses, even assuming there were some to spare.[2] And despite or because of the many subsequent repetitions of Sadat's warning by other Egyptian leaders, as yet there has not been large-scale bloodshed over the shared waters in the Nile basin. Nonetheless, if things continue progressing as they have been along and around the Nile River, and even if there are no major armed confrontations among the riparian states in the near future over water per se, it is almost certain that domestic upheaval—engendered by the increasingly scarce and deteriorating freshwater supplies—will further aggravate political instability and territorial fragmentation in this large and highly volatile river basin in Africa.

Hydropolitics in the Nile basin can be understood only if it is recognized outright that without the Nile's water Egypt would cease to exist as a viable state. No other country in the world is so dependent on the water of a single river that it shares with not two or three but eight other states,[3] all located upstream from Egypt. Thus, while Egypt may be the strongest state in the Nile basin—economically and militarily—it is also the most vulnerable when it comes to national water security. Anything that substantially affects the quantity and the quality of the Nile's waters upstream from Egypt, and within the country, has an immediate impact upon the country's environmental and economic well-being, domestic politics, international relations, and national security. This "Egyptian condition" has always been and will continue to be at the heart of hydropolitics in the Nile basin. For Egypt, geography, more specifically hydrology, *is* national destiny. Other countries sharing the basin also depend on the waters of the Nile for economic development, political stability, and social welfare, but not as crucially as does Egypt.

As is the case in many other international river basin in the Third World, hydropolitics in the Nile basin very clearly highlights the complex historical interplay of colonial legacies, superpower rivalry in the Cold War era, interstate relations, and domestic politics in shaping and circumscribing interstate conflict and cooperation over transboundary water resources. Many additional and unique factors and geographical features have also shaped, and continue to shape, the nature and conduct of hydropolitics in the Nile basin, as we shall see.[4]

GEOGRAPHY

Physical Geography

Stretching from Lake Victoria in south-central Africa to the Mediterranean Sea, the Nile basin, with a total area of 3.1 million square kilometers (1.2 million square miles)—an area as large as one-tenth of the whole African continent—mainly encompasses the sub-basins of two major rivers, the White Nile and the Blue Nile (see the map facing).[5] The catchment and drainage basin of the White Nile includes portions of territories of eight of the nine Nile basin riparian states, Burundi, Ethiopia, Kenya, Rwanda, Sudan, Tanzania, Uganda, and Congo (Zaire)—that is, all except Egypt. The territories of Burundi and Rwanda are almost entirely contained within this sub-basin. The Blue Nile basin, on the other hand, includes portions of territories of only three states, Egypt, Ethiopia, and Sudan, which, nonetheless, share almost 85 percent of the total area of the combined Nile basin. A little less than two-thirds of the whole Nile basin is within Sudanese

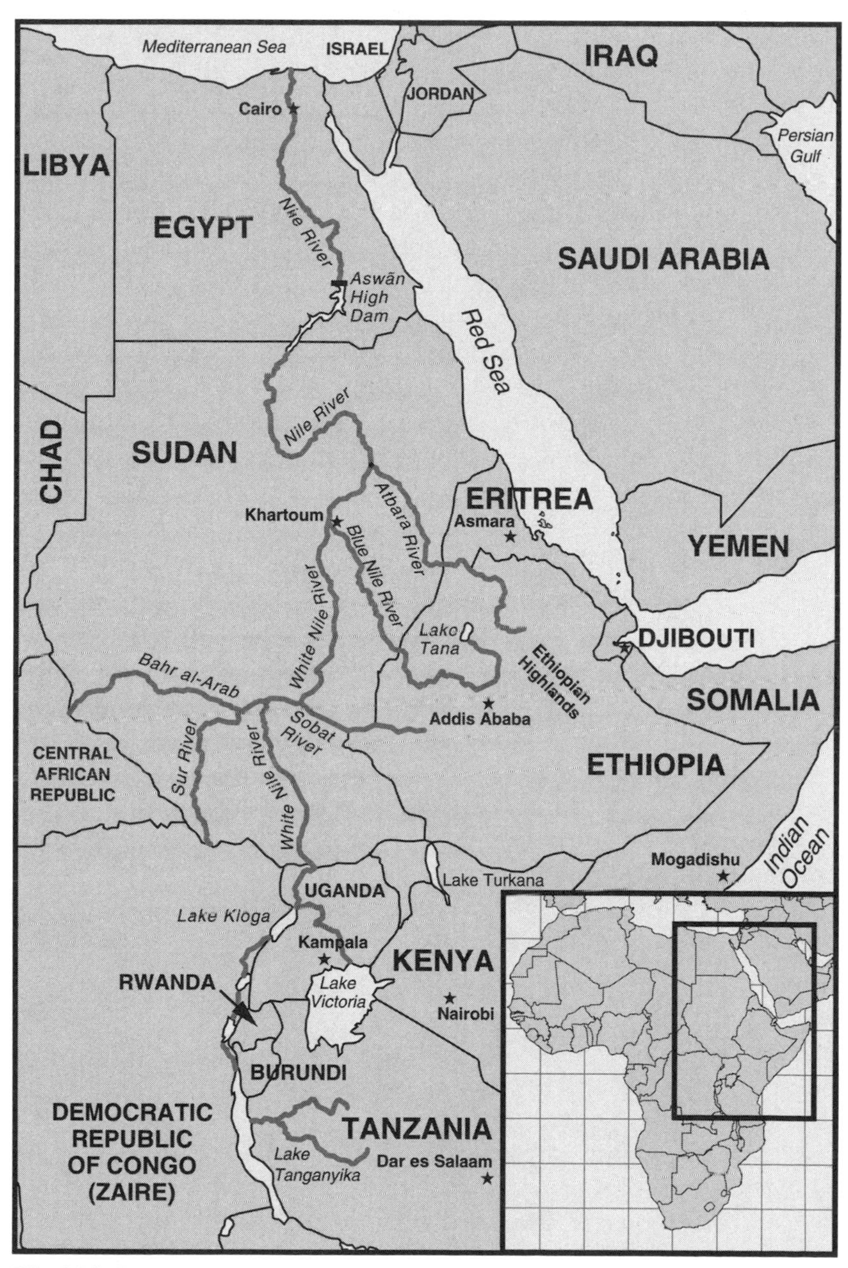

The Nile Basin

territory; however, close to 85 percent of the Nile's water reaching the Aswân High Dam in Egypt originates in Ethiopia.

The Nile basin also includes many large lakes: the main ones are Lake Tana (Tsana) in Ethiopia; Lake Mobutu (formerly Lake Albert) and Lake Idi Amin (formerly Lake Edward), which are shared by Congo (Zaire) and Uganda; Lake Kioga in Uganda; and Lake Victoria, which borders Uganda, Tanzania, and Kenya. The basin also includes the world's largest freshwater swamps, the Sudd in southern Sudan, with an area of 8,000 square kilometers (3,120 square miles).

The origins of the White Nile are in the Luvironza River in Tanzania, from where it traverses a course of 6,825 kilometers (4,230 miles) to the Mediterranean Sea.[6] However, its principle source is in Lake Victoria—a freshwater lake with a surface second in size only to Lake Superior in North America. Throughout its passage to the sea, the river's flow is joined by water from other sources, including the Sobat (Baro) River from Ethiopia and the Bahr el Ghazal lagoon in southwestern Sudan.[7] From its origin to the sea, the river drops in elevation by nearly half a mile, creating a huge potential for hydroelectricity generation in Tanzania and Uganda.

The principle source of the Blue Nile is Lake Tana in Ethiopia, with a surface area of 3,100 square kilometers (1,200 square miles) and an elevation of 1,800 meters (1.1 miles) above sea level. From the lake to the Sudanese capital, Khartoum, where it joins the Blue Nile, the river traverses nearly 1,500 kilometers (930 miles), and its elevation drops to less than one-third of a mile above sea level. This steep drop in elevation has created a vast potential for hydropower generation in Ethiopia. On the way to Khartoum, the Blue Nile is joined by two seasonal tributaries, the Rahad and the Dinda, and north of Khartoum, at Atbara, by the Atbara River, all of which also originate in the Ethiopian highlands.

Just to the north of Cairo the Nile splits into the Rosetta, which empties into the Mediterranean Sea near Alexandria, and the Damietta, which meets the sea near the mouth of the Suez Canal. The vast Nile Delta is completely within Egyptian territory.

An important physical geographic feature that distinguishes the Nile basin from some other international basins is that navigation is possible only on some short and distinct stretches of the basin's rivers. Moreover, these distinct navigable stretches are wholly contained within the territories of different riparian states. This has effectively eliminated one source of possible conflict in the basin, that is, the right to freedom of navigation on the shared rivers. However, for all other uses of the shared waters, the riparian states are dependent on one another to varying degrees.

Another important feature of the basin's physical geography, which, as we shall see, has substantial bearing on hydropolitics, is the highly varied pattern of rainfall and evaporation over the basin's vast stretch across the tropical and subtropical climatic zones. Almost all the flow of the Nile is derived from rainfall in Ethiopia and the lakes in the White Nile basin. There are great variations in precipitation over the whole basin over time and space; for example, the Blue Nile may discharge sixty times as much water during floods as during the rest of the year, bringing with it 60 million tons of silt per year in the process. These silts, which are now held back in large part by some dams and reservoirs, were primarily responsible for making the Nile basin habitable and productive. Overall, the Blue Nile contributes nearly 75 percent of the combined annual flow of the two Niles.

In the White Nile basin, countries south of Sudan have considerably more rainfall than both Sudan and Egypt combined. However, the fluctuations in rainfall and water extraction upstream do not seriously affect the downstream hydrological regime of the river, mainly because the large Sudd swamps help to mitigate any downstream impacts. Nonetheless, these huge swamps are also responsible for the evaporation of close to one-half of all the water brought down by the White Nile into Sudan; these evaporation losses have been estimated to be as much as 14 billion cubic meters a year, almost exactly the amount of water later added to the White Nile by the Sobat River from Ethiopia.

The lakes along the White Nile's path also have very high evaporation rates because of their large surfaces, which are exposed to a hot tropical climate. In addition, close to 10 billion cubic meters of the Nile's flow into Egypt is currently evaporated every year over Lake Nasser, the large reservoir behind the Aswân High Dam.[8] Altogether, the combined evaporation losses amount to nearly 40 billion cubic meters a year. As a result, the Nile delivers only 84 billion cubic meters of water on average every year at the Aswân High Dam. These high evaporation losses over Sudanese and Egyptian territories and over the lakes upstream have great significance for hydropolitics in the basin, as will shall see.

From Khartoum to the Mediterranean Sea, the Nile does not receive any substantial rainfall or other perennial source of water. Only 4 percent of Egypt's water needs are currently supplied by underground reserves; however, some geological surveys and estimates suggest there may be as much as 150 billion cubic meters of water stored beneath the soils of Upper Egypt and another 500 billion cubic meters under the Nile Delta. These reserves could conceivably satisfy Egypt's growing water needs for decades to come; however, even if these estimates turn out to be correct, only a fraction of these potentially huge supplies may be stored at sufficiently shallow depths to make their economic exploitation possible. In any case, unlike the fossil waters lying underneath the western desert of Egypt, in ancient aquifers it shares with Libya, aquifers in the Nile basin may be recharged only by the river itself.[9] Thus, any reduction in the river's flow may have a substantially degrading impact on the underground water reserves. Nonetheless, it is estimated that with proper recharge, up to 1 billion cubic meters of these reserves may be used annually.

There are also reported to be large aquifers underneath Sudanese and Ethiopian territories. But as in the case of Egypt, many economic, political and technical impediments stand in the way of these countries being able to fully exploit these reserves to relieve their ongoing and impending water shortages. In any case, any indiscriminate exploitation of the water stored in any of the Nile basin aquifers carries with it the risk of serious environmental damage as well as the potential for interstate conflict from the contested multilateral claims of ownership of these water resources.

And yet the Nile basin is one of the largest freshwater basins in the world. If only their full multiple-use potential could be developed and exploited in a cooperative manner, the basin's water resources could become the foundations for great economic prosperity and well-being in all the riparian states, both in the short run and the long run. Unfortunately, not only is this vast potential not being developed and exploited, environmental damage in the basin is seriously degrading even the existing freshwater supplies. Some examples of serious environmental damage in the basin include deforestation in the Ethiopian highlands, leading to severe topsoil erosion and silting of the river channels downstream; salinization and waterlogging of large tracts of the farmland in Sudan and Egypt from the spread of poorly drained perennial irrigation; a massive spread of water hyacinth and other weeds in the reservoirs and irrigation canals, requiring enormous amounts of toxic chemicals for eradication, which are, in turn, leached back into the water supply; depletion of the diverse fish species in Lake Victoria; and the spread of some debilitating waterborne diseases along the irrigation canals.[10] If these ongoing environmental calamities were not alarming enough, global climatic changes are projected to reduce the Nile's flow by as much as 25 percent in the future, by substantially altering the established pattern of precipitation and evaporation in the basin.[11] Even a rise of only a few feet in the sea level from global warming would not only destroy Egypt's underground water supply in the coastal areas, but it would also submerge large tracts of farmland in the Nile Delta. Altogether, the ongoing water practices and the anticipated climatic changes are likely to have devastating consequences for the already precarious economic geography of the basin as a whole and of the states sharing it.

Economic Geography

Historically, inhabitants of the Nile basin had husbanded their precious water and land resources to build some of the most developed and long-lasting civilizations and empires in the world. However, once regarded as the "cradle of civilization" and as the heart of the "breadbasket" of the Roman Empire, today the whole basin is characterized as food deficient, underdeveloped, and close to economic and political collapse.

In mid-1997, the combined population of the nine countries sharing the Nile basin was estimated to be close to 250 million, with a million people being added to the Egyptian population alone every seven to eight months. With growth rates as high as 3.6 percent per annum in some countries, the combined population of the riparian states is expected to rise to 327 million by the end of this century. This will be equivalent to an increase in population, in just one decade, larger than the *combined* current population of Egypt and Ethiopia. And by the year 2000, Ethiopia—the third-lowest per capita income country in the world after Rwanda and Mozambique in 1994 and already the third most populous country in Africa—is expected to have 10 million more people than will Egypt.[12]

Keeping in mind that the minimum per capita water needs for an efficient, moderately industrialized nation have been estimated as 1,000 cubic meters per year, the annual per capita water availability between the years 1990 and 2025 is expected to drop from 1,070 to 620 cubic meters in Egypt, from 2,360 to 980 cubic meters in Ethiopia, from 590 to 190 cubic meters in Kenya, from 880 to 350 cubic meters in Rwanda, and from 2,780 to 900 cubic meters in Tanzania, based solely on the anticipated increases in the respective populations and on the current rates of water extraction.[13] These dire projections do not take into account the rising water needs and intensities of urban settlements, agriculture, industries, power generation, and other economic activities in the basin.

In 1997 per capita annual incomes in the basin ranged from $110 in Ethiopia to $1,180 in Egypt, making it one of the poorest regions in the world. In 1995 annual energy consumption per capita varied from just 21 kilograms of oil equivalent (koe) for Ethiopia to 596 koe for Egypt, compared with 7,905 koe for the United States.[14] Nonetheless, in 1995 the nine countries together spent close to $6 billion on their military establishments, with Egypt alone spending $4 billion.[15] And despite being the second-largest recipient of aid from the United States, after Israel, Egypt owed $31 billion in external debt in 1996.[16] In 1996 Sudan owed $16 billion, Zaire $12 billion, and Ethiopia $10 billion to their respective international creditors. Altogether, in 1996 the nine riparian states had an external debt of about $90 billion. At the same time, in Egypt alone subsidies for irrigation were estimated to amount to $5 billion to $10 billion every year, in addition to energy subsidies of $4 billion to $6 billion.[17] Clearly, without radical economic restructuring and substantial external assistance none of the riparian states will be able to unilaterally undertake any large water project in the basin in the foreseeable future.

Agriculture is still the primary economic activity in all the riparian states, employing up to 93 percent of the labor force, mostly in subsistence agriculture and cattle raising, especially in Burundi, Rwanda, and Tanzania. Few countries have any semblance of modern industrialization, and that which exists is mostly to satisfy some domestic needs for consumer goods. Although some countries are exporters of cash crops, such as coffee and cotton, and some other primary commodities, the basin as a whole is now a net importer of agricultural commodities; Egypt, for example, currently imports more than one-half of its basic food requirements.

A rapid expansion of perennial irrigation since the beginning of this century had allowed food production in Egypt and Sudan to keep pace with their growing populations and to produce surpluses for export; however, in recent decades urban encroachment on precious arable lands and severe degradation of the farmland from salinization and heavy use of chemicals have greatly reduced the availability of agricultural land in both countries. Despite the massive extension of perennial irrigation for almost a century, arable land per person in Egypt declined from 0.21 hectares (0.5 acres) in 1900 to 0.06 hectares (0.15 acres) in 1990, while the population rose from 10 million to 52 million.[18] Thus, in Egypt both water and land have become highly scarce commodities; in the future a rapidly growing urban population will only exacerbate the problem of available agricultural land.

About 96 percent of Egypt's population currently lives in the narrow Nile Valley and in the Nile Delta, which together account for only 4 percent of the landmass of the country. In the south the valley is rarely more than 3 kilometers (2 miles) wide; in the north it averages 8 to 16 kilometers (5 to 10 miles) in width. Thus, except for the Nile Valley, the Nile Delta, and some settlements along the Suez Canal, Egypt is a vast and empty desert. No other comparably populous country in the world has such a narrow and concentrated economic geography that is so heavily dependent on the waters of a shared river.

Faced with this peculiar economic geography and with a projected doubling of the population by the year 2025, Egypt has drawn up grandiose plans for constructing new cities in the desert; for transferring populations away from the highly congested Nile Valley and the Suez Canal area; for extending irrigation to millions of new cultivated acres while making more intensive use of the old acreage; for promoting rapid industrialization of the country; for achieving self-sufficiency in the production of basic food items; and for promoting tourism.[19] However, it ought to be clear to all concerned that the implementation of each of these ambitious plans is contingent upon the availability of large amounts of freshwater, which Egypt currently does not have, nor is it likely to have anytime in the foreseeable future. It is also highly doubtful whether this heavily debt-laden country will be able to secure the external aid needed to implement these grand schemes, even if basinwide cooperation for the Egyptian projects were forthcoming. Facing growing environmental problems, most of which are related to the quantity and the quality of available freshwater, Egypt has also drawn up ambitious plans for improving its environment. However, these plans called for an investment of $300 million in Phase I (1992–97) and for an additional $3 billion in Phase II (1997–2002).[20] Again, it is difficult to see debt-laden Egypt managing to undertake these projects without substantial external assistance.

Sudan has also formulated some grand plans for extending irrigation and agriculture to vast tracts of land. Sudan does have a comparative advantage over Egypt in that its 2.5-million-square-kilometer (1-million-square-mile) territory, 49 percent of which is suitable for agriculture, is still very sparsely inhabited. However, with a vast potential for the extension of irrigated agriculture, Sudan currently irrigates less than 1 percent of its arable land. Some earlier irrigation projects, such as the Gezira Irrigation Scheme, which has extended agricultural land in Sudan from 300,000 to 2.1 million acres since its inception in 1920, have already run into serious problems.[21] Given Sudan's very precarious domestic security situation (discussed later) and huge external debt, it is difficult to visualize any significant improvement in the agricultural situation in Sudan, in the short run. Sudan is also heavily dependent on the imports of large amounts of petrochemical resources. This makes the country highly vulnerable to manipulations from the outside.

Some other Nile basin riparian states also have ambitious plans for implementing large economic development projects—all of which are again contingent upon the availability of water and substantial external financial and technical aid. With the assistance of the United Nations Development Program (UNDP), a comprehensive development plan has been formulated for the 60,000-square-kilometer (23,400-square-mile) Kagera River basin, which is shared by Burundi, Rwanda, Tanzania, and Uganda. Besides the generation of hydroelectricity, extension of agriculture to areas currently infested with tsetse flies, reforestation in the highlands, and training of technical and managerial personnel, the plan visualizes a vast network of roads and railways—costing several billion dollars—to provide access to the sea for the landlocked countries in the Kagera basin.[22] Many schemes for water transfer and for extension of irrigation have also been proposed for Kenya and Tanzania. However, it should again be clear that none of these plans can materialize without interbasin cooperation, external aid, and, most important, political stability in the basin as a whole.

The Nile basin riparian states, like many developing countries sharing other international river basins, are thus caught in a vicious cycle: the much-needed regional cooperation and economic development will not materialize without political stability in the basin, and political stability will remain elusive without regional cooperation and equitable economic development. In the meantime, the economies of nearly all the basin countries are stagnating or declining. Most of the countries lack the basic infrastructure and human resources that are usually needed to implement and maintain large development projects. Unfortunately, despite the vast but as yet only partially exploited developmental potential of the Nile's waters, the highly volatile political geography of the basin, and of the individual states sharing it, does not offer much hope that things will improve anytime soon.

Political Geography

Among the major international river basins in the Third World, the Nile basin not only has the distinction of being shared by the largest number of riparian states,[23] but it also contains some of the youngest sovereign states. It was less than five decades ago that Egypt became an independent republic after forty years of British rule and thirty years of monarchy, and Sudan gained independence from British rule only in 1956. The other upstream British colonies—Kenya, Tanzania, and Uganda—became sovereign states in the early 1960s, around the same time that three more upstream countries in the White Nile basin—Burundi, Rwanda, and Congo—became free from Belgian rule or "protection." Only Ethiopia has the distinction of never being fully colonized by a European power, although a region of the country, Eritrea, was occupied by the Italians for close to fifty years and by the British for a short duration after 1941. In May 1993, Eritrea became an independent nation after nearly four decades of armed rebellion against its incorporation into Ethiopia.

Since achieving independence from colonial rule, nearly all these countries have made many attempts to establish representative governments; however, these intermittent moves toward democracy have mostly been subverted by military coups, by the imposition of one-party rule, and by ethnic conflicts—often aided and abetted by the earlier colonizers as well as the Cold War superpowers. Colonial legacies of arbitrarily drawn and imposed international borders, with scant regard for geography or ethnically shared spaces; Cold War–era support by the superpowers for despotic client regimes; selective use of aid by donors to essentially further their own home-country interests; and a massive dumping of military hardware in a highly volatile region have greatly distorted both domestic politics and interstate relations in the basin. In addition, some disastrous experiments with different models of socioeconomic development have now brought the whole region to the brink of chaos, so dramatically illustrated by the millions of refugees now crisscrossing international borders in the basin. These upheavals have also impeded the emergence of much-needed basinwide cooperation for the development and sharing of the precious water resources.

Today, the Nile basin contains a most heterogeneous group of riparian states, in terms of their ideological orientations, political and economic systems, and ethnic and religious composition. Nearly all of the riparian states are now riven with domestic conflict and regime instability. For example, two of the three countries in the so-called Horn of Africa—Sudan and Somalia—are on the verge of collapse or fragmentation. Although Somalia does not share the Nile basin, there are cross-boundary rebellions for separatism across the Somali-Ethiopian border in the Ogaden region. Within Ethiopia the former central government had fought against the Eritrean secessionist movement for close to thirty years, and since the late 1970s it had been attempting to suppress another separatist movement in the Tigray (Tigre) region. The Ethiopian army—one of the largest in Africa—had used all means, including help from foreign (e.g., Cuban) troops, to suppress and destroy these rebellions for nearly three decades, without much success. As a consequence of these upheavals, until recently Ethiopians were the largest group of refugees in Africa. This has created further tensions between Ethiopia and its neighbors.[24]

In Sudan an active and very costly civil war rages on in the south between the Muslim-controlled central government in Khartoum and the Sudanese People's Liberation Army (SPLA), which seeks to reorganize the Sudanese government along nonconfessional lines. The rise of Islamic fundamentalism in both Sudan and Egypt represents a great threat to national and regional security. There has been "ethnic cleansing" in Congo and forced expulsion of refugees from Kenya. Uganda has yet to fully recover from the calamities perpetrated there since the 1970s by Idi Amin Dada and his successors. Currently, both Burundi and Rwanda are essentially dysfunctional states, and both are engaged in ethnic and cross-border conflict. Thus, overall, the Nile basin remains a highly unstable and potentially explosive region in the post–Cold War world. This ongoing regional instability is likely to be further compounded by the very real possibility that more than ten sovereign states may be sharing the Nile basin in the future. This would further complicate the already highly complex hydropolitical situation in the basin.

Ironically, almost all the insurgent movements in this food-deficient basin as well as the central governments trying to suppress them have used food as a weapon, by usurping the domestic and externally provided food supplies and by denying them to their opponents.[25] As always, the worst sufferers from these "food wars" have been the marginalized sections of the rural populations, who often have had no choice but to migrate across international borders at great personal risk. Persistent droughts, ongoing civil wars, and frequent ethnic bloodletting have devastated agriculture in many countries. By depressing the prices for indigenous produce, even the much-needed external food-aid has greatly diminished agricultural productivity.[26] Terrorist activity in some countries has destroyed much of their rudimentary infrastructure—roads, railways, power grids, and so forth. In recent years events in Burundi, Congo, Rwanda, Somalia, Sudan, and Uganda have most dramatically brought home to the larger international community the tragic consequences of these mostly man-made disasters.

But there have also been some attempts in the past, especially by Egypt, to form economic and political alliances and federations within the basin as well as with some countries in the Middle East. Recognizing Egypt's total dependence on the Nile's water coming out of Sudan, and that together Egypt and Sudan could become the largest state in Africa—in area, population, and economic and military might—from time to time the Egyptian leadership has tried to form a federation of the two countries. Guided by economic and strategic considerations and by the ideology of pan-Arabism, Egypt has also toyed with the idea of forming economic and political federations with Libya and Syria. However, as should have been expected, it has been impossible to sustain these misguided efforts to artificially and arbitrarily integrate highly disparate peoples, separated in the case of Egypt and Syria by other countries! Of course, if a union of Egypt and Sudan (or Egypt and northern Sudan) were to somehow come about in the future, hydropolitics in the Nile basin would change dramatically; but the very real possibility of the fragmentation of Sudan—into a predominantly Muslim north and a mostly Christian south—makes such a federation highly unlikely.

During the Cold War, both the superpowers and their allies had tried to woo Egypt into their respective camps, with substantial grants of economic and military assistance. In particular, following the signing of the Camp David Accords with Israel, Egypt became the second-largest recipient of economic and military aid from the United States. The fact that Egypt has been seen, rightly or wrongly, by other regimes in the Arab world as the only military power capable of seriously challenging the designs of Iran, Iraq, Israel, and Syria, and more recently of perhaps being able to confront the threat of growing Islamic fundamentalism in the region, means that Egypt's stability and interests have acquired added significance for some regional actors, in particular for Saudi Arabia. Thus, Egypt's internal vulnerabilities notwithstanding, it is difficult to imagine the other Nile basin riparian states mounting a direct challenge—individually or collectively—to Egypt's domination of the basin's hydropolitics in the near future.

The fact that Egypt has become a strategic link between the regional security complexes in the Middle East and northeast Africa by virtue of its involvement in the larger Arab-Israeli conflict, and more recently by its participation in the Gulf War against Iraq, means that hydropolitics in the Nile basin has not been and cannot be immune to developments in the larger geopolitical situation in the two regions. If comprehensive peace does come to the Middle East (see chapter 3), it is possible that the Nile basin may also benefit from the overall reduction in tensions in the region. However, whether the riparian states upstream of Sudan would derive any substantial benefits from peace in the Middle East remains an open question.

Given the particular riparian structure of the basin and the existing power imbalances between Egypt and all the other riparian states in the

Nile basin, it can be argued that Egypt has an interest in ensuring that the upstream riparian states remain weak, unstable, and underdeveloped and thus incapable of constructing large water projects upstream from Egypt or mounting a serious challenge to Egypt's disproportionate share of the basin's waters. In fact, Egypt has on occasion been accused of fomenting dissent and helping rebellions in Sudan and Ethiopia.[27] On the other hand, for reasons to be discussed later, political stability in the basin as a whole and basinwide cooperation are now essential if Egypt and the other riparian states want to develop the full potential of the Nile's waters for everyone's benefit.

HYDROPOLITICS

Compared with some other international river basins in the Third World, for example, the Paraná–La Plata basin (chapter 1) and the Ganges-Brahmaputra-Barak basin (chapter 5), the Nile basin would seem to have a very simple riparian structure; the Blue Nile and its tributaries flow successively through Ethiopia, Sudan, and Egypt, and the White Nile follows a successive course through all the riparian states in its sub-basin. And although some White Nile lakes, and the smaller rivers connecting them, do form international borders between some riparian states, on the whole the main channels of the two Niles follow successive courses through the riparians' territories. However, even though Egypt shares a border with only one other riparian state, Sudan, its overwhelming dependence on the Nile's water makes the effective riparian structure of the basin highly complex. To fully comprehend hydropolitics in the basin, one needs to conceptually modify the seemingly simple riparian structure to a more complex one in which Egypt is, in effect, surrounded by all the other riparian states. This is because Egypt needs to deal with all of them—individually and collectively—to ensure that its national interest and security are not jeopardized by any manipulation of the upstream river regimes.

As an upper riparian with Egypt but a lower riparian with every other state sharing the basin, Sudan would seem to have a classic middle riparian position in the basin's hydropolitics. However, because nearly two-thirds of the Nile basin lies within its territory, and because both the Blue and the White Niles and all their tributaries pass through it, Sudan potentially has a much stronger riparian position than its middle riparian status would otherwise dictate. If some day Sudan were to become militarily and economically more powerful than it is now, it could radically change interstate relations and the nature of hydropolitics in the basin. The fact that Sudan also shares borders with all other riparian states except Burundi, Rwanda, and Tanzania points to yet another arena of potential conflict in the basin, especially as large numbers of refugees continue to crisscross the contested and porous international borders.

Because of its unique physical geography and the upstream riparian position, Ethiopia would seem to have potentially the strongest position in the basin's hydropolitics, especially as the rivers originating within its territory contribute about 85 percent of the Nile's flow. Lake Tana, which has a much lower evaporation rate than any alternate storage reservoir that can be built within Egypt or Sudan or on the headwaters of the White Nile, could be developed as a large storage reservoir to help prevent floods downstream as well as create additional flow in the lean season for both Egypt and Sudan. The enormous hydroelectric potential of the rivers originating in Ethiopia could also be jointly developed and shared by the three countries.

But all the riparian advantages conferred upon Ethiopia by the basin's physical geography notwithstanding, it remains underdeveloped because it has not been able to tap even a tiny fraction of the multiple-use potential of the rivers originating in and flowing through its territory. This is mainly because Ethiopia has had to face constraints created by its peculiar economic geography and highly volatile political geography. For example, even if Ethiopia could somehow develop a substantial portion of its estimated 8,380 megawatts of hydroelectric potential,[28] the electricity generated would not be fully consumed within the country because domestic demand for it will continue to be suppressed from a lack of economic development as well as the concentration of whatever demand there is in some distant urban areas. Transmission of electricity to these settlements from the Nile basin would imply very high losses and costs. Thus Ethiopia, like Paraguay in the Paraná–La Plata basin, would have no choice but to sell any surplus hydroelectric power it may produce to its downstream neighbors. Since the Eritrean declaration of independence, Ethiopia has also effectively become a landlocked country. A substantially truncated Ethiopia has thus joined the ranks of the other landlocked countries—Burundi, Rwanda, and Uganda—in the Nile basin, and it is now forced to negotiate from a substantially weakened position with Eritrea and Djibouti for maintaining its overland access to the sea.

As for the other upper riparian states on the White Nile, until very recently none had developed any major plans for utilizing the basin's waters, nor have they been in a position—individually or collectively—to seriously challenge Sudan's and Egypt's water practices in the basin. For historical reasons, relations among them have also remained contentious. For example, Kenya has been hostile to Uganda, Uganda to Kenya and Sudan, and Congo (Zaire) to Ethiopia.[29] This has greatly reduced the possibility of any collective action by the upper riparian states on the White Nile. Such cooperation, were it somehow to come about, could seriously challenge the positions of their powerful but downstream neighbors in the basin's hydropolitics. And given the fact that international organizations and donors now require cooperation among all the riparian states in an international basin before granting loans for large water projects, these countries could yet exercise considerable influence on hydropolitics in the basin, if only by delaying one another's plans for constructing large water projects. Thus, in the absence of a multilateral agreement on their common water resources, hydropolitics among the Nile basin riparian states is bound to become more contentious and problematic than it currently is.[30]

Conflict and Cooperation

Throughout the colonial period, Great Britain had effectively controlled the Nile River from its origins to the Mediterranean Sea, despite Belgium's control of Burundi, Rwanda, and Congo; Italy's control of Eritrea; and Ethiopia's independence. This was possible mainly because the British controlled Egypt and Sudan, as well as the three upper riparian countries on the White Nile—Kenya, Tanzania, and Uganda—and because of Britain's military superiority over all other colonizers in the basin.

The British achieved full control over the Nile primarily by signing treaties with other colonizers and by establishing an Anglo-Egyptian condominium over Sudan in 1899 to ensure that no projects could be built in the basin and no water withdrawn upstream of Egypt without Egyptian and British consent.[31] The colonial treaties and the condominium over Sudan were designed mainly to protect Egypt's interests in the basin, since for many strategic and economic reasons Egypt had become the most important Nile basin riparian state for the British colonizers. The strategic importance of Egypt arose mainly because of the value of its Red Sea ports for Britain's colonial trade and of the Suez Canal for controlling the shortest route from Europe to India — the "Jewel of the British Crown." Consequently, political stability in Egypt acquired paramount importance for its British administrators. To a very large extent, this stability became contingent upon satisfying Egypt's growing water needs, without much regard for the interests of the other riparians. This colonial-era mentality, subsequently inherited by the rulers of independent Egypt, and the resentments it has generated in the newly independent nations have continued to circumscribe hydropolitics in the Nile basin in the post–World War II era.

The British discovered that both Sudan and Egypt could produce large surpluses of high-quality cotton for the textile mills in England. This realization gained greatly in value after the successful rebellion against British rule in North America in the late eighteenth century. Coffee and sugar were the other water-intensive cash crops, again mainly for export, developed in the basin by the different colonizers, who paid scant attention to developing any semblance of modern industrialization in any of the basin countries under their control. The cash crop–dominated economies introduced by the colonizers, over and above the rapidly growing indigenous needs for basic food, have continued to dictate a growing need for the Nile's water for irrigation. In the process, very powerful and highly subsidized agricultural (and construction) lobbies have become entrenched in the domestic power structures of several states, especially Egypt and Sudan. Consequently, it has become very difficult to rationalize agricultural practices, prices for agricultural inputs and produce, and energy use in the basin in order to make them conform to the scarcity value of its water resources.

Since Egypt is totally dependent on the waters of the Nile and since it has long been the largest consumer of the basin's waters, in conducting hydropolitics with other riparian states it has mostly emphasized the triple doctrines of primary need, prior use, and acquired water rights. As long as the colonial powers dominating the basin could guarantee compliance with Egypt's needs and designs in the basin, or as long as Egypt itself could exercise direct or indirect domination over the upper riparians, it did not have to be mindful of the interests of other riparian states. Not surprisingly, after achieving independence from colonial rule and acquiring some maneuverability vis-à-vis Egypt, the upper riparians states have, in principle, rejected all colonial-era treaties and accords as well as Egypt's right to dictate all aspects of hydropolitics in the basin.

The most relevant among the colonial-era agreements for sharing water resources in the Nile basin was a 1929 agreement between Egypt and Britain, which was then representing Kenya, Tanzania, Sudan, and Uganda. The most important clause of this legal regime stated that "no works or other measures likely to reduce the amount of water reaching Egypt were to be constructed or taken in Sudan or in territories under British administration without prior Egyptian consent."[32] The agreement also granted Egypt the right to construct waterworks and undertake other water-related measures within Sudanese and other East African territories. Thus, the agreement allowed Egypt a virtual monopoly over the development and use of the basin's water resources. And although subsequent attempts to apply the 1929 agreement to Ethiopia did not materialize, until very recently much of the Egyptian thinking and perceptions relating to the Nile have been guided by the provisions of this highly lopsided colonial regime.

After World War II, relations between Egypt and Sudan began to deteriorate for a variety of reasons, including a growing demand in Sudan for independence from British and Egyptian domination, and Sudanese opposition to Egyptian plans for building the Aswân High Dam rather than some projects proposed under the Century Storage Scheme (discussed below). Sudan also began to question the rationale for the highly inequitable water-sharing quotas under the 1929 agreement. Negotiations between the two countries began in 1954 but were soon broken off. Following Sudanese independence in 1956, an unsuccessful military campaign by Egypt in 1958 to reclaim some disputed border territory led to the abrogation of the 1929 agreement by Sudan. The same year, a change in leadership in Sudan following a military coup created conditions for more conciliatory negotiations between the two regimes, culminating in the 1959 Agreement for the Full Utilization of the Nile Waters. On Egypt's insistence, Britain's efforts to represent the interests and concerns of the other riparian states under its control were rebuffed.[33] After their own independence, these riparian states and Ethiopia have refused to accept the 1959 agreement as a legal regime for the Nile basin, whereas Egypt has continued to insist that any new agreement for water sharing in the basin must be based on the provisions of the 1959 agreement.

The Century Storage Scheme

In 1946 the Egyptian government had formulated a scheme for developing the vast potential of the Nile's waters to meet the future water and energy needs of Sudan and Egypt, with some side benefits going to the upper riparians. The major components of the plan, first proposed in 1920 by a Briton, Murdoch Macdonald, were the following: Water discharges from Lake Victoria would be controlled by a dam at the Owen Falls in Uganda, at the place where the White Nile leaves the lake. The dam would provide storage for the irrigation needs of Egypt and Sudan during the lean seasons and bad rainfall years, and would generate hydroelectric power for Kenya, Tanzania, and Uganda. Another dam was proposed for the point where the river exits from Lake Albert (now Lake Mobutu) to enable regulation of the amount of water flowing down to Egypt and Sudan from the East African Plateau. An additional dam was foreseen at the outlet of the Blue Nile from Lake Tana in Ethiopia to provide supplementary over-year storage for irrigation and flood protection for the two downstream countries as well as to produce hydroelectric power. On the Sobat River, the plan called for a continuation of the role of the existing Jebel Awlia Dam in Sudan to hold back water from floods, mostly for use in Egypt at the low-water time of the year. The last but the most important part of the comprehensive plan was the Jonglei Canal Project in southern Sudan, which would divert large quantities of water away from the Sudd swamps where nearly one-half of the river's flow otherwise disappears from evaporation or transpiration by plants.[34] Altogether, these Upper Nile projects were expected to produce an additional supply of 18 billion cubic meters of water for Egypt and Sudan.

An interesting feature of the Egyptian scheme was that although Egypt stood to gain the most from the proposed projects, all but one project—a flood-control barrage—would have been located outside Egyptian territory.[35] However, none of the other riparian states in the basin, or their colonial administrations at the time, was consulted prior to making these plans public. Further, all the central functions relating to the planning, implementation, and management for all the proposed projects were to be located within Egypt, and Egyptian officials were to be stationed at each project site to ensure compliance with the Egyptian plans and directives. In 1946 and for a few years afterward, all the upper riparian states, except Ethiopia, were under colonial rule (or domination), which greatly facilitated a tacit approval of the Egyptian scheme by all the basin countries. However, as it turned out, this did not guarantee the subsequent implementation of the full Egyptian scheme. Because of some political developments within the basin as a whole and within Egypt, in the end only the Owen Falls Dam and the Jonglei Canal Project were constructed according to the Century Storage Scheme, and the latter only partially.[36]

Six major structures now control the Nile's flow from Uganda to Egypt. In addition, innumerable dams and barrages now alter and control the river's flow. As a consequence, as John Waterbury has stated, "The Egyptian Nile is now fully domesticated and made as manageable as a water faucet."[37] Among the large projects constructed in the basin to date, the Jonglei Canal Project in Sudan and the Aswân High Dam on the Egypt-Sudan border best reflect the hitherto contentious nature and conduct of hydropolitics in the Nile basin.

The Jonglei Canal Project

The idea of a canal to drain the Sudd swamps was first conceived in 1904 by a Briton, Sir William Garstin, at a time when the British effectively controlled both Egypt and Sudan. Subsequently, it was taken up as a major project under the Egyptian Century Storage Scheme. According to the Egyptian proposal, the Jonglei Canal in southern Sudan was to be 300 kilometers (186 miles) long, 52 meters (about 170 feet) wide, and 4 meters (13 feet) deep. In addition to draining the Sudd swamps, the project was meant to produce hydroelectric power for both the countries as well as allow controlled irrigation for farming in the nearby areas in Sudan. It was also expected to mitigate the devastating effects of floods in the Sudd swamps and some areas downstream from the swamps. Moreover, the proposed canal and a paved road running alongside it were to become important transportation arteries for southern Sudan.

However, though proposed at a time when Sudan was under British domination, the Jonglei Canal Project generated considerable opposition from the colonial administrators in Sudan, who felt that Sudan's interests would not be safeguarded if the Egyptian proposal were accepted. Later, the government of independent Sudan also objected to some details of the proposed project. Within Egypt, the idea of the country becoming dependent on water projects outside its territory also came under criticism. Consequently, the first stage of the canal project was not taken up for formal negotiations by the two governments until 1974, and only after many modifications in the original plan had been made, mainly to address some Sudanese concerns. After protracted negotiations the two countries finally agreed on the details of the project and to share the costs and benefits from implementing and maintaining it. A construction contract was subsequently awarded to a French consortium for building a canal 360 kilometers (223 miles) long and other associated works. Construction on Phase I of the project began in 1978—a full three-quarters of a century after the idea was first conceived by Sir William Garstin. At no time during this long incubation period were any of the upper riparian states in the basin consulted by Egypt and Sudan, nor was domestic opposition in the two countries allowed to interfere with the decision to go ahead with the bilateral project.

As soon as the plans for constructing the canal were announced, opposition mounted in southern Sudan, with violent demonstrations led by students in Juba, the south's main town. The opposition argued that the canal would dry up the Sudd swamps and speed up the expansion of the Sahara Desert southward. Critics of the project also charged the government in Khartoum of conspiring with Egypt to settle a large number of mostly Muslim Egyptians in southern Sudan who would displace indigenous nomadic populations. It was also pointed out that the freshwater Sudd swamps were the largest in the world and, as such, home to millions of migratory birds and thousands of large herbivores.[38] It was feared the project would seriously jeopardize the annual migration of birds to the Sudd from southern Europe.

Some southern Sudanese liberals did, however, support the canal project, provided that social services, such as schools, hospitals, and roads, were built simultaneously to benefit the local people. Some also suggested the building of bridges to enable wildlife to cross over the canal. But the Sudanese government in Khartoum, long accustomed to treating the south as a virtual colony, paid no attention to the fears and demands of the southerners, and it proceeded to construct the project with the help of the French consortium. Consequently, just five years after construction began on Phase I of the project, in 1983 all excavation work was halted owing to the eruption of a violent civil war in southern Sudan. In 1984 a one-year-old rebellious group in the south, the Sudanese People's Liberation Army (SPLA), effectively terminated the contract of the French company. Ironically, the leader of SPLA, Colonel John Garang, who is from the Sudd area, had done his doctorate dissertation on the Jonglei Canal Project![39]

Thus, despite the bilateral agreement between Egypt and Sudan and despite a massive outlay of resources to date, it is not clear if the project can be completed. Throughout its implementation, rumors have floated that hostilities in the south have destroyed all or part of the project. For instance, on March 26, 1990, the Egyptian minister of works and water resources reported to the People's Assembly that implementing the project, which was then only 70 percent completed, would not be resumed until the "security disputes" in southern Sudan were resolved. However, he was able to assure the assembly that, despite rumors to the contrary, the equipment for the project had not been damaged.[40]

Apart from the domestic opposition within Sudan and Egypt, the Jonglei Canal Project has been criticized internationally on larger environmental grounds. First, it is feared that draining the huge swamps would lead to weather modification and changes in rainfall patterns not only in southern Sudan but also in the neighboring countries. Second, the volume of flow in the canal, amounting to about 20 million cubic meters, would back up the flow of the Sobat River at Malakal, resulting in flooding of the Sobat Valley in Ethiopia. Third, any control of floods in the Sobat Valley and in parts of southern Sudan would necessitate regulating the discharges from Lake Victoria by raising the level of water stored behind the Owen Falls Dam. This would, in turn, lead to serious environmental consequences in Kenya, Tanzania, and Uganda, owing to lake water backing up inland.[41] Naturally, these countries are not likely to be very enthusiastic about any extension of the Jonglei Canal Project unless they have a stake in its construction and functioning, and unless they are compensated for the damages they may suffer.

Thus, although initially conceived by Egypt and Sudan as a bilateral project for their mutual benefit, implementation of the full Jonglei Canal Project would require the cooperation and blessing of other riparian states in the Nile basin. A precondition for the project's success is also the continued integrity of Sudan as well as the cessation of all hostilities in the south. Many additional environmental, socioeconomic, and political concerns of the mostly non-Egyptian peoples likely to be affected by the project would have to be addressed before Egypt and Sudan can fully implement and benefit from the Jonglei Canal Project. International donors, increasingly concerned about the preservation of freshwater wetlands in their own countries, are also highly unlikely to finance any further development of the project unless their larger environmental concerns are adequately addressed. In short, the two lowermost riparian states cannot count on additional water supplies from the Sudd in the foreseeable future.

The Aswân High Dam

On January 15, 1971, the Egyptian president, Anwar al-Sadat, accompanied by the president of the Soviet Union, Nikolai Podgorny, presided over a ceremony marking the official inauguration of the Aswân High Dam. As it turned out, the ceremony also marked a denouement of the highly publicized Egypt-USSR friendship, which had made the gigantic project possible. Just eighteen months after the ceremony, Sadat expelled all Soviet military advisers from his country and, in 1976, just five years after its signing, the Special Friendship Treaty between the two countries was abrogated by Egypt.[42]

Despite many domestic and international controversies relating to the socioeconomic, political, and environmental impacts of the project, the Aswân High Dam has stood as a giant symbol of Egypt's long quest for sovereignty, national security, economic prosperity, and technical accomplishments. Branded as Nasser's "pyramid" by some critics,[43] and as "the most recent (and surely not the last) manifestation of Egypt's struggle to dominate rather than coexist with the Nile Valley,"[44] the dam has drawn fire and acclaim since its very inception in the late 1950s. The High Dam is also one of the most glaring monuments to the interplay of colonial legacies and post–World War II geopolitics in affecting and shaping hydropolitics in a Third World region.

The High Dam project was first proposed by a Greco-Egyptian engineer, Adrien Daminos, in 1948—the same year that the Egyptian government had officially endorsed the Century Storage Scheme. That was also the year of the first Arab-Israeli war, which led to a partial arms embargo on the region by the United States, France, and Great Britain. This embargo was strongly resented by the Egyptians and other Arab nationalists, who were then seeking freedom from colonial rule. Many Sudanese nationalists of the time were also inspired by the Egyptians' call for independence and for Arab unity in the face of what was then perceived to be Western hegemony in the region as well as bias against the Arabs. Thus, from the very beginning the Aswân High Dam proposal became embedded in the larger geopolitical dynamics in the region.

As pointed out earlier, the Century Storage Scheme had a major flaw from an Egyptian perspective in that all of the proposed projects were to be located outside its territory. This did not sit well with the highly nationalistic leadership that came to power in Egypt under Nasser in 1952, when three important upstream countries on the Nile—Kenya, Sudan, and Uganda—were still under the control of Egypt's chief adversary, Great Britain. In addition, Great Britain then had armed forces stationed on Egyptian soil in the Suez Canal area, which Britain effectively controlled. The new Egyptian leadership under Nasser felt a strong need to assert Egypt's national sovereignty and territorial integrity and concretely demonstrate to its own people and to the rest of the world its resolve to transform Egypt into a modern, industrialized nation.[45] In such a politically charged climate, the Aswân High Dam proposal, controversial though it was even then, came to signify and symbolize all the aspirations and capabilities of the new Egyptian republic. Any criticism of the project became an act of treason almost, since it was felt that the domestic and international adversaries of the new Egyptian leadership could use criticism of the project to undermine its credibility. The multiproject Century Storage Scheme proposal of 1946 was thus mostly put aside in favor of the plan for one giant water project within Egyptian territory.

In contemplating this huge project, the Nasserist regime's main concerns included establishing a secure source of water within Egyptian territory, achieving national food security, and creating a strong bargaining position in future hydropolitics with its neighbors. According to this thinking, construction of the High Dam and a huge storage reservoir behind it would mean that Egypt would no longer have to watch out for political developments in Sudan and the other riparian states. The dam would also establish a higher level of prior use of the Nile's water by Egypt, just in case water allocations were to be renegotiated with the other states in the future. Other Egyptian concerns at the time included an assured availability of water for expanding irrigation and producing hydroelectric power for industrialization in the future. By eliminating wild fluctuations in the downstream river flow, the dam would also enable easy navigation from the Mediterranean Sea to the Egyptian interior, in the process opening up for tourism many inaccessible historic sites along the Nile.

Within months of coming to power, and despite domestic and external criticism, the new regime in Egypt assigned the highest priority to the Aswân project by constituting a special committee to oversee its planning and implementation. Funding for the large project was sought from the World Bank, which, given the larger geopolitical climate of the time, agreed to finance only minimally an engineering feasibility study. However, the Federal Republic of Germany, stung at the time by Arab criticism of its decision to compensate Israel for Jewish suffering under Hitler, decided to save some face in the Arab world by helping Egypt, mainly by financing a project study and design for the High Dam by two German firms.

Egypt had hoped and preferred to secure full funding for the project from an international financial institution, such as the World Bank; however, under the domination of the United States, which was then involved in regional rivalry with the Soviet Union and which saw the project as embedded in the larger Arab-Israeli conflict, the World Bank dragged its feet. This was also the time when Egypt and Great Britain were negotiating the evacuation of British troops from the Suez Canal Zone. To complicate matters further, an Israeli raid on an Egyptian army post in the Gaza Strip in 1955 forced Egypt to seek arms from the USSR, mainly because the 1948 arms embargo imposed on the region by the Western powers was still in place.

All of these developments led to a chain of geopolitical maneuverings and manipulations by the two superpowers, and by Britain and France. In the end, the United States and Britain withdrew their offers to help Egypt construct the Aswân project. Seeing this as an attempt to humiliate his country and regime, Nasser nationalized the Suez Canal, precipitating a military assault on Egypt by Britain, France, and Israel. The British forces were finally withdrawn from Egypt in 1956, and in 1958 Egypt and the Soviet Union signed an agreement to finance the Aswân High Dam project.

After all these geopolitical ups and downs, there was still the problem of overcoming Sudanese objections to the project, especially after Sudan achieved independence in 1956. In essence, Sudan made its consent for the project conditional upon Egyptian compliance with three conditions: Sudan's share of the Nile's water should be agreed upon before construction could begin, the dam should not inhibit Sudan's own construction plans on the Nile or its tributaries, and Egypt should provide adequate compensation for any population displacement within Sudan.[46] These demands led to a series of negotiations between Egypt and Sudan, culminating in a bilateral agreement in 1959 and in the establishment of a Permanent Joint Technical Commission. In addition to some technical adjustments to its earlier plans, Egypt agreed to pay a sum of $43 million to Sudan as a compensation for the flooding of land and the dislocation of population that the Egyptian project would cause within Sudan.

The 1959 Agreement for Full Utilization of the Nile Water between Egypt and Sudan was based on the assumption that the mean annual flow at Aswân would be 84 billion cubic meters, which would be allocated to the two countries in a fixed proportion. Egypt, which was then drawing 48 billion cubic meters of water from the Nile and on whose territory the dam was to be built, would receive an additional 7.5 billion cubic meters while Sudan's share would also increase by an equivalent amount from 11 to 18.5 billion cubic meters. The remaining 10 billion cubic meters of water was expected to be lost from evaporation and seepage from the reservoir. Once again, like the 1929 agreement between Egypt and Britain, and like the case of the Century Storage Scheme, this bilateral agreement and project design did not take into account any claims of the other riparian states, nor was any provision made for addressing their future needs. Nonetheless, the 1959 agreement did establish certain procedures that Egypt and Sudan would jointly follow to settle any future claims by the other riparians for a share of the Nile's new bounty. To date, the procedure has not been tested because no other country in the basin has yet made any serious claim to a share of the benefits from the High Dam. But Ethiopia and the other upper riparian states do not explicitly recognize the legality of the 1959 agreement, and they continue to reserve the right to make claims on the Nile's waters in the future.

Construction of the High Dam was expected to be completed within eight years, with full employment provided to a large number of workers for twenty years. The project was expected to pay for itself within two years of completion by preventing floods and by generating huge economic returns for Egyptian agriculture and industry. Built according to a Soviet design, the dam was expected to produce 10 billion kilowatt hours of electricity annually. Construction of the dam began in 1961 and it was completed by 1968, but the entire project did not become fully operational until 1975. In 1974 it produced only 4.4 billion kilowatt-hours of electricity—slightly more than one-half of all the electric power then generated in Egypt. In 1976 electricity production at Aswân peaked at 6.6 billion kilowatt-hours; the highest recorded figure was close to 8 billion kilowatt-hours in the 1980s. The Aswân project now supplies less than 30 percent of Egypt's power needs and, if the available estimates for Egypt's future energy needs are correct, the share of the Aswân's contribution to Egypt's commercial energy supply will drop to 10 percent, reducing the value of the project in the country's overall energy balance.[47] In addition to producing electricity, the dam has been instrumental in increasing the total arable land in the Nile Valley from 2.4 million hectares (6 million acres) in 1970 to about 2.9 million hectares (7.2 million acres) in 1990, a 20 percent increase overall.[48] Some supporters have also argued that the project has paid for itself many times over just by preventing severe damage by droughts in Egypt.[49]

Like the Itaipu project in the Paraná–La Plata basin, every aspect of the High Dam project can only be described in superlative terms. Built on the second-longest river in the world, the dam is 100 meters high and 5 kilometers (3 miles) long, with a reservoir stretching nearly 700 kilometers (430 miles) in length (250 kilometers in Sudan), and covering an area of 6,000 square kilometers (2,340 square miles). It is also the world's highest rock-filled dam; if it were to ever break, 110 billion gallons of water would be sent downstream in massive waves, destroying everything in its path in Egypt all the way to the Mediterranean Sea.

The Aswân is also the most scrutinized and perhaps the most criticized dam in the world; its critics have blamed the project for causing many socioeconomic and environmental problems in the Nile basin. For example, the reduction in soil fertility downstream of the dam from the holding back of nutritious silts has now to be compensated by applying some 13,000 tons of chemical fertilizers every year, most of which is washed back into the river. In addition, by providing a very cheap and abundant supply of irrigation water, the dam has encouraged Egyptian farmers to overirrigate their farmlands, without making proper arrangements for adequate drainage. This has resulted in an increase in the groundwater level of the irrigated areas. Consequently, salinity and waterlogging have led to the abandonment of large tracts of farmland and to an overall decline in agricultural productivity. Further, the Mediterranean waters are reported to have cut into 14 square kilometers (5 square miles) of Rosetta's coastline because the High Dam now holds back silts that used to replenish and protect the shore. This has forced the Egyptian government to develop a $96 million plan to erect a rock-and-concrete barrier to protect the shore as well as some threatened historic sites from seawater intrusion.[50] The estimated loss of about 10 billion cubic meters of water a year from the high rate of evaporation over Lake Nasser, compared with a combined increase of only 15 billion cubic meters of water for Egypt and Sudan, has also raised serious questions about the overall water efficiency of the project. Finally, some critics have charged that by locking Egypt into a false sense of water security, the project may have impeded basinwide multilateral cooperation in the Nile basin.[51]

Overall, although the Aswân High Dam has created a semblance of water security in Egypt and produced substantial economic returns over time, it has also made the country vulnerable to long-term environmental, socioeconomic, and security problems. For instance, a reported threat by Israel to attack the High Dam during the 1967 war clearly highlighted Egypt's strategic vulnerability as a result of implementing the project.[52] Thus, the water security Egypt has long sought and now managed to achieve, albeit partially, has come at the high cost of strategic and environmental insecurity. It remains an open question whether Egypt would not have been better off had it pursued other cooperative projects elsewhere in the basin, as proposed in the Century Storage Scheme. In hindsight, summarizing the critical perspective on the Aswân High Dam, John Waterbury has remarked that "it is possible to place responsibility for the unforeseen consequences of the High Dam on such things as the exaggeration of socialist ideologues, the perfidy of the Soviet Union, lack of democracy, and police rule."[53] As for the question why more critical voices were not raised and heard within Egypt before the launching of the costly project, Waterbury quotes a couplet from the Rubáíyát of Omar Khayyám to the effect, "When the king says it is midnight at noon, the wise man says behold the moon."[54]

Other Projects

To this day, there is no truly multilateral agreement or regime for developing and sharing the multiple-use potential of the Nile's waters. All the colonial-era agreements and accords are unacceptable to the successor states, and there is only a contingent acceptance by other riparian states of the 1959 agreement between Egypt and Sudan. However, though the question of riparian rights in the basin has not been settled, there have been ongoing consultations between all the riparian states. And while not directly addressing riparian rights, some attempts at multilateralism on issues of mutual concern are proceeding. For example, a UN-sponsored Hydromet (hydro-meteorological) survey project of 1961 to evaluate the water balance in the catchment area of Lake Victoria was initially backed by Egypt, Kenya, Sudan, Tanzania, and Uganda, and later extended to include Burundi and Rwanda. A multilateral technical commission comprising representatives of all the riparian states except Ethiopia was established in 1967. In 1978 the Kagera Basin Development Organization was formed by Burundi, Rwanda, and Tanzania, and was later joined by Uganda in 1981. Subsequently, a basinwide Hydromet survey sponsored by the U.S. Agency for International Development was begun in 1990. Over time, a number of water agreements have also been signed by the East African states. Finally, since 1983, under the auspices of the Organization of African Unity (to which all the countries belong), the Undugu group (which includes all the riparian states except Ethiopia) has met regularly to discuss a framework for basinwide cooperation.[55] Many other efforts, supported by the international community, to develop basinwide multilateral cooperation are ongoing.

These growing efforts at multilateralism notwithstanding, the fact remains that a basinwide cooperative regime for developing and sharing the Nile's bounty does not yet exist. Whether this situation will change remains to be seen. What is beyond doubt is that without basinwide cooperation over the shared waters, the potential for domestic upheaval and large-scale human suffering and deprivation will keep rising in this highly volatile region of the Third World.

SUMMARY AND CONCLUSION

Among the international river basins in the Third World, the Nile basin has the distinction of being shared not only by the largest number of riparian states but also by some of the youngest sovereign states in the Third World. In no other basin is the strongest riparian state so totally dependent on the waters of a single river that flows into it from sources outside its territory and to which its own territory adds so little water. With Eritrea's independence, the region also has the distinction of having one of the only two sovereign states that have emerged as independent entities in the Third World as a result of civil wars in the post–World War II era.[56] At the same time, three countries sharing the basin—Burundi, Congo, and Rwanda—and perhaps more, face the danger of state collapse.

These specific features of the Nile basin point to the possibility of very volatile hydropolitics in the future. However, despite the current water scarcity for multiple uses in some countries and the rapidly growing demand for water and energy across the basin, and despite very clear links between water scarcity and national security for some of the riparian states, the possibility of armed interstate conflict, especially between Egypt and other riparian states, in the foreseeable future remains low. This is primarily because of the hydropolitical advantages Egypt has inherited from the earlier colonizers, Egypt's overwhelming military superiority in the basin as well as its diplomatic clout in the international system, and continuing underdevelopment and political instability in the upstream riparian states. For the same reasons, it has so far been impossible to develop a comprehensive regime for collectively developing and sharing the vast potential of the Nile's waters.

Like that of the Paraná–La Plata basin, the case study of the Nile basin again underscores the centrality of geography in defining and shaping hydropolitics among states sharing a river basin. Specifically, the geographically determined, almost total dependence of the strongest but lowermost riparian state on the shared waters has turned a potential regional hegemon into an aggressive but highly vulnerable riparian. This dependence has also effectively modified the simple, mostly successive, riparian structure of the basin into a complex one as Egypt must deal with all the other riparian states, bilaterally or multilaterally, to ensure that its water security is not jeopardized. And although physical geography has endowed both Ethiopia and Sudan with substantial potential advantages in hydropolitics, their economic and political geography has so far rendered these powers ineffective. The volatile political geography of the other upstream riparian states has also effectively negated their potential advantages in the basin's hydropolitics.

The fact that the most cost-effective solutions for the strongest riparian state's water-related problems lie outside its borders means that it must keep a wary eye on every development upstream that may affect its lifeline. However, despite such dependence, the nature, timing, and outcome of any bilateral or multilateral water accord in any international basin are likely to be subject to the initiative and approval of the strongest riparian state.

The Nile basin presents a clear case of the intricate play of domestic politics, interstate relations, and geopolitical factors in shaping hydropolitics in the Third World. Acrimonious legacies left behind by the colonizers, the quest for sovereignty by the newly independent states, and continued fears about and resentments against manipulations by external actors are likely to be at the heart of hydropolitics in all the international basins in the Third World. On the other hand, the need for external financial and technical assistance to implement large water projects inevitably means some loss of sovereignty. Although the salience of these factors and issues may vary from basin to basin, there seems to be no escape from this "hydropolitical dilemma" for the Third World states that share international river basins.

Further, as the checkered history of the Jonglei Canal Project clearly demonstrates, even a bilateral accord worked out after a long period of negotiations between two willing riparian states can be made highly problematic if the divergent domestic interests in the respective riparian states are not reconciled and if the differentiated impacts of implementing such accords on certain groups of people in certain locations are not taken into account. The project further shows that ultimately it may not be possible to implement even a bilateral project in an international basin, especially one between two lower riparian states, if the interests and concerns of the other riparian states are not addressed in some acceptable manner.

On a more general level, the Aswân High Dam Project shows that though a large water project may improve a state's water security over the short to medium term, it may also make a state more vulnerable in the long term. Further, it shows that even a militarily superior riparian state in an international basin may not want to be totally dependent on the goodwill or compliance of its upstream neighbors when it comes to such an essential resource as water; that a very high value may be placed on water projects within a state's territory, no matter what the short- and long-term economic, political, and environmental costs; and that a combination of domestic and international political imperatives may lead to the choice of nonoptimal solutions to the water-related problems faced by the riparian states in an international basin.

Unlike the Paraná–La Plata basin, where the economic, political, environmental, and security interests of the riparian states have been converging over time and spurring concrete steps toward multilateralism in hydropolitics, the Nile basin presents a dismal outlook for hydropolitical cooperation. The international community is making substantial efforts to bring all the parties together to recognize that their water-related problems are interrelated and are likely to worsen in the future in the absence of cooperation, but these efforts have yet to generate much response. Given that hydropolitics in the Nile basin is closely tied to hydropolitics in the Jordan basin, a critical look at developments in the latter should be instructive.

3

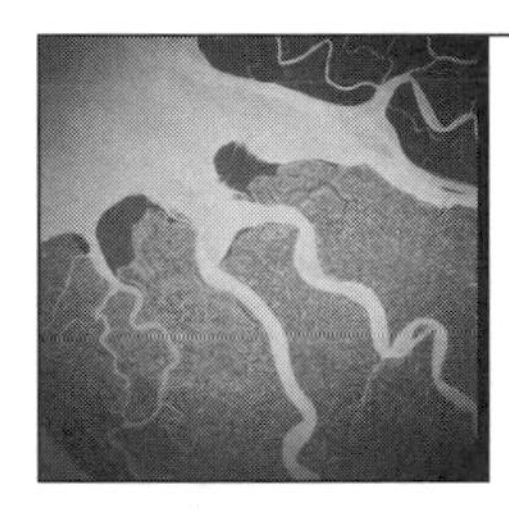

The Jordan Basin

On September 13, 1993, in a grand ceremony at the White House in Washington, D.C., two erstwhile sworn enemies, the Israeli prime minister, Yitzhak Rabin, and the chairman of the Governing Council of the Palestine Liberation Organization (PLO), Yassir Arafat, shook hands for the first time. This unprecedented—and for some viewers in the Middle (Near) East, shocking—event was witnessed by the president of the United States as well as nearly three thousand international dignitaries who had gathered for the historic occasion. The same day, representatives of Israel and the PLO signed the Declaration of Principles (DOP), which recognized—for the first time since the establishment of Israel as a sovereign state in 1948—each other's right to exist, in the process setting in motion the likely future emergence of yet another sovereign riparian state in the Jordan basin.[1] Following this long-sought Palestinian-Israeli peace accord, on July 25, 1994, Israel and Jordan also ended a state of war that had lasted between them for about a half-century.[2] In the aftermath of these developments a "peace process" between Israel and the Palestinians has been ongoing, albeit in great fits and starts, and bilateral and multilateral meetings and talks on several substantive issues among different combinations of Middle Eastern states and peoples have taken place from time to time.

Despite all the obstacles yet to be overcome on the way, the friends of the Middle East continue to hope that peace will some day settle over the region. However, peace in the Middle East cannot, and will not, be sustainable unless and until the problems relating to equitable sharing of the scarce transboundary surface and underground water resources of the Jordan basin are fully addressed and resolved to the satisfaction of all the peoples who share the basin. In fact, peace in the Middle East may actually exacerbate the impending water crisis and hydropolitical conflicts in the Jordan Valley by luring millions of Palestinian refugees and Jewish immigrants to settle in the already water-scarce basin.

Contested claims over surface and underground water resources continue to permeate all major concerns relating to ideology and national security, economic and social well-being, and domestic and international politics in the Jordan basin. This is also one of the very few international basins where conflicts over water have led, very directly, to armed hostilities between some riparian states and peoples in the post–World War II era. Rather than being a "low-politics" issue, water is deeply and inextricably intertwined with all the "high-politics" concerns in the basin. According to Thomas Naff—a longtime observer and analyst of conflict over water in the Near East—"Though physically shallow, politically Middle Eastern waters do run deep."[3] What is also very important to note is that hydropolitics in the Jordan basin is intimately linked to hydropolitics in the Nile basin (chapter 2) and the Euphrates-Tigris basin (chapter 4), making it one of the most complex hydropolitical problems for the international community to help resolve.

Shared by four sovereign states—Israel, Jordan, Lebanon, and Syria[4]—as well as the hitherto stateless Palestinian people, the transboundary water resources flowing above and below the ground in the Jordan basin are the lifeblood for all its inhabitants. Without these water resources, no settlement or economic activity is possible in this arid, mostly desert region. These water resources have been a prize catch for all occupiers and colonizers of the basin throughout history, and they continue to be eyed by all the riparian states and peoples now settled there. In no other international river basin in the world have contested claims over scarce water resources generated as much study, controversy, and hostile emotions in the post–World War II period as they have in the Jordan basin; nowhere else has a riparian state improved its water security by occupying and holding on to the territories of its neighbors.

But opinions differ about how severe water shortages in the basin currently are or likely to become. According to one expert, the Jordan basin "is a case of scarcity rather than maldistribution."[5] Another expert has estimated that Israel, Jordan, and the Palestinians are already deep within the "Water Stress Zone,"[6] the boundary of which has been defined as the availability of at least 500 cubic meters of water per person per year.[7] Other analysts have questioned the idea that the basin suffers from permanent water deficiency.[8] However, what is very clear is that, *if things continue as they are*, the problems of water scarcity and maldistribution in the Jordan basin are bound to be further compounded by growing populations, poor water management practices, and great imbalances in military and economic power among its riparian states. In the absence of a basinwide water accord among all the riparian states and peoples sharing the basin, growing pressures on the basin's scarce water resources will keep fueling tensions and hatred among its current and future inhabitants.

What factors and circumstances drive the hitherto highly acrimonious hydropolitics in the Jordan basin? What role does hydropolitics play in shaping and defining relations between the respective riparian states and peoples? What are the stands taken and strategies adopted by different players in conducting hydropolitics in the basin? Under what circumstances would the preeminent military power in the basin decide to relinquish control over the lands and water resources it has long desired and won as war prizes? Will the prophecies of impending "water wars" in the basin in the near future become discredited or will this danger continue to lurk in the background?[9] Do the nature and conduct of hydropolitics in this conflict-prone basin hold any lessons for other international basins or is this such a unique case that no generalizations can be usefully derived? These are some of the questions to be tackled in this chapter.

GEOGRAPHY

Physical Geography[10]

The Jordan Valley forms the northern portion of the Dead Sea drainage basin, which lies in the great rift extending from the Gulf of Aqaba on the Red Sea to the mountains of Lebanon (see the map on p. 88). Within this drainage basin, with an area of 40,650 square kilometers (15,850 square miles), the Jordan River system per se drains an area of about 17,300 square kilometers (6,750 square miles). There are four main sources of water in the Jordan basin: the flow of the main rivers, the perennial flow of the wadis, the flood flow of the wadis, and the well supply from groundwater.[11] All of these water resources, except the flow of some wadis, are shared by two or more riparian states and peoples.

The Jordan Basin

The drainage system of the upper basin is composed of the Banyas, Bareighit, Dan, and Hasbani Rivers, which together form the Upper Jordan above Lake Huleh in Israel, at an elevation of about 70 meters (230 feet) above sea level. The water discharges that these rivers feed into the Upper Jordan are derived primarily from a group of springs located on the western and southern slopes of Mount Hermon. The Dan spring lies wholly within Israel, near its border with Syria. The Hasbani's source is in Lebanon and that of the Banyas within Syria. However, some hydrologists believe that all three springs may actually represent the outflow of a single large aquifer. In a typical year, these springs provide 50 percent of the flow of the Upper Jordan; the rest comes from winter rainfall runoff. In a dry year, as much as 70 percent of the Upper Jordan's flow may be made up of spring outflow. Among the other minor springs and seasonal water courses, Wadi Bareighit is the most important for its contribution to the flow of the Upper Jordan.[12]

The Yarmuk is the principal tributary of the system. It originates in Syria, flows west along the Syria-Jordan border and through the Adisiyeh triangle, which borders Israel, and then joins the Jordan 10 kilometers (6 miles) below Lake Tiberias.[13] Of the 7,252-square-kilometer (2,828-square-mile) area of the Yarmuk basin, 19.6 percent lies within Jordan and the remainder is in Syria. The river forms a border 40 kilometers (25 miles) long between Syria and Jordan before it becomes a border between Jordan and Israel. All the water of the Yarmuk originates outside Israeli territory.

The Lower Jordan forms a border 40 kilometers (25 miles) long between Israel and Jordan before it becomes the border between Jordan and the West Bank. It flows through the deepest depression in the basin, entering the Dead Sea at 398 meters (1,305 feet) below sea level. Only about 20 percent of the Lower Jordan's flow originates within Israel. According to Naff and Matson, only 3 percent of the total area of the Jordan basin lies within the pre-1967 Israeli territory, and "the annual flow of the Jordan is almost double the amount of water available from *all other sources* in Israel, and three times the amount of water available from *all other sources* in Jordan" (original emphasis).[14]

The drop of nearly 2.5 kilometers (1.6 miles) in the elevation of the Jordan during its 360-kilometer (223-mile) journey from Mount Hermon to the Dead Sea has created substantial potential for water storage and generation of hydroelectric power in some mountainous parts of the basin. This sloping topography also favors gravity-based distribution of irrigation water, in both upper and lower sections of the valley. Further, the Jordan is the only river studied here that does not flow to an ocean.[15] This unique physical feature of the basin has important implications for hydropolitics because it has effectively eliminated the possibility of conflict over international navigational rights on the shared river. Fishing rights are also not a contentious issue in the basin.

The mean temperature in the upper valley can range from 30°F to 104° F whereas in the Lower Jordan Valley the climate varies from tropical to subtropical and the mean temperature can vary from 39° F to 112° F.[16] The average annual flow of the Jordan and Yarmuk Rivers at their junction has been estimated to be about 538 and 475 million cubic meters, respectively. However, whereas the Dan has a mostly uniform flow, there are considerable variations in the mean annual flow of the Hasbani and Banyas Rivers, which on average supply 572 million cubic meters of water.[17]

In addition to the flows of the Jordan and Yarmuk Rivers, Israel and the West Bank Palestinians rely heavily on three major groups of aquifers. The Yarqon-Taninin aquifer is the most abundant of the three: it extends from north to south, along the western edge of the West Bank. Its water flows down in a westerly direction toward Israel. This aquifer currently supplies more than 25 percent of Israel's water consumption. A minor group of aquifers is located in the northern part of the West Bank and drains areas in both the West Bank and Israel. Only one of the three groups of aquifers, which Israel relies so heavily upon, is located within Israeli territory, beneath its coastal plain.[18] Yet another group of aquifers forms the eastern edge of the West Bank; its water does not flow into Israel but is discharged into the Jordan River.[19]

The other major water body in the basin, the Dead Sea, has a surface area of about 1,015 square kilometers (396 square miles), with a maximum depth of 400 meters (1,312 feet) in the northern section declining to 10 to 11 meters (32 to 36 feet) in the southern section. Evaporation over its large surface drops its level by up to 2 meters per year, making this water body considerably more saline than any ocean. It would require an annual flow of 990 million cubic meters of water to maintain the level it had in 1953. If all the projects proposed in a 1953 UN report (discussed later) were to be implemented in the Jordan basin, the water level in the Dead Sea would drop by an additional 85 meters before a new equilibrium between the reduced flow and the losses from evaporation could be established. This would take up to two hundred years to accomplish.

The extreme variability of surface water flows in the basin makes it imperative that large storage facilities be developed upstream to ensure a regular water supply and to provide reserve storage capacity for drought relief and flood mitigation. A central feature of the basin is Lake Tiberias (the Sea of Galilee), a body of freshwater about 166 square kilometers (65 square miles) in area, at an elevation of 212 meters (695 feet) below sea level. Lake Tiberias is the most strategically located potential water storage facility in the basin, in terms of its storage capacity and potential to irrigate large tracts of agricultural lands. In 1953 it was estimated that the total inflow into Lake Tiberias was 838 million cubic meters, of which about 300 million cubic meters evaporated and the remaining was available downstream. As we shall see, a long-standing proposal to develop the lake as a common regional storage facility has played a substantial role in the basin's hydropolitics.

Compared with the other riparian states sharing the basin, Jordan is in the most precarious position because of water scarcity. Of the total area of Jordanian territory, nearly 91.4 percent receives an annual rainfall of less than 200 millimeters (8 inches) and only 3 percent of the land, mostly in the northwest highlands, registers an average annual rainfall greater than 300 millimeters (12 inches). Overall, total annual precipitation hovers around 7,200 million cubic meters, but 85 percent of this sizable precipitation evaporates in the dry climate. Close to 36 percent of water available to Jordan comes from the surface and underground sources it shares with Israel, Syria, and the Palestinians.[20] In addition, Jordan shares an ancient aquifer with Saudi Arabia; however, the two countries have a running dispute over this nonrenewable and environmentally controversial water supply.[21]

A worsening problem in the Jordan basin is the progressive deterioration in water quality in the Jordan River from Mount Hermon to the Dead Sea, naturally and from increasing pollution from human (mostly agricultural and waste disposal) activities. Whereas the headwaters of the Jordan and the Yarmuk are generally of high quality, Lake Tiberias has much higher salinity as a result of the inflows from salty springs. The Lower Jordan's water is essentially unusable because of very high salinity. The river also carries a large sediment load: about 2 percent of its volume in normal years and about 5 percent in dry years. In addition to its other consequences for the human habitants of the basin, environmental degradation—engendered by heavy pesticide use in agriculture, by habitat loss, and by developmental projects of all kinds—now threatens the resting grounds for millions of migrating birds that pass through the area every spring and fall, attracting thousands of birdwatchers.[22]

To sum, the peculiar physical geography of the Jordan basin has established certain overall parameters and constraints within which hydropolitics among the riparian states and peoples sharing the basin has been and will continue to be played out. In combination with the basin's economic geography (to be discussed next), the basin's physical geography establishes the following simple facts: *if things continue as they are*, the water supply in the basin will not be sufficient to meet the needs of all the states and peoples who currently share and will share the basin in the future; there are substantial transboundary interdependencies in the availability of water for different peoples as well as use categories; there are no purely "national solutions" for the basin's water problems; and Israel, the most powerful state sharing the basin, is highly dependent, and will continue to be, on the waters that originate outside its internationally recognized borders. Further, as the following sections will demonstrate, if peace does come to the basin, any collective solution for the problem of water scarcity would require substantial restructuring of the economic and political geography of the basin as a whole, as well as the individual riparian states that share (and will share) it.

Economic Geography

Nearly 80 percent of the Jordan basin lies within the boundaries of Israel, Jordan, and the West Bank; their populations are also the most dependent on its waters. These populations are growing at rates substantially above the world average—naturally and from immigration and return of refugees. With an annual growth rate as high as 3.6 to 3.8 percent, Jordan's population is expected to double within eighteen years. The Israeli population is growing at a rate of about 2 percent per year. If some day a comprehensive and sustainable peace is finally made between the Palestinians and the Israelis, a large number of Palestinian refugees and Jewish immigrants may settle in the basin. Among the other problems associated with the expected large-scale in-migration, these new settlers will considerably increase the pressures on the basin's scarce water resources.

At the present rates of growth, Jordan's 1997 population of 4 million may grow at the rate of 4.8 percent per year; Israel's population of 6 million may grow at the rate of 3.2 percent, including new immigration; and over the next two decades the Palestinian population may jump to 4.2 million. Syria's 1997 population of about 15 million is currently estimated to be growing at a rate of 2.9 percent a year. Lebanon was estimated to have about 4 million people in 1997, with a growth rate of 1.9 percent a year.[23]

Thus, if the currently available population projections can be trusted, between the years 2015 and 2020 the population of the Jordan basin would be about 16 million to 18 million people. According to Thomas Naff, "Given ideal conditions of cooperation and of conservation and efficient use of water, the basin might sustain fourteen million people. A more realistic estimate . . . is about twelve million, *if all of these other conditions obtain*" (emphasis added).[24]

If the populations of the riparian states keep growing at the present rates, and if the amount of water currently withdrawn by each riparian does not change, there will be a drastic reduction in per capita water availability in Jordan and Syria in the first decades of the twenty-first century, as well as a substantial drop in water availability in Israel. It should also be pointed out that further industrialization and urbanization in Israel, Jordan, and Syria will significantly increase the demand for water in the basin, as will economic development within the territory governed by the Palestinian people. Great disparities currently exist in per capita water use by the different riparian states, and these are likely to substantially worsen in the near future. The World Bank data for 1997 showed almost all the urban and rural populations in Jordan and Israel to have access to a safe drinking water supply, and 95 percent of the urban and 77 percent of rural population in Syria to have such privilege.[25] However, these estimates, even if accurate, do not indicate how often and in what amounts safe drinking water was being made available to the Palestinian, Jordanian, and Syrian populations.

Not only are there great disparities among the riparian states and peoples in the per capita availability and use of water, there are also substantial disparities in their levels of economic development. For instance, the gross national product (GNP) per capita in the basin in 1997 ranged from $1,570 for Jordan to $15,810 for Israel.[26] Estimates for Syria and Lebanon available from the World Bank show that the 1997 per capita GNP of Syria was about $1,150 and of Lebanon about $3,350.[27] These numbers clearly show the wide gaps that have developed, and continue to grow, between the standard of living in Israel and the other riparian states since 1948. The estimates also point to the disparities in the level of financial resources available to each riparian state to deal with the growing water scarcities.

Despite the wide gaps in economic development and water availability, one economic characteristic that all the Jordan basin riparian states and peoples share is that for decades they have all been receiving massive external financial aid from different donors; Israel has been supported with massive aid from the United States and other Western countries, whereas the Arab and Palestinian inhabitants of the basin have received substantial aid from some oil-exporting Arab countries as well as other international donors. It is questionable whether the economies of these states and peoples would have developed to the extent that they have in the absence of this aid. A common economic problem all the riparian states now face, to a lesser or greater degree, is the burden of external debt that each has accumulated over the years. For example, Jordan's external debt in 1996 was estimated at about $8 billion and Syria's at about $21 billion.[28] In 1996 Lebanon owed $4 billion, while Israel had an external debt of about $25 billion.[29] The commonalty of this problem should not, however, obscure the fact that Israel has long been the largest recipient of public and private aid from the United States, and is very likely to continue to be so. Nonetheless, the heavy debt burden in the Jordan basin does imply that none of the riparian states, except Israel, can undertake a large water-related project without substantial external financial aid. On the other hand, these financial constraints may provide one incentive for all the riparian states to begin to cooperatively solve the problem of water quantity and quality in the Jordan basin.

Jordan's economic situation is particularly precarious: debt relief was the most urgent need Jordan had repeatedly expressed to the international community during its peace negotiations with Israel. The loss of control over the West Bank since 1967, the influx of refugees throughout the last four decades, and the cutoff of aid from other Arab countries since the Gulf War are only a few of the economic woes that this country has had to suffer. Although the area of the West Bank was only about 6 percent of the pre-1967 Jordanian territory, before the 1967 Arab-Israeli war it had accounted for 45 percent of Jordan's GNP and 25 percent of its cultivated agricultural area. Annexation of the West Bank and East Jerusalem in 1950 had doubled Jordan's population, greatly increased its agricultural productivity, and added numerous tourist attractions for economic exploitation. Since 1967, in addition to the very direct and substantial economic losses that Jordan has suffered as a result of Israel's annexation of the West Bank, it has had to cope with an additional three hundred thousand Palestinian refugees. Nonetheless, largely because of the aid received from some oil-producing Arab countries as well as remittances from a large number of Jordanians working abroad, the country experienced steady economic growth from 1974 to 1980. After the signing of the Egyptian-Israeli peace treaty in 1979, Iraq replaced Egypt as Jordan's major trade partner, but this trade suffered a serious blow during the 1980–88 Iran-Iraq War and later during the Gulf War when an international embargo was imposed on trade with Iraq. If an independent Palestinian state is established in the Jordan basin some day, it is likely to compete with Jordan for external financial resources and aid, employment opportunities, and regional and international markets.

After the 1991 Persian Gulf War, thousands of Jordanians who had been working in Kuwait were expelled. The loss of employment opportunities and of the money that the Jordanians were repatriating have been severe blows for the Hashemite Kingdom. In addition to Jordanian citizens, a large number of Palestinians arrived in Jordan during 1990–91 from Kuwait and other Arab countries. This increased the population of Jordan by 12 percent within a very short time—equivalent to about 30 million people being added to the population of the United States within a year! The same year, the unemployment rate in Jordan was estimated at about 30 percent.

About 40 percent of Jordan's population is concentrated in the capital city, Amman, which regularly faces severe shortages of water and electricity. Water shortages in 1991 led to severe rationing in the city, such that water was made available to households for only 48 hours in a week. The Jordanian farmers were given less than one-third of the irrigation water they had normally been receiving. Industrial water use had to be severely curtailed also.[30] Jordan's heavy reliance on imported petroleum for its energy needs also burdens the country with a hefty import bill, especially after losing the support of most oil-producing Arab countries after the Gulf War.

A notable feature of the economic geography of Jordan is that most sources of water supply for the country are located far away from the big cities and major consumers of water. For instance, Amman is supplied drinking water from three pipelines: from Azraq in the northeast, via a 102-kilometer (63-mile) pipeline; from Dair-Alla in the Jordan Valley, via a 36-kilometer (22-mile) pipeline; and from Sawaqa in the southeast, via a 72-kilometer (45-mile) pipeline.[31] Desalination is not a solution for Jordan's overall water deficits for the primary reason that it is a costly option and the only access Jordan has to the sea is at Aqaba on the Red Sea, which is located 400 kilometers (250 miles) away from Amman and far from other domestic, agricultural, and industrial water users. Lacking petrochemical resources, Jordan would also have to incur very high energy costs for desalination of seawater, even if other hurdles to transporting water over long distances could be overcome. Under the 1994 peace accord, Jordan and

Israel agreed to develop a desalination plant in the Aqaba area but, for the reasons stated here, its benefits will be confined to the nearby area.[32]

Israel too has a mismatch in the location of its water resources vis-à-vis the geographical concentrations of water demand in the country. If the Negev Desert is excluded, Israel is one of the most densely populated as well as one of the most urbanized countries in the world. This spatial concentration of settlements and economic activities, and of the resulting water demand, away from sources of freshwater requires transportation of water over long distances. Whereas 85 percent of its water supply originates in the north, about one-half of the land that can be irrigated is located in the south, as are most of the large cities and industries. Israel has dealt with this problem by constructing the highly controversial National Water Carrier (discussed later) to carry water of the Jordan River to the different demand sites outside the Jordan basin. Further, the average elevation of land suitable for irrigation in Israel is 100 meters (330 feet) above sea level, whereas all the water that can be transported to these lands is found at or below 55 meters (180 feet) elevation. This necessitates pumping water uphill, using electricity along the National Water Carrier. Consequently, about 17 percent of the total energy used by Israel in a year is currently estimated to be spent on transporting water to the different demand centers.

Israeli agriculture is generally regarded as one of the most efficient water users in the world. However, although exact data on the amount of subsidy to water users in Israel are hard to come by, estimates for 1962–63 had shown the price charged to farmers for a unit of irrigation water to have ranged from 8 to 59 percent of the cost of providing water in different regions.[33] In 1987, 40 to 45 percent of irrigation water was sold to farmers below production cost.[34] Whether Israeli agriculture would still be a viable enterprise without these large subsidies remains an open question. In any case, the Israeli agricultural sector has been in decline since the 1960s; in the 1980s especially, it went through a dramatic slump. Agriculture now accounts for only about 7.6 percent of Israel's GNP, about 3 percent of all export earnings, and just 5.3 percent of total employment.[35] Nonetheless, in 1990 almost 67 percent of the water use in Israel was for agriculture, while only 6 percent was used by industries and the remaining by the domestic sector.[36] Facing impending water shortages, Israel plans to gradually reduce water allocation to agriculture by as much as 37 percent of the current usage, to enforce strict cost-based water pricing for irrigation, to shift the cropping pattern away from high water-use crops, to make increasing use of waste water and brackish water for different crops, and to continue practicing cloud seeding in the Lake Tiberias area. To what extent Israel can continue to make use of the West Bank aquifers and of the Jordan River in the future will not be clear until a multilateral peace and water accord is signed in the basin.

After facing initial hardships, including rationing of all kinds owing to resource scarcities, from the second half of the 1950s to the early 1970s the Israeli economy grew at an annual rate of 10 percent. After the oil crisis of 1973, the growth rate declined sharply because of inflation, devaluation of the currency, and high military expenditures. During the 1980s, the country faced a very high rate of inflation, a huge foreign debt, and a severe balance-of-payments deficit. An embargo imposed by the Arab countries on foreign investments in and trade with Israel in the aftermath of the 1973 Yom Kippur War also hurt the nation's economy substantially. However, the Israeli economy has made a remarkable recovery, such that by the mid-1990s Israel's per capita income was estimated to be close to $16,000, making it a candidate for a "high-income" country designation by the World Bank. At the same time, Israeli exports of goods and services amounted to more than $25 billion every year.[37] If peace does come to the basin, Israeli government and businesses hope to attract large foreign investment as well as claim a growing share of the market for goods and services in the region and internationally. What implications these hoped-for developments will have, if they do indeed materialize, for Israel's and its neighbors' water balances are not clear at the moment.

Syria, with a total area slightly larger than the state of North Dakota in the United States, including the area under Israeli occupation, has some natural resources, including crude oil, phosphates, and minerals. However, the Syrian economy turned out only slightly more goods in 1990 than it did in 1983, when its population was 20 percent smaller. Its economy has suffered from severe droughts in recent years, from high military expenditures, from a falloff in aid from other Arab countries, and from insufficient foreign exchange earnings. Lacking self-sufficiency in both cereals and food grains, Syria has been experiencing an increasing food deficit: between 1970 and 1985 the country's import of wheat increased from 28 percent of its total supply to 41 percent. In 1989 imports of wheat grain and flour amounted to 9 percent of the total value of all commodities imported by the country.[38]

A highly uneven geographical distribution of water resources has historically dictated an unbalanced land settlement pattern in Syria, such that there is an excess of population in relation to water resources in the western region while the eastern parts are mostly peopleless steppes and desert (also see chapter 4). Recognizing the importance of irrigated agriculture for national economic development, since the mid-1950s the government has taken a highly active role in initiating large projects to bring together the country's land and water resources; however, progress on these projects has been slow. The Ba'th government, in particular, has viewed government-supported irrigation projects as a key to rural social transformation, and has vastly increased investments in irrigation and reclamation.[39] However, despite these efforts, the total irrigated area today is actually smaller than the peaks reached in the 1950s and early 1960s, the main reason being that as new irrigation projects were coming on line, formerly irrigated areas were being abandoned because of the buildup of salinity on lands lacking adequate drainage. Indiscriminate private exploitation of the underground water supply, highly ambitious state-sponsored projects that were badly implemented, bureaucratic incompetence, and widespread corruption led to a situation where in 1989 only 11 percent of the cultivable land in Syria was under irrigation, the remaining was cultivated with rainwater.[40]

On the more positive side, under the socialistic Ba'th regime, a sizable number of villagers have benefited from land reforms, electrification, and other rural development programs. Recent finds of light oil have also allowed Syria to cut its oil imports. Whereas agriculture still accounts for about 27 percent of Syria's gross domestic product (GDP), industry accounts for almost one-fifth of the GDP, recording growth rates as high as 19 percent in some years.[41] However, state control, corruption, and bureaucratic inertia and meddling continue to plague industrialization in Syria.

Nonetheless, unlike the other major Jordan basin riparian states, Syria does have other sources of water supply outside the basin, the main ones being the Orontes River and the Euphrates-Tigris system.[42] However, both of these river systems originate outside Syrian territory, in Lebanon and Turkey, respectively. Faced with a growing food deficit for its expanding population, Syria would like to substantially increase the cultivated area under irrigation; however, as we shall see in this chapter and the next, this expansion of irrigation is seriously constrained by a lack of cooperation over the major water resources Syria shares with its neighbors.

In Lebanon, the national economy and the infrastructure have suffered severely from the 1975 civil war and its aftermath. Lebanon's capital, Beirut, was known as the "Paris of the Middle East" and as the financial hub of the region, but its economy lay in ruins until the relative peace of the 1990s, which has allowed the government to have some semblance of control and to start reconstructing the economy in an organized fashion. Remittances from expatriate Lebanese, foreign financial support for different political factions, trade in narcotics, and international emergency aid have been the main sources of foreign exchange for the national economy. It is now expected that peace in the Middle East and a growing control over the nation's economic affairs by the government may again raise the country to a place of prominence. Rebuilding Beirut alone, if the resources can be obtained for the gigantic task, may provide a great stimulus to the national economy. Its traditional industries—in particular, banking, food processing, textiles, cement, oil refining, jewelry making, and metal fabrication—may also benefit substantially from the overall regional economic growth. However, meddling in Lebanese affairs by outsiders will have to cease for the government to be able to achieve some semblance of normalcy in the economic sphere. If that happens, Lebanon will hold a highly valuable comparative advantage over the other riparian states sharing the Jordan basin: it will be the only water-rich and, perhaps, water-surplus state located close to the basin.[43]

As for the economic geography of the landlocked West Bank, it continues to be dominated by agriculture and small industrial production. Its terrain comprises mostly hilly regions in the north, west, and center; valley lands in the east; and desert in the south. Until the 1967 occupation by Israel, under Jordanian jurisdiction the Palestinian people had relied primarily on rain-fed agriculture. Only a few wells, mainly for domestic water supply, were dug in the West Bank; nonetheless, by June 1967 there were 314 functioning wells on the western slopes and in the Jordan Valley.[44] Great restrictions were, however, placed by Israel on Palestinian water use and irrigation development after the 1967 occupation. On the whole, the West Bank economy continues to rely heavily on repatriation by outside Palestinians, and on financial aid from international development agencies and other donors. The Palestinians hope to attract sizable foreign investment once they have acquired an independent state; however, an increasing replacement of Palestinian workers by other foreign workers in Israel, including from places as far away as Thailand, is likely to worsen the unemployment situation for the Palestinians. The unemployment rate in Gaza in 1994 was estimated to be about 45 percent.[45]

Before we end this discussion of the economic geography of the Jordan basin in relation to its hydropolitics, it is important to highlight the major role that agriculture has played and continues to play in shaping the many ideological, political, and economic imperatives for the nature and conduct of hydropolitics in the basin. Agriculture has historically been at the core of the identity and ideology of all the peoples sharing the basin; today agricultural production and associated activities continue to account for a very large proportion of employment and water withdrawal in the basin overall. Deeply sensitive to the political clout of the agricultural interest groups and lobbies domestically, and afraid of becoming overtly dependent on external food supplies that may not be available in times of crises and conflict, all the riparian states and peoples have attempted to develop food self-sufficiency or food security within their respective territories. This has meant that other, less water-intensive and more economically efficient alternatives have not been fully explored at the basinwide level. Some recent research suggests that by cutting down on agricultural production and relying on imported food, which is a source of "virtual water," the region may be able to solve most of its water-related problems.[46] But a prerequisite for abandoning the individualistic quest for food security on the part of some or all the parties is an environment of peace and trust among the neighbors.

Thus, overall, the economic geography of the Jordan basin is characterized by great spatial mismatches in the location of water resources and demand, substantial disparities in the withdrawal and use of water, widening gaps in the level of economic development between Israel and its neighbors, and large debt burdens of all the riparian states. The quest by all the parties for food security has, thus far, further complicated hydropolitics in the basin. Nonetheless, in an era of sustained peace in the region, if the financial and energy resources of other Arab countries could be gainfully combined with the natural and human resources of the Jordan basin, the prospects for transforming the region into one of great prosperity seem limitless. For this to happen, however, the political geography of the basin will need to undergo substantial restructuring.

Political Geography

The origins of all sovereign states now sharing the Jordan basin lie in a post–World War I settlement, after the collapse of the Ottoman Empire, which partitioned the formerly unified river basins in the Middle East between British and French Mandates, and a residual Turkish state. Later, Lebanon and Syria emerged as sovereign states from the French Mandate in 1943 and 1946, respectively, and Iraq, Jordan, and Israel were formed from British Mesopotamia and Palestine in 1932, 1946, and 1948, respectively. These colonial legacies of new state formation, and the many international borders in the region that were drawn by the colonizers in a mostly arbitrary fashion, have left behind several unresolved boundary disputes in the Jordan basin.[47] Whereas most of the land boundaries in the Middle East were drawn between about 1880 and 1930, even today only about half of the boundaries have been formally agreed upon and demarcated on the ground. As a comprehensive geographical study of the region points out, as an aftermath of colonization "three major types of disputes can be recognized in the Middle East: *positional disputes*, over the precise location of the boundary; *territorial disputes*, when neighboring states claim the same border area; and *functional disputes*, when the boundary creates problems associated with the movement of goods and people, or the allocation of resources such as water, oil, or minerals" (original emphasis).[48] However, the study also points out that "Talk of boundary disputes should not obscure the fact that many states have made considerable progress towards the elimination of boundary problems with their neighbors in recent decades."[49]

At the heart of any discussion of the political geography of the Jordan basin since the end of World War II has to be a recognition of the profound implications of the division of Palestine and the creation of Israel, as well as the occupation of Palestinian and Arab lands by Israel since 1967. Such a discussion should also recognize and highlight the larger geopolitical forces and actors that substantially impacted the evolution of the basin's political geography in the Cold War era.

The story of the creation of the state of Israel cannot be repeated here. What is important for this study is how Israel's coming into being as a riparian state in the Jordan basin impacted and changed the water balances of the states and peoples earlier sharing the basin.[50] In particular, the West Bank and East Jerusalem were designated as Arab areas by the United Nations in 1947 when its members voted to divide Palestine into Arab and Jewish states. The area was occupied by Jordan during the first Arab-Israeli war in 1948 and formally annexed in 1950. This annexation was, however, not formally recognized by the members of the United Nations at the time, with the exception of Great Britain and Pakistan. Later Israel managed to occupy the area during the 1967 war and has managed to hold on to it for more than three decades. Jordan implicitly renounced its claims to the West Bank in 1974 at an Arab summit in Rabat, which declared the Palestine Liberation Organization (PLO) as the sole legitimate representative of all the Palestinian people. After tensions developed between the Hashemite Kingdom and Palestinians living in Jordan, in 1988 Amman announced that it was officially severing all legal and administrative ties to the West Bank and surrendering its claims to the PLO.

Guided by a mission to claim Palestinian lands as ancient homes of the Jewish people, since 1967 Israel has followed settlement policies for Jewish immigrants that have allowed it to establish highly contentious and controversial "facts on the ground" relating to the land and water resources of the occupied territories. From 1967 to 1977, under Labor governments, Israeli settlement activity in the West Bank had mainly followed military considerations, as outlined in the Allo Plan, which envisaged a line of settlements overlooking the Jordan Valley away from the hills to the west. After the 1977 election, pressed by some right-wing and religious extremist groups, the Likud government approved several unofficial settlements that had sprung up in the meantime and encouraged many new settlements in the interior. A massive purchase of private Arab lands was also permitted and encouraged. As a consequence, by 1985 there were fifty-two thousand Jewish settlers in 155 villages in the West Bank, and Israeli authorities had effective control of 52 percent of the Palestinian lands. And since 1982, Israel's national water company, Mekorot, has been integrating the West Bank's water supplies into an Israeli water network.[51] Under Israeli occupation, severe restrictions have been placed on Palestinian water use and well-digging activities in the West Bank. As a consequence, some analysts have estimated that Jewish settlers in the Palestinian lands have been using at least four times as much water as the Palestinians. Since 1967 the irrigated area in the West Bank is reported to have dropped from 27 percent of the total cultivated area to a mere 3.5 to 6 percent.[52]

What is generally not known outside the region is that the PLO came into being at an Arab summit in 1964, which was called to discuss, among other things, the rising water problems in the Middle East as a consequence of Israel's water appropriation activities in the Jordan basin. What is also significant to note is that the first, and as it turned out unsuccessful, act of sabotage by the PLO was directed against Israel's National Water Carrier.[53] Restoration of Palestinian sovereignty over the surface and underground water resources in all the Palestinian lands has since been a central demand of the PLO.

The Golan region of Syria, popularly known as the Golan Heights, has been the most attractive of the occupied territories for Israel; it will likely be the last area Israel would be willing or able to give back in a peace agreement with Syria. Not only is it strategically located—overlooking as it does many settlements in northern Israel, the Huleh Valley, and the Tiberias basin—but it has been a prize catch because of its water resources and agricultural potential. It was one of the first occupied areas to be settled by Israel after the 1967 war; with only nine settlements built there during the first year of occupation, by 1987 there were forty Jewish settlements in the area with a total population of about ten thousand.[54] In addition to agriculture, many of these settlements are engaged in industrial activity, and massive investments have been made by the Israeli government to provide infrastructure—roads, electricity, water, and sewage facilities—for the settlements. These "facts on the ground," including the associated water withdrawals, are bound to make it very difficult for any Israeli government to completely withdraw from all the occupied territories *until* there is a clear agreement on water sharing in the Jordan basin.

In addition, opposition to a substantial restructuring of the established water practices in Israel is likely to come from various special interest groups as well as certain bureaucratic agencies. For instance, management of Israel's water system has traditionally rested with the Water Commission, which is under the authority of the minister of agriculture, who is near the top of the bureaucratic hierarchy. This arrangement clearly implies that water policy in Israel has been subordinate to agricultural policy, making it difficult in the past to reorient water use away from agriculture toward more economically efficient sectors. According to some estimates, water was being sold to Israeli farmers at highly subsidized rates: as low as $0.16 per cubic meter compared with $0.40 for domestic use in 1990, whereas the actual cost of supplying water was $0.36 per cubic meter.[55] Clearly, other water users have been heavily subsidizing irrigation by the Israeli farmers. In the 1980s these practices began to attract criticism, and in 1990 the state comptroller charged the Water Commission with "25 years of mismanagement" and raised serious questions about the nation's wasteful irrigation practices.[56] As the Israeli economy expands, mostly in the industrial and service sectors, the political clout of the agricultural and irrigation lobbies may decline substantially, allowing water use to be rationalized according to calculations of its scarcity value and the economic returns it can produce in alternative sectoral uses. Significant movements in this direction have already begun, creating some tension among different stakeholders and ideological groups. Thus, it is clear that the Israeli economy as well as Israel's established water practices will require further restructuring in its political geography.

Compared with the other riparian states in the Jordan basin, Lebanon has certainly suffered the greatest political turmoil over the past two decades. In addition to several changes in national leadership, often accompanied by violence, large portions of the country continue to be effectively occupied or controlled by different outside powers. For instance, though separated from Israel by the 1949 Armistice Line, southern Lebanon has been effectively occupied by Israeli forces since June 1982. Israel did withdraw a large part of its forces from the area in 1985, but it continues to occupy a "security zone" 10 kilometers (6 miles) deep within southern Lebanon.

In addition to Israel, Iran and Syria have continued to meddle in Lebanon's internal affairs to serve their own political and strategic interests and needs in the Middle East. Syrian troops, constituted as the Arab Deterrent Force by the Arab League following a civil war, have remained in north Lebanon since October 1976. Iran is reported to maintain a small contingent of revolutionary guards in the Bekaa Valley and southern Lebanon to support Islamic fundamentalist groups there. Syria has also been accused of supporting Kurdish rebels stationed mostly in the Bekaa Valley, and of using these rebels to harass the Turkish government.[57] Occasional attacks on northern Israel by the Hezbollah and Hamas extremists located in Lebanon and, in return, bombardments of their strongholds by Israel, continue to undermine the capacity of the Lebanese government to exercise effective control within its territory.

As for the political geography of the West Bank, its structure and dynamics are not likely to become clear for some time to come. Whatever its composition and ideology, an autonomous Palestinian state is likely to face considerable difficulties in consolidating its control over the domestic polity and in fulfilling the demands of the "revolution of rising expectations," which usually accompanies state formation, especially after decades of occupation and repression. It remains to be seen whether the PLO will be able to consolidate its rule in the West Bank and Gaza, and to build the kind of civic consensus needed to launch large and small development projects, mostly with external aid. It may be that a Palestinian state in the West Bank, endowed as it would be with a highly valuable store of human capital, would be able to attract the kind of foreign investment and aid that would enable it to transform a primarily agrarian economy into a thriving industrial and service economy; however, the road to such transformation in a highly competitive global economy is not likely to be smooth, especially if Palestinian goods and services have to compete with Israeli and Jordanian products. On the other hand, economic cooperation between Israel and its neighbors, similar to the ongoing developments in South America (chapter 1) and southeast Asia (chapter 6), can open up vast opportunities for regionwide prosperity. But a basinwide peace accord that necessarily includes equitable sharing of the basin's water resources will remain a prerequisite for the full realization of the great economic potential of the West Bank.

In conclusion, it needs to be emphasized that although the recent peace initiatives in the Jordan basin have engendered the hope of resolving many outstanding disputes between Israel and its neighbors, including the contested claims over the shared water resources, successful implementation of any peace accord would require much more economic and political restructuring in the whole basin and within each riparian state than has yet been contemplated. Such restructuring is likely to be resisted by the entrenched economic and political interests in all the riparian states and by extremist political parties and religious zealots. The hopes created by the ongoing peace process in the Middle East should not blind anyone to these harsh hydropolitical realities in the Jordan basin.

HYDROPOLITICS

Before this chapter proceeds to develop an analysis of hydropolitics in the Jordan basin, it should be pointed out that most data pertaining to water supply and usage that have been made available from time to time by the different riparian states and peoples sharing the basin or by their international supporters have been highly self-serving. For long, such data have been regarded as "state secrets" by some of the major players in the basin's hydropolitics, and have been used selectively to further their own claims on the shared waters. Over the last four decades, some regional and international scholars and experts have attempted to provide objective and accurate water balances for each riparian state and for the basin as a whole; however, there is as yet no consensus in the basin about the validity of such data. Consequently, hydropolitics in the basin is driven by suspicions and accusations based on partial, controversial, and contested hydrological data.

The second distinguishing characteristic of hydropolitics in the Jordan basin has been the highly antagonistic and often demeaning perceptions the different peoples in the Middle East in general, and in the basin in particular, have long held about one another. The discourses, if they can be so called, between Palestinians and Jews, and between Jews and different groups of Arabs, have been tainted by the worst stereotypes about each other, by racism, and by outright hatred and mistrust.[58] These perceptions continue to fuel religious bigotry, ideological battles, bloody terrorism, and armed conflict in the basin: they also impact hydropolitics in the basin in very substantial ways.

Before World War I, no systematic study relating to the development and sharing of the water resources in the Jordan basin had been carried out, and water resources were used by the inhabitants of the basin in a mostly laissez-faire manner. This was primarily because there were no major population pressures in the basin at that time, nor any pressing water needs for large-scale irrigation and industrialization. The earliest systematic studies, therefore, began during the Mandate period, mainly to determine the absorptive capacity of the basin's land and water resources for future Jewish immigration. Since then, the Jordan basin has been one of the most studied international river basins in the world. However, inasmuch as most of these initiatives have originated with political institutions in the different basin and nonbasin countries, many of which have had vested interests in particular outcomes, the findings of all water-related studies in the Jordan basin remain controversial and contested.

As in most other international river basins in the Third World, the stands taken and strategies adopted by each riparian state in the Jordan basin reflect, very directly, its riparian status on the water resources it shares with others. For example, as the uppermost riparian state on the Litani River, Lebanon bases its claims on the principle of absolute territorial integrity and sovereignty. Lebanon refuses to have its rivers and water resources included in any water negotiation in the Jordan Valley. Syria, as the uppermost riparian on the Yarmuk and the Banyas, also claims the privileges of absolute territorial integrity and sovereignty. However, these claims, developed only since 1964, mostly to reflect Syria's hostility toward Israel, have created some problems for Syria in conducting hydropolitics in the Euphrates-Tigris basin where it is a middle riparian on the Euphrates River and a co-riparian on the Tigris River (see chapter 4).

Jordan—the state most dependent on transboundary water resources in the basin, a middle riparian on the Yarmuk, and a co-riparian on the Jordan—emphasizes absolute integrity of the river system and has opposed any diversion of water from the basin to the outside, as, for example, by Israel's National Water Carrier, which transports the Jordan's water to locations outside the Jordan basin (more on this later). Jordan has another major concern that no other riparian state in the basin has: only a 19-kilometer (12-mile) southern coastline on the Gulf of Aqaba prevents the country from being completely landlocked. If this access is ever denied to it, Jordan would be in a similar situation as Iraq is in today.[59]

In addition to the problems Jordan has faced in hydropolitics of the Jordan basin proper, an ongoing Jordan-Saudi Arabia competition for groundwater withdrawals now threatens to prematurely deplete one of Jordan's strategic water reserves, the Disi aquifer, located on its border with Saudi Arabia. This ancient and nonrenewable underground source can produce up to 100 million to120 million cubic meters of drinking water per year at safe yield, which can be pumped to Aqaba and eventually to Amman and Zarqa. Saudi Arabia began drawing water from this aquifer in 1983, at a rate of 25 million cubic meters per year; it is reported to have increased water withdrawals to 250 million cubic meters per year. At this rate, this precious and nonrenewable source of Jordan's water supply would be exhausted within twenty-five years.[60] No formal agreement currently exists between the two countries for sharing this ancient water supply.

Water claims of the Palestinian people in the West Bank have in the past been based on absolute territorial integrity and unalienable rights over all the waters flowing over and stored underneath their lands. If an independent Palestinian state does emerge in the basin, this new entity will almost certainly demand a fair share of the Jordan's water as well as the right to tap more deeply into the West Bank aquifers to enhance its agricultural potential and provide drinking water for its growing population. Whether the new state will be able to link the issue of water availability in Gaza to water rights in the West Bank remains an open question at this stage.[61]

The case of Israel in the hydropolitics of an international river basin is a unique one. Although the state came into existence only in 1948, aware of future competition for Palestinian and Arab water, as early as in 1919 at the Paris Peace Conference the Zionist leaders who conceptualized the state of Israel in Palestine had argued for a larger Israel that would include most of the water resources as well as fertile lands in the region. Earlier, in a 1902 novel, the founding father of political Zionism, Theodor Herzl, had envisioned the use of Lebanon's rivers and the headwaters of the Jordan to generate electricity and to irrigate the future national home for the Jewish people scattered around the world.[62] Some have argued that this early Zionist dream of a larger Jewish state, encompassing the major sources of freshwater in the Jordan basin, has been a driving force, a "hydraulic imperative" as it were, behind Israel's occupation of the Arab and Palestinian lands in Syria, Lebanon, and the West Bank since the 1967 war, but this remains a controversial issue.[63]

Between 1922 and 1931 a significant growth took place in both the Arab and Jewish populations in Palestine, leading to Arab-Jewish conflicts over the basin's water supplies. On the Jewish side, a nonprofit company was formed in 1937 to provide water to the growing Jewish community. From 1937 to 1948, myriad unsuccessful British proposals also attempted to resolve conflicts over water and land between Palestinians and Jews. As David Wishart points out, there were three main factors responsible for water conflicts between 1931 and 1948. First, no progress was made toward a uniform system of water rights. Second, while there were significant improvements in water use efficiency in the Jewish sector, the rate of improvement in the Palestinian economy remained low. Third, there was a simultaneous rapid growth in the Arab and Jewish populations.[64] In the end, of course, Palestine was divided in 1948 to establish the state of Israel, without much regard for the hydrological integrity of the Jordan basin.

For two decades after its founding, as the lowermost riparian on the Jordan River, Israel asserted the principle of community of property; however, after occupying the uppermost position on most of the water sources in the basin in 1967, it began advocating the principle of absolute territorial integrity and sovereignty, just as Lebanon, Syria, and the Palestinians have done. Through substantial settlement activity and water withdrawals in the occupied lands, Israel asserts that it has acquired de facto prior-use claims since 1967 to the waters of the Jordan River as well as to the West Bank aquifers, claims that the Israeli government now maintains as legitimate and established.

As Egypt has often done in the Nile basin, before the mid-1960s Israel had consistently warned its neighbors that any attempt by them to significantly alter the flow of the Jordan River would invite a military response. During the Six Day War in June 1967, Israel made the threat real by using repeated air strikes to destroy the partially completed Mukhaiba Dam as well as damage Jordan's East Ghor Canal.[65] The Israeli air force also took out Syrian fortifications in the Golan Heights and pushed back Syrian forces that had earlier prevented Israel from carrying out dredging on a stretch of the Jordan River above Lake Tiberias.[66] Some analysts have hypothesized or asserted that Israel's occupation strategy was driven by the fact that by 1964 Israel was reported to be already making full use of all the surface and underground water resources within its territory as well as 540 million cubic meters of water from the Jordan River—an amount it would have been allocated had the Johnston Plan (discussed later) been implemented.[67]

Israel is the only state since World War II that has improved its water security as well as riparian position in an international basin—from a lowermost to an upper riparian status—by occupying neighboring territories for close to three decades.[68] Similar to the earlier French and British Mandates in the basin, by occupying strategic lands in Lebanon, Syria, and the West Bank, Israel has in effect created a new mandate covering the whole of the Jordan River from its source to the Dead Sea. In particular, since the 1967 war, Syria and Lebanon have effectively become nonriparians on the Jordan River even though their claims to land and water in the basin continue to be internationally recognized.

Further, "occupation of the Golan Heights allowed Israel to open up a large tract of fertile land in the Huleh, to open up some new springs, to channel Huleh Valley floodwaters into Lake Tiberias (because of substantial decline in its salinity level) and into the National Water Carrier."[69] But according to some analysts, Israel's withdrawals from the Jordan River system have remained within the limits set for Israel in the Johnston Plan.[70] A study prepared by the Jaffe Center for Strategic Studies at the Tel Aviv University, which was earlier suppressed by successive Israeli governments, came to the conclusion that Israel could give up significant portions of the Golan Heights and the West Bank and still protect its access to vital water resources.[71] Whether domestic opposition within Israel, especially from the settlers and right-wing political parties, would allow any Israeli government to completely withdraw from all the occupied territories remains an open question at this stage. What can be said with confidence is that Israel is highly unlikely to sign any peace agreement that does not guarantee it secure and adequate sources of freshwater in the near and distant future, especially given Israel's claims that it has invested about $30 billion to improve water management in the Jordan basin, including the occupied territories, over the past four decades.[72]

Some observers of the peace process in the Middle East have wanted to marginalize Syria for various reasons; however, what they fail to realize is that because of its strategic location Syria may prove to be the most important agent for unleashing comprehensive water accords not only in the Jordan basin but in the Euphrates-Tigris and Orontes basins as well. For instance, construction of the proposed "Peace Pipeline" from Turkey (see chapter 4) to the West Bank and Israel, overland transfer of water between the two basins, and development of multilateral storage reservoirs in the

Jordan basin will depend largely on Syria's cooperation. This is to imply not that Syria is the most influential riparian state in the Jordan or the Euphrates-Tigris basin, but that without its cooperation, comprehensive solutions for the water woes of its neighbors would be very difficult to fashion.

Syria's position in the Jordan basin's hydropolitics is bolstered also by the Treaty of Brotherhood, Cooperation, and Coordination, which it has signed with Lebanon. This treaty gives Damascus virtual veto power over any project that could transfer surplus Lebanese water from the Litani or Orontes Rivers to the Jordan basin, assuming that Lebanon agrees to such transfer in the first place. If nothing else, by dragging its feet in the peace negotiations with Israel and developing its own water projects in the Yarmuk basin, Syria can continue to frustrate all attempts at achieving anything close to a regional water accord. By fomenting trouble both in Lebanon and Turkey—the only water-rich countries in the region—and by backing different rebel factions in the region, Syria can continue to keep water problems from being resolved in a cooperative manner in the whole of the Middle East, not just in the Jordan basin. However, faced with its growing marginalization in regional politics, combined with domestic discontent and a worsening economic situation, Damascus may finally be impelled or forced to seek some kind of regional water and peace agreement with its neighbors in the Jordan basin, but this remains to be seen.

Finally, in the absence of a multilateral water accord in the Jordan basin, the Palestinians are very unlikely to secure international funding for any unilateral, large-scale project to develop their underground water resources, even assuming that they do acquire some semblance of statehood. Securing such funds will also be a problem for Jordan. And as long as the Jordanians and the Palestinians remain caught in this situation, Israel may continue to draw from the surface and underground water resources it shares with them, perhaps even at an accelerated pace as its water needs rise. The same may be the case of Israel with Syria on the headwaters of the Jordan River in the Golan Heights. Nonetheless, in the 1994 peace agreement with Jordan, Israel did agree to supply about 50 million cubic meters of water (about 13.2 billion gallons) a year to arid Jordan.[73]

Because "facts on the ground" have played such an important role in the stands taken by some riparian states, especially Israel, in the Jordan basin's hydropolitics, a discussion of some of the large water projects proposed and implemented in the basin should be illuminating. This discussion must begin with the earliest attempts by the United States and other Western powers to resolve the problems of water scarcity and water sharing in the basin, efforts undertaken mainly to ensure that water conflicts would not lead to large-scale violence in this geopolitically strategic region.

Hydropolitics and the Great Powers

In 1918, the King-Crane Commission sent to the Middle East by U.S. president Woodrow Wilson to study the disposition of the old Ottoman territories had recommended that despite all due sympathies for the Jewish cause, any settlement of Jewish migrants in the region be limited and gradual, and that "the project for making Palestine distinctly a Jewish Commonwealth be given up."[74] The following year, at the 1919 Paris Peace Conference, the Zionists wishing to establish a larger Jewish homeland in Palestine claimed that with the use of efficient and scientific methods for agriculture and water use, the land and water resources of Palestine could support several times the number of people then living in the basin.[75] For obvious reasons, the Arabs were strongly opposed to this Zionist idea as well as to the possibility of a Jewish national homeland in Palestine.

Arab resistance to Jewish immigration led to bloody riots in 1929 and 1936. A British commission looking into the genesis of these riots concluded that animosity between Arabs and Jews had reached such an alarming level that partition of Palestine was the only solution to the problem. The Peel Commission also recommended a full hydrological survey of the region to determine its actual carrying capacity. Following these developments, another British commission reversed the Peel Commission recommendations in 1938 for the main reason that the findings of some surveys had raised serious questions about Zionist claims relating to the availability of land and water resources in the region. These recommendations and other developments convinced the British government to abandon the idea of partitioning Palestine. However, large-scale Jewish immigration did take place subsequently, and Israel came into existence as a sovereign state in Palestine. Since 1948 many plans and proposals have been put forward by different individuals and organizations for developing and sharing the precious water resources of this arid region. None of the integrated plans have yet been implemented, but one of the plans, the Johnston Plan, continues to reverberate through all the discussions of conflict and cooperation over water in the Jordan basin.

The Johnston Plan[76]

Just five years after the creation of Israel, a 1953 report commissioned by the United Nations to resolve water problems in the Jordan basin had envisaged the construction of twenty large and small projects, to be constructed in five phases at a 1953 cost of $121 billion to $135 billion. Five hydroelectric projects were also proposed in the plan.[77] This report became the basis for a plan developed by an emissary of the U.S. government with the aim of bringing about cooperative development and sharing of the water resources in the Jordan basin.

As mentioned earlier, the involvement of the United States in international attempts to resolve conflicts over water in the Jordan Valley dates back to 1918; however, only in 1953, following an incident between Syria and Israel that involved Syrian shelling of a water facility then being developed by Israel, did the U.S. government attempt to become actively engaged in Jordan Valley water management.[78] Recognizing the danger of water disputes leading to armed conflict in the basin, facing the problem of shouldering the financial burden of maintaining about eight hundred thousand Palestinian refugees, and inspired by the ongoing large-scale Tennessee Valley project in the United States, in October 1953 President Eisenhower dispatched an ex-president of the U.S. Chamber of Commerce (and then a motion picture magnate), Eric Johnston, to the Middle East to negotiate a basinwide water agreement.[79] Referred to variously as the Main Plan, the Unified Plan, and the Johnston Plan, an integrated water management proposal, titled *The Unified Development of the Water Resources of the Jordan Valley Region*, was then carried by Johnston to Egypt, Israel, Jordan, Lebanon, and Syria in October 1955.[80]

The Johnston Plan was a basinwide, integrated plan. The main provisions of the plan included small dams on the Banyas, Dan, and Hasbani Rivers; a medium-size dam at Maqarin; gravity-flow canals on both sides of the Jordan Valley (including the East Ghor Canal that was later built by Jordan with U.S. assistance); draining of the Huleh swamps (later carried out by Israel); and additional storage in the Sea of Galilee in Israel. Following a tenet of international law that, regardless of political boundaries, water from one basin should not be diverted outside the area until all water needs of those living within the catchment or basin are satisfied, the Johnston Plan excluded from consideration the Litani River in Lebanon, and it opposed the idea of transferring water from the Jordan basin to areas outside the basin.[81] Further, it allocated 394 million cubic meters per year to Israel, 774 million cubic meters per year to Jordan, and 45 million cubic meters per year to Syria. The Palestinians were allocated 100 million cubic meters per year. To facilitate acceptance of the plan, the United States also offered to fund up to two-thirds of the cost of implementing the plan.

After two years of intense negotiations, the plan was approved with some modifications by the Israeli cabinet in July 1955, but rejected by the Arab League Council in October 1955. The council saw the plan as yet another imperialist and Zionist scheme for territorial expansion at the core of the Arab heartland and for controlling vital resources of the Arab peoples. The Arab states also wanted more water as well as an international board to supervise the allocation of regional water resources. Israel too asked for more water and rejected giving a supervisory board, with several Arab members, control over its water supply. A subsequent Arab League Plan (1959), which included a short tunnel to divert Lebanon's Hasbani River where it passed close to the Litani River, was also rejected by Israel.

In hindsight, David Wishart arrives at the conclusion that the Johnston negotiations failed for the following reasons: negative opportunity costs for Jordan of rejecting the Unified Plan, Arab reluctance to accept a plan that involved acquiescence to Israel's development goals and to the abandonment of traditional principles for water rights assignment; Arab refusal to allow the transfer of Jordan's water to places outside the basin; Arab displeasure at the possibility of a U.S. security pact with Israel; and the lack of adequate leverage for Johnston in relation to the Arabs. The large number of parties involved in the negotiations also made an agreement highly problematic.[82]

In the end, what is interesting about the failed Johnston Plan is that even though it never became an official treaty or accord, the Jordan basin riparian states keep invoking it selectively to serve their own purposes. For example, Israel does so to justify its considerably expanded water withdrawals while Jordan invokes the plan's proposed water allocations to demand more water from the Jordan and Yarmuk Rivers. Thus, notwithstanding all its faults and biases, the Johnston Plan may yet become the basis of a regionwide water accord, definitely not in its original form but at least as a starting point in bilateral and multilateral negotiations over water. Another interesting outcome of the Johnston Plan was that Jordan and Israel agreed to send technical experts to informal but regular "Picnic Table Talks" to determine day-to-day hydrological operations at the confluence of the Yarmuk and Jordan Rivers.[83] Despite the ups and downs in the overall relationship between Jordan and Israel, these talks have continued over the years and may have paved the way for the 1994 peace agreement, which includes water sharing between the two countries.[84]

Notwithstanding the failure of the Johnston Plan, U.S. involvement in the hydropolitics of the Jordan basin continued beyond the 1950s. In 1967, immediately after the Six Day War, officials of the Atomic Energy Commission and the Oak Ridge National Laboratory, under the leadership of President Eisenhower, developed a massive water and power project for the Middle East.[85] The plan included a series of nuclear desalination plants that would provide electricity and water for immense agro-industrial complexes in the region. It was hoped that these projects would ease political tensions in the Middle East, then being caused by refugees and water scarcity. The U.S. Senate, through Resolution 155, supported the idea of such projects in Egypt, Israel, and Jordan, as well as at a site in Gaza. In the end, economic and political objections to the plan, and the fear of introducing nuclear energy in a volatile region, doomed the plan.[86] After the failure of these attempts to help fashion and sustain basinwide water accords, the United States has mostly supported several water-related projects within different countries. Since the 1994 peace agreement between Israel and Jordan, the United States has been supporting the joint desalination plant in the Aqaba area.

Among the various agencies of the U.S. government that have, over time, been directly or indirectly involved in water-related issues in the Middle East are the Department of State; the U.S. Agency for International Development (USAID); the Department of the Interior, the U.S. Geological Survey (USGS) and the Bureau of Reclamation; the Department of Agriculture (Office of International Cooperation and Development, Soil Conservation Service, and Agriculture Research Service); the Department of Defense (Defense Intelligence Agency, Army Corps of Engineers); and the Environmental Protection Agency.[87] Between 1975 and 1987, USAID is reported to have provided $184.8 million worth of capital and technical assistance for water projects to Jordan, $18.2 million to Lebanon, $20 million to Israel for a desalination plant, $5 million to the West Bank and Gaza, and $2,540 million to Syria, even though the Syrian programs were discontinued in 1983 after a political falling out between the two countries. Between 1964 and 1986, the USGS also carried out six survey projects in Jordan that were sponsored by USAID and Saudi Arabia.[88] Thus, it is not for lack of international initiatives that the problems of water sharing in the Jordan basin have remained unresolved for so long. Among the many reasons for this impasse have been the controversial water appropriations for some large water projects.

The Israeli National Water Carrier

Mostly completed by 1964, entirely within the pre-1967 Israeli borders, this unified system of pumps, canals, and tunnels transports about 500 million cubic meters per year of water from Lake Tiberias to places as far away as 200 kilometers (125 miles) in southwestern Israel. This project is one of the very few examples in the world where water is being diverted from an international river basin by one riparian state to areas outside the basin, without the consent of other riparian states and peoples sharing the basin.

At a 1964 summit organized by the Egyptian president Nasser, several Arab countries had considered various options, including going to war, in response to the Israeli diversion of "Arab" water from the Jordan basin. In the end, they decided to support and finance upstream diversion projects in Lebanon and Syria, and to help Jordan build a dam on the Yarmuk. The main idea behind these projects was to divert or store water on Arab soil before it reached the Jordan River and Lake Tiberias in Israel. It is also at this first Arab summit that the PLO was born.

In 1965 the Israeli army attacked the diversion projects in Syria, though avoiding a full-scale war mainly because of warnings from the U.S. government. These attacks, combined with other animosities, led to a chain reaction of hostilities, culminating in the 1967 Arab-Israeli war. Here is a clear case of a conflict over transboundary water resources that has contributed substantially to armed hostilities between the riparian states in an international basin.[89] According to some analysts, in the post-1967 era also, many military operations in the Jordan basin can be traced back or linked to conflicts over water.[90]

The East Ghor Canal

Proposed under the Johnston Plan, ground for this Jordanian irrigation canal was broken on August 8, 1958. Financed jointly by the United States and Jordan, the project was expected to cost $12 million and require three to five years to complete.[91] Finished in June 1963, it is the largest single irrigation scheme ever undertaken in Jordan, consisting of a 70-kilometer (44-mile) main canal that taps the waters of the Yarmuk River by gravity diversion to irrigate about 30,300 acres of agricultural land along the eastern slope of the Jordan Valley. The Yarmuk provides about 123 million cubic meters of water to the canal; additional water is tapped from the Zarqa River and from several seasonal streams within Jordanian territory. The point of diversion for the canal from Yarmuk is about 10 kilometers (6 miles) from the confluence of the Yarmuk and Jordan Rivers below Lake Tiberias. Its entire course is below sea level, with the point of diversion from the Yarmuk being 203.6 meters (665 feet) below sea level.

It is noteworthy that in signing the agreement with the United States for this project, the Hashemite Kingdom accepted the need for equitable apportionment of irrigable lands, for clearly defined procedures for determining land values and water rights, and for improvements in farming and marketing methods and facilities. Jordan also agreed to address the needs for housing, education, and communal facilities for the affected population. To implement the project, the independent East Ghor Canal Authority was established and a law was passed to vest exclusive power and responsibility in this authority for managing all aspects of the canal project. What is also significant is that the tunnel to carry the Yarmuk's water was built to accommodate twice the amount of water that the canal would usually carry. This reflected a hope for the future when the canal would become part of a regional water system. In the end, U.S. contributions to the project have amounted to $18 million, with Jordan contributing another $5 million.

In addition to the Israeli National Water Carrier and the Jordanian East Ghor Canal, many other water projects have been implemented, are ongoing, and have been proposed in the Jordan basin. The following is a brief description of some of these projects and proposals.

Other Projects and Proposals

In the Yarmuk sub-basin the major uses of the river's waters are for hydropower generation and irrigation. Syria currently withdraws about 90 million cubic meters of these waters to irrigate about 15,000 hectares, Jordan withdraws another 158 million cubic meters for the East Ghor Canal to irrigate 12,000 hectares, and Israel diverts 100 million cubic meters on average to Lake Tiberias, leaving virtually no Yarmuk water to reach the Jordan River.

Syria already has several earthen dams on the Yarmuk.[92] If it goes ahead with the plans to build additional dams, not enough water may be available for a proposed Jordanian-Syrian dam, the al-Wahda, as Syria is already in the process of capturing for its own exclusive use much of the water that was to have been stored in the al-Wahda.[93]

Major projects within Jordan include the King Tala Dam on the Zarqa River (capacity 48 million cubic meters) and an 18-kilometer (11-mile) extension of the East Ghor Canal. In addition there are some smaller projects in progress on some wadis that drain into the Jordan River.[94]

The Med-Dead and Red-Dead Canal Proposals

Designed to take advantage of the difference in the surface levels of the Mediterranean Sea and the Dead Sea (current surface level about

409 meters—1,350 feet—below sea level), the Med-Dead Canal was first proposed around 1938–39. According to the original proposal, with a total length of 70 kilometers (43 miles), this water carrier would carry 80 cubic meters of saline water every second (700 million cubic meters a year) from the Mediterranean Sea to a desalination plant in the Beisan Valley at the head of the Dead Sea.[95] The water carrier would commence on the Mediterranean shore on a thinly populated strip. An underground water carrier 2 kilometers (1.2 miles) long would cross the seashore eastward to the first pumping station, which would raise the water into a tunnel 13 kilometers (8 miles) long at an elevation of 40 meters (132 feet). From there, the water would follow an eastward course into the Jezreel Valley Canal at an elevation of 30 meters (99 feet). A second pumping station, located 11 kilometers (7 miles) from the tunnel exit, would raise the water into a 40-meter- (132-feet-) high canal, and a third pumping station, located 13 kilometers (8 miles) from the tunnel exit, would raise the water to a canal at an elevation of 55 meters (182 feet). This last canal would cross the Afula plateau in Israel through an underground carrier 5 kilometers (3 miles) long into another canal, the Ramat Zvaim canal, which would then carry the water to the regulating reservoir overlaying the Beisan Valley at an elevation of 50 meters (165 feet). From there, the water would flow by gravity into a desalination facility, installed along the western shore of the Beisan Lake. An additional desalination plant would be located on the eastern shore of the lake.

It was estimated that making use of the hydrostatic gravity pressure in the Beisan Valley would save about 70 percent of the energy required for desalination. Overall, the desalination facilities in the larger Jordan Valley, including the ones proposed for the banks of the Jordan River, were estimated to cost about $4.5 billion (at 1991 prices) for a throughput of about 1,300 million cubic meters per year. It is now reported that this canal proposal is part of the ongoing bilateral talks between Jordan and Israel.

Yet another proposal under discussion is a project known as the Red-Dead Canal or the Jordan Rift Valley Project. The project would require the construction of a canal along the Israel-Jordan border from the Dead Sea to the Red Sea.[96] One to three hydroelectric plants in both Israel and Jordan would take advantage of the drop in elevation from the Red Sea to the Dead Sea (from sea level to 400 meters—1,320 feet—below sea level) to produce up to 600 megawatts of electricity, and a series of desalination plants would produce about 800 million cubic meters of additional water for both countries along the way, using the electricity produced by the hydroelectric plants. This project is also reported to be under serious consideration in the bilateral talks between the two countries. A consortium of companies from Britain, Germany, Italy, Israel, and the United States is said to be preparing feasibility studies for the project.[97]

Other Developments

Under the 1993 Protocol on Israeli-Palestinian Cooperation in Economic and Development Programs, the two sides agreed to establish an Israeli-Palestinian Continuing Committee for economic cooperation, focusing, among other things, on cooperation for water sharing. It includes designing the Water Development Program, to be prepared by experts from both sides, which would also specify the mode of cooperation in the management of water resources in the West Bank and Gaza and would include proposals for studies and plans on water rights of both parties, as well as equitable utilization of their transboundary water resources.[98]

Going beyond these bilateral developments, the first multilateral talks on water sharing under the current round of peace negotiations in the Middle East were held in May 1992 in Madrid. At the subsequent rounds of the multilateral talks, held in different locations, the participants agreed to form working groups on five substantive issue areas—refugees, the environment, economic development, arms control, and water resources. Under the leadership of the United States, the water resources group has since met several times at different locations around the world. The talks have, at times, been attended by twenty countries, each of which has agreed to prepare a regional development plan of its own to be examined by the United States for compatibilities and identifying areas of cooperation. However, progress in these multilateral talks has, to date, been tardy at best; now it is not clear whether such talks can be held in the future or achieve any concrete results in the absence of a successful culmination of the peace process between Israel and the Palestinians.

In the end, Israel, Jordan, and the Palestinians may be able to work out at least some form of cooperative arrangements for the development and sharing of their common water resources. It is clear that for this to happen the United States will once again have to play a major, proactive role in the hydropolitics of the Jordan basin. But it is also clear that a settlement of the conflict over the Golan Heights between Israel and Syria still will remain a prerequisite for designing and implementing optimal and multilateral solutions for the basin's growing water woes.

Before we close this section, we should point out that, in addition to the formal negotiations among the riparian states and peoples, many concerned individuals and nongovernmental regional and international organizations have long been playing very active roles in bringing together scholars, opinion leaders and policymakers, and other concerned citizens from the Jordan basin, in many different forums, to develop common understandings of the water problems faced by all the riparians and to seek out collective solutions for these problems. These efforts have sensitized many inside the basin and outside to the severity of the common natural resource and environmental problems in the Jordan basin, as well as set the stage for more informed interactions among the potentially influential actors in the hydropolitical game. To these individuals and groups must go the credit for creating an environment, despite many hurdles, wherein the erstwhile enemies can begin to take a broader perspective on their common resource and environmental problems, and to search for cooperative solutions for these problems.

SUMMARY AND CONCLUSION

Water has been, is, and will continue to be deeply and inextricably intertwined with the issues of identity, ideology, national security, interstate relations, and domestic polity in the Jordan basin. *If things continue as they have been*, the potential for acute conflict over water will keep growing because all the major water resources in this mostly arid basin flow across and under the different international borders, and water availability for all the basin's current and future inhabitants is likely to get much worse. There cannot be peace in the Jordan Valley for long without collective solutions for the water crises that all the riparian states and peoples are currently facing and are likely to face.

Although some constraints imposed by physical geography on the supply and the distribution of surface and underground waters in the Jordan basin can be alleviated by unilateral means, such as improving the agricultural and irrigation practices, imposing cost-based pricing for different uses of water, and so forth, the overall deficit can be made up only by multilateral cooperation within the basin or by importing water from outside the basin. The latter option does not seem to be politically or economically feasible for the foreseeable future. Major improvements in the quality of water will also require basinwide accords because of the hydrological interdependencies between the different water resources in the basin. But cooperation over water would also necessitate a substantial restructuring of the existing economic and political geography of the basin as a whole.

To solve the problems of growing water deficits, all the states and the peoples sharing the Jordan basin will need to abandon food security as a national goal, mainly because agriculture consumes such a large portion of all water withdrawals in the basin, and because total food security is not a feasible goal for any of the riparian states. Even in Israel, there are ecological and technical limits to improvements in water efficiency of irrigated agriculture and food production. The abandonment of food security by the riparian states, however, would require major changes in the ideologies and practices of all the peoples sharing the basin. Unless the overall regional economy develops rapidly, the unemployment situation in the basin will become worse. In particular, the return of Palestinian refugees to the West Bank and further Jewish immigration to Israel will greatly exacerbate the already explosive unemployment situation in some areas of the Jordan basin.

According to Naff and Matson, resolution of water disputes and forging of cooperation in the Jordan basin would require substantial cognitive restructuring, that is, reshaping or radically altering the cognitive maps different parties currently hold about their common water resources as well as each other.[99] The strides made in the recent peace initiatives between Israel and its neighbors clearly show that many psychological and ideological barriers earlier standing in the way of cooperation have been crumbling, and that many cognitive maps are already being redrawn. However, while this cognitive restructuring is needed for the erstwhile enemies to begin to move along the road to peace and cooperation, a substantial restructuring will also be needed "on the ground" to ensure that the hard-won peace in the cognitive realm is not lost to very down-to-earth resentments engendered by the unequal distribution of water resources and associated scarcities. The geography and hydrology of the Jordan basin dictate that a sense of fairness and a sensitivity to the needs of others have to be essential parts of any cognitive restructuring, especially when it comes to sharing the basin's scarce water resources.

What generalizations can be derived from this case study? First, in the arid and semiarid areas that are already facing or are likely to face absolute water scarcities, it is not possible to separate issues of low politics, especially water sharing, from issues of high politics. Second, while the strongest riparian state in an international basin may be able to improve its water security in the short to medium term by occupying the neighbors' land and water resources, this solution is not viable over the long run. Third, premature international or third-party attempts to fashion basinwide cooperation over transboundary water resources, especially in situations of deep-rooted ideological and territorial conflicts, are likely to be unproductive; only when the riparians themselves reach a situation and place from which they can begin to negotiate on water issues can there be a substantial role for any third party or honest broker. Fourth, even in the absence of a formal water accord, overt and covert understandings between two or more riparian states can exist to mitigate conflicts over water sharing. Fifth, though some purely national efforts may solve the water problems of one or more riparian states in the short to medium terms, there cannot be an optimal solution for water scarcity in an international basin in the long run other than a multilateral water accord. However, even bilateral accords take a long time to bring about and implement; truly multilateral agreements mostly remain distant goals. Sixth, the nature and conduct of hydropolitics in an international basin, over time, are bound to be circumscribed by the intricate play of both domestic and geopolitical forces and circumstances.

How does hydropolitics in the Jordan basin compare with hydropolitics in the La Plata and Nile basins? The findings here support the earlier findings about the conduct of hydropolitics by the strongest riparian state in an international basin. Like Brazil and Egypt, Israel has also taken many unilateral actions in the basin, and it has preferred to deal with its neighbors on a bilateral basis rather than collectively. Israel has also managed to ensure that its water security is not jeopardized by any manipulation of the water inflows to its territory by other riparian states, if necessary by attacking their water projects. But a combination of geopolitical and domestic factors and circumstances has finally forced it to at least begin to seek collective solutions for the impending water shortages it faces. Thus, water may force yet another hegemon in an international basin to become a benevolent neighbor.

In conclusion, though peace may yet break out in the Middle East some day, deep-seated hatreds—both ancient and modern—will continue to jeopardize the development of amicable relations among the different peoples of the region as long as the scarce transboundary water resources of the Jordan basin are not developed and shared in an equitable manner. At the very least, inequities in the access to and appropriation of the shared water resources will keep fueling resentments among the peoples sharing the basin. This would allow ideologues, religious zealots, or fundamentalists of different hues to keep fermenting discontent among their followers and, perhaps, to instigate renewed waves of terrorism, including attacks against the major waterworks in the basin. In the end, no one can sleep peacefully for long in the Jordan Valley until all the peoples are assured a fair share of the basin's scarce water resources, now and in the future. As a Turkish proverb has it: "When one man drinks while another can only watch, doomsday follows."

4

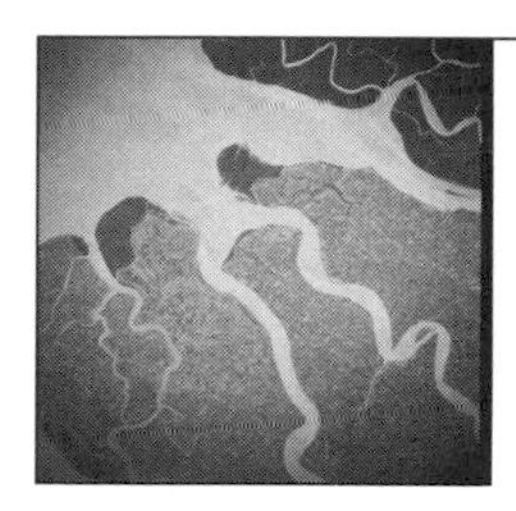

The Euphrates–Tigris Basin

In January 1991, armed with a mandate from the United Nations Security Council, a multinational military force commanded by a general of the United States Army mounted one of the largest military campaigns since World War II against a country that had occupied another country in the Middle East. Close to half a million soldiers from such near and distant lands as Syria and Bangladesh took part in the operation, code-named Desert Storm, to oust the occupying Iraqi forces from Kuwait. In the end, Iraq suffered a devastating defeat and was forced to withdraw from the occupied territory. The Gulf War, which followed the deadly, eight-year-long (1980–88) Iran–Iraq War, destroyed much of Iraq's military and civilian infrastructure located in the Euphrates-Tigris basin. Among its other casualties, the war also destroyed the myth of an "Arab nation" as well as any nascent complacency about the emergence of a peaceful post–Cold War "new world order."

The Gulf War has drastically altered the balance of power in favor of Iraq's adversaries in the Middle East for the foreseeable future; it may also have serious implications for the already highly contentious hydropolitics among the riparian states sharing the Euphrates-Tigris basin. And if the hitherto stateless Kurdish people living in the basin are able to establish one or more independent Kurdish states on the headwaters of the basin's major rivers in the future, hydropolitics in the basin would go through further convulsions.

Shared by four riparian states—Iran, Iraq, Syria, and Turkey—the Euphrates-Tigris basin has been driven to the brink of war in the recent past by unresolved conflicts over its transboundary water resources. It may well become the arena for acute interstate conflict in the future as the water and energy needs of its riparian states keep multiplying, and if the states continue to proceed with some highly ambitious plans for diverting and/or developing the basin's transboundary water resources in a noncooperative and ad hoc manner. In this particular basin, water has the very real potential to one day ignite fires that would seriously threaten regional and international security. On the other hand, the struggle to survive and prosper in this mostly semiarid region, combined with the altered geopolitical situation in the Middle East in the post–Cold War era, may some day persuade or compel the riparian states to cooperatively develop and share the multiple-use bounty that their transboundary water resources can help produce.

Will peace and prosperity finally come to this cradle of civilization or will the peoples sharing the basin, who are collectively so well endowed by nature with two essential resources—water and energy—continue to suffer violence and deprivation? What characteristics make hydropolitics in this basin similar to or different from hydropolitics in other international basins? Why have the riparian states in this resource-rich basin not wanted to or been able to cooperate with one another in the arena of hydropolitics? Will the post–Cold War, post–Gulf War era be one of enlightened cooperation among the riparian states or will hydropolitics in the basin remain as contentious as it has been in the past, or perhaps deteriorate further and lead to war? Are there lessons here that the states and peoples who share other river basins can and need to learn? Once again, physical geography provides the best entry point for exploring these questions.

GEOGRAPHY

Physical Geography

The Euphrates-Tigris basin comprises the catchment and drainage areas of two major rivers, both of which originate in Turkey; however, some tributaries of the system originate in Iran. With a total length of 2,700 kilometers (1,674 miles), the Euphrates is the longest river in southwest Asia. It is formed in southeastern Turkey by two tributaries—the Karasu, which originates at an elevation of 2,744 meters (1.7 miles), and the Murat, which originates at an elevation of 3,135 meters (2 miles). The two streams meet 45 kilometers (27 miles) northwest of the city of Elazig in Turkey. The combined stream then flows through the southeastern Taurus Mountains and crosses into Syria at Karkamis, downstream of the Turkish town of Birecik (see the map on p. 126). Farther down, the Euphrates is met by two tributaries, the Balikh and the Khabur, both of which also originate in Turkey. Near Qurna in Iraq, some channels of the Euphrates meet the Tigris flowing down from the east, and from this confluence to the sea—a distance of about 179 kilometers (111 miles)—the main stream is known as the Shatt al-Arab. About 32 kilometers (20 miles) below Basra in Iraq the Shatt is joined by the Karun River and by other smaller tributaries flowing westward from the Zagros mountains in Iran. From there to the Persian Gulf, the river traverses a course of 72 kilometers (45 miles) and forms a short but contested border between Iraq and Iran.[1]

The catchment basin of the Euphrates in southeastern Turkey, a mostly mountainous region, is 82,330 square kilometers (32,160 square miles); in addition, the river drains an area four times as large downstream. About 63 percent of the annual flow passes down the river between March and June; it takes only two months, July and August, to reach a minimum whereas it may take up to nine months to reach the maximum. During the flood season, the river carries huge amounts of silt to the delta, enough to cover six hundred acres of land with a layer of 0.25 centimeter (one-tenth of an inch) in a day. For thousands of years, these silt deposits have made Mesopotamia one of the most intensively farmed and productive agricultural regions in the world.

The Tigris is the second-longest river in southwest Asia. It originates in eastern Turkey near Lake Hazar at an elevation of 1,150 meters (0.72 mile) and forms the border between Turkey and Syria for 32 kilometers (20 miles) before entering Iraqi territory. The river enters its delta in the swamplands in Iraq between Tikit and Samarra, later forming the eastern part of the Tigris-Euphrates system.[2] Owing to the location of the Tigris near the foot of the Zagros Mountains, the tributaries joining it carry both melting snow and rainfall in the warmer months. Consequently, depending on the phasing of the two types of flows, the Tigris's flow also shows great variation over the year. The river carries about 40 million cubic meters of sediment past Baghdad every year, of which only one-tenth reaches the Persian Gulf. However, compared with the Euphrates, the Tigris is less important for

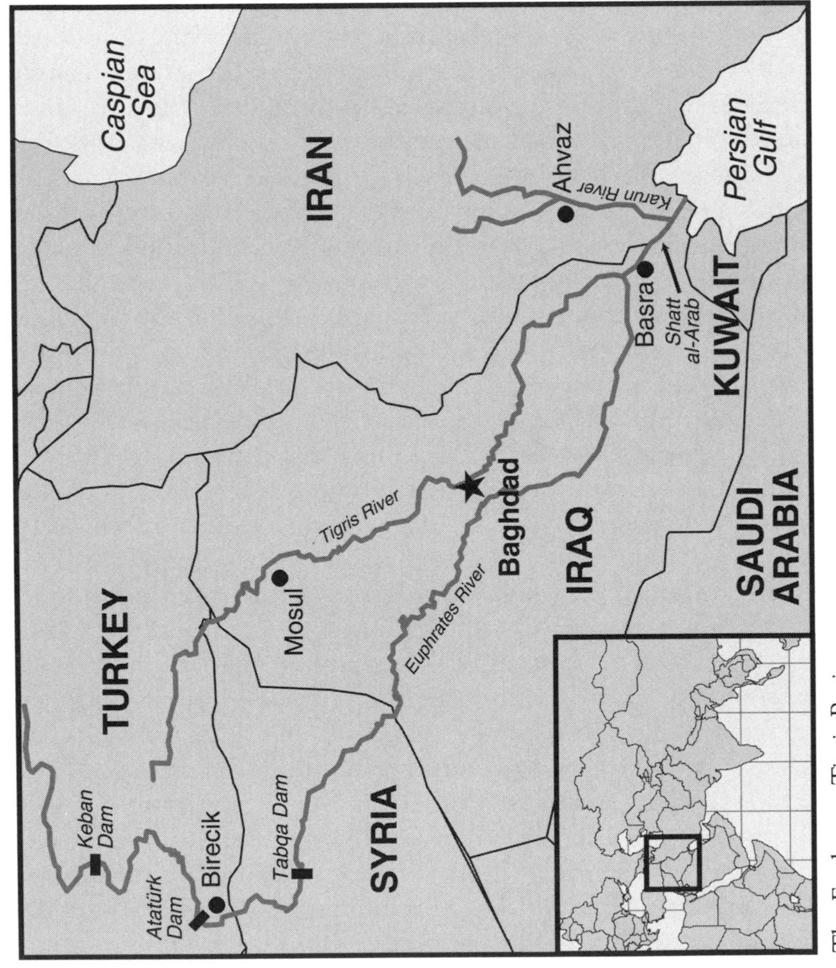

The Euphrates-Tigris Basin

agriculture because of a high concentration of sedimentation in its water and because of the violent nature of its main stream.[3]

The flow in the Euphrates can be as high as twenty-eight times its low flow and in the Tigris almost eighty times its low flow. As we shall see later, these wild fluctuations in river flows have substantial implications for hydropolitics in the basin since they necessitate construction of large storage facilities to ensure a steady availability of water for household, agricultural, and other needs downstream. It should be noted, however, that the available estimates for the average annual flow of the two rivers vary widely, depending on the sources of data. As is the case in most international river basins, each of the riparian states in this basin also has its own best estimates for the volume of flow of the two rivers as well as the many tributaries that feed these rivers.[4] Based on the best available information, Kolars and Mitchell have provided the following estimates for average annual flows at three chosen sites in the basin: Birecik (Turkey)—26,990 million cubic meters; Tabqa (Syria)—28,400 million cubic meters; and Hit (Iraq)—27,230 million cubic meters.[5] Considering the contributions of some underground aquifers and the main tributaries to the water supply in the combined basin, as much as 98 percent of the Euphrates' water may originate in Turkey. About 45 percent of the Tigris's water also originates in Turkey; the remaining is contributed mostly by tributaries that originate in Iran. Thus, not only are Turkey and Iran the uppermost riparian states on all the major rivers and tributaries in the basin, but also their territories contribute most of the water flowing in the basin's streams.

The Shatt al-Arab is the only major navigable waterway in the basin and it is shared by two riparian states, Iran and Iraq. Only small steamers can go up from the Persian Gulf as far as Basra;[6] limited steamer transportation is possible on the Tigris within Iraq as far as Baghdad and Mosul. Thus, except for the Shatt al-Arab, navigation rights on the shared rivers are not an arena of interstate conflict in the basin. However, since the Karun River flowing down from Iran meets the Shatt, Iran has a strong interest in ensuring its navigational access on the Karun and the Shatt to the Persian Gulf.

Another important geographical feature of the basin, with substantial implications for interstate relations and hydropolitics, is the extremely narrow access Iraq has to the sea. Iraq's coastline on the Persian Gulf is only about 15 kilometers (9 miles) long, and Shatt al-Arab provides its only riverine access to the sea. The Iraqi ports of Basra and Al Faw are located adjacent to the Shatt. Before the Gulf War, Basra was Iraq's principal deepwater commercial port and Al Faw was the main petroleum shipping terminal. Damage from the Iran-Iraq War and from bombardments during the Gulf War effectively closed this waterway as well as the port facilities. Iraq has also constructed a canal, the Shatt al-Basra Canal, connecting the town of Basra to the Persian Gulf. The northern end of the canal connects to a waterway of the Euphrates about 13 kilometers (8 miles) northwest of Basra, the southern end of the canal is about 31 kilometers (19 miles) north of the Umm Qasr seaport, located on a tributary flowing into the Persian Gulf. This and another seaport located on the canal had for a while served as alternatives to the port of Basra during the Iran-Iraq War, but they later had to be closed because of extensive damage to the canal and other facilities. The ports were reopened in 1988; however, damage from Desert Storm bombardments has again rendered these ports and waterway inoperable. The waterway remains clogged by debris that includes unexploded ordnance and mines, and sunken vessels.

In a 1991 study, the U.S. Army Corps of Engineers estimated that it will take hundreds of millions of dollars and many years to repair the damaged port facilities, dredge the channels, and make navigation on these waterways possible again.[7] Until that happens, Iraq will remain an effectively landlocked country, the only riparian state to be saddled with such a fate in the Euphrates-Tigris basin. If the UN embargo on Iraqi oil exports is lifted before the ports and other facilities are repaired, Iraq will have to rely on pipelines running through Syria and Turkey to ship its oil out to the Mediterranean Sea. This will further reduce Baghdad's bargaining power in conducting hydropolitics with its upstream neighbors, all of whom have independent access to the sea outside the Euphrates-Tigris basin.

As in many other international basins in the Third World, in this basin environmental degradation, pollution, and deterioration of water quality have also begun to emerge as issues of great concern. Dumping of untreated sewage in the two rivers and their tributaries has already led to serious health problems in Syria and Iraq. Although some sewage treatment plants have been built in Syria in recent years, the level of pollution downstream remains a grave concern in the lower basin. Since the destruction of Iraqi infrastructure during the Gulf War, dumping of untreated sewage in the Tigris has created serious pollution in Iraq. To deal with the problems of waterborne pollution, a multilateral agreement, signed by Bahrain, Iran, Iraq, Kuwait, Oman, Qatar, Saudi Arabia, and the United Arab Emirates, has existed in the region since 1978 to prevent, abate, and combat pollution caused by waterborne discharges reaching the sea. The agreement also provides for assessing civil liabilities and compensation for damage from pollution of the marine environment.[8] However, as far as is known this agreement is not being effectively implemented in the Euphrates-Tigris basin.

The deteriorating quality of water reaching the Persian Gulf substantially affects important fisheries and shrimping areas at the head of the gulf. The marshes and waterways of the basin are also vital resting and feeding stops on a major flyway for birds migrating between the polar regions. Poor water quality in the basin and reduced flow in the rivers are bound to substantially impact this migration process. This particular issue may provide some leverage to the international environmental community to influence the way large water and hydroelectric projects are designed and implemented in the basin. The fact that all the riparian states are currently debt ridden and would require substantial external assistance to launch large water projects in the basin also means that international donors, financial institutions, and other organizations may also be able to exercise considerable influence on hydropolitics in the basin in the future (more on this in the next section).

Thus, overall, the physical geography of the Euphrates-Tigris basin has endowed different riparian states with different sets of advantages and disadvantages in conducting hydropolitics with their neighbors. From all accounts, the lowermost and effectively landlocked riparian, Iraq, now seems to be the most vulnerable to any manipulation of the river regimes in the basin, whereas Turkey and to a lesser extent Iran seem to have all the advantages in hydropolitics. At the same time, this physical geography has also created substantial grounds for interstate cooperation in the basin: for exploiting the water supply, flood mitigation, drought relief, irrigation, and hydroelectric potential of the shared rivers. However, whether this potential is ever fully developed and shared among the inhabitants of the basin will be determined largely by the evolving economic and political geography of the individual riparian states, and of the basin as a whole.

Economic Geography

A distinguishing feature that the Euphrates-Tigris basin shares with the Nile basin in Africa and the Indus basin in South Asia is the length of time the basin was occupied by highly developed civilizations that were supported by the bounty that the water could produce. The basin has been populated for close to seven thousand years or more, and construction of waterworks in the basin dates back to as early as 3000 B.C. However, much of the irrigation system then existing in the basin was destroyed during the

Mongol invasions in the thirteenth century. In recent times, Iraq has undertaken massive projects to repair and revitalize the earlier irrigation infrastructure, with notable successes until the Gulf War when much of this infrastructure was destroyed.

The combined mid-1997 population of the four riparian states was estimated to be around 160 million, projected to grow to about 190 million by the year 2000.[9] If these projections turn out to be correct, the growth in population over a period of less than a decade will be larger than the current population of Iraq. Of course, not all the citizens of these countries currently live in the Euphrates-Tigris basin, nor would the additional population concentrate exclusively in the basin. However, the high population growth rates do point to the rising water and energy needs in all the riparian states. What proportion of these needs each riparian state would want to or be able to satisfy from the waters of the two rivers and their tributaries would depend on how the economic and political geography of the basin evolve. What is certain is that pressures on the shared water resources in the basin will keep multiplying, more so in Iraq and Syria than in Iran and Turkey, for reasons to be discussed.

Agriculture is still the main economic activity in the basin, providing employment and sustenance for a significant portion of its inhabitants. Iraq, in particular, has the second-largest agricultural potential in North Africa and the Middle East, after Sudan. However, by the mid-1980s Iraq was importing 80 percent of its food requirements; in 1987 food imports accounted for 26.7 percent by value of Iraq's total imports. Iraq's growing dependence on food imports has been further accentuated by the damage its irrigation system has suffered in the recent wars and by the trade embargo imposed by the United Nations since August 1990. A side effect of this embargo may be to impel Baghdad to seek total food security within its territory in the future. However, this will only put more pressure on its water resources, even assuming that Iraq continues to receive the amount of water it currently does. Already, about 80 percent of all water currently withdrawn in Iraq goes to agriculture and related activities.

Iraq is richly endowed with petrochemical resources, however. The total national petroleum reserves are estimated at about 6 percent of the world total. From 1972, Iraq was capable of producing up to 500,000 barrels of oil per day; however, it suffered a severe blow during the eight-year-long war with Iran when oil shipments through the Persian Gulf were halted and again during the Gulf War when much of the country's oil refining and export capacity was destroyed. The continuing UN embargo on the export of petroleum products has also deprived the country of the much-needed financial resources for reconstructing its damaged infrastructure.

The Gulf War also destroyed much of Iraq's waterworks. Only one major project, the Derbandi Khan Dam was relatively (50 percent) undamaged; the Dokan and Haditha Dams were 75 percent destroyed, and the Ramade Barrage, Saddam, and Samarra Dams were made inoperable altogether.[10] In addition, the war destroyed much of the infrastructure for supplying water to Iraqi households and industries.[11] Although Iraq has managed to repair some of these facilities and infrastructure, restoration of full water supply capacity is likely to take many years, even assuming that the resources needed for such an enterprise become available. Another problem yet to be fully faced by Baghdad is the gainful resettlement of hundreds of thousands of Iraqi soldiers who had participated in the Iran-Iraq War and the Gulf War. This would require an opening up of large tracts of new land for agriculture and settlements. This goal can be achieved only if sufficient amounts of freshwater as well as the needed financial resources become available on a sustained basis.

Deteriorating water quality is a serious problem Iraq now faces. A consequence of irrigation over thousands of years, salinity has become a major problem and currently affects 65 percent of all irrigated lands. Without an adequate supply of running freshwater the soils cannot be washed of the accumulated saline deposits. These problems will be further compounded if some Turkish and Syrian projects (discussed later) are completed that could well reduce the Euphrates' flow into Iraq substantially. Iraq would be able to irrigate only 37 percent of the farmlands that were irrigated in 1990.[12] But Iraq will not be alone in facing the dire economic and environmental consequences of large water withdrawals upstream.

In Syria the region surrounding the Euphrates is known as al-Jazira. Sparsely populated until the end of World War II, it is now home to about one-fifth of the Syrian population, attracted there by the employment opportunities and wealth generated by the introduction of mechanized dry farming, discoveries of oil, and expansion of agriculture, made possible by some Syrian dams on the Euphrates. Various crops, including rice, are now grown in the area, but cotton and wheat are the main cash crops.[13] However, if the planned upstream projects in Turkey (discussed later) are fully implemented, Syrian agriculture may also be severely affected. Already, Syria has had to seriously curtail its very ambitious plans to extend irrigation to large tracts of cultivable land in the Euphrates-Tigris basin because of water shortages.

In recent years the Syrian economy has also suffered greatly from severe droughts, costly attempts to keep up with and match Israel's military strength, a falloff in Arab aid, and insufficient foreign exchange earnings to buy the needed inputs for agriculture and industries. Bureaucratic regulations and corruption have discouraged or driven underground the mercantile and entrepreneurial spirit for which Syrian businessmen have been historically renowned. Syria's involvement in Lebanon and support for the Kurdish rebellion in Turkey also deprive the economy of the much-needed resources for investment. The reduction of Syrian exports, which had earlier gone primarily to the Soviet Union and some Eastern European countries, has also dealt a serious blow to the economy in the post–Cold War era. Thus, in the altered geopolitical and geoeconomic environment, Syria is being forced to face the challenge of radically restructuring and reorienting its economy or risk losing out in the regional and global competition for capital, technology, and markets. These economic reforms, if implemented, will also have substantial implications for Syria's need for water and energy.

In Iran the Karun is the only navigable river and its valley is among the most productive agricultural lands in the country. A significant portion of Iran's population is concentrated in the river valley and the Euphrates-Tigris delta. As the Iranian population continues to grow, the need for water and agricultural land around the Shatt will also multiply. Freedom of navigation on the Shatt and the Karun and control over the river waters that originate within its territory and flow down to the Shatt are, thus, two primary determinants of Tehran's stand in hydropolitics with Iraq. Maintaining access to the huge reserves of oil as well as fish stocks in the Persian Gulf is an additional concern that will continue to have substantial import for Iranian conduct in hydropolitics.

Pressures on the water and energy resources of the Euphrates-Tigris basin are rising also because of the accelerating growth of urban centers in the basin. As pointed out earlier, Iraq, Syria, and Turkey now have population growth rates that will double their populations in two to three decades. In all likelihood, a large portion of this anticipated growth will continue to be concentrated in the cities in each country. Historically, guided mainly by the availability of water, most of Iraq's urban centers and a large portion of its population were located along and near the Euphrates and Tigris Rivers. This trend has continued in the modern times and is not likely to change significantly in the foreseeable future. A high rate of urbanization, propelled by natural growth of the urban population and internal migration, implies a rising demand for water for households and for industrial and service sector needs. After the destruction brought about by the Gulf War, Iraq is in dire need of good-quality drinking water as well as water for maintaining sewage and waste disposal systems for its urban population.

The largest Iraqi cities located in the basin are Baghdad and Mosul; populations in several other cities located along the Euphrates are growing at rates far higher than the rural areas. This is fast multiplying the demand for freshwater in the urban areas. In Mosul alone, per capita water consumption is expected to rise from 230 liters (60 gallons) per day in 1974 to 330 liters (85 gallons) per day by the year 2000. All the urban centers in Iraq are currently supplied mainly from surface water sources, which are the most vulnerable to upstream manipulations.

In Syria in nearly all the major cities, including the capital, Damascus, water and energy shortages have led to strict rationing and long "blackout" periods. Food shortages have, from time to time, led to riots that have been brutally suppressed by the ruling regime. Faced with growing water scarcities, Damascus has implemented very strict water conservation laws in the country in recent years. These restrictions have engendered additional hardships for certain sections of the population and have led to political tensions.

More than half the population of Turkey currently lives in urban areas, most of which are already overcrowded because of natural population growth and large-scale migration to the cities since the midcentury. Most Turkish cities also suffer from serious energy and water shortages. Even in the water- and energy-rich southeastern region surrounding the headwaters of the Euphrates and the Tigris, which is mostly rural and sparsely populated, potable water and electricity have been and continue to be in short supply.

The southeast Anatolia region of Turkey, though abundant in natural resources, including water, rich agricultural soil, and minerals, has long remained the least developed part of the country; six of the eight southeastern provinces together have only 1.9 percent of the nations' medium- and large-scale industrial establishments, 1.92 percent of industrial workers, and 1.98 percent of the industrial value added.[14] And despite the region's abundant water resources, severe water deficiencies exist in most urban and rural areas in these provinces.

With some nascent industrialization in two of the six southeastern provinces, the economy of the region is based primarily on agriculture. Given the low productivity of much of the cultivable land, animal husbandry is an important supplement to agriculture for the regions' population. It should also be pointed out that ownership of agricultural land in the region shows a highly skewed distribution (only 8 percent of the farmers own 50 percent of the land). This highly uneven distribution of land is one more factor that engenders political tensions in the region.[15]

Turkey imports about one-half of its annual energy requirements, and a quarter of its electricity production depends on imported fuel; in 1990 its oil bill was $3.5 billion.[16] As urbanization, industrialization, and mechanization of agriculture proceed, accompanied by the continuing growth in population, the demand for electricity and water in Turkey, overall, and in the southeast, in particular, is expected to keep growing at a fast pace. To deal with these shortages, Turkey has launched a massive project in the basin that has not only run into serious financial problems but has also greatly accentuated tensions in Turkey's relations with the downstream riparians. (See the later discussion on "The GAP Project.")

The severity of impending water shortages in the downstream riparian states, if the planned Turkish projects on the headwaters of the two rivers are implemented as planned, is highlighted by some projections of per capita water withdrawals in different riparian states over the next thirty-five years.[17] Considering only the projected increases in populations in the downstream countries and decreases in river flows caused by the upstream Turkish projects, by the year 2000, Syrian per capita water withdrawals would be only 31 percent of what they now are; by the year 2025 they would have dropped to 16 percent of the current withdrawals. For Iraq, by the year 2000 per capita withdrawals would be 51 percent of what they are now; by the year 2025 they would have dropped to just 27 percent of the current withdrawals. And though the per capita Iraqi withdrawals in 2025 would still be substantially higher than the withdrawals in Turkey, the quality of water reaching Iraq would be much worse. If these dire projections are anywhere close to the actual outcome for water availability in the basin in the future, it should be clear that there will certainly be great socioeconomic and political turmoil in the two downstream countries and in the basin as a whole. Looking at these future estimates, Kolars and Mitchell have described the situation as one with "the general pattern of impending crisis."[18]

One additional economic factor impinging on hydropolitics in the basin is that, in the absence of a basinwide water accord, the unilateral actions the different riparian states may want and can take to develop large water and energy projects in the basin will depend largely on the financial resources they can mobilize domestically. In 1996 the total external debt of Turkey was estimated to be $79 billion, of Iran about $22.7 billion, and of Syria $21 billion.[19] The per capita incomes in the basin in 1997 ranged from $1,150 per year in Syria to $1,780 in Iran.[20] Since the Gulf War, Iraq's economy, in particular, has deteriorated greatly, and it may be a long time before Iraq can reach even the 1989 per capita income level of about $2,000 per year. Certainly, Iraq will not be in a position to launch any major water or energy projects in the basin for some time to come; whether Iran, Syria, or Turkey can do so unilaterally remains to be seen, particularly since some ambitious projects launched in the basin in the recent past have run into serious problems. Whether the riparian states can collectively overcome these economic constraints to cooperatively develop the multiple-use potential of their shared water resources, even with external assistance, will depend on the evolving political geography of the basin and of its individual riparian states.

Political Geography

The political geography of the Euphrates-Tigris basin since the end of World War II has been shaped by the legacies of colonization in parts of the basin; by rivalries and contingently formed alliances among its riparian states; by Cold War–era manipulations of interstate relations and domestic polity in the region by the two superpowers and other external agents; by military coups, violent rebellions, and revolutions, at different times and in different riparian states; and by intermittent attempts at democratization in some riparian states. Because the basin is contiguous with the Jordan basin, with Syria sharing both the basins, hydropolitics in the Euphrates-Tigris basin has not been and cannot be immune to political developments in the Jordan basin.

In addition to the unresolved water disputes, interstate relations in this basin have been plagued by border disputes, transboundary ethnic and religious affiliations and loyalties, and allegations of support for each ruling regime's opponents by one or more of the neighboring states.[21] The riparian states have not hesitated from suppressing domestic opposition, often brutally, and from meddling in the internal affairs of the others in a variety of ways. More recently, the rise of Islamic fundamentalism and growing ethnic conflict in some of the riparian states have made the Euphrates-Tigris basin a potential powder keg. At the same time, the collapse of the Soviet Union, the defeat of Iraq in the Gulf War, and the moves toward peace between Israel and its neighbors have created the potential to radically restructure the political geography of the basin as well as its hydropolitics in unprecedented ways.

Formerly called Mesopotamia, Iraq was the center of one of the most ancient civilizations in the world. From the seventeenth century to the end of World War I it was under Ottoman Turkish rule, followed until

1932 by the British Mandate of the League of Nations. A monarchy at the time of independence from British rule, Iraq in 1958 suffered a violent revolution that led to the overthrow of the Western-oriented Hashemite family then ruling the country, and to the establishment of a socialist republic. This was followed by a succession of revolutionary socialistic regimes that ruled the country under a provisional constitution, culminating in the mid-1960s in the coming to power of the socialist Ba'th Party and the formation of a coalition in 1973, known as the National Progressive Front. Since 1979, the country has been ruled by a self-proclaimed "socialist" regime led by Saddam Hussein.[22]

Historically, Iraq was a much-prized catch for all the empire builders and colonizers in the region because of its strategic location at the head of the Persian Gulf and the high productivity of its agricultural lands. The expansions and contractions of different empires in the region, and manipulations of Iraq's borders by the European colonizers, left behind a legacy of disparate ethnic and religious groups needing to be incorporated into a modern nation-state. Consequently, a tension has always existed between the Iraqi state and its people.[23] The ruling Ba'th Party has striven over time to consolidate diverse interests within Iraq and to enhance economic and social welfare throughout the country; but, as Georges Roux, a historian of Iraq, has pointed out, "Iraq required, to be viable, two conditions: perfect cooperation between the various ethnic and sociopolitical units within the country itself, and a friendly or at least neutral attitude from its neighbors. Unfortunately, neither one nor the other ever lasted for any length of time."[24] As we shall see, the absence of these conducive domestic and external conditions for the long-term viability of the Iraqi polity continues to substantially impact hydropolitics in the Euphrates-Tigris basin.

The existing borders of Syria were demarcated by the French colonizers after World War I. The French Mandate over the country was formally approved by the League of Nations in 1922; only in 1946, after a long struggle, did the country achieve independence. The Ba'th Party came to power in Syria in 1963 through a military coup, followed by another coup in 1966 that temporarily brought to power a neo-Ba'thist party. The new regime's unpopularity, fueled by the loss of the Golan Heights to Israel in the 1967 Arab-Israeli war for which the regime was blamed, contributed to the coup of 1970 that brought Hafez al-Assad to power. Assad has ruled the country ever since with an iron hand.

In contrast to the colonial roots of the modern states of Iraq and Syria, Turkey was founded as a successor state to the Ottoman Empire in 1923. It was under military rule from 1960 to 1961, and again from 1971 to 1973. From 1973 to 1980 it was governed by a series of weak governments that were unable to tackle the economic and political problems the country was then facing. In 1980, in the third coup since the proclamation of the Turkish republic, the military deposed the ruling government. This was followed in 1982 by the approval of a new constitution by the Turkish voters and establishment of a presidential system. Since 1983, when elections for a national assembly were held, the country has been governed by elected one-party or coalition-based prime ministers.

Iran also has a checkered political geography. Historically known as Persia, it was ruled by many dynasties and empires and was itself often the center of vast empires extending through much of the Middle East. In 1907 an Anglo-Russian entente divided the country into a Russian zone of influence, a British zone, and a neutral zone. After World War I, under the strong leadership of an allegedly pro-German leader, Reza Shah Pahlavi, many legal, political, and economic reforms were instituted in the country. However, under joint Russian-British pressure the shah was forced to abdicate the throne in 1941 in favor of his son, Mohammad Reza Shah Pahlavi. Known internationally as the shah of Iran, this new leader was forced to flee the country in 1953 by a highly nationalist leader, Mohammad Mosaddeq, but returned to power shortly afterward with strong Western backing. In 1979 the shah was deposed by an Islamic movement led by Ayatollah Khomeini and Iran became an Islamic republic; the national polity has since been dominated by the Islamic clergy. However, since the mid-1990s a movement toward a more moderate and liberal Iran has scored some notable successes, both at the national and the local levels.

About 93 percent of the Iranian population follows the Shia sect of Islam, whereas most ethnic minorities in the country, including Arabs, Baluchis, Kurds, and Turks, are members of the rival Sunni sect. These divisions have led to great tensions in the relationship of the minorities with the state; one religious minority in particular, the Baha'is, have been severely persecuted by the government since the 1979 revolution. The so-called Hostage Crisis of 1979, in which many American citizens were held captive in Iran for more than a year; Iran's alleged support for international terrorism; and some other domestic and international postures and actions condemned by the West in recent years have led to Iran being branded a "rogue state." This has effectively prevented the country from participating fully in the international community of states.

An episode that clearly demonstrates the relationship of water to armed hostilities in this basin occurred during the 1980–88 Iran-Iraq War. South and east of the marshy region in the Euphrates-Tigris basin is a contested area that the Iranians refer to as Khuzistan and the Iraqis as Arabistan. Both countries claim the area as their own. It was the main locale for substantial military activity during the war, and water played a significant role in military planning by both sides. Iraqi forces, supported by tanks, moved freely over this flat plain until the winter and spring rains transformed it into mud. The Iranians also flooded part of the plain by releasing water from a dam, forcing the Iraqis to build raised roads and dikes in order to maintain their positions.[25] According to an Iraqi press release, about 37 million cubic meters of earthworks and 2,400 kilometers (1,500 miles) of roads were built between October 1980 and May 1981 to support military action in the area.[26] Now, Iran-Iraq relations continue to be adversely affected by the boundary dispute in the Shatt al-Arab that has not been resolved despite the long war.

Within this broad political geographic context, a common issue faced by all the riparian states in the Euphrates-Tigris basin is the commonly referred-to "Kurdish problem" or "Kurdish question." These 20 million or so people, culturally and ethnically very distinct from other citizens of the four riparian states, account for about 19 percent of the population in Turkey and about 23 percent in Iraq.[27] They are also among the close to 10 percent minority population in Syria. The Kurds are politically represented by the PKK (Kurdish Workers' Party) in Turkey, and by the KDP (Kurdish Democratic Party) and the PUK (Patriotic Union of Kurdistan) in Iraq. All three parties have significant military wings and, at different times, different factions of the parties have been backed and supported by Turkey, Syria, Iraq, and Iran with the aim of destabilizing one another. Turkish-Syrian relations, in particular, have been overshadowed by allegations of Syrian support for the PKK rebellion in Turkey. In the mid-1970s, following Iraq's refusal to reach an agreement to demarcate the mutual border on the Shatt al-Arab, Iran supported the Kurdish rebellion in northern Iraq. This support continued until 1975 when an agreement between the two countries in Algiers ended the clandestine Iranian support for the rebels. And, before the Gulf War, Iraq and Turkey were known to have collaborated to "take care" of their respective Kurdish rebellions. Baghdad is reported to have even allowed the Turkish army to pursue the Kurdish fighters within Iraqi territory.[28]

Now, in the aftermath of the Gulf War, international efforts have created a seemingly autonomous "safe haven" for the Iraqi Kurds, the so-called No-Fly Zone north of the 32d parallel. However, this has not prevented either Iraq or Turkey from using their military forces to suppress the Kurds. Factionalism and opportunism have also long plagued the Kurds' search for freedom, and it is by no means certain whether these people will be able to establish one or more sovereign states in the Euphrates-Tigris basin. One thing is clear though: as long as the riparian states are unable to fully suppress (or eliminate) the Kurdish people and as long as the Kurds themselves are unable to achieve an acceptable degree of autonomy or independence, hydropolitics in the basin will remain highly contentious. This is inevitable given the location of the Kurds on the headwaters of the two rivers, as well as the hitherto unexploited mineral reserves in the lands they occupy. If one or more independent Kurdish states were to somehow emerge in the basin, as uppermost riparians they would certainly demand a substantial share of the bounty the shared water resources of the basin can and may produce. In this sense hydropolitics in the Euphrates-Tigris basin is directly related to issues of national independence and sovereignty, domestic politics and interstate relations, and human rights within each of the riparian states.

With the end of the Cold War and the breakup of the Soviet Union, geopolitics and interstate relations in the Middle East, in general, and in the Euphrates-Tigris basin, in particular, have been undergoing substantial restructuring. With the coming into existence of several independent Central Asian nations, Turkish foreign policy has begun to be reoriented toward developing friendly relations with the new nations. But whatever its final outcome, this reorientation does not mean that Turkey can afford to be complacent about developments on its southern flank, especially given its ongoing problems with the Kurds. Whether these new geopolitical developments will lead to Turkey changing its stand in conducting hydropolitics in the Euphrates-Tigris basin remains to be seen.

HYDROPOLITICS

An important hydrological fact to keep in mind when analyzing the nature and conduct of hydropolitics in the Euphrates-Tigris basin is that Turkey—the uppermost riparian on both the rivers—is also the only major source of surplus water in the whole of the Middle East. And substantial as they are, waters of the Euphrates and Tigris Rivers together constitute only 28 percent of Turkey's total water supply. This has substantially boosted Turkey's maneuverability and clout in hydropolitics, not only in the Euphrates-Tigris basin but in the Jordan basin as well (see the later section on "The Peace Pipelines"). Iran is also well endowed with additional water resources and, as pointed out earlier, some of the tributaries feeding the Euphrates-Tigris system originate in Iran. Thus, whereas Turkey and Iran are only partially dependent on the two rivers, for the two lower riparians, Syria and Iraq, these resources are of vital importance. Iraqi territory adds virtually nothing to the flow of the two rivers, and Syria's contribution to the basin's water resources is also minimal, further underscoring the importance the two rivers have for the downstream riparians. Syria does have other water resources outside the basin (see chapter 3), but for Iraq, waters of the two rivers have the same crucial importance as the Nile's water has for Egypt; without them much of Iraq would turn into a desert. Iraq can certainly try to implement several purely national solutions for its water woes, but in the long term there is no escape from this structural "Iraqi condition" except the goodwill and cooperation of its upstream neighbors.

If we look only at the main streams of its major rivers, the Euphrates-Tigris basin would seem to be a classic case of a successive upper-middle-lower riparian structure. As pointed out earlier, except for forming a short stretch of the border between Syria and Turkey, the Tigris flows through Turkey and Iraq in succession and never enters Syrian territory proper. The Euphrates' riparian structure is also a simple one, with Turkey as the uppermost riparian, Syria the middle riparian, and Iraq the lowermost riparian. However, this does not mean that hydropolitics in the two sub-basins and in the larger combined basin is simple in any way. It should be remembered that, at least for a stretch of the Shatt al-Arab and on some of the tributaries, Iran too has co-riparian and upper riparian claims. Thus, Iraq is and will always be forced to deal with all the other riparian states sharing the basin to ensure its water security. Syria also shares other river basins with Jordan, Lebanon, Israel, and Turkey, thus adding to the complexity and contentious nature of hydropolitics in the Euphrates-Tigris basin. As we shall see, these hydrologically determined interdependencies and power asymmetries as well as some historical developments in the basin help to explain the stands taken and strategies adopted by the different riparian states when conducting hydropolitics in the Euphrates-Tigris basin.

Historically, the Euphrates basin was mostly administered by a unitary authority under the different empires and colonizers that had ruled Mesopotamia. Only after the Ottoman Empire withdrew and the subsequent British and French Mandates in the region were dismantled did water disputes acquire a nationalistic character. And even though sovereign states came into being in the basin in the aftermath of World War I, interstate water sharing did not become a problem until recently, mainly because Iraq alone was traditionally withdrawing any substantial amount of the river's water. The same has historically been true of the Tigris's water.

Before World War II, a number of treaties affecting national borders and natural resources were signed by the nations and mandates then existing in the Euphrates-Tigris basin. Among these, in 1913 Great Britain, Russia, Persia, and Turkey signed a treaty for the regulation of the Shatt al-Arab, followed by two treaties in 1921 and 1923 between France and Turkey for the Euphrates and Kuveik Rivers. In 1930 the Commission on the Demarcation of the Turco-Syrian Frontier on the Tigris was established, and in 1937 Iraq and Iran signed a treaty for demarcating their border and for regulating navigation on the Shatt al-Arab. None of these colonial-era treaties now has much import for contemporary interstate relations and hydropolitics in the basin.

The only seemingly legal regime currently in place in the basin is the Treaty of Friendship and Neighborly Relations between Iraq and Turkey. It was signed in 1946, the same year that Syria achieved independence. The treaty states that Turkey will, in the event of constructing any water conservation project on the Euphrates, consult Iraq and make adjustments to such projects so that the needs of both nations are satisfied as far as possible.[29] The treaty is theoretically still in operation; however, by leaving Syria out and by not specifying how the terms of consultation will be defined or adjudicated, the treaty falls far short of being a legal regime to govern water sharing in the basin or for resolving disputes among the riparian states. Consequently, according to one scholar, "the present legal regime can best be categorized as a chaotic regime of claim and counterclaim governed more by political than legal concerns."[30]

The claims regarding the amount of water each riparian state is entitled to revolve around some contested "facts" and assertions. The average annual flow of the Euphrates at the Syrian-Iraq border is estimated to be about 29 billion cubic meters. In a tripartite meeting in Baghdad in September 1965, Iraq was reported to have demanded 18 billion cubic meters of the Euphrates' flow, Turkey 14 billion cubic meters, and Syria 13 billion cubic meters.[31] Clearly, these demands and claims far exceeded the average low-flow capacity of the river. The Iraqis continue to base their claim, by and large, on two reports prepared by the World Bank (1965) and the Soviet Union (1972); however, neither Syria nor Iraq has accepted the contents of either report.[32]

Because Iraq has historically been the major user of the waters of the two rivers, and because it is the lowermost riparian in the basin, not surprisingly

Iraqi claims relating to the shared waters are based on the doctrines of prior use, established rights, and projections of current and future needs. Baghdad points out that both Syria and Turkey have other freshwater resources whereas it alone is completely dependent on the two rivers. As a middle riparian, Syria tends to base its claims on the notion of "rightful share." Syria emphasizes that since both Turkey and Iraq make use of the Tigris's water, it should have a greater say in how the Euphrates' water should be shared and utilized. And Turkey has often claimed the waters originating in and flowing through its territory as its exclusive property.

Negotiations between Syria and Iraq for sharing the water of the Euphrates have been going on since 1962, when Syria first announced its intention to construct the Tabqa Dam. As the uppermost riparian on the river, Turkey joined these negotiations from time to time, primarily because it too was planning to build dams within its territory upstream. According to Baghdad, Syria agreed in 1962 to exchange hydrological and technical information concerning the dams that would be built on the Euphrates in the future and to recognize the "established rights" of the two countries. However, no record has so far been made available of a formal agreement between the two riparians. In 1965 bilateral talks between Syria and Iraq began in anticipation of the completion of the Tabqa Dam in the early 1970s. In 1972, Saddam Hussein, then Iraqi vice president of the Revolutionary Command Council, and President Assad of Syria held comprehensive talks on economic cooperation between the two countries and on an Iraqi proposal for political union among Iraq, Syria, and Egypt to counter plans by King Hussein of Jordan for the creation of a United Hashemite Kingdom.[33] In the end, nothing concrete came out of these high-level talks, except that the failure of the talks marked a turning point in the stands taken by the two countries in their disputes over water. Essentially, both began to assert and seek individual gains as opposed to the seemingly accommodative approach during the 1962–72 period. In 1973 Iraq concluded an agreement with Turkey for the construction of an oil pipeline from some Iraqi oil fields, across Turkey to the Mediterranean. This infuriated Syria because it felt its own interests were compromised by the pipeline.

In 1974 Syria completed the construction of the Ath-Thawrah Dam, at the same time that Turkey built its Keban Dam. The following year, Syria impounded a large portion of the spring flood in order to fill the reservoir behind the dam, resulting in the Euphrates' flow entering Iraq being reduced from about 920 cubic meters per second to just 197 cubic meters per second. This allegedly created a severe water shortage for millions of Iraqi farmers downstream. In a clear demonstration of the water scarcity–acute conflict relationship in arid and semiarid areas, Iraq nearly went to war with its upstream neighbor. Airline links between the two countries were broken, and both dispatched armed soldiers to their borders. In the end, mediation by Saudi Arabia and the Soviet Union led to Syria releasing additional water from the Tabqa Dam; however, a Saudi proposal for the proportionate division of the Euphrates' water was not followed up. Here is one clear instance of a conflict over water almost leading to armed hostilities between two riparian states in an international river basin. This episode also shows that although, in some circumstances, influential third parties may be able to help resolve an immediate international crisis over water, they cannot guarantee longer-term survivability of any agreement they may have brokered.

In the spring of 1974, stung by Iraqi criticism of its handling of the aftermath of the war with Israel, Syria further slowed down the flow of water of the Euphrates toward Iraq. According to Baghdad, this caused havoc in the Iraqi part of the basin. Iraq launched protests with Syrian authorities while continuing its criticism of the Syrian leadership. Syria slowed down the flow again in March 1975 and did not restore it until the sowing season for summer crops in Iraq was over.[34]

Relations between Iraq and Syria became even more problematic in 1975, when Iraq signed the Algiers Agreement with Iran. This development unsettled Syria since it felt that a resolution of the outstanding problems between Iraq and Iran, especially the so-called Kurdish problem they shared in common, would allow Iraq to be more assertive toward Syria in all matters of dispute between them, including the waters of the shared rivers. During the drought-prone 1980s, on several occasions Iraq accused Syria of withholding the Euphrates' water. Nonetheless, in 1983 Syria joined the Joint Technical Committee formed by Turkey and Iraq in 1982. This committee has met several times since, but other than some exchange of technical information, it has failed to resolve conflicts about the quality and the quantity of water to which each riparian state claims it is entitled.

In 1987 Turkey and Syria signed the Protocol of Economic Cooperation, including a Turkish guarantee for minimum flow in the Euphrates in return for Syria's cooperation on border security.[35] However, the same year Syrian officials began to become acutely aware of the serious implications a Turkish project known as GAP (discussed below) may hold for their country. Consequently, during a 1987 visit by the Turkish prime minister Ozal to Damascus, a protocol was signed guaranteeing Syria a minimum flow of 500 cubic meters per second (amounting to about 16 billion cubic meters per year) in the Euphrates, across the border at Karkamis. This amount was well within the range demanded by Syria in earlier negotiations. However, although Syria may have been satisfied with this amount of water coming down the river, the amount was also exactly equal to the flow demanded by Iraq. Thus, even if the protocol between Turkey and Syria could hold, under this bilateral agreement any consumptive use of the Euphrates' water by Syria would not be to Iraq's liking.

In 1986 a tripartite meeting of senior ministers from the three countries was held to discuss the problem of collectively sharing the Euphrates' water; however, other than settling some bureaucratic matters very little was achieved at the meeting. Yet another meeting in 1989, this time between Turkish and Syrian ministers, is reported to have yielded an agreement to jointly construct a dam on the Euphrates on the Syrian side of the border. However, in late 1989 Turkey announced plans to begin filling the reservoir behind the then nearly completed Atatürk Dam, by closing the gates on the dam for a period of thirty days. Although Turkey claimed to have released additional water downstream before the date of closing the gates (January 15, 1990), both Syria and Iraq strongly objected to the Euphrates' flow being reduced to a trickle during the filling of the Turkish dam. A tripartite meeting held to resolve once again the issue of how much water Syria and Iraq were entitled to stalled when Iraq insisted on claiming a flow of at least 500 cubic meters per second. In April 1990 Syria and Iraq signed an accord on sharing the Euphrates' flow. Under the terms of this bilateral accord, Syria would receive 42 percent and Iraq 58 percent of the annual flow, irrespective of its variation from year to year. However, the occupation of Kuwait by Iraq shortly after the tripartite meetings and the Iraq-Syria agreement led to the suspension of all negotiations and agreements for sharing the Euphrates' bounty.

The old dispute between Syria and Turkey over the waters of the Euphrates surfaced again in July 1992 when the Turkish prime minister, Suleyman Demirel, rejected Syrian (and Iraqi) complaints that Ankara's massive irrigation and hydroelectric projects on the two rivers, especially the GAP projects, threatened to deny them their fair share of water. According to the *Mideast Mirror,* Demirel is quoted as having said, "We do not say we share their oil resources. They cannot say they share our water resources. This is a matter of sovereignty. We have a right to do anything we like."[36] Although a spokesperson for the Turkish government later denied that Ankara had any intention of using water as a lever or threat against its neighbors, and further asserted that Turkey is always ready to cooperate with them, the leaders, media, and public opinion in both downstream countries were outraged by Demirel's remarks, seeing in them a sinister design to use water as a weapon. Although some saw in Demirel's remarks a tactic to pressure Syria into crushing the Kurdish PKK movement, a more sober assessment of Demirel's remarks suggested that perhaps Turkey was indicating a desire to trade water for oil with its downstream neighbors. Whatever their real intent, these and some earlier remarks by Turkish officials continue to reinforce the feeling in Syria and Iraq that a "water tap" in the hands of the uppermost riparian state on both the rivers may not be a good thing to agree to.

As pointed out in the previous chapter, Syria's stand on water rights in the Euphrates basin is complicated by the fact that while it is a middle (lower) riparian on the Euphrates, Syria is the upper riparian on the Jordan. In 1964, guided by animosity toward Israel, Syria began to press its claim of absolute territorial sovereignty in its use of the Jordan's water; a claim that continues to pose a dangerous precedent for Syria because, if accepted, it would allow Turkey to claim the same right and privileges in the Euphrates-Tigris basin. Thus Syria, like several countries in other international basins, such as Brazil and India, that share multiple international river basins from different riparian positions, finds itself in a rather complicated and uncomfortable position when claiming rights in the respective basins. Had Syria been as powerful vis-à-vis its neighbors as India is in South Asia (chapter 5) or had the geography of the basin been similar to the Ganges-Brahmaputra-Barak basin, this Syrian predicament may not have mattered. But Syria has neither of these advantages. Consequently, as the uppermost riparian on the two rivers and on some of the tributaries, Turkey, despite its 1946 agreement with Iraq, continues to treat the waters of the two rivers mostly as its exclusive property, as reflected in the lack of consideration for the lower riparians' interests and consent in the formulation of the GAP project. Not surprisingly, even the release of additional water in the Euphrates by Turkey before the filling of the Atatürk Dam was interpreted by Iraq and Syria as one more example of Turkey's affirmation of absolute sovereignty on the headwaters of the rivers originating within its territory.

Turkey's refusal to recognize either of the two rivers as an international river adds to the contentious hydropolitics of this basin. Further, in the negotiations with Syria, Turkey links the issue of sharing the Euphrates' bounty to a deal on the waters of the Orontes (Asi) River, which the two countries share with Lebanon.[37] Syria refuses this issue linkage as well as all Turkish claims over the Orontes because Syria has irredentist claims over the province of Hatay, formerly known as Alexandretta, through which the Orontes flows. This province, earlier a part of the French Mandate of Syria, was ceded to Turkey in 1933.

This larger context provides some understanding of the forces impinging on interstate conflict and cooperation over the transboundary water resources in the Euphrates-Tigris basin. However, for a more grounded understanding of hydropolitics it is necessary to look at some large water projects that have been launched and proposed in the basin.

Water Projects

Iraq was the first riparian state to construct a major water project in the Euphrates basin in this century. Completed in 1913, the Hindiyah Barrage was primarily intended to resurrect a system of canals that had been inoperable since the Middle Ages.[38] Another barrage was installed within Iraqi territory in the 1950s for controlling floods, and for diverting water to some storage facilities and distant demand centers. Three dams—the Dokan, the Derbendi Khan, and the Hamrin—were finished in 1958, 1962, and 1981, respectively. Another three dams—at Mosul, Dahuk, and Bikhma—were expected to be completed in the 1990s. The most significant project launched in the last two decades in Iraq is a reservoir north of Hindiyah. Started with Soviet assistance, this project was expected to be completed in 1982. However, many of Iraq's ongoing water projects in the basin have been delayed indefinitely owing to the chaos created by the Iran-Iraq War and the Gulf War. Nonetheless, Iraq has managed to construct the 500-kilometer (300-mile) Main Outfall Drain to drain about 2 million hectares of irrigation water into the Shatt al-Arab. What impact this drainage has or will have on the ecosystem of the Shatt is not known.

The latest and most controversial Iraqi project in the basin is a scheme to link the Euphrates and Tigris upstream from their confluence near Basra, with the professed aims to alleviate expected water shortages in the Euphrates, to prevent flooding along its most intensely irrigated lands, to drain salt from the region between the two rivers, to extend irrigation to large tracts of new agricultural land, and to provide water to new settlements. However, critics of the project have pointed out that the real intention behind the project is to dry out the marshes where the so-called Marsh Arabs have lived for centuries.[39] Unlike the Iraqi rulers in Baghdad, who are followers of the Sunni faith of Islam, these people follow the Shia faith, similar to the majority of the population in bordering Iran. They have long resisted and actively fought against all Baghdad regimes. If the marshes dry out, the Marsh Arabs' existence as a distinct and cohesive social group is likely to come to an end.

In Syria, three dams have already been built on the Euphrates River: the Tabqa Dam (14.2-cubic-kilometer storage capacity, 860-megawatt power generation capability) completed in 1975, the al-Ba'th regulatory dam, and the Tishreen hydroelectric project (1.9-cubic-kilometer storage capacity, 630-megawatt power generation capacity) completed in 1991. The largest lake in the country, Lake Assad, was formed by the construction of Tabqa Dam, which is also the second-largest dam in the northeast Africa–Middle East region after the Aswân High Dam, and like the Aswân it too was constructed with Soviet assistance. Its reservoir has substantial storage capacity when filled to the height of 40 meters. However, with a surface area as large as 625 square kilometers (244 square miles), there are substantial losses from evaporation. An agricultural area as large as 64,500 hectares (159,000 acres) was lost to the floodwaters of Lake Assad, another 31,000 hectares (77,000 acres) were disrupted by land reclamation, and an additional 7,500 hectares (18,500 acres) of dry-farming land was flooded.[40] The reservoir is the only source of water for the city of Aleppo, which faces fast rising demands for water from households and industries. As pointed out earlier, the sewage system in the city is totally inadequate.

Syria constructed the Ath-Thawrah Dam on the Euphrates in 1974—the same year that Turkey built its own Keban Dam on the river upstream. However, in 1986 original plans for irrigating 640,000 hectares (1,581,000 acres) of agricultural land were drastically revised downward. Only 240,000 to 260,000 hectares (593,000 to 642,000 acres) can now be irrigated, if all the ongoing Syrian projects come on line. Overall, Syrian activities on the Euphrates were expected to reduce the flow by 2,100 million cubic meters by 1990. By the year 2000, Syrian withdrawals and evaporation losses from its reservoirs are expected to amount to as much as 12,100 million cubic meters.[41]

In Turkey one hundred multipurpose dams were operational by 1985. Their functions included providing water for irrigation, flood control, generation of hydroelectricity, and domestic and industrial needs. An additional sixty-six new water projects were under construction. Eventually, Turkey hopes to construct five hundred more dams, 85 percent of which will be hydroelectric dams.[42] The projects planned by Turkish developers are expected not only to make Turkey self-sufficient in food production but also to provide an agricultural surplus that Turkey can trade with the rest of the Middle East. These projects are also expected to make the country less and less dependent on imports of energy.

The centerpiece of Turkey's waterworks is the Atatürk Dam, designed to produce 8.9 billion kilowatt-hours of electricity per year; however, electricity production will be reduced to 8.1 billion kilowatt-hours per year when the proposed irrigation projects become fully operational.[43] A significant portion of the power generated will also be used up locally for pumping irrigation water to the agricultural fields. At its full capacity, the Atatürk Dam may lose as much as 1,470 million cubic meters of water per year from evaporation over its large surface. Estimates for evaporation, water loss, and evapotranspiration by the year 2000 show an astonishing loss of about 13,437 million cubic meters per year along the lower Euphrates within Turkey. Only about one-half of this water is expected to return to the reservoir and as flow to downstream areas in Syria.[44] About seventy thousand people from 117 villages were displaced by flooding of the Atatürk Dam. These people had to be monetarily compensated by the state; however, rather than buy agricultural lands with the compensation they received as part of the resettlement package, most used the money to buy houses in Sanliurfa.[45]

It is important to underscore the interdependencies among the national water projects in the basin. Syria has claimed that its Tabqa Dam hydropower plants have operated at only 10 percent of the full capacity because of the filling of the Atatürk Dam upstream. Yet another problem Syria faces is the depletion of flows in some of the tributaries flowing into the country from Turkey, owing to the pumping of water by Turkish farmers upstream from aquifers located within Syrian territory that supply some of the largest springs in the world. Although a substantial portion of these withdrawals does finally reach Syria, the water is too polluted with fertilizers and other toxins to make it usable downstream. The water-related problems faced by Syria are likely to get much worse if a highly ambitious project launched by Turkey, popularly known as GAP, ever gets fully implemented. GAP is likely to seriously reduce the downstream flow of both rivers. And all together, the Turkish and Syrian projects on the Euphrates, by decreasing both the quantity and the quality of the water, could jeopardize as much as 1 million acres of irrigated land in Iraq.

The GAP Project

The initial thinking about a project of the vast scope and long duration of the Southeast Anatolia Development Project (Guneydogu Anadolu

Projesi), known as GAP, began around 1963 as a part of the regular five-year national development planning in Turkey; however, actual planning for the project did not begin until 1970 and a formal proposal was issued only in 1980. The project was to be implemented in a region covering about 9.5 percent of the area and population of Turkey. More than 5 million people currently live in the eight GAP provinces. The regional economy is dominated by agriculture, and the economically irrigable areas account for about one-fifth of the total irrigable land in the country.

As envisioned in the master plan, the GAP project includes thirteen groups of major projects—seven in the lower Euphrates sub-basin and six in the Tigris sub-basin. From the initial goal to develop the hydroelectric and irrigation potential of the two sub-basins within Turkey, the project has come to be seen as a comprehensive regional development program, including schemes for the development of agriculture, industry, social infrastructure, transportation, education, and health.[46] When completed, twenty-two dams, nineteen hydropower plants, and many irrigation projects are expected to make the area one of the leading economic regions in Turkey. Specifically, the projects are expected to help irrigate 1.7 million hectares (6,600 square miles) of agricultural land, an area larger than the total area previously opened by the state to irrigation in the entire country; to produce 27 billion kilowatt-hours of electricity (equal to the total national production from all sources in 1983); to create 3.3 million new jobs; and to provide a boost to urbanization while slowing down rural-urban migration in the region.[47] GAP is expected to cost $30.26 billion (1981 prices), and to contribute $933 million (1981 prices) to the Turkish economy every year, in the process raising the national income by 12 percent. The symbolic importance of this highly ambitious project is underscored by the observation that two prominent Turkish politicians, Suleyman Demirel and Turgut Ozal, who have both served as prime minister, had worked on the development of the two rivers before taking up politics. Both have subsequently claimed credit for the Keban Dam and for the inception of GAP.[48]

As it is, this highly ambitious project, especially for a developing country, has run into serious difficulties. Lack of domestic and international funding, heavy cost overruns, and some technical impediments have considerably slowed down progress on the projects already started, and on launching new ones. Some projects have had to be considerably scaled down, especially schemes for extending irrigation to large tracts of cultivable lands; about others there are now serious doubts. Success of the overall project is also dependent on serious land reforms in the project region and on finding domestic and international markets for the additional agricultural production the irrigated lands may produce. Thus, though initially expected to be completed by 1994, the full project is now expected to take until the year 2030 or even 2040 to become operational.[49] The total cost for implementing the project is also likely to be much higher than estimated initially. It is also noteworthy that, given a growing reluctance on the part of international donors and organizations to get involved in large-scale developmental activities in an international basin where contending claims to the shared waters have not been resolved, Turkey will be forced to foot the bill for this highly ambitious project from its own national resources. Already, the project accounts for about 6.9 percent of the national budget; the $1.5 million spent on the project every day has contributed substantially to the very high rate of inflation the national economy has recently faced. Nonetheless, although GAP, or a major portion of it, may yet be completed some day, there does not seem to be much hope for yet another ambitious project Turkey had once proposed.

The Peace Pipelines

In early 1987, recognizing the water woes of its neighbors in the Middle East as well as the centrality of water sharing for the prospects for peace in the region, the Turkish prime minister Ozal put forward a proposal, popularly known as the Peace Pipelines, to use Turkey's surplus freshwater resources to supply water to several Arab nations as well as Israel. As then visualized, one pipeline would carry surplus water from two Turkish rivers, the Seyhan and the Ceyhan, through Syria and Jordan to such faraway places as Mecca and Medina in Saudi Arabia. Yet another pipeline would take water from the Tigris through Iraq and Kuwait to the Persian Gulf countries, including the United Arab Emirates.

According to the project design, the first pipeline would carry 3.5 million cubic meters per day (1.28 billion cubic meters per year) and the second pipeline would supply up to 2.5 million cubic meters of water per day (0.9 billion cubic meters per year). Estimates for the total cost of this highly ambitious and controversial enterprise have ranged between $17 billion and $20 billion; the international contractor for the project has claimed that the pipelines can deliver water to the distant lands at one-third the cost of desalinated water of comparable quality.[50] These claims notwithstanding, the political problems that would need to be resolved on the way to implementing the project are so daunting that the project may never get to the stage of serious consideration. On the other hand, if peace is made between Israel and its neighbors in the Jordan basin, the idea of regionwide peace pipelines, transporting water from Turkey (and perhaps Lebanon) to the parched lands of the Middle East, may find renewed support. The key to materializing this visionary dream, of course, will be the onset of cooperative interstate relations in the Euphrates-Tigris basin, especially Syria's cooperation with its neighbors.

As things stand, a battered Iraq and a troubled Syria may not have much choice in the near future but to let Turkey have its way in the basin's hydropolitics. However, for all the reasons discussed, Turkey too will continue to play a heavy price for noncooperation. The hope is that growing water scarcities for multiple needs in all the riparian states, and deteriorating water quality downstream will impel the Euphrates-Tigris basin riparians to develop and share, in an equitable manner, the bounty their common water resources can produce.

SUMMARY AND CONCLUSION

Conflicts over transboundary water resources have brought the Euphrates-Tigris basin to the brink of war on several occasions. Water disputes have played, and will continue to play, a major role in conditioning interstate relations in the basin. If the projections for future water scarcity in Iraq and Syria, resulting from population growth and ad hoc implementation of large water projects on the headwaters of the major rivers in Turkey, can be believed, the possibility of a war over the transboundary water resources in the basin cannot be ruled out. Absolute water scarcities engendered by a fast-rising demand for freshwater for multiple uses, the lack of economically viable alternatives for the shared water resources of the basin, deteriorating water quality, and ad hocism in exploiting the shared water resources without much consideration for the needs or sensitivities of others are bound to continue poisoning relations among the mostly antagonistic regimes in the region. The situation is likely to be made worse by the unsettled status as well as the continuing economic and political deprivation of the minorities in the basin, especially the Kurdish people.

Similar to the Jordan basin, with which this basin's hydropolitics is intricately linked through Syria, water conflicts have been, are, and will continue to be inextricably intertwined with the issues of identity, national sovereignty, and security; interstate rivalry and ideological competition;

and demands for autonomy and independence, economic well-being, and political power in the Euphrates-Tigris basin. Water issues already impinge very directly on the quest for environmental, economic, and food security in all the riparian states. Even if the riparian states do not go to war over water, contested claims over the transboundary water resources will continue to be used by the ruling regimes in the basin to justify whatever antagonistic stands and strategies they may otherwise want to adopt in their dealings with each other.

But despite all the predictions of impending "water wars" in the Middle East, and in the Euphrates-Tigris basin in particular, what is encouraging is that, despite their historical rivalries and animosities, and despite the contested claims over the waters of the two rivers, multilateral and bilateral dialogues among Iraq, Syria, and Turkey have taken place from time to time. And while no international regime currently exists for cooperatively developing and sharing the transboundary water resources of the basin, a tacit understanding seems to exist among the riparian states that the waters carried down by the shared rivers have to be divided among them in some acceptable fashion. However, the irony is that a water war may not take place in the basin not because the riparian states agree to cooperate with one another, but because the uppermost riparian state, Turkey, and the middle riparian, Syria, may not be able to implement all the large-scale water projects they would like to construct in the basin. Although the physical and economic geography of the basin and the support Turkey has from its Western allies have certainly endowed Turkey with seemingly unlimited advantages in conducting hydropolitics in the basin, the uppermost riparian is prevented from playing a hegemonic role in the basin by the domestic political and economic vulnerabilities it faces, and by the ability of the lower riparian states to stir up trouble in its sensitive southeastern provinces.

This case study supports the finding from earlier case studies that, in general, the uppermost riparian in an international basin emphasizes the principle of absolute sovereignty over the water resources originating in and flowing through its territory. The lowermost riparian, on the other hand, usually claims water rights under the theory of absolute territorial integrity, interpreted to mean that the resources available to each riparian state must be preserved at their status quo levels according to the doctrine of prior appropriation. The middle riparian's dual upstream and downstream status makes its stand in hydropolitics ambiguous, often emphasizing the doctrine of equitable distribution and rightful share. This case study also supports the finding that, driven by their historical experiences and facing uncertainty in their future relations with their neighbors, the lower riparian states in an international basin do not like to become dependent on the goodwill of their upstream neighbor(s). When they can, they prefer to explore and implement purely national solutions for their water scarcities or seek binding water-sharing agreements. However, in the end, geography dictates the limits to which these options are available and can be explored by the lower riparian states.

This case study also demonstrates that whereas third parties may be able to defuse an immediate water crisis in an international basin, as they did in the 1974–75 confrontation between Iraq and Syria, they cannot guarantee the long-term survival of any understanding or agreement reached with their assistance. In the end, it is the riparian states themselves who must reach a place from which they can begin to move away from a path of confrontation toward the goal of cooperation.

5

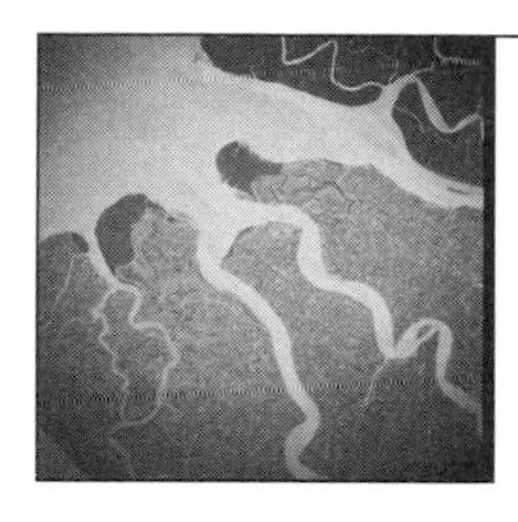

The Ganges-Brahmaputra-Barak Basin

Located on two sides of the tallest mountain range on earth, the Ganges-Brahmaputra-Barak basin, with an area less than one-fifth the size of the United States but with twice its population, is one of the richest regions of the world in terms of the multiple-use potential of its abundant water resources. It is also one of the least developed regions of the world, where millions continue to languish in abject poverty and suffer from severe environmental degradation. Commenting on this tragic state of affairs, a former foreign secretary of India once remarked, "Nowhere is the problem of cooperation between riparian neighbors as critical as in the Ganges-Brahmaputra basin in South Asia. Nowhere are the benefits from cooperation as spectacular for the futures of the countries involved, and nowhere is the penalty for non-cooperation as devastating."[1]

Why has this dismal state of affairs persisted in this large basin for so long? Why have the riparian states sharing the basin continued to fritter away the vast economic potential of the precious water resources that nature has so generously endowed them with, collectively? What specific factors and circumstances, alone and in combination, have made it so difficult for some of the poorest nations on earth to unleash and share cooperatively the vast developmental potential of their common water resources? Are there reasons to hope that this dismal situation may change radically some time in the foreseeable future? These are some of the primary questions this case study attempts to address from a geography-centered perspective.[2]

GEOGRAPHY

Physical Geography

The Ganges-Brahmaputra-Barak basin, named after its three major rivers,[3] and shared by four sovereign states—Bangladesh, Bhutan, India, and Nepal—and Chinese-occupied Tibet, covers an area of roughly 1.6 million square kilometers (624,000 square miles). About 80 percent of the basin is in India, 7 percent is in Bangladesh, and the remainder is shared by Bhutan, Nepal, and Tibet.[4] The Ganges and the Brahmaputra originate in India and Tibet on the southern and northern slopes of the Himalaya Mountains, respectively, and the Barak has its source in eastern India. The three rivers eventually meet in Bangladesh to flow to the Bay of Bengal as the Meghna River.

The Himalayas, with the highest summit in the world, Mount Everest, is also one of the youngest mountain ranges on earth, and is still rising owing to tectonic activity.[5] It constitutes the largest reservoir of snow and ice in the world outside the polar regions. Nearly fifteen thousand Himalayan glaciers, as well as the large snow cover, estimated to be 1,400 cubic kilometers (341 cubic miles) in volume,[6] constitute a vast water storage system, accumulating over the winter and draining into many rivers and tributaries through the summer. For all practical purposes, this virtually insurmountable mountain range also physically separates Bhutan, India, and Nepal from Tibet.[7] These geographic features of the basin, combined with the fact that two of the five riparian states sharing the basin, Bhutan and Nepal, and Tibet are landlocked, and that for the most part Bangladesh is surrounded by Indian territory, have significant implications for hydropolitics in the basin, as we shall see.

The Ganges is formed mainly by two Himalayan head streams; the smaller of the two is the Bhagirathi, the other is the Alakhnanda, which rises near the Indo-Tibetan border at an altitude of about 7 kilometers (4.3 miles). However, many tributaries coming down from Nepal and Tibet account for close to 45 percent of the Ganges' flow.[8] Counting the delta but not the basin it shares with the Brahmaputra, the Ganges has a length of over 2,600 kilometers (1,620 miles) and it drains an area of nearly 1.04 million

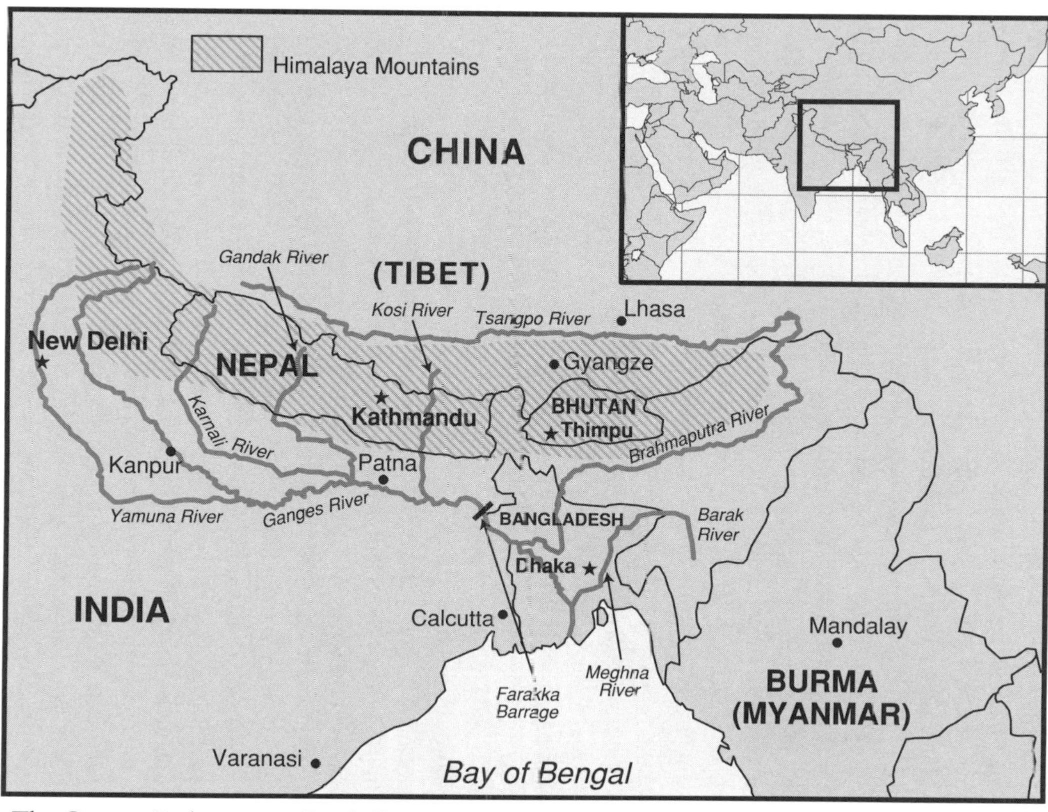

The Ganges-Brahmaputra-Barak Basin

square kilometers (405,600 square miles) in northern India, Bangladesh, Nepal, and southern Tibet. The great drop in the elevation of the Ganges and of its northern tributaries from the Himalayas to the sea has created a vast potential for generating hydroelectricity within India and Nepal, and on the India-Nepal border.

The Brahmaputra flows for about 2,900 kilometers (1,800 miles) successively through Tibet, India, and Bangladesh, and it drains an area of about 935,000 square kilometers (364,650 square miles). It rises in the Kailash Range of the Himalayas, flows eastward across Tibet for about 1,127 kilometers (704 miles), crosses through deep Himalayan gorges, enters India in the northeast, takes on two tributaries, and then flows through the Assam Valley. After crossing the Assam it flows south through Bangladesh and then enters the complex and densely populated Ganges-Brahmaputra Delta. From its source in Tibet to the northeastern Tibet-India border, the Brahmaputra's elevation drops from 3.6 kilometers (2.2 miles) to 150 meters (0.1 mile) above sea level, creating the potential for generating a tremendous amount of hydroelectricity along the way. The same is true of the river's many tributaries originating in Bhutan and Tibet.

Compared with the mighty Ganges and Brahmaputra, the Barak is a small river; however, it too is of great importance for India and Bangladesh because of its irrigation, navigation, and hydroelectric potential. The river originates in the Mizoram state of India and follows a northwestern course for some distance before entering Bangladesh to join with the Old Brahmaputra River. It then flows through the delta into the Bay of Bengal as the Meghna River.

In addition to the three main rivers, more than fifty smaller rivers and tributaries enter Bangladesh from India.[9] As a result, about 94 percent of Bangladesh's aboveground freshwater supply originates outside its territory. As the lowermost riparian state on all the shared rivers and tributaries in the basin, Bangladesh is the most susceptible to water withdrawals and ecological degradation upstream. Further, a third of Bangladesh is below the high-tide level, making it highly vulnerable to saline water intrusion inland. For the same reason, any sea level rise from global warming would have devastating consequences for Bangladesh's land and water resources.[10]

Over a vast period of geological time, the Ganges and the Brahmaputra have been eroding the Himalayas to build a vast plain, which is historically one of the largest continuously farmed areas in the world.[11] All together, the three rivers carry a phenomenal load of 2.9 billion metric tons of sediment into the Bay of Bengal every year,[12] with a flood discharge second in the world only to the Amazon River. Consequently, the basin has the distinction of the world's largest delta formation, the Sundarbans, most of which is in Bangladesh. With its extensive network of interconnected waterways and a wide variety of fauna, this delta hosts the greatest mangrove forest in the world. Silts brought down by the basin's rivers are also responsible for new land formation in the Bay of Bengal, whose ownership is now contested by Bangladesh and India.[13]

The climate of the Ganges-Brahmaputra-Barak basin is temperate subtropical monsoon. The highest annual rainfall in the world, 1,115 centimeters (434 inches) on average, is recorded at Cherrapunji in Assam. Bangladesh itself has a semitropical monsoon climate, with one of the world's highest annual rainfalls, averaging as much as 215 centimeters (84 inches) in the northeast. There is, however, great seasonal variability in the total amount of rainfall and in its areal distribution in the basin: three-quarters of the yearly precipitation occurs within just three monsoon months, June to August, and the average annual precipitation can vary from 1,600 millimeters (64 inches) in the east to 990 millimeters (40 inches) in the west. Consequently, some areas in the basin suffer from severe drought in the dry months, while floods inundate large areas during the monsoon season.[14] Given the dependence of most agriculture in the basin on adequate and timely rainfall, the success or failure of the monsoon has great economic and political impacts in all the basin countries.

In addition to the large annual precipitation, groundwater is extensively available in the Indo-Gangetic plain, stretching all the way from Bangladesh to Pakistan, though in parts of northwestern India some of the water is heavily saline. Elsewhere in peninsular India, groundwater availability is more sporadic and very restricted in volume. In some areas in the basin, the rate of groundwater use is now much faster than the rate of natural replacement. Nonetheless, according to some World Bank studies, there may be a series of deep aquifers underneath Nepalese territory and the Gangetic plain in India and, separately, in the Bengal basin—both in India and Bangladesh—at depths of 1 to 3 kilometers (0.6 to 1.8 miles). These aquifers may constitute the largest single groundwater resource in the world.[15]

Because of abundant rainfall and groundwater availability in the basin, historically there was virtually no storage of the Ganges' waters before India's independence in 1947; even today there is only minimal storage on the Himalayan stretches of the river. Substantial storage capacity is now planned for some ongoing projects in Nepal and India, which could conceivably capture some of the annual rainfall for regulated releases during the dry season.

However, whether this kind of storage is the best means of dealing with the lean-season shortages of water for irrigation remains a controversial issue.[16]

The lack of storage upstream and the deforestation in the Himalayan foothills in India and Nepal have often been blamed for aggravating flooding in both countries and in Bangladesh; however, this too remains a controversial issue.[17] Nonetheless, satellite imagery shows only 15 percent of South Asia to be forested, covering about 9 percent of Bangladesh, 60 percent of Bhutan, 15 percent of India, and 34 percent of Nepal.[18] These forests are being depleted at an alarming rate by indiscriminate cattle grazing, commercial logging, infrastructure construction, and fuelwood extraction. Having recognized the danger of losing this locally and globally valuable resource, all countries are now trying to severely curtail deforestation and to promote reforestation. However, the abject poverty of hundreds of millions of their citizens, especially those living in the hills and mountain ranges, and widespread corruption and mismanagement are frustrating many local and international attempts at stopping severe deforestation and loss of biodiversity in the basin.

Rapid population growth and severe environmental damage, combined with some natural processes such as mass wasting and flooding, are putting severe constraints on the availability of land and freshwater in large parts of the basin. Ironically, even some badly needed infrastructure projects are compounding the problem of flood control in the basin. For example, according to a 1988 World Bank report, Bangladesh had 143,820 kilometers (90,000 miles) of surfaced and unsurfaced roads, with one of the highest road densities per unit area in the world. Many of these roads cut across and block the drainage channels that need to be kept open for flood flow in low-lying areas. The same is true of roads, dams, and other infrastructure projects already constructed and under construction in Bhutan, India, and Nepal.

Overall, although the dynamic physical geography of the basin continues to create problems of water scarcity and flooding at different times and at different places in the basin, it has also endowed the shared waters with a vast, multiple-use developmental potential, as we shall see. However, this potential is mostly being frittered away at a great opportunity cost, despite the fact that the basin's economic geography has created ample scope for a convergence of the economic interests of all its riparian states.

Economic Geography

The Ganges-Brahmaputra-Barak basin is one of the richest basins in the world in terms of the economic potential of its water resources for irrigation, power generation, industrial development, fisheries, and navigation. In addition, some areas in the basin—Bangladesh, India, and Tibet—are well endowed with minerals, oil, and gas. Nonetheless, all the basin countries currently rank among the lowest per capita income economies in the world. On all other socioeconomic indicators, these countries also rank among the least developed in the world.[19] Perhaps most relevant for the present study is that although all the countries are richly endowed with internal renewable water resources, only a very small percentage of these supplies is currently withdrawn.

Close to 500 million people—nearly one-tenth of the world's population and a very large proportion of the world's poor—live in the basin. By the year 2000, population in the basin is estimated to reach 625 million, with the prospect of doubling again before stabilizing by the middle of the next century. In particular, by the year 2050 Bangladesh may have a population larger than that of the United States, and India's population may stabilize around 1.6 billion, making it perhaps the most populous country in the world ahead of China.[20] Although efforts at population control are continuing in all the countries, the effectiveness of the various measures adopted is being greatly undermined by a host of religious, cultural, economic, and political factors. A large portion of the future population growth in all the countries is expected to concentrate in the Ganges-Brahmaputra-Barak basin and, if things proceed as they currently are, in the future much of this population is expected to continue living in abject poverty.[21] The food, water, and energy needs of these growing populations, especially the poor who often have no choice but to overexploit and degrade their natural resources and environment, are bound to severely strain the already precarious food, economic, and environmental security of all the riparian states.

Some of the largest cities in South Asia are located in the basin. These include the five national capitals—Dhaka (Bangladesh), Kathmandu (Nepal), Lhasa (Tibet), New Delhi (India), and Thimpu (Bhutan)—as well as many other large cities in India, including Calcutta, which alone is expected to have a population of 15.7 million by the year 2000. The 1994 populations of Delhi/New Delhi and Dhaka of 8.8 million and 7.5 million, respectively, are expected to rise to 13.2 million and 12.2 million by the year 2000.[22] All these cities currently suffer from severe shortages of drinking water, domestic fuel, and electricity. Most lack even the most rudimentary sewage facilities for millions of their inhabitants. These shortages are bound to accelerate as the urban populations keep rising naturally and as more and more people from the rural areas continue migrating to the cities. The rising urban populations will create additional problems of sanitation and waste disposal, with severe environmental impacts all across the basin. Already, pollution of the Ganges' water, still regarded as sacred and self-cleansing by the Hindus, has reached alarming proportions; it is now the most polluted river in the world during the summer season.[23] Given the urban biases in the development programs of all the riparian states, further urbanization would not only lead to encroachment into the valuable and increasingly scarce farmlands, but would also create severe problems of water allocation between rural and urban areas.

Farming, cattle raising, and agribusiness are still the main economic activities in the basin, employing as much as 80 percent of the total population in some countries. Agriculture also accounts for nearly one-half of all freshwater usage in the basin. This makes the amount and timing of water supply for agriculture the most significant single constraint on economic development. Nonetheless, irrigation efficiencies remain as low as 40 percent in most agricultural areas in the basin.

Because of a massive spread of perennial irrigation since gaining independence in 1947, and because of the adoption of "green revolution" technologies, including heavy use of electric power, chemicals, and fertilizers, India has gradually become self-sufficient in basic food production, and it has managed to ward off large-scale famine.[24] However, agriculture in large parts of the country still depends heavily on timely monsoonal rains, on traditional technologies of production, and on large inputs of cheap labor. In Bangladesh irrigated farmland still amounts to only a fraction of the country's arable land; however, despite many constraints it faces, the country has managed to achieve remarkable increases in rice production over the past twenty years. In the future, Bangladesh is expected to produce growing surpluses of rice for export.[25] Nonetheless, the country's growing population continues to impose an immense burden on the availability of land and its productive capacity, periodically confronting the government with a small but chronic food deficit that must be overcome through food aid and commercial imports. Nepal has so far managed to irrigate barely 5 percent of its arable land, and both Nepal and Bhutan currently import a substantial portion of their food requirements. Tibet is now reported to be importing close to one-third of its own food requirements from other parts of China. Clearly, all these countries would benefit substantially if the vast irrigation potential of the basin's waters could be developed in a cooperative and sustainable manner.

In addition to the benefits from an extension of irrigated agriculture, large-scale development of freshwater fisheries in the basin can generate an important dietary supplement as well as substantial new employment and income in all the lower riparian states. The basin has a very rich natural resource base for such an enterprise, and fish already provide a large portion of the protein consumption in the basin, as high as 80 percent in the Assamese and Bangali diets. The potential for expansion of fisheries in the Indian and Bangladeshi portions of the basin is especially large.[26] Bhutan and Nepal can also benefit greatly from developing fisheries in the lower reaches of some Himalayan rivers and in large reservoirs. However, construction of large dams and reservoirs upstream to control floods, to produce hydroelectric power, or to develop fisheries may have serious consequences for fish catch in Bangladesh where floodwaters over farmers' fields provide a major source of freshwater fish.

The shared waters also have the potential to contribute substantially to the economic development in the basin by providing an abundant, inexpensive, and renewable source of energy through hydroelectric generation. The basin is endowed with tremendous hydroelectric potential of the order of 200,000 to 250,000 megawatts, of which nearly one-half could be easily harnessed.[27] However, only a very minuscule portion of this vast potential is being tapped, despite the fact that Bangladesh, Bhutan, Nepal, and Tibet do not have any significant deposits of easily exploitable coal for producing electricity in thermal power stations, nor do they have nuclear power stations. Most of their demand for energy is presently met by noncommercial sources, such as fuelwood, animal dung, agro-waste, and animal and human draft power for agriculture and transportation. India does meet some of its power needs by generating electricity in nuclear power plants and coal-fired thermal stations; however, a large portion of its energy needs is also met by noncommercial sources. India currently taps only 12 percent of the hydroelectric potential of the Ganges, 10 percent of the central Indian tributaries, and a mere 1 percent of the vast potential of the Brahmaputra.[28] Nepal has so far developed a meager 0.2 percent of its 83,000-megawatt hydroelectric potential—equivalent to the combined installed hydroelectric capacities of Canada, the United States, and Mexico. Although some progress is gradually being made in exploiting its substantial hydroelectric potential, Nepal also needs external assistance to substantially improve its transmission and distribution system. India and Nepal have been negotiating several joint hydroelectric projects, which, if implemented, would make Nepal not only self-sufficient in electricity but also a major exporter of electricity to India. In the meantime, as one scholar has pointed out, "Topsoil washing down into India and Bangladesh is now Nepal's most precious export, but one for which it receives no compensation."[29]

In addition to Nepal, the tiny kingdom of Bhutan has the potential for abundant power generation, since its hydroelectric potential has been estimated to be close to 20,000 megawatts. Like Paraguay in the Paraná–La Plata basin, Bhutan could become one of the largest exporters of electricity in the world, but only a very tiny portion of this potential is currently being exploited. Bangladesh, in particular, feels a substantial need for electricity, but because of its mostly flat terrain, the hydroelectric potential within its territory is small even though controversial proposals for producing up to 1,000 megawatts of mostly peak power from the Ganges and the Brahmaputra have been floated from time to time. In any case, given the peculiar physical geography of the basin, implementation of major hydroelectric projects to supply power to Bangladesh would inevitably require cooperation with India and Nepal as well as substantial technical and financial aid from the international community. Overall, Bangladesh stands to benefit the most from multilateral development of the basin's hydroelectric potential.

In Tibet the giant U-bend on the Tsangpo (Brahmaputra), in its easternmost reaches as it cascades down 2.5 kilometers (1.5 miles) into India, has long excited the imagination of engineers as the biggest potential storehouse of hydroelectric power in the world. A preliminary study by the Electric Power Development Company of Japan had envisaged the construction of up to eleven large dams around the Brahmaputra loop to harness the river's full potential. According to the plan, tunnels through the Himalayas would drop the water into India to generate about 70,000 megawatts of electricity, more than five times the output of the Itaipu project in South America.[30] Because of the remoteness of the area, practically no displacement of population would take place and all the electricity generated would be sold to India, as the Chinese load centers in the Sichuan province are very distant and more difficult to access.[31] Japan, some other industrialized nations, and the World Bank have in the past shown great interest in the project, and the process of formulating and forging an international structure and secretariat was proceeding at one time. However, realization of the grand U-bend project would now require cooperation among China, India, and Bangladesh, the lowermost riparian state on the Brahmaputra.

The economic potential of the basin's rivers also includes their contribution to national economies through navigation.[32] Historically, the Barak and the Brahmaputra were the main waterways providing access to the sea for most of the northeastern region of undivided India. This important access was disrupted after the partition of India in 1947, which resulted in the isolation of the northeast region, with severe and ongoing economic impacts. Furthermore, the upstream diversion of water from the Ganges for irrigation in India has diminished the river's usefulness for navigation. Thus, India, in particular, has not exploited the great navigational potential of the basin's rivers, despite the fact that many northeastern cities in India are much closer to a Bangladeshi port at Chittagong than to the nearest Indian port at Calcutta.[33]

In Bangladesh, however, river transportation continues to play a crucial role in the economic and social life of the country. For example, in 1985 Bangladesh had 5,600 kilometers (3,470 miles) of inland waterways compared with 2,900 kilometers (1,800 miles) of railways. These waterways link the two main ports of Chittagong and Chalna with five major inland ports as well as serve the vast rural heartland. Faced with energy shortages and severe environmental degradation from the construction of roads and railways, Bangladesh could benefit substantially from the expansion of year-round navigable waterways in the basin.

Within Tibet, the Tsangpo is navigable for about 600 kilometers (372 miles) at a high altitude of 4 kilometers (2.5 miles) above sea level. This stretch of the river passes through some of the most productive agricultural land and through the most populous parts of the region. A high barrage across the river, as conceptualized by a Japanese company, would greatly extend navigation not only on the main river but also on the tributaries, like the Lhasa River, thus connecting the two largest cities of Tibet, Lhasa and Shigatse. Until the late 1950s, when relations between India and China deteriorated, Calcutta was Tibet's only port of entry. It still remains the closest ocean outlet for Lhasa, nearer than any of the Chinese ports on the Pacific Ocean.[34] If navigation on the shared rivers could be extended northward to the India-Nepal border, or if new navigation channels could be constructed, Tibet could benefit greatly from regaining easier and cheaper access to the sea over land and water through India and Nepal than through China or Pakistan.[35]

In Nepal, mostly because of the mountainous terrain, navigation is currently not as important; however, it would like to develop and keep open the waterways for recreational (mostly tourism) and other uses. Landlocked Nepal also has great interest in acquiring permanent and secure access to the Indian Ocean for bringing in essential supplies and for international trade; the same goes for landlocked Bhutan.[36]

The development plans of all the riparian states face yet another constraint, however. Although separate data for Tibet are not available, all other riparian states are currently heavily in debt. All together, their combined external debt in 1996 amounted to a staggering $116 billion.[37] This debt is unlikely to be settled anytime in the foreseeable future, making it virtually impossible for the riparian states, except perhaps India, to unilaterally or multilaterally undertake the construction of much-needed, large water projects. A stark example of this is the cancellation by the World Bank of $700 million in grants and loans, which would have enabled Nepal to build a 201-megawatt hydroelectrical project, named Arun 3. Among the reasons for this cancellation was Nepal's inability to raise $155 million in matching funds from the domestic sources.[38] In any case, the required external assistance for such projects will not be forthcoming until the interstate water disputes in the basin are resolved and until the riparian states are able to come together for multilateral cooperation.

Finally, even though the level of industrialization in the basin, especially in the smaller riparian states, is currently very low compared with East Asia, Western Europe, and North America, India is gradually beginning to be recognized as a newly industrializing nation.[39] Much of India's mineral and oil reserves and a significant portion of its heavy industries are already located within or near the basin. As all the basin countries attempt to transform and modernize their economies, water and energy needs of the industries located in the basin would multiply. Industrial development would also create serious environmental pollution, especially if industrial waste continues to be dumped in the rivers.

Thus, overall, the physical and economic geography of the basin has created ample scope for a convergence of national interests of all the riparian states in developing the full potential of their shared river waters, especially given their urgent needs for economic development and external assistance. However, a mere recognition of mutually reinforcing national interests has never been a guarantee for the emergence of riparian relations that would foster peaceful resolution of conflict and nurture basinwide cooperation in any international river basin. This is especially so among riparian states with a short but contentious history of interstate relations and with highly polarized domestic polities.

Political Geography

The political geography of South Asia changed radically in 1947 when, after nearly two centuries of colonial domination, the British were forced to relinquish their control over the Indian subcontinent. Over a period of thirty years following World War II, the South Asian subcontinent witnessed not only the emergence of three sovereign states—Bangladesh, India, and Pakistan—after much bloodshed, but also the assimilation of two other states—Sikkim and Tibet—by India and China, respectively.[40] Most significant for this study, colonial legacies of unresolved boundary disputes and the division of British India into India and Pakistan in 1947 without much regard for the geography and integrity of the major river basins, followed by the breakup of Pakistan and the emergence of Bangladesh as a sovereign state in 1971, lie at the heart of the contentious post–World War II hydropolitics in the Ganges-Brahmaputra-Barak basin.[41]

Central governments in three of the five states sharing the basin, in Bangladesh, India, and Nepal, are now run by democratically elected administrations. Bhutan remains a constitutional monarchy while Tibet is ruled by the Chinese government as a special (autonomous) province.[42] All the riparian states, except Tibet-China, are members of the United Nations, the World Bank, and the International Monetary Fund, as well as many other international organizations. All except Tibet-China also belong to the South Asian Association for Regional Cooperation (SAARC).[43]

India has remained the world's largest secular democracy from the beginning of its independence, and regular elections have been held in the country to choose the central and state (provincial) governments.[44] Despite its immense diversity, the central administrations have so far managed to keep the country together, although separatist movements have on many occasions threatened India's territorial integrity—the latest being movements for autonomy and separatism, accompanied by great violence, in the northwestern states of Jammu and Kashmir, and Punjab. If these rebellions do succeed in creating independent nation-states, the prospects for further disintegration of India (and perhaps Pakistan) cannot be dismissed. Independent Punjab and Kashmir, located as they would be on the headwaters of some of the major rivers in the Indus basin, will further complicate the already contentious hydropolitics in South Asia. If an independent nation-state were to emerge in the volatile northeastern region of India, for example, in Assam, hydropolitics in the Ganges-Brahmaputra-Barak basin would also be seriously affected.

From the Indian side, hydropolitics in the basin is also made problematic and contentious by the Ganges flowing through many states (provinces) in India and forming the boundary between two large states, Uttar Pradesh and Bihar. The centrally administered territory of Delhi–New Delhi also lies within the Ganges basin. The Brahmaputra basin, on the other hand, covers portions of territories of eight northeastern Indian states. Given the democratic and federal polity in India, especially state-level jurisdiction over all water projects and water allocations, conflicting needs and interests of the different states have to be reconciled before any international agreement with the neighboring countries can be arrived at or ratified. Whereas on some occasions New Delhi has been successful in dissuading the states from implementing water projects, which could harm India's neighbors, on other occasions some states have objected to the central administration's moves toward cooperation with the neighbors.[45] Center-state and state-state cooperation over water in India also depend on the relationships between the political parties in power at the two levels of administration, at any particular time. Consequently, many water disputes among the Indian states remain unresolved, often engendering violent domestic upheaval and, in some cases, helping to crystallize rebellions and separatist movements around water-related issues.[46]

With the massive extension of irrigation since independence, powerful agricultural lobbies in the Indian states have developed a vested interest in ensuring a continuation of their water rights as well as the huge subsidies they receive for irrigation water and electric power. The democratic polity of India also allows different political parties to emotionalize and politicize all domestic and international water disputes and to use these to gain votes in the elections. Thus, the ups and downs of center-state and state-state relations in India continue to have substantial impact on hydropolitics in the basin. Increasingly, the concerns of domestic and international environmental movements and nongovernmental organizations have also to be taken into account and reconciled before large water projects can be launched and completed.[47]

The nature and vagaries of domestic politics in Bangladesh, Bhutan, and Nepal add further to the basin's contentious hydropolitics. For example, after becoming a sovereign and secular state in December 1971, with India's help, Bangladesh went through one-party rule and a series of military coups, installing General Zia as president, who in 1977 declared the country to be an Islamic state. This declaration and the defiant attitude of the new regime toward secular India led to further deterioration in Bangladesh-India relations, which were already strained by the assassination of the first and allegedly pro-Indian leader of Bangladesh, Sheikh Mujib. Later, after Zia's assassination in 1981, Bangladesh entered a decade of political turmoil, which also adversely affected its relations with India. Thus, despite recent democratization, Bangladesh's polity remains problematic, also owing to the recent rise of Islamic fundamentalism in the country.[48] This makes it very difficult for the leaders in Dhaka to proceed toward cooperation with India, without seeming to compromise national sovereignty or interests.

Many Bangladeshis continue to suspect India of hegemonic ambitions in South Asia, and different political factions and interest groups in Bangladesh continue to exploit any dispute with their powerful neighbor to create domestic upheaval and to gain political leverage with the ruling party. Bangladesh's abject poverty, its near total dependence on waters originating outside its borders, and its extreme vulnerability to floods and droughts have made its domestic politics and international relations highly susceptible to hydropolitics in the basin. As we shall see, unresolved water disputes have constituted the core of Bangladesh's contentious relations with India and Nepal.

In Nepal, the post–World War II period until 1981, when the first national election since 1959 was held, was one of great political turmoil. Over the next decade there were many clashes between the various political parties and the monarchy. Under the provisions of a new constitution promulgated in 1990, Nepal remains a constitutional monarchy; however, a new multiparty democratic order was instituted in the country through elections in June 1991. In November 1994, a coalition led by a communist party came to power in Kathmandu, the first such occurrence at the national level in South Asia.[49] The new government professed to take a pragmatic stance on all issues toward its neighbors, including India. However, the new leadership also called for negotiating substantial modifications to the 1951 Treaty of Friendship with India as well as reexamining bilateral cooperation for several joint water and hydroelectric projects proposed over the years. In 1995 this government was dissolved and Kathmandu has been moving toward more friendly relations with India.[50] However, in the end, as in Bangladesh, any attempt by the Nepalese leadership to cooperate with India over the shared waters remains vulnerable to exploitation by various political factions who may accuse the ruling party of compromising Nepal's sovereignty and national interest.

In Bhutan a hereditary monarchy was founded in 1907, followed in 1910 by the Anglo-Bhutanese Treaty, which placed Bhutan's foreign relations under the supervision of the government of British India. After India became independent, that treaty was replaced in August 1949 by the Indo-Bhutanese Treaty of Friendship, whereby Bhutan agreed to seek the advice of the Government of India with regard to its external relations, but it remained free to decide whether or not to accept the advice. Bhutan is now governed by the king, a council of ministers, a national assembly, and the powerful head of Buddhist lamas. On the whole, Bhutan has benefited greatly from friendly relations with India, as we shall see, but here again some Bhutanese have questioned the country's near total dependence on India for security, trade, and aid.[51]

Relations between Bhutan and Nepal have also seen some ups and downs in recent years. Nepalese settlers, most of them Hindus, now compose nearly a quarter of the predominantly Buddhist population in Bhutan. Since mid-1988, when the king initiated a program for the revival of Bhutanese identity and culture, there has been strong opposition to the monarchic rule from the Hindu Nepalese. Because of the eviction of noncitizens from Bhutan, thousands of refugees continue to languish in camps in India and Nepal.[52] This has further fueled an ongoing violent movement for establishing a greater Nepalese nation, Gorkhaland, comprising the existing territory of Nepal and parts of Bhutan as well as some Indian territory. However, some recent indications do point to attempts by both countries, especially by the king of Bhutan, to bring down the tension in their relationship.

In the case of Tibet, treaties signed in 1906 and 1907 between Britain and China had recognized the latter's sovereignty over Tibet. However, Tibet declared its independence in 1911 and maintained it until 1950, when the Chinese army forcibly occupied the country. In 1951 a defeated Tibet signed a treaty making it once again a part of China, and in 1965 it was officially constituted as an "autonomous" region of China. Renewed protests against Chinese rule erupted in 1987, and in 1989 martial law was imposed in Lhasa. Nonetheless, the exiled Dalai Lama has continued his efforts to build international support for some form of autonomy for Tibet. In the meantime, the Chinese are allegedly continuing to exploit Tibet's vast mineral resources as well as settle large numbers of Han Chinese in the region. Thus, it is not clear how the political and economic geography of Tibet would evolve in the future and what impact it would have on hydropolitics in the Ganges-Brahmaputra-Barak basin.

Within this context of highly contentious domestic politics and interstate relations in this volatile basin, a hopeful sign, perhaps presaging more tolerant and cooperative relations among the riparian states, has recently been provided by a growing rapprochement between India and China. In 1962 the two Asian giants had fought a brief war over their unsettled borders, a war in which India suffered a humiliating defeat. Over the next three decades there were occasional skirmishes between their armies stationed in the Himalayas. However, in the post–Cold War era both countries have made several moves to normalize their relations, to open diplomatic channels, and to promote travel and trade. It is to be hoped that this rapprochement between two erstwhile enemies and rivals for regional domination will open up the space for all riparian states in the basin to put aside their differences and suspicions, and to begin to explore genuinely the possibility of multilateral cooperation.

In summary, the political geography of the basin, especially the contentious nature of domestic politics in each of the riparian states and their interstate relations, has so far prevented the emergence of riparian relations conducive to basinwide cooperation. The relations of the smaller and weaker riparian states with their powerful neighbor, India, continue to be adversely affected by domestic political concerns as well as fear, resentments, and envy engendered by the unbridgeable power imbalances in the basin. Without substantial and credible military arms of national security, the smaller countries are forced to pursue mostly political, environmental, and economic concerns and contentions with India.[53] However, geography, in combination with other factors, has also made the potential hegemon in the basin highly vulnerable in the conduct of hydropolitics, as we shall see.

HYDROPOLITICS

The analysis of hydropolitics in this chapter focuses mainly on Bangladesh, Bhutan, India, and Nepal for the primary reason that, although China shares the basin by virtue of its occupation of Tibet, to date China has not made any substantial claims relating to its acquired uppermost riparian status on the Tsangpo-Brahmaputra or on any of the tributaries originating in Tibet. The main reason for this is the unique physical geography of the basin, which does not allow China to substantially manipulate the rivers' waters. Chinese inability (or disinclination) to participate in hydropolitics is also partly due to the special status of Tibet in Chinese polity as well as to other domestic and international preoccupations of the Chinese leadership. Further, even were China to fully develop the hydroelectric potential of the Tsangpo in Tibet, the mostly coastal and southeastern orientation of its mainland economy would extract very high costs (and losses) for transmitting electricity from Tibet to Chinese cities and industrial areas. Because of the Himalayas, navigation on the Brahmaputra is also not a concern for China. Thus, the physical and economic geography of the basin has effectively shut China off from playing a major direct role in hydropolitics. However, this does not mean that China's presence on the borders of South Asia does not cast long shadows on hydropolitics in the Ganges-Brahmaputra-Barak basin.

Without China's active involvement in the basin's hydropolitics, India is by far the strongest riparian state in the basin. India's size, both in terms of its area and population and its far superior economic and military capabilities, have placed it in a potentially hegemonic relationship with its weaker neighbors. These power imbalances have often engendered fear, suspicions, and envy in the smaller states. Emerging out of colonial experiences, the smaller states in South Asia have been especially sensitive to issues of national sovereignty, identity, and autonomy, and to the very real possibility of cultural and economic domination by their big neighbor. In turn, the contentious and defiant attitude of Bangladeshi and Nepalese leaders from time to time, mainly to appease their domestic constituencies, and some attempts on their part to seek extraregional support to balance India's clout on certain issues have irritated the Indian leadership. In the end, physically separated from China by the Himalayas and from each other by Indian territory, the smaller states have had no choice in the past but to seek bilateral accommodations with India as best as they can.

On certain occasions in the past, India has selectively used its strong riparian position to unilaterally construct water projects despite objections from other riparian states; to withhold hydrological data in the name of national security; to control the nature and timing of negotiations over water sharing; to delay and block international efforts (and aid) for implementing water-related projects in other countries; and to curtail the degrees of freedom of the smaller neighbors in the international arena, as evidenced by the restrictive nature of the Indo-Bhutanese Treaty of Friendship, and by a 1989 episode in which India blocked Nepalese purchase of arms from China by severely restricting Nepal's access to the sea.[54]

In conducting hydropolitics in the basin, India has often taken an upper riparian position vis-à-vis Bangladesh and a lower riparian position vis-à-vis Nepal, especially when it comes to claims of prior water withdrawals. Thus, on occasion, India has opposed construction of some upstream water projects in Nepal while denying a similar claim by Bangladesh on Indian projects. By not recognizing the Ganges and the Brahmaputra as international rivers, and by attempting to dissuade the smaller countries from internationalizing any conflict over the shared water resources, India has sought to prevent outside powers and international agencies from actively participating in the basin's hydropolitics. Mainly because of India's reluctance to be bound by any legally enforceable cooperative regime, no multilateral accord for sharing the transboundary water resources is as yet in place in the basin. And even though India is a member of SAARC, it has tried to ensure that contentious bilateral issues, including water rights, are kept out of SAARC's agenda.[55] On the whole, India has preferred bilateral and project-by-project negotiations rather than a holistic approach to cooperation with its neighbors over the shared water resources, and it has opposed any issue linkage.

But India's potentially hegemonic position in the basin is undermined by its staggering poverty and regional disparities; by its tremendous cultural, ethnic, religious, and linguistic diversity; and by class and caste differences among its large population. These divisions have created highly volatile grounds for domestic instability in India. In addition, India's secularism is threatened by the fact that it is surrounded by Islamic Bangladesh and Pakistan, Hindu Nepal, and predominantly Buddhist Bhutan, Sri Lanka, and Tibet.[56] These domestic and external sources of instability continue to seriously challenge India's potentially hegemonic position in the basin's hydropolitics.[57]

India's dominating position in hydropolitics is moderated also by some maneuverability the smaller riparian states have with India, owing mostly to some physical and economic geographic features of the basin. For example, as the uppermost riparian on some of the major tributaries of the Ganges, and because of its mountainous terrain, Nepal has the potential to help India with substantial hydroelectric supplies, especially given that some Indian states sharing the Ganges basin continue to suffer from serious power shortages. By controlling environmental degradation in the Himalayas, Nepal can also help enhance the ecological and economic security of its downstream neighbor. Most of the remaining sites for building large water storage capacity in the Ganges basin are within or on the borders of Nepal, making the country a potentially stronger riparian than its size or economic and military strength would allow.[58] At the very least, by withholding cooperation for bilateral water projects, Nepal can further delay economic development in India's northern states since external financial assistance for any large-scale water project India may want to launch unilaterally would then not be forthcoming. This delay will be increasingly costly for India as it pursues the dream of becoming a global economic power and as the demand for electricity in its northern states keeps skyrocketing.

Despite its lowermost riparian status in the basin, and despite its economic, political, and environmental vulnerabilities, Bangladesh also has some clout in the basin's hydropolitics. At the very least, it can delay economic development in the troubled and underdeveloped northeastern regions of India by denying navigational and transshipment rights to India through its territory and, as we shall see, by withholding cooperation on an Indian scheme for constructing a canal to link the Ganges and the Brahmaputra through Bangladeshi territory. By not doing much to stem the tide of illegal migrants to India, or by actually encouraging such migration, Bangladesh can also seriously undermine political stability in India's northeast.[59] Both Bangladesh and Nepal can thus continue to "export" their own poverty to India through the migrants. By raising the issue of water sharing in different international forums from time to time, as they have done on several occasions in the past, both Bangladesh and Nepal can jeopardize India's quest for the status of an internationally accepted regional and global power.

Thus, the overall contours of hydropolitics in the Ganges-Brahmaputra-Barak basin are circumscribed largely by the basin's geography, by domestic politics in the riparian states, and by the overwhelming power imbalances between India and its smaller neighbors. It is made contentious by the fears and suspicions the smaller and weaker riparian states have, rightly or wrongly, about India's allegedly hegemonic and exploitative intentions. However, despite the unresolved conflicts between them over the shared waters, the riparian states have managed to cooperate with one another on some occasions. It is to the specifics of such hydropolitical conflict and cooperation in the basin that we now turn.

Conflict and Cooperation

The first post–World War II interstate conflict over transboundary water resources in South Asia arose almost immediately after the independence of India and Pakistan in 1947, over the sharing of six rivers in the Indus basin. Starting in 1948, the dispute was resolved more than a decade later with the signing of the Indus Water Treaty in 1960. The initiative and honest broker role of a third party, the World Bank, and the sizable financial and technical help from a consortium of international donors were crucial in arriving at a solution that the two hostile countries could accept. However, although the treaty is often cited as a prime example of internationally mediated interstate cooperation over transboundary water resources, what is often not recognized is that the unique physical geography of the Indus basin played an important role in resolving the conflict in that, after many proposals for sharing the transboundary river waters in an integrated manner were rejected, the two countries were awarded the waters of three rivers each for their exclusive use. Thus, even though the Indus Water Treaty has survived two subsequent wars between India and Pakistan in the Indus basin, by no stretch of the imagination can it be called a cooperative regime.[60] The treaty has also not engendered cooperation between the two countries on other issues of mutual concern nor has it led to the resolution of other bilateral problems. Nonetheless, what is important for the analysis here is that, as far as is known, at no stage during the protracted negotiations for the Indus Water Treaty was the issue of sharing the waters of the Ganges-Brahmaputra-Barak basin in the east seriously linked to the resolution of the Indus dispute, even though as early as in 1951 Pakistan had objected to India's plans for diverting a portion of the Ganges' flow before it reached East Pakistan. Among other reasons for this nonlinkage by Pakistan may have been a lack of concern for East Pakistan's welfare that many East Pakistanis subsequently blamed the leadership in West Pakistan for, leading to the liberation struggle that created Bangladesh.

In any case, unlike the Indus basin, not only are there more than two riparian states sharing the Brahmaputra-Ganges-Barak basin, but the physical geography of the basin makes it impossible to divide waters of the many rivers and tributaries among the riparian states in an exclusive manner. Consequently, the complex and multilateral hydrological interdependencies in the basin have engendered many disputes over the shared waters: disputes that continue to plague interstate relations, making it difficult to develop multilateral cooperation for the much-needed water projects.

Before we turn to the specifics of conflict and cooperation among the riparian states in this basin, it must be emphasized that in no other international basin in the world is a river so deeply tied to the myths and ritual practices of a living religion followed by hundreds of millions of people as is the Ganges within India's majority religion, Hinduism. Despite the professed secular nature of the Indian state, in no other contemporary state does a river have as much psychological, religious, and cultural importance in the lives of the majority population as does the Ganges in the lives of the Hindus. Through mythology and daily rituals, the river and its water are intractably intertwined with deeper issues of identity, spirituality, faith, culture, and many other aspects of this and "other-worldly" existence for the Hindus. This is one among many reasons why the Indian leadership has been reluctant to declare the Ganges an international river. Thus, an additional factor to take into account in the analysis of hydropolitics in this basin is religious sensitivities of the peoples sharing the basin's waters.

Bangladesh–India Hydropolitics

Water disputes between Bangladesh and India concern more than just equitable sharing in terms of quantity; they are also intimately linked to issues of flood control and drought mitigation in both countries, but much more so in Bangladesh than in India. Until the signing of the 1996 Ganges Water Treaty by the two states (discovered later), the main dispute focuses on the construction of a barrage by India in the early 1970s on the Ganges, at a location 250 kilometers (155 miles) north of Calcutta and just 18 kilometers (11 miles) from the place where the river enters Bangladeshi territory.[61] Bangladesh has continued to object strongly to the implementation of this scheme and to India's allegedly unilateral diversion of about 40,000 of the estimated 55,000-cubic-feet-per-second average dry-season flow of the Ganges. While India has consistently argued, for more than four decades, that the Farakka Barrage was needed to divert some of the Ganges' lean-season flow to the Hooghly River to keep the silted Calcutta port open year-round,[62] Bangladesh has maintained that this unilateral act by India not only deprived it of the much-needed flow for the economic and ecological well-being of the region served by the Padma River—also its most important waterway—but that it also smacks of India's disregard for Bangladesh's sovereignty, needs, and interests. Consequently, a senior Bangladeshi minister once ranked a permanent Farakka settlement near the top of the bilateral agenda between the two countries.[63]

But there was a period earlier when a bilateral agreement relating to the Farakka Barrage was in force in the basin. After protracted negotiations for twenty-five years, between India and Pakistan earlier, and between Bangladesh and India after 1971, the Ganges Water Agreement was signed between Bangladesh and India on November 5, 1977, for sharing the Ganges' water at Farakka from 1977 to 1982.[64] This bilateral agreement was significant on several counts, including its tacit recognition of the Ganges as an international river and its guarantee of a certain fixed percentage of the Ganges' flow to Bangladesh. To placate Nepal, the agreement also provided in its side letters that any Indo-Bangladeshi scheme for augmenting the dry season flow of the Ganges would not preclude any scheme or schemes for constructing storage dams in the upper reaches of the river in Nepal. Thus, the bilateral Ganges Water Agreement also recognized, albeit indirectly, the multilateral interdependencies and rights in the basin.

What is also important to note is that this agreement was reached following the first defeat that the Congress Party suffered in India's parliamentary elections since independence. This change of leadership came about as a result of the two-year-long (1975–77) "Emergency" imposed on the country by Indira Gandhi, a period during which many freedoms guaranteed by the Indian Constitution were suspended, opposition leaders were arrested and harassed, and a humiliating campaign of forced birth control was imposed on the Indian masses. Facing great domestic upheaval as a result, Mrs. Gandhi lifted the emergency in 1977 and called for a general parliamentary election, hoping to reestablish legitimacy for her party and for her administration. Instead, the Indian electorate handed her a humiliating defeat, installing a coalition of opposing political parties to power in New Delhi. This coalition did not last long in power for several reasons; however, in the brief duration it was in power the new leadership tried to establish better relations with India's neighbors than had been the case earlier.[65] The 1977 Ganges Water Agreement was one outcome of these efforts.

At the expiration of the first five years of the agreement, in 1982 it was extended for another five years through a bilateral Memorandum of Understanding (MOD), with some modifications to the earlier agreement. The MOD expired in 1988 and no official agreement for sharing the water of the Ganges existed until very recently. In the meantime, India continued to release water downstream of the Farakka Barrage in a unilateral manner. Some in Bangladesh also blamed India for opening the gates at Farakka during floods without adequate prior warning.[66]

Yet another dispute between the two countries has crystallized around two substantially differing proposals for constructing large projects in the basin to augment the lean-season flow of the Ganges. The Indian proposal calls for building a canal across Bangladeshi territory to link the Brahmaputra with the Ganges, at a site above the Farakka Barrage. India argues that in addition to reducing flooding and intrusion of saline water into Bangladesh, the project would contribute substantially to India's own industrial and irrigation needs in the Gangetic plain as well as produce hydroelectric power for the two countries and facilitate navigation to India's northeast region. India also argues that the combined water resources of the two rivers are in excess of the projected needs of the two countries and, therefore, the project could supply additional water to West Bengal without affecting Bangladesh's water supply.

According to the Indian proposal, 128 kilometers (79 miles) of the 324-kilometer (201-mile) canal would be within Bangladeshi territory. Bangladesh argues that the canal would not only violate its territorial integrity and sovereignty, especially if India controls the project at both ends, but that it would also enhance India's military capabilities within Bangladeshi territory and in the hitherto remote northeast region by providing an easy means of transporting military personnel and supplies upstream. Additionally, the canal would cause serious social, economic, and environmental disruptions by dividing and separating many communities and natural habitats. Further, it would displace a large number of people, who would have to be resettled elsewhere and provided alternate means of earning a livelihood. Bangladesh also fears that by agreeing to the Indian scheme, it may be seen to be legitimizing India's continuing withdrawal of the Ganges' water at Farakka. According to some reports, China has also expressed concerns about the military-strategic implications of the canal, especially as it would allow India to move military supplies to Arunachal Pradesh, where India and China have contesting territorial claims. Bangladesh's reluctance to approve the Indian scheme is thus partially a reflection of its desire to maintain good relations with China, which it considers as a friend and as a counterweight to India's economic and military domination of South Asia.

Bangladesh's own $20 billion counterproposal visualizes the construction of a series of dams and reservoirs in the Himalayan foothills in India and Nepal to store floodwaters, to control salinity intrusion from the Bay of Bengal, and to generate hydroelectricity in Nepal for domestic use and export. Further, the reservoirs could be connected by a link canal across Indian territory to provide a navigational channel to the sea for Bhutan, Nepal, and Tibet. Bangladesh argues that these projects would benefit all the riparian states without causing too much social, economic, and environmental disruption, and that these would be cheaper to construct than the canal and associated works proposed by India.

India has been cool to the Bangladeshi proposal for the primary reason that it would violate India's established policy of dealing with water-related problems in a strictly bilateral manner. India also does not find very attractive the idea of building canals across and along its very narrow (14-mile-wide) and strategically important territory between West Bengal and Nepal. After some initial enthusiasm, Nepal has also been reluctant to take the Bangladeshi proposal seriously. Among the many reasons for this reluctance are Nepal's own negotiations with India for constructing other joint projects and its need to maintain good relations with a powerful neighbor, especially one that controls its access to the sea. Nepal would also like adequate financial compensation for implementing projects on its territory that benefit Bangladesh and India.

Among the other water-related disputes between Bangladesh and India are the contested claims to a land formation in the Bay of Bengal as a result of the tremendous amount of silt brought down from the Himalayas by the Ganges and the Brahmaputra. This island, which varies in size from 2 square kilometers (0.8 square miles) at high tide to 12 square kilometers (4.7 square miles) at low tide, was first discovered and claimed by India in 1971. Subsequently, in 1978 Bangladesh staked its claimed to the new land. Despite some attempts to resolve the issue amicably, it continues to cause considerable tension between the two countries, leading in one instance to the dispatch of gunboats and frigates by the two navies to assert control over the tiny island. This dispute does have potentially serious repercussions, especially for Bangladesh, as the issue has now become intertwined with the larger conflict between the two countries regarding the delimitation of their maritime boundaries and of exclusive economic zones (EEZs).[67] Because of the ongoing tectonic activity in the Himalayas and soil erosion from other activities in the basin, more disputes of this kind may emerge in the future, making it even more problematic to resolve conflict between the two riparian states over the shared waters.

The many water-related problems between Bangladesh and India notwithstanding, the Bangladesh government's refusal to participate in a European parliamentary conference on flood-action planning, for the primary reason that it may offend India, and some movement on India's part to treat the problem of water resources in the basin as a multilateral problem provide some hope that the two neighbors may become more sensitive and open to each other's views about hydropolitics in the basin.[68] However, whether these developments would lead to a resolution of outstanding conflicts and to cooperation between the two riparian states in the hydropolitical arena remains subject to congenial domestic political developments within the two countries, as clearly demonstrated by the recent signing of a water treaty between the two countries.

In December 1996, India and Bangladesh signed the Ganges Water Treaty, which allocates the river's water according to a complex formula. Under this treaty, the two states each receive 50 percent of the Ganges flow (measured at Farakka) when the water flow is less than 70,000 cusecs; if the flow is between 70,000 and 75,000 cusecs, Bangladesh is guaranteed 35,000 cusecs and India receives the balance. If the flow exceeds 75,000 cusecs, India is guaranteed 40,000 cusecs and Bangladesh receives the rest. Between March 1 and May 10, the two parties receive their respective allocations in alternating ten-day periods. The treaty establishes the Joint Committee, with the responsibility for implementing the treaty and measuring and recording the daily flow at Farakka and other specified points along the river. All water-related disputes are referred to the Indo-Bangladesh Joint Rivers Commission for resolution.[69]

Although hailed as a major breakthrough by the political leadership in both countries, the treaty does not address or resolve all the issues relating to the Ganges' waters. Pollution of the river from sewage and chemicals discharge in India remains a serious problem despite the Ganga Action Plan initiated in 1985. There also remains the need to construct additional barrages, link canals, and storage dams in both countries to augment and regulate seasonal water supplies and avoid continued storage as water stress increases. And some vested interests in Bangladesh continue to charge that India secretly diverts a portion of the flow of the Ganges upstream during dry months, causing acute water stress and environmental damage in Bangladesh when the dry-season flow is low. These suspicions and allegations continue to fuel criticism of the treaty by nationalists and Islamic opposition parties in Bangladesh and create tensions in the bilateral relationship.

The unresolved problems and allegations notwithstanding, what is important to note is that the Ganges Water Treaty was negotiated and signed after new, democratically elected governments took over power at the center in both countries. What is interesting is that under the so-called Gujral Doctrine, promulgated by an earlier Indian prime minister Gujral for improving India's relations with its neighbors, India did not insist on any kind of reciprocity from Bangladesh nor did it try to link the Ganges issue to other bilateral matters. And rather than send an official from New Delhi to negotiate the treaty, India sent the chief minister of West Bengal state, who also happens to be the leader of the Communist Party Marxist (CPM), to negotiate with the Bangladesh government, which was headed by the daughter of the founding father of Bangladesh and a friend of India. Following the treaty, amicable negotiations are reported to be continuing on a range of bilateral problems and issues, including the other transboundary water resources. However, substantial progress toward integrated development of the basin will not be possible without the full engagement and cooperation of Nepal, because of the hydrological interdependencies in the basin that were mentioned earlier.

India–Nepal Hydropolitics

Following the democratization of Nepal in 1951, as early as in 1954 and 1959 agreements were signed between Nepal and India for constructing two diversion schemes on the Kosi and Gandak Rivers.[70] Reflecting the amicable relations between the political parties then ruling the two countries, the entire cost of the Kosi project, which was completed in 1963, was borne by India. Nepal also received some water for irrigation, protection against floods, an estimated 10 megawatts of electricity, and a valuable bridge that linked the eastern and western regions of Nepal. Similarly, on the Gandak project, once again financed by India, Nepal received water for irrigation and 15 megawatts of power. However, some Nepalese have subsequently felt that India benefited disproportionately from these projects and that Nepal could have received greater benefits had the projects been constructed within its own territory. These critics maintain that had Nepal been in a better economic situation at the time, it could have constructed the projects unilaterally and then sold water and electricity to India at much higher rates than it was able to negotiate earlier.

Notwithstanding this rather questionable hindsight, the fact remains that Nepal was and remains unable to construct large water projects on its own. In any case, physical geography of the basin dictates that any surplus water and electricity Nepal may be able to generate can be sold only to India.[71] This has often created a standoff over price in a "one seller–one buyer" market, especially one with a great imbalance in power between the buyer and the seller. Consequently, many plans for the development of Nepal's full hydroelectric potential have been stymied, preventing it from becoming a potential "Opec [*sic*] of the Subcontinent."[72] Nepal's inability to unilaterally construct large water-diversion projects on its own territory also means that India can continue to use the river waters downstream without having to compensate Nepal. Thus, it may seem to some that India does not pay any significant opportunity cost for not cooperating with Nepal; however, this highly simplistic algebra does not take into account the great economic, political, and internal security costs that a continuing state of underdevelopment in the basin extracts from all its riparian states, including India.

Another ongoing Nepalese grievance relates to an agreement reached in 1920 between Nepal and the then British Indian government pertaining to a barrage across the Sharda (Mahakali) River on the border with Uttar Pradesh. Under this agreement, Nepal traded some territory with India on the understanding that it would be provided with fixed amounts of water during the main agricultural seasons. These supplies were to be increased in the future until Nepal's own irrigation system could be developed. However, when Nepal was able to obtain credit for an extended irrigation scheme of its own, India, claiming the right of prior appropriation, refused to release additional water from the barrage it now controls. In other instances, in a kind of "seesaw" diplomacy, India and Nepal have frustrated each other's attempts to develop water projects, unilaterally or with the help of international organizations and donors. Many projects of great potential benefit for both countries have not been constructed because of mutual suspicions and bureaucratic foot-dragging on both sides.[73]

It is crucial for Nepal, as a landlocked country, to maintain unimpeded access to the sea, and for the most part India has facilitated the flow of goods and crucial supplies to and from Nepal. However, following a deterioration of bilateral relations, in 1989 India decided not to renew two earlier treaties concerning trade and transit, insisting that a common treaty covering both issues be negotiated. Nepal objected, stressing the need to keep the treaties separate on the grounds that while bilateral trade issues were negotiable, the right of transit for a landlocked country was an internationally recognized right. Further, taking an objection to Nepal's intended purchase of some weapons from China, India closed most of the transit points through which Nepal's international trade is conducted. This resulted in severe shortages of food and fuel in Nepal, and its foreign trade deteriorated noticeably. Kathmandu was also forced to lift an earlier ban on the use of firewood for household fuel needs, leading to further deforestation in the Himalayan foothills. Following this dispute, several rounds of senior-level talks were held and, as a goodwill gesture, Nepal agreed to postpone indefinitely the purchase of arms from China. Subsequently, in 1990, during the Nepalese prime minister's visit to India, a joint communiqué was signed, restoring trade relations and reopening the transit points. Though peacefully resolved, this conflict further reinforced the view some Nepalese hold of India's disregard for their country's sovereignty and national interest. Summarizing this acrimonious legacy of bilateral relations, especially as they relate to the shared waters, a Nepalese scholar has commented that "now the situation is such that no politician or bureaucrat (in Nepal) will ever dare to stake his career and fame in dealing (with) the sensitive issue of water resources which involves the question of sharing between and among (the) co-riparians."[74]

Given its strategic buffer-state location between the two formerly antagonistic Asian giants, China and India, Nepal in the past was able to bargain with both countries for technical and financial aid, infrastructure projects, and so forth. For example, with its huge hydroelectric potential, Nepal managed to get both India and China to build and finance power projects and other infrastructure on its territory. Thus, while India constructed and financed the Trisuli (21 megawatts) and Devighat (14 megawatts) projects, China built the Sunkosi (10.5 megawatts) project.[75] Its strategic location also enabled Nepal to attract aid from other nations and from international organizations for large and small development projects. However, this Nepalese maneuverability, in particular in relation to India, is likely to be curtailed in the future if relations between China and India improve, as seems very likely in the post–Cold War era.

The legacies of the past notwithstanding, India and Nepal have made substantial progress in resolving their water disputes and moving ahead with cooperation. In particular, the renegotiation in 1996 by the two countries of an earlier agreement on the Tanakpur Dam and the signing of the Mahakali Treaty, which aims at an integrated development of the Mahakali River system, indicate that progress on water-related and other bilateral issues is more likely in the future.[76] The two countries are also reported to be considering several joint projects, with hydropower production as the primary purpose, and with potential for added benefits, including irrigation, flood control, and navigation.

Among the other national and regional interests cited by the Nepalese officials relating to the shared waters are watershed management and soil conservation; development of an international power grid and a regional transportation network, based on waterways and "electrically propelled" land transportation; creation of regional cold storage and refrigerated transportation facilities; and better utilization of the primary natural resources of the region, namely water, coal, and natural gas.[77] In addition, Nepal has an interest in training water engineers at some universities in India. Starting out in 1983, with a Water Resources Ministry report that set out the parameters for the hoped-for international cooperation with other basin countries, Nepal has invited expertise from international organizations, and from consultancy groups from various countries, including Australia, Canada, and Japan, for developing hydroelectric projects. There are some indications that India may be softening its stand against third-party involvement in Nepalese water projects.

Finally, the recently formed Indo-Nepalese Joint Commission has a subcommission on water resources development. This subcommission has worked out a joint program, with India's help, to upgrade Nepal's infrastructure and early warning system for floods for the benefit of both countries. However, embedded as the subcommission is in a larger system for managing Indo-Nepalese relations, its effectiveness has been circumscribed by the vagaries of political relations between the two countries. What is needed is a permanent and autonomous Indo-Nepalese Commission similar to the Indo-Pakistani Indus Commission, which has endured and been effective despite two wars in the Indus basin. However, whether such a development comes about will again depend on how the domestic political situation in Nepal and India evolves, and on the nature of their larger interstate relations.

Bhutan–India Hydropolitics

Without China's active participation in the basin's hydropolitics, and given the fact that its special relationship with India constrains it from seeking external support and alliances, the tiny kingdom of Bhutan has had no choice but to deal amicably with India in all matters relating to the shared waters. On the whole, Bhutan seems to have benefited greatly from cooperation with its powerful downstream neighbor. The historically friendly relations between the two countries, combined with Bhutan's landlocked geography and its near total dependence on India for trade and aid,[78] have created a situation where any conflict between the two countries tends to be resolved in a peaceful manner. Bhutan's strategic location between the two Asian rivals and India's eagerness to keep at least this tiny South Asian state firmly within its own sphere of influence have resulted in a high level of sensitivity in India to the economic and social well-being of its small neighbor. In this bilateral relationship at least, India seems much closer to be acting as a benevolent hegemon than a bullying neighbor, which many Nepalese and Bangladeshis see it as.

Among the projects jointly constructed by the two countries is the 360-megawatt Chukkha hydel plant, which was fully financed by India, with 60 percent of the project's cost as a grant to Bhutan and with the balance being treated as a loan at 5 percent interest rate, repayable over fifteen years.[79] The plant commenced full production in 1987. Since Bhutan is currently able to absorb only a minuscule fraction of the plant's full production, most of the electricity generated by the project is bought by India, at a price negotiable every two years under an arrangement that is to last for ninety-nine years. These exports currently account for about one-third of Bhutan's domestic revenue. Another large project on the Kuri-chu River has been investigated by India, primarily to supply electricity to eastern Bhutan. Yet another 1,000-megawatt bilateral project on the Wang-chu River, below Chukkha, is also being considered. Competing projects are some storage dams on the Wang-chu and Amo-chu Rivers, which could yield up to 850 megawatts of electricity for the development of export-oriented industries in southern Bhutan. Thus, cooperation on water projects between India and Bhutan seems to be proceeding smoothly. For the reasons of geography and diplomacy this situation is not likely to change any time in the foreseeable future.

SAARC and Hydropolitics

As mentioned earlier, all the riparian states, except China, belong to the South Asian Association for Regional Cooperation (SAARC), which was set up in 1985 in Dhaka during a summit-level meeting of the heads of seven states—Bangladesh, Bhutan, India, the Maldives, Nepal, Pakistan, and Sri Lanka.[80] According to its mandate, the primary aim of SAARC is to promote economic growth with social justice in each of the member countries by facilitating regional cooperation, collective self-reliance, and peaceful coexistence. Since its inception, SAARC has developed a long list of possible areas of cooperation, including agriculture; rural development; intraregional tourism; problems relating to the fulfillment of basic needs for food, clothing, and shelter; population control; and so forth. Recognizing the growing environmental problems South Asia faces, the 1992 SAARC summit at Male also declared 1992 as the SAARC Year of the Environment to coincide with the Earth Summit in Rio de Janeiro.[81]

However, despite the long list of possible areas of cooperation and despite the repeatedly expressed desire by all the member countries to move ahead with regional cooperation, the real achievements of SAARC to date have been disappointing.[82] In addition to the vagaries of interstate relations and domestic politics in South Asia, two provisions of the SAARC mandate have stood in the way of substantial progress—the requirement of unanimity for all collective decisions and the exclusion of all contentious bilateral issues from the deliberations of SAARC. These provisions were included in SAARC's mandate mainly to ensure that the other countries do not "gang up" on India (or Pakistan) and that India, in turn, is not able to impose any undesired decisions on the other countries. What is most relevant for this study is the earlier exclusion of the shared water resources as a possible area of cooperation from the mandate of the only multilateral organization that could be an ideal agency to promote such cooperation. It is to be hoped that as the awareness of the high cost of noncooperation over transboundary water resources grows, wiser heads will prevail in the region.

In the end, a more enlightened and effective SAARC; strong and effective national leaders; efforts by individuals and nongovernmental organizations in all the riparian states and internationally to educate the public as well as national leaders about the urgency of the problem; a "carrot-and-stick" approach by international organizations and donors; some new imperatives engendered by economic liberalization in all the riparian states in a highly competitive and globalizing international economy; and a growing urgency to redress problems of economic disparities within the basin may all be necessary to unleash the tremendous potential of the shared waters in the Ganges-Brahmaputra-Barak basin in a cooperative manner.

SUMMARY AND CONCLUSION

The physical geography of the Ganges-Brahmaputra-Barak basin has bound five developing countries and about one-tenth of humanity together in environmental, economic, political, and security interdependencies, and it has endowed the shared rivers in one of the least-developed regions of the world with an unmatched, multiple-use developmental potential. The evolving economic geography of the basin continues to create favorable conditions for the convergence of national economic interests of all the riparian states. However, some unique physical features of the basin, combined with its peculiar history and political geography, have frustrated all past attempts at multilateral cooperation for developing and sharing the abundant potential of its transboundary water resources.

Unlike the Paraná–La Plata basin, where two potential regional powers, Argentina and Brazil, had some semblance of power balance in hydropolitics, geography has effectively prevented a regional power, China, from balancing or affecting the dominant position of another regional power, India, in this basin's hydropolitics. By effectively separating the two upstream but landlocked riparian states, Bhutan and Nepal, from China, the Himalayas have also substantially curtailed their relative powers and maneuverability in hydropolitics. Vulnerability of the lowermost riparian state, Bangladesh, to water withdrawals and ecological degradation upstream has made it highly dependent on the benevolence of the upstream states. Additionally, the very large number of shared rivers and tributaries in the basin, a feature that, in theory at least, should enhance the possibility of making trade-offs across the many sub-basins and across multiple uses of the shared waters, has in fact made the task of calculating the costs and benefits of all possible trade-offs, for each riparian state, very difficult. Thus, whereas some unique features of the physical and economic geography of the basin have created substantial grounds for cooperation among the riparian states, other features continue to frustrate the quest for multilateral development of the basin's full economic potential.

Among the major political factors that have impeded multilateral cooperation in the basin are colonial legacies of unresolved boundary disputes; a highly skewed distribution of power resources among the riparian states; the salience of issues of identity, sovereignty, and recognition for the smaller riparian states; and the contentious nature of domestic politics and interstate relations in the basin. Religion too has played a role in frustrating the attempts at cooperation, by adversely affecting domestic politics and interstate relations in the basin.

Faced with a potentially hegemonic neighbor, and locked into vulnerable geographic locations, the smaller riparian states have tried to make use of the usual "weak-nation" strategies—collective action, power balancing, internationalization of conflict, and selective noncooperation—in the basin's hydropolitics. However, the strategic advantages the strongest riparian state enjoys—locationally, economically, and militarily—have enabled it to effectively thwart all attempts by its neighbors to act collectively or to internationalize the contentious regional issues. The strongest riparian state has also used its dominating position in hydropolitics to selectively reward compliance and to punish noncompliance by other riparian states with its larger geopolitical agenda.

To date, most interstate cooperation in the basin has been bilateral, and mostly on a project-by-project basis, primarily because the strongest riparian state has wanted it that way and because physical geography of the basin is such that the other riparian states cannot directly cooperate with one another.

Nonetheless, the dominant riparian state also pays an increasingly high price for noncooperation since the opportunity costs of delayed economic development and growing environmental degradation within its own territory continue to accumulate. Domestic instabilities within its own territory and in the rest of the basin, engendered by water and energy scarcities, and economic underdevelopment and ecological degradation, inevitably threaten even the strongest riparian state's national security and territorial integrity. Thus, it is that the potentially hegemonic power of the strongest riparian state in a basin's hydropolitics is moderated by ecological, economic, and security interdependencies in the whole basin.

An interesting finding to emerge from this case study is that the fashioning of cooperative agreements among the riparian states has been possible when there have been changes in the central government(s) in one or more states. It may be that changes in national leadership open up new politico-psychological spaces for fresh approaches to interstate relations, which may, in turn, make it possible to cooperate in hydropolitics. This may be because the new leaders and regimes feel a need to demonstrate to their domestic constituencies and to the world community their good intentions and capabilities to resolve outstanding conflicts with their neighbors. However, this case also demonstrates that after an initial period of fresh explorations following leadership changes, attempts at conflict resolution and cooperation can often be frustrated by the vagaries of domestic politics, bureaucratic inertia and haggling, and the resurgence and exploitation by vested interests of accumulated frustrations and suspicions of the past.

This case study also shows that although a progressive democratization of the states sharing an international basin may be a laudable goal on many counts, it can also make it more difficult for national leaders to reconcile the increasingly diverse domestic water-related interests, and to develop and sustain the kind of domestic constituency and consensus required for cooperation with their neighbors. The analysis here also shows that third parties may be able to play a very marginal role in a basin's hydropolitics until the time when the riparian states themselves are able or forced to develop the willingness and ability to cooperate with one another.

Similar to the Jordan and Euphrates-Tigris basins, this case study also shows that in some international basins, water disputes may be so intimately tied to issues of identity, recognition, and ideology that a clear delinking of contentious high- and low-politics issues may not be possible. Further, if the shared waters also have religious significance for one or more groups in an international basin, the demarcation of high- and low-politics issues may be made even more problematic. There is little evidence from this case study to support the hope that cooperation on such low-politics issues as water sharing necessarily facilitates resolution of other contentious high-politics issues among the states sharing a river basin. In fact, this case shows that some forms of low-politics cooperation may actually engender resentments and suspicions that may cast long shadows over the possibility of further cooperation, even in the same issue area. This is especially so if the nature and vagaries of domestic politics allow the low-politics compromises to be exploited by different interest groups or political parties in one or more riparian states.

In sum, in the Ganges-Brahmaputra-Barak basin, enlightened multilateral cooperation over the shared waters is not possible without strong political will and authority at the highest levels of national leadership, supported by an environment of domestic stability in all the riparian states. However, these conditions cannot be fully achieved unless there is multilateral cooperation over the shared waters. Unresolved conflicts over water will continue to adversely affect interstate relations, domestic politics, and quality of life in the Ganges-Brahmaputra-Barak basin. Nonetheless, the fact remains that to date the riparian states have not gone to war over the shared waters, nor is there any possibility of this happening in the foreseeable future. But there is a very real possibility that a continuing state of noncooperation in the basin will engender acute domestic conflict in one or more riparian states, with very high probabilities of spillovers across the international borders. Thus, interstate conflicts over shared waters may lead to domestic upheaval rather than outright war. In this sense, water is and will continue to be a national security issue in the Ganges-Brahmaputra-Barak basin.

6

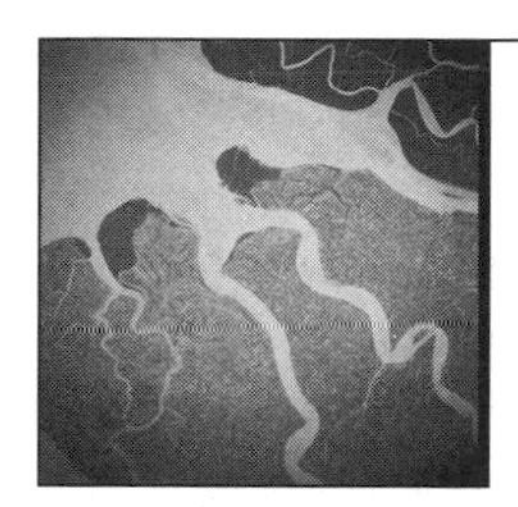

THE MEKONG BASIN

On February 4, 1994, after a long and often acrimonious domestic debate, and despite strong opposition from some quarters, the Clinton administration lifted the economic embargo against Vietnam that had been in place since 1975, the year the United States ended its active military engagement in Southeast Asia.[1] This long-awaited first step toward rapprochement between the two erstwhile enemies, following the end of the Cold War and the collapse of the Soviet Union, opened up the way to a full normalization of relations between them; it also helped to draw Indochina, comprising Vietnam, Laos, and Kampuchea (Cambodia), into the fold of the Association of Southeast Asian Nations (ASEAN).[2] If the international community is successful in helping to bring about a resolution to the ongoing turmoil in Kampuchea, peace may finally come to the Mekong basin after decades of bloodshed. These developments may also help unleash the tremendous, but as yet largely unexploited, multiple-use potential of the waters of one of the largest river basins in the world. However, many historical animosities and other hurdles will have to be overcome before basinwide cooperation in the Mekong basin becomes a reality.

Shared by six riparian states—Burma (Myanmar), China, Kampuchea (Cambodia), Laos, Thailand, and Vietnam[3]—the Mekong basin remains one of a handful of large river basins in the world that have not yet been developed to any significant extent. But after more than four decades of regional and international efforts, it may well turn out to be one of the few examples in the Third World where the changing geopolitical and regional circumstances, and local and international efforts, may yet lead to the integrated and sustainable development of an international basin for the benefit of all the riparian states sharing it. For this to happen, however, an extraordinary degree of trust and cooperation will need to develop among neighbors who have in the recent past rattled sabers at one another and who continue to be watchful of one another's actions and intentions.

Why has the Mekong basin remained underdeveloped for so long? Can the states and peoples sharing the basin realize the cherished dream of equitable, integrated, and sustainable development of their shared hydrological resources? What circumstances and factors may lead to such an outcome? What are the lessons this case study holds for understanding hydropolitics in other international river basins in the Third World? These are some of the questions to which we now turn.

GEOGRAPHY

Physical Geography

Like the Ganges and the Brahmaputra in South Asia, the mighty Mekong originates in the Himalayan mountain ranges in Tibet, at an elevation of more than 5 kilometers (3 miles). In Tibet it is known as Dza-chu, the Water of the Rocks. The river then flows through the southern Yunnan province of China, under the name Lan-Tsan Kiang, the Turbulent River. Through Tibet and China the river traverses a course about 2,000 kilometers (1,250 miles) long—nearly one-half its total length from the Himalayas to the sea—through a 174,000-square-kilometer (67,860-square-mile) subbasin known as the Upper Basin.

After flowing through Tibet and southern China, the Mekong forms short stretches of borders between Burma and China, Burma and Laos, and Thailand and Laos, before entering northern Laos. From the Laotian capital, Vientiane, it flows 840 kilometers (520 miles) to reach Cambodia, forming a 662-kilometer (415-mile) border between Laos and Thailand on the way. Finally, after traversing a course of nearly 4,200 kilometers (2,600 miles) from its snow-capped Himalayan origins, the river flows into the sea through the Mekong Delta. (See map facing.)

The northern edge of the Lower Basin begins where the boundaries of Burma, Laos, and Thailand converge, an area popularly known as the Golden Triangle.[4] Through this basin the Mekong flows mostly placidly for another 2,400 kilometers (1,490 miles), comparable in length to the

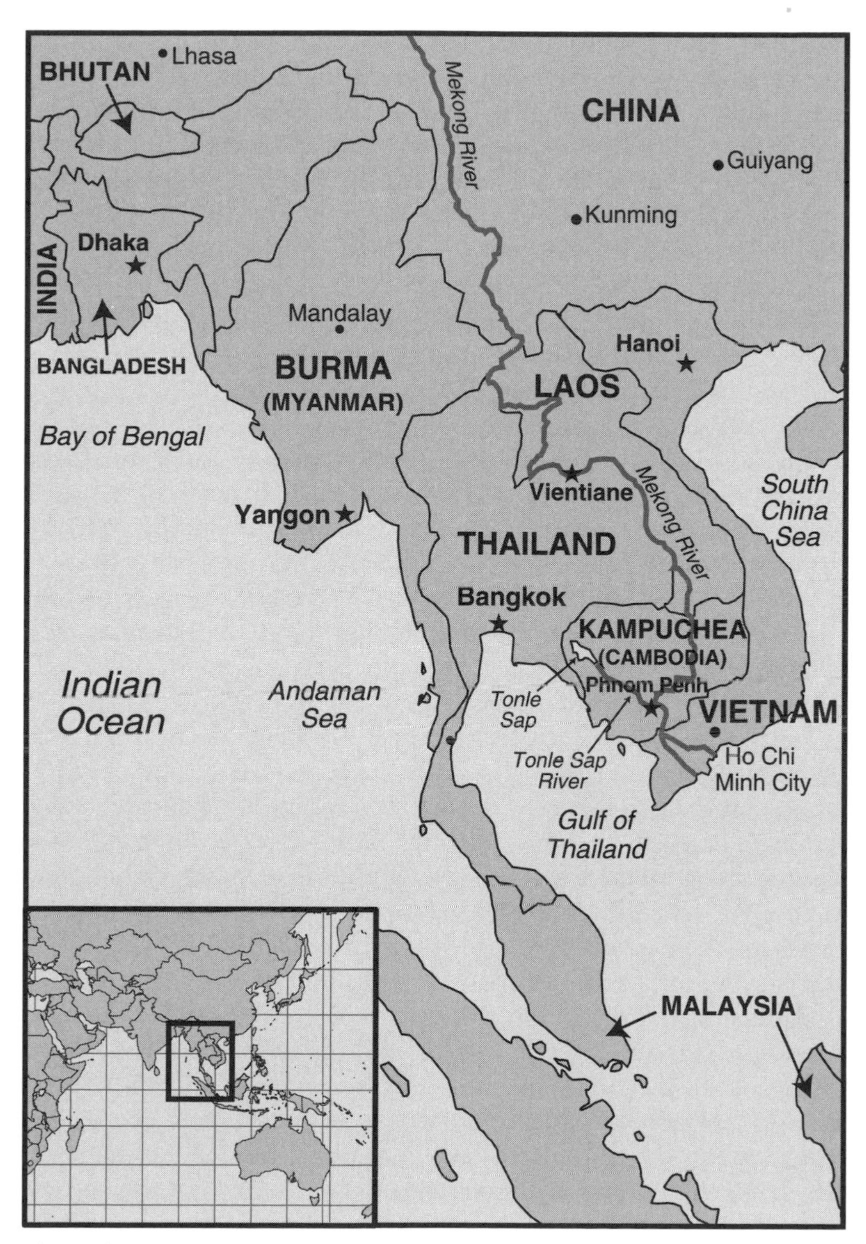

The Mekong Basin

full course of the Danube River from its source to the Black Sea.[5] Of the total drainage area of about 786,000 square kilometers (307,000 square miles) of the whole Mekong basin, some 77 percent is in the Lower Basin—an area larger than the states of New York and California combined, or larger than France. The Lower Basin comprises almost the whole national territories of Laos and Kampuchea, one-third of Thailand, and one-fifth of Vietnam.

In Laos and Thailand the river is known as Mae Nam Khong—Mother of Waters—from which its westernized name, the Mekong, derives. The Khmers in Kampuchea call it Tonle Thom, the Big River. Farther down, the Vietnamese call it Cuu Long Giang, the River of the Nine Dragons.

The Mekong is among the world's ten largest rivers: in terms of the volume of water discharged it ranks first in Southeast Asia and tenth in the world. Three-fourths of its annual discharge stems from monsoon rains falling on the Lower Basin, only one-fourth of the flow is contributed by the Upper Basin in Tibet and China. Consequently, the hydrological regime of the Lower Mekong is not markedly affected by the climatology of the Upper Basin. As we shall see, this feature, combined with some topographical features of the terrain the river passes through, has a substantial bearing on the nature and conduct of hydropolitics in the basin.

The Mekong's flow shows great seasonal variability: the flow can be as low as 1,764 cumecs in the dry season and as high as a flood flow of 52,000 cumecs during the monsoons, with the typical average flow hovering around 14,116 cumecs. Thus, comparing only their low-water discharges, the Mekong stands third in Asia after the Yangtze and Ganges-Brahmaputra systems. At the peak of the Mekong floods there is generally extensive flooding in the lowlands of Kampuchea and Vietnam. Fortunately, owing to some farming practices that have evolved in the basin over centuries, regular floods do little damage and even facilitate cultivation. However, severe floods do cause serious damage to crops and property, both in the lowlands and sometimes in the riverine areas upstream.[6] Every year, more than 475,000 million cubic meters of water, on average, flow almost completely unutilized through the mouth of the Mekong Delta to the sea. If fully developed to generate hydropower, this free-flowing water could help produce 500,000 gigawatts of electricity annually, enough to supply the projected needs of all the riparian states for decades to come.[7]

About 40 percent of the Lower Basin receives an annual rainfall of 100 to 150 millimeters (40 to 60 inches); in other parts of the Lower Basin annual rainfall reaches 150 to 200 millimeters (60 to 80 inches). Taking a well-distributed rainfall of 150 millimeters as the minimum required for rice cultivation throughout the growing period, rainfall in the basin varies from less than adequate to just adequate for rice production. Consequently, years of less-than-average rainfall lead to acute shortages in food production. If the full irrigation potential of the Lower Mekong could be harnessed, millions of acres of land could be brought into cultivation without affecting navigation or hydroelectricity production in the basin.

Throughout its long course through the Lower Basin, the Mekong is joined by numerous tributaries originating in different countries. About 80 percent of the runoff in the Lower Basin comes from the Mekong's left-bank tributaries in Laos, Cambodia, and Vietnam, and the remaining originates in the west, in Thailand and Cambodia. These tributaries form an extensive network of channels in the basin, with substantial potential for irrigation and hydroelectricity generation. Among the major tributaries, near Phnom Penh the Mekong is joined by the Tonle Sap flowing from northwestern Kampuchea. At the head of this river is the largest lake in Asia, also known as Tonle Sap (meaning "great lake"), which changes size from 2,600 square kilometers (1,014 square miles) in the dry season to about 24,600 square kilometers (9,594 square miles) at the height of flooding. The lake serves as a natural reservoir for part of the Mekong's flow during the wet season when, owing to the high volume of flow in the Mekong, the Tonle Sap River changes direction and carries the Mekong's water northward to fill the lake.[8] Later, as the Mekong's flow subsides the Tonle Sap River changes direction again, and the stored water is released downstream. A short distance below the confluence of the Mekong and the Tonle Sap, the main stream splits into two parallel channels, the Mekong (Tien) and the Bassac (Hau), which flow independently through the delta in Cambodia and Vietnam to the South China Sea.

The terrain through which the Mekong passes from its origins to the sea is, for the most part, highly mountainous. The mountain ranges stretch from north to south, creating formidable barriers to the movement of people and goods between the riparian countries. Laos is predominantly a mountainous land, with only one-tenth of its territory suitable for permanent agricultural settlement; in Kampuchea less than one-fifth of the land is currently cultivated. Parts of the basin shared by Burma, China, and Thailand are also mostly mountainous; only the plateau shared by Laos and Thailand, and the delta in Cambodia and Vietnam are flatlands.

Historically, the mountains surrounding the Mekong were well endowed with dense forest cover and minerals; however, indiscriminate logging and mining in the past three decades have led to serious environmental problems throughout the basin. The mountains in southern China are now mostly bare of forest cover, and Thailand is reported to have lost 75 percent of its forest cover since records have been kept.[9] Consequently, silting has considerably reduced the storage and power-generating capacity of the existing dams in Thailand and Laos, as well as substantially reduced fish production in both countries and in Kampuchea.[10]

Major environmental problems are now encountered regularly in the Mekong Delta. The mangrove forests in southern Vietnam, once considered the largest and most productive in the world, have been devastated by war and by unplanned development. In just one southern Vietnamese district alone, chemical spraying by the U.S. military during the Vietnam War is estimated to have reduced the mangrove cover from some 58,000 hectares in 1965 to 26,000 hectares in 1972; close to 70 percent of the remaining cover in that particular province has disappeared over the last two decades. These mangroves are now further threatened by some indiscriminate economic activities, such as shrimp raising.[11] Environmental degradation also poses serious threats to the diversity of fauna inhabiting the delta, including 23 species of mammals, 386 species of birds, 35 species of reptiles, 6 species of amphibians, 260 species of fish, and large breeding colonies of herons, egrets, storks, and ibises.[12] In the future, many of the large water-related projects proposed to be developed in the basin, if implemented, are likely to have severe environmental impacts in the whole basin (see the section "International Efforts").

These mostly man-made calamities are especially ironic in a basin where physical geography has created a tremendous potential for food production, development of fisheries, hydroelectricity generation, industrial development, and navigation. Whether the riparian states and peoples sharing the Mekong basin are willing and able to reverse the process of environmental decay and to collectively develop the multiple-use potential of their shared waters in a sustainable manner will depend mainly on the evolving economic and political geography of the basin.

Economic Geography

Today, the economic geography of the countries surrounding the Mekong presents a mosaic of very rapidly growing national and subnational economies existing side by side with some chronically underdeveloped ones. Whereas the regional economies in parts of southern China and Thailand have recently recorded some of the highest growth rates in the world, most of Burma and large parts of Indochina continue to suffer from severe poverty and unemployment.[13] Within the basin itself, abject poverty, combined with high population growth rates, accelerating urbanization, and massive internal migrations, is creating the potential for acute conflict. Rapidly growing demands for potable water, food, electricity, and transportation, as well as some highly ambitious plans for industrialization and for resettlement of populations in some countries, are fast multiplying the pressures on the shared water resources in the basin.

In the Upper Basin, the ongoing liberalization of the Chinese economy and the growing transboundary economic linkages of the southern provinces with Southeast Asia and the rest of the world have engendered rapid economic growth that now requires larger and larger inputs of water and electricity. At the same time, large-scale migration to these thriving regions from other parts of China is multiplying, manifold, the demand for water for household consumption, sanitation, and so forth. These areas also need easier and cheaper access to the sea for their rapidly growing imports and exports than is currently provided by the eastern Chinese seaports on the Pacific Ocean or through Hong Kong. Access to the South China Sea over the Mekong would also allow China to exploit the fast-growing markets in the downstream countries as well as their considerable stocks of natural resources, particularly in Burma and Laos. Despite major physical barriers to overcome on the way, smuggled goods from southern China are already flooding the markets in the lower riparian countries, giving rise to fears of Chinese domination over their national economies. At the same time, smuggling of stolen cars, agricultural produce, and natural resources, including hardwood and minerals, from the Lower Basin into China has created an economic boom in the northern parts of Laos and Vietnam.[14]

Facing severe shortages of electricity for the rapidly growing industrial sector in its southern provinces, and plagued by debilitating environmental pollution from its outdated coal-fired power plants, China would like to fully develop the hitherto unexplored hydroelectric potential of the Upper Basin within its territory and, if necessary, to import surplus electricity from its downstream neighbors. According to some Chinese estimates, the Upper Basin has a potential of generating about 20 million kilowatts of hydroelectric power, with a gross reservoir volume of 38 billion cubic meters if, as proposed, fifteen dams can be built on the main river within Chinese territory.[15] According to available reports, a 1,250-megawatt mainstream dam, the Manwan, has already been constructed in the Yunnan province and work on two additional dams, the Xiaowan and Dachaoshan, is to be completed by the year 2000. Together these dams will create the potential for generating about 4.5 million kilowatts of electricity within Chinese territory. Earlier it was mentioned that only about 25 percent of the Mekong's flow originates in Tibet; however, if all the Chinese projects are implemented as proposed in the Upper Basin, they will substantially impact the downstream river regime. In the absence of basinwide consensus and cooperation, these unilateral developments have the potential to make hydropolitics in the Mekong basin much more contentious than it has been in the past.

The overall demand for electricity in the Lower Basin over the past few years is estimated to have increased at a rate of 10 percent per year, and is projected to reach 24,000 megawatts a year by the year 2000. Thailand alone may account for about 70 percent of this projected demand and it may require an additional power-generating capacity of about 1,000 megawatts *per year* from the year 2000 onward.[16] However, the potential for hydropower generation within Thailand is very limited and the two indigenous fuel sources, lignite and natural gas, are likely to be exhausted in the near future; most of the country's forests have already been felled. Thailand already imports some electricity from Laos, and its dependence on outside sources of energy is bound to grow as its population and economy continue to expand. In 1994 Thailand was reported to have signed an agreement for importing natural gas from Burma. With the growth of populations, accompanied by urbanization and industrialization, the demand for electricity in all the other Lower Basin riparian states is bound to grow rapidly.

The total electricity-generating capacity of the Lower Basin has been estimated to be close to 200,000 million kilowatt-hours per year (the equivalent of 1 million barrels of oil per day); however, the per capita supply and the consumption of electric power in the basin are currently among the lowest in the world. About one-half of all the potential hydroelectric capacity in the Mekong basin is located within and on the Laotian borders; nonetheless, as much as 60 percent of Laos's energy needs are currently supplied by fuelwood, resulting in substantial deforestation. Because of its small population and low level of economic development, for the foreseeable future the country can absorb only a tiny fraction of its full hydroelectric potential, assuming that it could be developed. Thus, although Laos, like some other small, poor, and landlocked countries in other developing regions—for example, Bhutan and Nepal in South Asia and Paraguay in South America—has the potential to become one of the largest exporters of electricity in the world, its precious forest wealth is rapidly being depleted, leading to dire environmental consequences for the Lower Basin.

Cambodia has the second-largest hydropower potential in the Lower Basin, in excess of 8,000 megawatts. However, only a few small hydropower projects have been constructed in the past, and some have been destroyed in wars. Like Laos, the primary source of energy in Cambodia is the fast-depleting stock of fuelwood, still accounting for close to 90 percent of all energy consumption. Consequently, the Mekong Secretariat believes that an acute shortage of energy will be one of the main constraints for the planned reconstruction and socioeconomic development of the country.[17] Facing some of the same problems as Laos and Cambodia, the Vietnamese, in turn, are interested in promoting and developing the 700,000-kilowatt Yali Falls project, the most promising hydroelectric project in the Lower Basin. If it is implemented, the project could make substantial contributions to the less developed middle region of the country. Of course, given the hydrological interdependencies in the basin, whether the Yali project can be fully implemented will depend upon what happens to the flow of the river upstream from Vietnam.

Despite its vast developmental potential, the Lower Basin continues to be sparsely populated, even though nearly one-half of the combined population in the four riparian countries—upward of 52 million people—lives in the basin. It is also one of the least urbanized river basins in the Third World, with Phnom Penh as the largest among the few cities located in the basin proper. Although this low population density and the nascent urbanization partly reflect the rugged mountainous terrain as well as the overall underdevelopment of the basin, in the Mekong Delta population density is as high as 400 or more people per square kilometer. In contrast, the highest population density in the Thai part of the basin is 160 people per square kilometer. In Laos and Kampuchea, with estimated 1996 populations of roughly 5 million and 10 million, respectively, about 93 percent of the total population lives within the basin. Vietnam, in particular, with an area about the same as New Mexico but with a 1996 population estimated to be about 74 million, is already the twelfth most populous country in the world: by the year 2025 its population is expected to reach 168 million.[18] As the economies of the Lower Basin riparian states grow and as political and economic liberalization proceeds in the basin, it is very likely that a large number of people will migrate to the basin from other areas, further amplifying the pressures on its underdeveloped water resources.

All the riparian states sharing the Lower Basin now have nascent industrial sectors, with Thailand beginning to be looked at as the next newly industrializing country (NIC) in Asia. However, for the most part, these economies are based primarily on the processing and manufacture of agricultural products. Nearly four-fifths of the region's population is employed in agriculture, with the estimated 1995 national per capita incomes ranging from $1,100 in Laos to $6,900 in Thailand. Within the agriculture sector, production of single wet-season rice crops has traditionally been the most significant activity. Food production has historically not only kept pace with the rapidly increasing populations in the basin but has provided an export surplus.[19] However, expansion of rice production now requires opening up of new lands for cultivation as well as extensive application of chemicals and irrigation.[20]

Laos, in particular, has an immense water supply for domestic, agricultural, and industrial use; however, as mentioned earlier, a large part of the country is mountainous and only a tiny fraction of its arable land is currently irrigated. Additionally, navigation on the Mekong and access to the sea are important concerns for the landlocked country. If its hydroelectric resources could be developed, not only could it earn valuable foreign exchange, but also it could use the electricity to process its agricultural produce and other natural resources for export. Surplus electricity generation could also attract foreign investment in large power-consuming industries, such as aluminum processing.

In Thailand, the northeastern region within the Mekong basin has roughly half the country's arable land, but only a very limited water supply. As a Thai official has remarked, "The single factor making the northeast the poorest part of the country is the shortages of water."[21] Frequent droughts and floods in the northeast are the primary reasons for many farmers migrating to Bangkok in search of jobs. Close to 7 million people and nearly 70 percent of the country's manufacturing industries are located in and around the national capital. Faced with this explosive growth of population and with severe infrastructure deficiencies, Thailand would like to develop the multiple-use potential of the Mekong's waters in the northeast as well as divert some water to another river flowing through Bangkok.[22] However, these projects cannot be implemented without the consent and cooperation of the upper and lower riparian states. As we shall see, this has already emerged as a point of contention between Thailand and Vietnam.

In Kampuchea, the amount of irrigated land has fallen by 80 percent in the last two decades because of wars. Before the 1970s the country was one of the major exporters of rice; today less than 7 percent of the rice fields are irrigated because of damage to the irrigation systems, and because of a mass exodus of farmers from war-ravaged areas. The economic development planners intend to make irrigation-based food security their major priority.[23] Plans also exist for implementing some of the irrigation-cum-hydroelectric projects that were initiated in the 1960s but later halted by the Khmer Rouge.[24] However, one of the major difficulties the country now faces is a shortage of trained managers and technicians to run large developmental projects. Given the current state of the national economy and because of ongoing domestic conflict, some developmental schemes have had to be abandoned, one of which would have provided water to southern Vietnam to deal with the problems of saline water intrusion in the delta during the dry season.[25] In any case, none of the proposed Kampuchean projects can be implemented without substantial foreign aid, domestic tranquility, and cooperation from other riparian states in the basin.

The Vietnamese may have been one of the first peoples in Asia to have mastered the art of irrigation. In the modern era, under French rule, the marshes of the Mekong Delta were drained, resulting in a substantial increase in wet-rice production. Today, the delta is the most important rice-producing area of Vietnam, accounting for one-half of the nation's annual production; it is also home to about 15 million people. However, indiscriminate deforestation and commercial logging upstream, over decades, have sharply reduced the agricultural potential of the delta: about 1.6 million hectares are now plagued by saltwater intrusion from the sea, another 1.5 million hectares suffer from acidic soils. Consequently, the Vietnamese government is focusing its attention on developing the delta to cope with problems of flooding, seawater intrusion, coastal erosion, and soil acidity, and to achieve two or even three irrigated rice crops a year. These goals can be achieved with a regular supply of 2,000 to 3,000 cumecs of water coming down the Mekong, which could also irrigate the fertile fields of the delta during the dry season. However, given the great seasonal variation in the Mekong's flow, combined with the low elevation and flatness of the delta, this water supply can only be ensured on a regular basis by building upstream reservoirs in the neighboring countries. In this sense, Vietnam faces a situation similar to that of Bangladesh in the Ganges-Brahmaputra basin and Egypt in the Nile basin in that the major solutions for its water-related problems lie within the territories of its upstream neighbors. This "Vietnamese condition" has substantial implications for hydropolitics in the basin, as we shall see.

In addition to its vast hydroelectric and irrigation potential, the Mekong can be developed as a major source of marine produce in the Lower Basin. Fisheries contribute about 4.5 percent of the GNP of the Lower Basin.

These sources supply 40 to 60 percent of the animal protein intake of the basin's inhabitants; they are also a major source of employment. Of a total catch of fish estimated at about 360,000 tons for the whole basin, nearly 90 percent still comes from traditional capture fisheries. Unfortunately, these fisheries are now seriously threatened by overfishing, other destructive fishing practices, and overall environmental deterioration.[26]

The inland waters of Cambodia, in particular, have been exceptionally productive, with estimated fish catches of 160,000 tons in 1968 and 130,000 tons in 1991, representing up to 70 percent of the total animal protein intake by the population. The Tonle Sap Lake is renowned as the most productive freshwater ecosystem in the world; it supports about 60 to 75 percent of the inland fishery in Cambodia. The fish harvest from the lake has historically been as high as 100,000 tons a year. This valuable natural resource for a poor country has, however, been seriously depleted by wars, by deforestation and land reclamation, and by the construction of dikes and canals. Siltation of water bodies and out-of-season fishing or overfishing have further depleted the fish stocks in some areas, including in the Tonle Sap Lake.

All the Mekong riparian states also have growing needs for riverine transportation. In the Upper Basin navigation from southern China is impeded by some falls and rapids on the border between Burma and Laos. In 1992 some Chinese officials were reported to have proposed blowing up these obstructions to facilitate navigation all the way down from southern China to the Gulf of Siam and the South China Sea. China would also like to see the development of a highway linking its southern provinces with the large cities and national capitals located in the Lower Basin.[27] However, if these projects are ever approved by the lower riparian states and if they are implemented, they would inject China very directly into the hydropolitics of the Lower Basin. Navigation on the Mekong will also provide China a much-prized access to the sea for possible power projections. As we shall see, given a history of conflicts with its downstream neighbors, and given their apprehensions about Chinese intentions in Southeast Asia and in the South China Sea, it is not surprising that at least some of the lower riparian states in the basin, especially Vietnam, would want to proceed very cautiously on a course that will bring China geopolitically even closer.

The Lower Mekong is currently navigable from the delta to the Laos-Kampuchea border, where further navigation is impeded by Khone Falls. Consequently, the navigation system on the river in the Lower Basin is divided into two stretches: one above the falls in Laos and the other below in Kampuchea and Vietnam.[28] Above Khone Falls in Laos, the Mekong already plays an important role in the country's transportation system, with an estimated 4,000 tons of goods being carried over the river every year. Nearly two-thirds of Laos's foreign trade is also carried over the Mekong from Thailand. The navigational needs of Laos are expected to fast accelerate as its trade with the upstream and downstream neighbors grows. To cope with its growing transportation needs, Laotian plans call for construction of two bridges spanning the Mekong, at Savannakhet in southern Laos and at Vientiane.[29] By linking the two sides of the mighty river, these bridges will greatly facilitate the movement of people and goods throughout the basin.

In Thailand, because of an extensively developed road transportation network, little use is currently made of the Mekong for navigation. However, with the mushrooming of trade between Thailand and its neighbors, this situation is changing rapidly. Estimates show that by the year 2000 the volume of trade among the upper riparians—China, Thailand, Laos, and, to a lesser extent, Myanmar—will have grown to 250,000 tons. Of this total, about 210,000 tons of cargo are expected to be transported on the Mekong and the remaining on its tributaries.[30]

In Kampuchea—a country with extensive rivers and other water bodies, but with a highly inadequate land transportation infrastructure—river transportation of people and goods has traditionally played a central and crucial role in the socioeconomic structure of the country. A significant amount of Cambodia's intraregional and international trade relies heavily on ferries plying the Mekong. These ferries are also Cambodia's gateways to Vietnam and Laos; however, after twenty years of war much of the Cambodian infrastructure for river transportation lies in ruins.

Farther down, the lowest part of the basin between the sea and Phnom Penh is already a very busy navigation artery, with the volume of traffic estimated at some 6 million tons a year. This is expected to grow to 7.2 million tons by the year 2000. With a fairly well developed river transportation system in the delta in Vietnam, ships of up to 2,000 dry weight tonnage (dwt) can travel as far as Phnom Penh; however, the meandering nature of the river in the upper reach and sedimentation in the lower reach create frequent changes in riverbed configuration. These problems may be solved only by constructing storage and flow-regulation facilities upstream of the delta.

Thus, overall, the existing and evolving economic geography of the Mekong basin provides substantial grounds for the convergence of disparate national interests of the riparian states in sustainable development of the full potential of the basin's water resources. Nonetheless, although this fact has been clearly recognized for more than four decades by some international organizations and donor countries, as well as some of the riparian states, the peculiar political geography of the individual riparian states and of the basin as whole has, in the past, put formidable barriers in the path to forging cooperation among them. Whether the recently altered geopolitical and geoeconomic situation in the region, and the ongoing political changes within each riparian state, will lead to an integrated and cooperative development of the basin is an issue to be taken up next.

Political Geography

Like its economic geography, the contemporary political geography of the Mekong basin presents a mosaic of regime types that are organized along different political ideologies, ways of governance, state-society relations, and so forth. Thailand remains a constitutional monarchy; China and Vietnam are communist states but with great differences in polity; Laos is ruled by a communist-controlled government; the Kingdom of Cambodia is struggling to become a democracy with the help of the international community;[31] and the military rulers of Burma continue to profess and practice their own peculiar brand of socialism.[32] The peoples sharing the basin are divided also by religion, ethnicity, and language, as well as widely differing levels of socioeconomic development. Nonetheless, in the aftermath of the Cold War and in a radically altered geopolitical and geoeconomic environment in Southeast Asia, all the riparian states are being forced to rethink and restructure their domestic polity and international relations. And despite many acrimonious legacies, ancient animosities seem to be giving way to cautious cooperation among the riparian states on a number of issues of common concern. Consequently, there are reasons to hope that the evolving political geography of the basin will finally lead to cooperation among the riparian states for developing and sharing the bounty that their shared water resources can help produce.

The political geography of the Mekong basin has historically been characterized by deep-seated animosities and rivalries among the three large riparian states, China, Vietnam, and Thailand, engendered mainly by expansions and contractions of their respective empires on the landscape of Southeast Asia. In this drama, though Laos and Kampuchea have often played the role of buffer zones between their powerful neighbors, their own empires have, from time to time, also expanded and contracted.[33] At different times in history, Indian culture as well as two major religions originating in India—Hinduism and Buddhism—and Chinese culture have held sway over the more indigenous cultures in some countries. These ups and downs of the indigenous empires over millennia and the cultural and religious influences originating outside the region have created a variegated political geography in the Mekong basin and within the countries sharing it. They have also left behind deep animosities and suspicions as well as transboundary affiliations among the peoples of Southeast Asia, which continue to affect relations among the states now sharing the basin.

The history and the political geography of the Mekong basin have been influenced by European domination and colonization since the mid-eighteenth century; by Japanese occupation during World War II and subsequent movements for independence in all the countries; by ravages produced by the Vietnam War, the most brutal proxy war between the superpowers in the Cold War; by Sino-Soviet, Thai-Vietnamese, and Sino-Vietnamese rivalries for ideological and strategic domination of the region; and by a plethora of conflicts among the different tribes and peoples occupying parts of the basin. Before the end of World War II, Southeast Asia had already suffered from three major wars that directly involved the great powers, and at different times parts of the region were fought for and occupied by nearly all the colonizing European powers and by Japan.[34] Thailand alone was able to escape colonization by using its traditional diplomatic skills and by making deals with the colonizers, including Japan.

Until 1954, three of the Lower Basin countries—Cambodia, Laos, and Vietnam—were French protectorates even though the Japanese had briefly occupied Vietnam between 1940 and 1945. During the time of French domination, the legal regime of the Lower Basin was based mainly upon agreements between France and Siam (Thailand), especially a treaty signed by the two in 1856. And although the Lower Mekong served as a boundary between French Indochina and Siam from 1893 onward, only in 1926 was the exact delineation of the river boundary finally decided upon by the two powers. In this respect the Lower Basin resembles the Nile basin where a local power, Egypt, and a colonial power, Britain, had together controlled a large river basin and later delineated national borders in a bilateral agreement.[35]

With the end of World War II and the eviction of Japanese forces from Southeast Asia, the European powers, especially France, attempted to regain their colonies but were met with growing movements for independence, which the Europeans tried to suppress militarily. Although the British, the Dutch, and the French, like the Japanese earlier, were all finally driven out of Southeast Asia, the region fell prey to the ideological conflict between the Soviet Union and the United States, and between China and the United States. Consequently, from the 1950s until recently, the Mekong basin has presented the most tragic and horrific examples of the ravages brought about by the Cold War. During the Vietnam War, for example, more bombs were dropped over Indochina—on Vietnam, Laos, and Kampuchea—than the total tonnage dropped by all the combatants in Europe, Asia, and Africa during World Wars I and II combined.[36] Close to sixty thousand American lives were lost in that undeclared war, mostly in the Mekong basin; estimates for non-American casualties place the number of dead and wounded in millions. While media attention in the United States has often focused on the two thousand or so American MIAs (missing in action) in Indochina, in Vietnam alone close to three hundred thousand people are still unaccounted for.[37] Countless deaths and maimings by millions of land mines that still lie buried in the region's soil continue to this day.[38] The Cold War also left behind legacies of bloody oppression and rebellions in the region, the most horrific example being the "killing fields" in Kampuchea in which upward of a million people were brutally massacred by the Khmer Rouge. The Cold War poisoned the emerging postcolonial interstate relations among the countries sharing the Mekong basin, especially relations between Vietnam and its neighbors.

Enmity between China and Vietnam has its roots in China's thousand-year-long occupation, under the Han dynasty, of the newly emergent Vietnamese civilization. Only in A.D. 939 were the Vietnamese able to restore their independence and to expand southward from their original homeland in the north. In the nineteenth century Vietnam was again defeated, this time by the French colonizers, and absorbed, along with Laos and Kampuchea, into French Indochina. After decades of struggle by communist-led guerrillas against French rule, in 1954 at the Geneva Conference the country was divided into communist-led North Vietnam and pro-Western South Vietnam. Although the Vietnamese rebellion against the colonial power was supported by communist China, some Vietnamese continue to harbor resentments against their ideological ally for agreeing to the division of their country.

During the ensuing Vietnam War, both China and the Soviet Union supported North Vietnam in its struggle against South Vietnam, and against the forces of the United States and its allies; however, historical Sino-Vietnam animosities and rivalries began to surface almost immediately after

Vietnamese reunification in 1976. A brief border war between them in 1979;[39] Chinese support for the Khmer Rouge in their struggle against the pro-Vietnamese government installed in Cambodia in 1979; Chinese claims and muscle flexing over some contested islands in the South China Sea; and the ongoing modernization of Chinese military, with greatly enhanced potential for power projection in the region are among the reasons for the continuing state of tension in Sino-Vietnamese relations. Growing links between China and other Mekong riparian states are also viewed as threatening by Vietnam; any attempts by ASEAN to integrate Laos and Cambodia into its fold without Hanoi's consent would likewise provoke Vietnamese concern.

Enmity between the Vietnamese and the Khmer people of Cambodia has existed for centuries for several reasons, among them the loss of Cambodian territory during the times of Vietnamese expansion,[40] identification of Vietnamese culture as belonging to the Chinese sphere rather than to the Indian sphere to which the Thais and the Khmers presumably belong, and adherence by the two peoples to different sects of Buddhism. Many Cambodians have resented the influence Vietnam tried to exercise over their country's affairs after the withdrawal of the French and American forces from Indochina. In more recent times, less than two months after Vietnam and the Soviet Union signed the Treaty of Friendship and Cooperation, the invasion of Cambodia by Vietnamese forces in 1978,[41] presumably to restore order in the war-ravaged country, initiated what is sometimes known as the Third Indochina War. The war pitted Vietnamese forces against the highly nationalistic and extremely brutal Khmer Rouge. The Vietnamese forces were finally forced to withdraw from Cambodia in 1989; however, this did not by any means end the historical animosity between Vietnam and the Khmer Rouge, nor did it stop the fighting between the Cambodian government and the Khmer Rouge.[42] The international community was able to broker a peace agreement between Phnom Penh and the Khmer Rouge in October 1991; the Khmer Rouge no longer exists as a fighting force but the process of democratization and national reconciliation continues to face serious challenges.

Relations between Kampuchea and Thailand have also experienced many ups and downs over time. Since the withdrawal of Vietnamese forces from Cambodia in 1989, there seems to have been some improvement in their relations; however, many areas of contention still remain. For instance, the Kampuchean government blamed Thailand for continuing to help the Khmer Rouge by giving shelter to their leader, Pol Pot, after a largely successful raid on his hideout by the Cambodian army.[43] Bangkok vehemently denied these charges, but the general feeling in the region is that some elements of the Thai business community and the army collaborated with the rebel forces in Kampuchea for personal gains.

Relations between Thailand and Vietnam continue to be affected by their traditional rivalry for domination—military, economic, and ideological—of the region, especially over the buffer states of Cambodia and Laos. Thailand has long seen itself as a natural leader in Southeast Asia, given its central location, large territory, and natural resources, and the fact that it is the only country in the region not to have been colonized. Many times in the past Thailand has collaborated with extraregional powers to boost its own status regionally and internationally and to keep Vietnam from enhancing its prowess in the region. From the Vietnamese side, the main methods for thwarting Thai ambitions in the region have been to keep Laos and Kampuchea in its camp and to exercise influence over their economies, domestic polity, and international relations. This Thai-Vietnamese rivalry has greatly impacted bilateral and multilateral relations in the Mekong basin, making it difficult in the past to achieve cooperation in developing the shared water resources.

Interstate relations in the basin are plagued also by numerous unresolved boundary disputes among the riparian states, mainly because the modern concept of clearly demarcated national boundaries did not exist in Southeast Asia until the nineteenth century. Similar to many other regions in the Third World, in modern times European colonization was instrumental in the demarcation of national borders in Southeast Asia; consequently, almost all international borders in the basin are contested by two or more parties. For example, Cambodia's current boundaries for the most part were fashioned in agreements signed by France and some countries in Southeast Asia during the colonial era. Except for a stretch of border it shares with Thailand in the north, large stretches of its national boundary do not follow any major natural features. This colonial legacy of arbitrarily drawn borders has engendered border disputes between Cambodia and Thailand, and between Cambodia and Vietnam.[44] Similarly, Laos, a country that has the distinction of sharing borders with every other riparian state in the Mekong basin, has an ongoing conflict over its border with Thailand, among others.[45]

Unresolved claims by Thailand, Vietnam, and China, and by other Southeast Asian nations, over some islands in the South China Sea are a constant source of tension in the basin.[46] These hotly contested claims may become particularly ominous as large stocks of oil begin to be discovered in the South China Sea, and as different states attempt to extend their exclusive economic zones (EEZs) by claiming territorial jurisdiction over the islands.[47] On the other hand, there is the growing possibility that some recent bilateral and multilateral efforts for resolving these complex territorial problems may facilitate cooperation in other problem areas also.[48] However, this may depend mainly on how willing China is to accommodate the interests of other claimants in exploiting and sharing the bounty of the South China Sea.

A factor further complicating relations between China and other Mekong riparian states is the presence of a large number of ethnic Chinese among the populations of the other countries. On the whole, these Chinese minorities belong to the wealthier strata in their respective countries of domicile and, for that very reason, are resented by some not-so-well-off indigenous ethnic groups.[49] Some past attempts by China to "reach out" to these expatriates and, allegedly, to incite them against rulers of other southeastern countries have engendered lingering suspicions about the loyalty of the overseas Chinese during times of possible conflict with China. The fact that three of the consistently fast-growing economies in Asia, Hong Kong, Singapore, and Taiwan, are also identified with the Chinese people only adds fuel to these resentments. The exodus of a large number of Chinese from Vietnam since the late 1970s, especially during the movement of the so-called boat people, and a spate of riots against the Chinese population in Indonesia in 1994 are just two examples of such social tensions boiling over.[50] If the mainland Chinese economy continues to grow at a faster pace than the economies of other Mekong riparian states, relations between overseas Chinese and other ethnic groups in the latter countries may well be further strained.

Relations among the Mekong riparian states are made problematic also by the process of nation building in Southeast Asia, which continues to face substantial hurdles. As Chandler and Steinberg have pointed out, "It is only quite recently that the rulers of the traditionally dominant societies have sought to establish a modern sense of allegiance to the notion of a nation-state identity, with its concomitant demand of loyalty from all its citizens living within sharply defined national boundaries."[51] As to whether this experiment in state building has been successful, another scholar, Hari Singh, has this to say, "Nation-building in Southeast Asia has been far from complete: ethnic conflict, social stratification, secessionism/irredentism, center-periphery tensions and regional parochialism are issues that refuse to go away and continue to compete with the state for loyalty." And, "Even if a case is made that the state is better able to absorb internal shocks, a number of other vulnerabilities arising from foreign debt, capital outflow, brain drain, refugee influx, natural calamities and ecological destruction will continue to undermine Southeast Asian security."[52]

Domestic politics in the Mekong riparian states has been complicated by the fact that, notwithstanding many episodic experiments with democratization, from the end of World War II to the end of the 1980s Southeast Asia had gradually drifted toward greater authoritarianism, often under very charismatic and strong leaders. As Chandler and Steinberg describe it, "By the 1980s militarized political parties controlled the government of Burma and Vietnam while politicized armies held power in Thailand and Indonesia."[53] Only recently have movements for democracy begun to acquire resilience and to have some sway in domestic politics in the region. However, as demonstrated by the recent debate over human rights, current leaders in these countries hold quite different ideas about democracy, justice, and human rights than what the West, particularly the United States, would like to see them embrace.[54] Nonetheless, as the region becomes more and more integrated in the global economy, and barring any major political setbacks, domestic politics in nearly all the Mekong riparian states is likely to become increasingly democratized. Whether further democratization and decentralization of decision-making powers in the riparian states would make cooperation easier or more difficult in the arena of hydropolitics remains an open question.

If we look at the larger picture, as far as the balance of power in the basin is concerned, although the defeat of the United States in the Vietnam War and withdrawal of American forces from Indochina had bestowed the status of a potential regional power on Vietnam,[55] the collapse of the Soviet Union has substantially weakened its regional clout by removing from the scene its powerful military ally as well as its main source of military and economic aid. At the same time, in some quarters at least, China is beginning to be seen as one of the emerging great powers of the next century.[56] Though Vietnam's ability to dominate the domestic politics of Laos and Cambodia and to dictate their international relations is on the decline, the ability of Vietnam's historical adversaries, China and Thailand, to do so is on the rise. And despite Burma's relative isolation from the larger international community, its military and economic links with China and Thailand are also growing.[57] These growing links among the two uppermost riparian states and a middle riparian state are likely to have great import for hydropolitics in the Mekong basin, as would the reentry of another actor to the scene, Japan.

Since the 1970s Japan has become the main extraregional economic actor in Southeast Asia; it is now the largest source of investment, aid, and trade for the region. The region now accounts for close to one-half of all Japanese trade and is an important source of raw materials for Japan. If large quantities of oil and hydropower can be produced in the region, Tokyo may be able to reduce its dependence on other sources, such as the Middle (Near) East, by importing energy or locating large energy-consuming industries there. However, even as the Southeast Asian countries, in general, and the poorer countries in the Mekong basin, in particular, continue to welcome these developments, nearly all fear the growing domination of their economies by Japanese capital and goods. In some quarters at least, the Japanese are seen to be again reviving the infamous "Greater East Asian Co-prosperity Sphere," a slogan they had used before and during World War II to persuade the Southeast Asian nations to move away from the Western alliance.[58] If some day Japan does decide to rearm offensively and to project military power in the Pacific Ocean and in the South China Sea, the dynamics of power balancing in the Mekong basin would undergo substantial changes.[59] Already, the ongoing modernization of Chinese military capabilities, among other strategic dynamics, is propelling Southeast Asia to become the largest importer of sophisticated weapons in the world.[60] Recent plans by Thailand to expand its navy are also causing concerns among its neighbors.[61] Thus, absent substantial American or Russian military power from the region, it may well turn out that an economically and militarily powerful Japan is welcomed by some as a balancing force in the Mekong basin while it is seen as a threat by others. Nevertheless, Japan's financial and technical means to help develop the tremendous potential of the basin's water resources, as well as its demonstrated inclination to do so given an opportunity, may well become a catalytic factor in bringing about cooperation among the riparian states.

To round up this discussion of the changing political geography of the Mekong basin, we need to point out that despite their political differences and despite the lingering suspicions and animosities from the past, all the Mekong riparian states now face some common social evils, such as the accelerating spread of AIDS, drug addiction, corruption, and prostitution, including child prostitution. Although these growing problems need to be solved individually by each country, there is a great deal of transboundary interdependence in these problem areas. For example, the growth of prostitution in Thailand, and the demand for younger and younger children it generates because of the patrons' (mostly foreign tourists) fear of contracting AIDS from older prostitutes, now impels the perpetrators of prostitution to secure their young victims not only from different parts of Thailand but also from China, Laos, Cambodia, and Burma. Many of these prostitutes contract AIDS and are then sent back to their respective countries and villages where they spread the HIV virus in their native communities.[62] Similarly, the growing trade in narcotics and the fast-spreading drug addiction in one country invite cross-border drug smuggling, in the process engendering corruption and violence throughout the region. As the level of affluence rises for some sections of their populations, leaving others economically marginalized, and as free trade and international tourism are promoted throughout the region, these social evils are likely to multiply and spread to new areas in all the countries. In this context, although interstate cooperation over the waters of the Mekong may not solve these problems, it may help create an overall environment where the riparian states can begin to deal collectively with their common and growing social problems.

Taken together, these ongoing developments are leading to significant changes in the political geography of Southeast Asia, and of the Mekong basin in particular, with the potential to radically restructure the earlier power imbalances as well as interstate and state-civil society relations. These changes have substantial implications for hydropolitics in the Mekong basin, as we shall see.

HYDROPOLITICS

Any discussion of hydropolitics in the Mekong basin must begin with the recognition that although history certainly weighs heavily on contemporary interstate relations in the basin, it has been only in the past twenty-five years—after the withdrawal of American forces from Southeast Asia and the reemergence of Vietnam as a unified state—that the riparian states have had the opportunity to directly deal with conflict and cooperation over their common water resources. And only recently have two of the six riparian states, Burma and China, which also happen to be the two uppermost riparians, become part of the basinwide dialogue for developing the hitherto unexploited potential of the Mekong's water. Significant also are efforts by the international community to help develop this potential, at least in the Lower Basin, that have continued for the past four decades, albeit with very mixed results. And as we shall see, geography continues to play a critical role in this evolving drama.

Similar to the case of the Ganges-Brahmaputra-Barak basin, historically China did not play a *direct* role in hydropolitics in the Mekong basin because physical geography of the basin prevented it from doing so. Until very recently, China's economic geography also did not require the resources and markets of Southeast Asia, nor riverine access to the South China Sea over the Mekong. Today, though China undoubtedly is the most powerful riparian state—militarily and economically—sharing the Mekong basin, its potentially hegemonic role in hydropolitics is circumscribed by some domestic and strategic imperatives it now faces. China needs domestic tranquility and rapid economic growth, as well as stability and peace on its southern borders, in order to achieve its stated goal of emerging as a global power in the next century.[63] It can thus be argued that Beijing is unlikely to use its potentially coercive power in Southeast Asia in a blatant and reckless manner for fear of alienating its downstream neighbors, who, as they have done in the past, may then be impelled to build alliances among themselves and with extraregional powers to thwart and balance the Chinese prowess. In the arena of hydropolitics, in particular, China's growing needs for hydropower, other natural resources, and access to the southern sea, all of which its downstream neighbors can make available, place China in a less hegemonic relationship with them than its uppermost riparian status and economic and military prowess would suggest. Despite its uppermost riparian status, China can only manipulate 25 percent of the Mekong's flow, which also limits its potential hegemonic role in the basin. However, this does not mean that China's strong influence on current and future hydropolitics in the Mekong basin can be ignored, especially if its ties with and influence over some downstream neighbors continue to grow.[64]

Historically, Burma has played only a marginal role in the Mekong's hydropolitics for three main reasons. First, except for forming short stretches of its border with Laos and China, the Mekong does not pass through Burmese territory. Second, the country is only recently beginning to emerge from its self-imposed political and economic isolation, and only very recently has it been able to negotiate peace agreements with some rebels in the Burmese part of the basin. Third, like China, until recently Burma's economic geography was such that the Mekong did not play a major role in its economy or polity. However, as Burma continues the process of opening up to its neighbors and looking for ways to develop its northeast region, it too is bound to be drawn more directly into the basin's hydropolitics. As we shall see, these two upper riparian states have already made some overtures in this direction, and the lower riparian states, especially Thailand, seem to be responding positively to these moves for reasons of their own.

Without China's direct involvement, Thailand could have been a major player in hydropolitics in the Lower Basin; however, it too has been prevented from playing a coercive role. As pointed out earlier, during the colonial era the river regime and international borders in the Lower Basin were regulated and demarcated primarily by agreements between Thailand and France. French control over Indochina meant that no major water projects could be launched in the Lower Basin that could adversely affect Thailand's interests. Later, during the Vietnam War and until the withdrawal of American forces from Southeast Asia, the other three Lower Basin riparian states were in no position to take any unilateral actions on shared waters that could seriously undermine Thailand's position in the basin's hydropolitics. However, the physical geography of the basin dictated that Thailand too could not develop common water resources for its own benefit without the cooperation of other riparians. Until recently, this stalemate was one of the primary reasons for the basin remaining underdeveloped for so long.

Thailand's need for water and energy has grown dramatically in the last two decades; however, its development plans for the Mekong remain constrained because, other than forming a long stretch of its border with Laos, the river does not enter Thai territory. Any major development of the river's bounty for Thailand's benefit thus remains contingent upon the cooperation of other riparian states, especially its coriparian, Laos. Although Thailand has been developing unilateral projects on some tributaries originating in and flowing through its territory, the potential benefits from developing the multiple-use potential of the Mekong mainstream continue to outweigh all the benefits from these unilateral projects. Two major projects already built in the basin to benefit Thailand, the Nam Ngum Dam and the Nong Khai Friendship Bridge,[65] required cooperation between Laos and Thailand, which bears ample testimony to this "Thai condition."

Tiny Laos has some additional advantages in the basin's hydropolitics. First, it shares borders with all the other riparian states in the basin. Whereas this makes Laos vulnerable to border conflicts with its neighbors, it also means that all the neighbors are and will be forced to interact with it indefinitely. Second, unlike Nepal and Bhutan, which are prevented from playing a balancing game or pendular diplomacy between India and China in hydropolitics because of the unhelpful physical, economic, and political geography of the Ganges-Brahmaputra-Barak basin, the geography of the Mekong basin will continue to enable Laos to benefit from its locational advantages, despite being landlocked. Given the traditional rivalries among its powerful neighbors and their growing needs for its unexploited resources and cooperation, Laos can gain substantially from the same kind of pendular diplomacy that, as we saw in the case of the Paraná–La Plata basin, has served the interests of landlocked Paraguay so well in conducting hydropolitics with its own powerful neighbors—Argentina and Brazil.[66] A significant difference in the Mekong basin of course is that as long as Laos continues to coordinate its domestic and foreign policy with Vietnam it will need to be sensitive to Vietnamese perceptions of the changing interstate relations in the basin. Laos thus needs considerable diplomatic and negotiating skills to fully benefit from the bounty that nature has so generously bestowed upon it.

Geographically, the situation of Cambodia in the basin's hydropolitics seems similar to that of Uruguay in the Paraná–La Plata basin. Historically, both countries have been buffer zones between their respective powerful neighbors, and neither is landlocked. Both are also relatively underdeveloped. There are some significant differences between their hydropolitical situations in the respective basins, however. One major difference is that Cambodia is still struggling to emerge as a viable nation-state after decades of war; the second is that neither Brazil nor Argentina currently exercises the kind of influence on the domestic politics and international relations of Uruguay as do Vietnam and Thailand over Cambodia's. Nonetheless, as Vietnamese influence in Indochina weakens, and as Cambodia begins to be independently interlinked with other neighbors and with the larger international community, it is likely to have a bigger say in the basin's hydropolitics than in the past, especially given its vast hydroelectric potential. The return of Cambodia as a full-fledged member of the Mekong Committee is also bound to impact the nature and conduct of hydropolitics in the basin substantially (see the section "International Efforts").

As the lowermost riparian on the main river, Vietnam would seem to be the most vulnerable player in the basin's hydropolitics, especially given its growing developmental needs and environmental woes in the Mekong Delta and its diminishing military prowess in the region. Some of the most cost-effective solutions for Vietnam's water-related problems in the delta may lie outside its borders, also making it highly dependent on the cooperation of its upstream neighbors. The major hydropolitical cards it currently holds are a possible denial of navigational rights up the Mekong Delta to the other riparians and withholding of consent for any large water-related project upstream. However, Vietnam is party to a long-standing agreement among the Lower Basin riparian states that recognizes the Mekong as an international waterway. Consequently, an outright or selective denial of navigation rights by Vietnam to the other riparian states would certainly lead to international protest and recriminations. As a last resort, Vietnam can try to persuade or coerce Laos and Cambodia not to cooperate with the other upstream riparian states; however, for many of the reasons mentioned above, this strategy, even if it could be successfully implemented, would now have increasing political and economic costs for Vietnam.

Thus, given the common economic needs, environmental problems, and social evils that the Mekong riparian states now face, and the fact that geography of the basin has created substantial interdependencies in these issue areas, it seems reasonable to assume that there are real incentives for all the states to develop cooperatively the full potential of the basin's hydrological resources. This understanding is further supported by our analysis of the constraints and the opportunities each riparian state faces and is likely to face in conducting hydropolitics in the basin. However, as the following historical account shows, until recently most attempts at developing the multiple-use potential of the Mekong's waters in a cooperative and integrated manner have failed. This failure and the reasons behind it are especially noteworthy in the light of more than four decades of sustained international efforts to forge cooperation in the basin.

International Efforts

In the Third World the Mekong basin stands out as a glaring example of the most extensive involvement by the international community in the efforts to develop an international river basin. Unfortunately, with few successes over a period of more than four decades, this well-intended engagement also points to the futility of such attempts, and to the mistakes and shortcomings of such endeavors, especially during the hostile climate of Cold War geopolitics.

The involvement of international organizations, especially some agencies of the United Nations, in attempts to develop the Mekong basin goes back to the end of World War II, after the withdrawal of Japanese forces from Southeast Asia.[67] As early as in 1949, recognizing the immense developmental needs of the riparian states as well as the substantial and mostly untapped hydroelectric and irrigation potential of the Lower Basin, the Economic Commission for Asia and the Far East (ECAFE, now ESCAP) had established the Bureau of Flood Control for the basin.[68] In 1952, in a report on flood control and water resources development in the basin, the principle of the river as an international waterway was clearly recognized. It is important to note, however, that in the 1950s China was not a member of the United Nations, hence precluded from participating in all UN-sponsored activities, and the isolationist Burmese leadership then showed no interest in participating in any international organization or arrangement. Thus, the two upper riparian states were excluded from the earlier international efforts to forge interstate cooperation in the Mekong basin.

Shortly after the initiation of ECAFE's efforts in the basin, in 1954 Vietnam was divided and the bureau's work was interrupted by the war between North and South Vietnam. The war also brought in the United States as a mostly disruptive player, at least in the beginning, that injected a Cold War element into the basin's fragile and evolving hydropolitics.[69] In 1957, mainly to thwart some attempts by the United States to steer the United Nations' efforts in a direction of its own liking, and to facilitate receiving international aid, the Lower Basin riparian states and the United Nations formally established the Committee for the Coordination of Investigations of the Lower Mekong Basin, popularly known as the Mekong Committee, comprising representatives of Cambodia, Laos, Thailand, and the Republic of Vietnam (South Vietnam).[70] The technical and planning branch of the committee has since been known as the Mekong Secretariat.

In the early 1960s relations among the Lower Basin riparian states were, on the whole, quite harmonious. During that period, under the Johnson administration, the United States was also very enthusiastic about helping to develop the basin in an integrated manner, along the lines of the projects undertaken by the Tennessee Valley Authority (TVA) back home. President Johnson, in particular, saw multilateral cooperation in the Mekong basin as an alternative to armed conflict and in 1965 promised a hefty sum of $1 billion to support ECAFE's initiatives in the basin.[71] However, the same year U.S. involvement in the Vietnam War escalated dramatically and U.S. funding for developing the basin began to wane and then to level off.[72] Nonetheless, efforts by the United Nations and by some philanthropic organizations continued during this period of turmoil. In particular, a report prepared by a renowned geographer, Gilbert White, with Ford Foundation support, helped broaden the scope of investigations beyond purely project-centered engineering and technical concerns to include the adverse socioeconomic impacts of large projects.[73] The United Nations, and Asian Development Bank, and a group of donor countries, including

Australia, Canada, France, Germany, Japan, New Zealand, the Netherlands, the United Kingdom, and the United States, also continued to provide funds to cover the cost of planning, scientific investigations, and feasibility studies initiated by the Mekong Committee. The World Bank came into the picture in 1969 when U Thant, the secretary-general of the United Nations, requested the bank's assistance to review the Indicative Basin Plan then being prepared by a team of international consultants hired by the Mekong Committee.

Some of the mainstream projects proposed in the 1970 Indicative Basin Plan, such as Pa Mong (4,800 megawatts), Sambor (3,400 megawatts), and Strung Treng (7,200 megawatts), would have been among the largest hydroelectric power projects in the world at the time.[74] In addition, by 1970 the Mekong Committee had developed a giant scheme for building a cascade of seven dams on the Lower Mekong to store 142 billion cubic meters of water, which could be released in the dry season to irrigate 4.3 million hectares of rice fields and to generate 24,200 megawatts of electricity.

These ambitious plans notwithstanding, in the volatile political climate of the 1970s the Mekong Committee was forced to concentrate on smaller tributary projects within the respective territories of the Lower Basin riparian states. In 1975, following the victory of the Khmer Rouge, Cambodia withdrew from membership in the committee, bringing all work on the projects involving that country to an immediate halt. Consequently, in 1978 the other three lower riparians were forced to constitute the Interim Committee, with the understanding that the full Mekong Committee would be revived when Cambodia agreed to return as a full-fledged member.

After 1978 regular consultations on projects relating to the Mekong were held by the Interim Committee, and the Mekong Secretariat continued to carry out research, to develop new projects, and to coordinate the members' activities in the basin. However, new problems arose in 1991 when Thailand, using the occasion of Cambodia's request for reviving its membership in the Mekong Committee, tried to bring about a change in the responsibilities and obligations of the members that had been in place since a 1975 agreement among them. That agreement, signed by the four member states, required each to provide the others with detailed information on any project involving the waters of the Mekong as well as its tributaries. Any project on these waters also required the approval of all members before it could be implemented. This particular clause thus gave every member state a virtual veto power over all the intended projects in the basin.[75] Mainly to circumvent this clause, in 1991 Thailand began to insist that the 1975 agreement be fully superseded by a less restrictive 1978 agreement that would enable it to divert the Mekong's water to its northeast region. Around this time, Thailand also took some steps to involve Burma and China in the discussions for developing the basin and to suggest that these upper riparian states should be allowed to join the Mekong Committee. In response, Vietnam, while accepting in principle some revision of the existing agreements, refused to go along with Thailand's maneuvers. As things stand, Burma and China have not become full-fledged members of the regional institution and Vietnam continues to object to Thailand's plans for diverting any water from the Mekong's mainstream.[76]

In the end, more than four decades after the initiation of international efforts in the basin, most plans for developing the full potential of the basin's waters remain mere blueprints. Not a single dam has yet been built across the Lower Mekong; the only hydroelectric project built under the Mekong Committee's sponsorship is at Nam Ngum within Laotian territory.

The failure of international efforts, especially the plans prepared by the agencies of the United Nations, to bring about an integrated and cooperative development of the Mekong basin has been a subject of much critical scrutiny. Among the critics, Syed S. Kirmani has identified the following reasons for the ineffectiveness of the United Nations' efforts.

> First, the objectives of the U.N. for developing the Mekong for promoting economic development and peace in the region were not shared by the riparian countries. . . .
>
> Second, the role of the riparian countries (themselves) in the Mekong Secretariat was rather nominal. . . .
>
> Third, the projects prepared by the Secretariat were too grand and too inconsistent with the current and foreseeable needs of the countries. . . .
>
> Fourth, the considerable external resources devoted to planning and investigations of the projects did not benefit the riparian countries. The assistance of donor countries was utilized mostly to finance their own experts and consulting firms while the United Nations funds were applied mainly to support the administrative costs of the Mekong Secretariat which was managed by foreign experts.[77]

Thus, overall, "the Mekong project was a classic example of external effort, external management and external planning with little involvement of the (supposed) beneficiaries. Lastly, the water resources of the basin were so vast that there was no conflict over their use."

Now, many of the projects supported and proposed by the Mekong Committee are coming under increasing attack for their likely environmental and socioeconomic impacts in the basin.[78] Growing sensitivity of international organizations and donors to protests by local and international environmental groups is likely to make it very difficult to launch large water projects, especially dams and hydropower projects, in the basin. Consequently, more sustainable and equitable alternatives, which also engage and involve all peoples affected by such projects, will need to be explored if the multiple-use potential of the basin's water resources is ever to be realized.[79]

What the critical appraisals of international efforts in the Mekong basin fail to take into account, however, are the geopolitical situation in Southeast Asia during the Cold War and the acrimonious history of interstate relations among the riparian states. These appraisals also do not pay due consideration to the changing economic and political geography of the basin, nor to the earlier lack of consciousness of environmental implications of developmental activities—a consciousness that has only recently begun to enter the sustainability discourse, not only in the basin but globally. Seen in this light, some observers of the situation are inclined to conclude that under the difficult circumstances it has faced, the Mekong Committee did a reasonably good job.[80] Not only did it bring about cooperation between Thailand and Laos for the Nam Ngum project, it has also supported numerous scientific and technical studies that will be needed if basinwide cooperation becomes possible. Most important, perhaps, the mere survival of the committee through nearly four decades of acrimonious relations among the riparian states has been instrumental in keeping the idea of basinwide cooperation alive.

The failures of past international efforts notwithstanding, the Mekong Secretariat, clearly recognizing the emerging problems of sustainable development of the basin as a whole, prepared a progress report in February 1993 that identified the following objectives for an integrated environmental program for the basin:

- to ensure that projects for the development of water and related resources are planned and implemented in such a manner that sustainability is achieved and negative impacts are minimized;
- to help create better understanding in the riparian countries and the Mekong Secretariat about environmental problems and risks in the (Lower) Mekong Basin;
- to increase the capability of the riparian countries for investigation, analyses, and evaluation of environmental parameters; and environmental planning, screening, and impact assessment;

- to continue the integration of Cambodia in the environmental program; and
- to assist the riparian countries in achieving the goals in their national plans for sustainable development.

Toward this aim, the Mekong Secretariat set in motion a series of initiatives relating to the development of databases, procedures, and tools for environmental impact assessment, monitoring of key environmental parameters, and training of technical personnel.[81]

Clearly, the ambitious plans for a long-term, comprehensive, and sustainable development of the basin's hydrological resources cannot be realized without an extraordinary degree of trust and cooperation among the riparian states, and without substantial financial and technical aid from the international community. However, notwithstanding all the hurdles to be overcome on the way, recent changes in the geopolitical situation and in interstate relations in the basin do offer substantial hope that an enlightened beginning on the road to prosperity and welfare for the basin's inhabitants can be made soon and sustained over the long run. For instance, in April 1994, following the inauguration of the Friendship Bridge between Thailand and Laos, high-level ministers representing all the six riparian states met in Hanoi under the auspices of the Asian Development Bank (ADB) to approve, in principle, more than a dozen projects involving cross-border cooperation in the basin. These projects span such areas as transportation, power generation, and environmental protection, among others. The price tag for these projects is estimated to be more than $12 billion. The ADB was reported to be very hopeful of securing the required financing for these projects. Further studies are planned for several priority road projects, including a Bangkok–Phnom Penh–Ho Chi Minh City–Vung Tau highway; an east-west road link between Thailand, Laos, and a Vietnamese port; and a highway between Chiang Rai in Thailand and Kunming in China through Burma and Laos.[82]

Going further, on April 5, 1995, the Lower Basin riparian states entered into the Agreement on the Cooperation for the Sustainable Development of the Mekong River Basin. This agreement, signed by the foreign ministers of Laos, Thailand, and Vietnam, and by the deputy prime minister of Cambodia, replaces the 1957 statute of the Mekong Committee, the 1975 Joint Declaration, and the 1978 Declaration concerning the committee, as well as all rules of procedure adopted under those agreements. Under the new agreement, the four signatories have agreed:

> To cooperate in all fields of sustainable development, utilization, management and conservation of the water and related resources of the Mekong River Basin including, but not limited to irrigation, hydro-power, navigation, flood control, fisheries, timber floating, recreation and tourism, in a manner to optimize the multiple-use and mutual benefits of all riparians and to minimize the harmful effects that might result from natural occurrence and man-made activities.[83]

The 1995 agreement reconstituted the Mekong Secretariat and the Interim Committee as the Mekong River Commission, with the status of an international body. The commission comprises three permanent bodies—the Council, the Joint Committee, and the Secretariat—and is composed of one member from each participating riparian state at the ministerial and cabinet level who are empowered to make policy decisions on behalf of the respective governments. The chairmanship of the council is for a rotating term of one year, according to the reverse alphabetical listing of the participating countries. What is highly significant for the nature and conduct of hydropolitics in the Mekong basin in the future is that the 1995 agreement makes provision for any other riparian state that agrees to accept the riparian rights and obligations stipulated under the agreement to become a party to the agreement with the consent of the existing members. In essence, this has opened the way for Burma and China to seek membership in the Mekong River Commission. These continuing international and regional efforts to bring all the riparian states together, despite their other differences, do offer concrete hope that the worst days of the Mekong basin may be over.

SUMMARY AND CONCLUSION

After more than four decades of international and regional efforts, the Mekong remains one of the least developed international rivers in the world. Although lamentable from the perspective of the missed opportunities for enhancing the welfare of millions of its inhabitants, this lack of development also means that the opportunity to develop the abundant multiple-use potential of the basin's waters in an integrated and sustainable manner still lies ahead. The Mekong basin thus presents a unique opportunity to its six riparian states and the international community to design and implement more enlightened and cooperative developmental programs to exploit the basin's hydrological resources than has been and is the case in other international basins in the Third World.

What lessons does hydropolitics in the Mekong basin hold for other international basins in the Third World? First, as some critical appraisals of the long-standing regional and international efforts in this basin have highlighted, unless there is a real or perceived severe water-related crisis in a basin, and unless the riparian states are themselves fully involved in all institution building, plan formulations, and so forth for the development of the basin, cooperation among them is not possible. External efforts to prematurely bring some or all the parties together or to fashion policies and programs without their full participation are not likely to bear fruit. International organizations and donors can play only a facilitative and supportive role in bringing the parties together and in instigating cooperation among them. This is particularly the case for a basin where historical animosities and an unhelpful geopolitical situation had, until recently, not allowed international efforts to move beyond the level of advocacy.

Second, this case study shows that if the power balance in an international basin is not conducive to the emergence of a powerful regional hegemon, cooperation over the shared waters cannot be fashioned by coercion from the outside or from within the region. In the past, without China's direct involvement in the Lower Basin's hydropolitics, the presence of two almost equally strong riparian states, Thailand and Vietnam, had prevented either from fully dominating hydropolitics in the Lower Basin. However, this situation could change radically if Thailand were to pursue a highly aggressive foreign policy, perhaps with the aid of China, and if the power of Vietnam to influence events in the region, militarily if necessary, were to decline radically. An interesting outcome of this semblance of a power balance between the two large states in the Lower Basin is that it may allow the two weaker states, Laos and Kampuchea, to benefit from playing a balancing game or practicing pendular diplomacy between their powerful neighbors. In this sense, this case is similar in some respects to the case of the Paraná–La Plata basin where Argentina and Brazil have played similar roles in hydropolitics as Thailand and Vietnam have done in the Lower Basin. In the former basin, cooperation between Brazil and Paraguay impelled Argentina to court Paraguay and Uruguay, finally leading to cooperation among all the riparian states. In the Mekong basin, bilateral cooperation between Laos and Thailand, and Cambodia and Thailand, on the one hand, and between Laos and Vietnam, and Cambodia and Vietnam, on the other hand, seems to be leading to a similar outcome, in the Lower Basin at least. The major difference, of course, is that hydropolitics in the Paraná–La Plata basin is not clouded by the shadow of a real or potential great power, such as China.

Third, the findings here again underscore the substantial role, both facilitative and constraining, that geography has played, and continues to play, in shaping hydropolitics in an international basin. Thus, while the physical geography of the Mekong basin and the changing economic geography of the riparian states sharing it have created substantial grounds for the convergence of national interests in developing and exploiting its hydrological resources, until recently the same geographical features have also prevented China from playing a direct role in the basin's hydropolitics. In the past, political geography of the basin was also not conducive to engendering bilateral or multilateral cooperation. Now, the changing political and economic geography of the basin in the post–Cold War era is impelling the riparian states to explore ways of cooperating with one another in a myriad of ways, including the sharing of the bounty their shared water resources can help produce. But as shown by other cases also, geographical factors do not operate in isolation. The importance of geographical variables continues to be circumscribed by the larger geopolitical situation and by the evolution of interstate relations in an international basin.

Fourth, like the previous case studies, this case study also shows that despite unresolved conflicts in other issue areas, as, for example, the territorial conflict between Thailand and Laos, cooperation in hydropolitics is still possible under certain circumstances. However, bilateral cooperation on specific projects is easier to achieve than multilateral cooperation. Nonetheless, for certain purely scientific and data-gathering projects, which may later become inputs into a multilateral plan, it may be possible for the international community to get the parties together and achieve a semblance of cooperation. In any case, in the end, a situation is inevitably reached in every international basin when all states sharing it have to come together at least to consider basinwide cooperation. Whether such cooperation does actually emerge remains, of course, subject to the specific circumstances and factors impinging on hydropolitics in the specific basin.

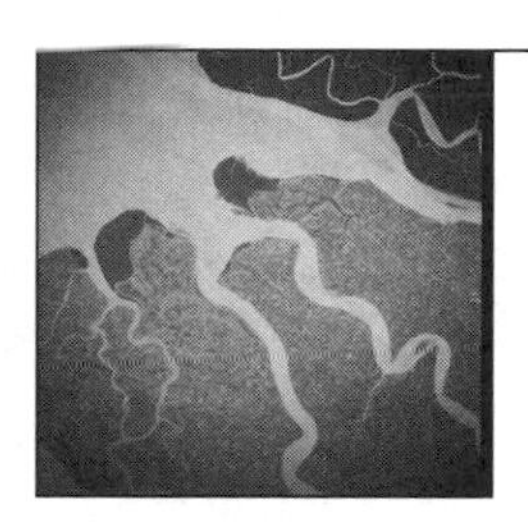

Conclusion

This long journey through six major international river basins has plainly demonstrated the urgent and growing need for the international community in general, and for Third World states in particular, to acquire a sophisticated and nuanced understanding of hydropolitics. This is because while the demand for water for multiple societal needs is growing rapidly in all the arid and semiarid regions of the Third World, water is becoming an increasingly scarce, economically prized, politically charged, and environmentally degraded natural resource. Most of the remaining major sources of freshwater that can be further developed to serve the growing and competing demands in such regions are in river basins that are shared by two or more sovereign states—a state of affairs that gives hydropolitics a promethean potential to ignite acute interstate and intrastate conflicts, but that also impels states to seek ways to cooperate with their neighbors.

In a situation of growing competition for transboundary water resources, the riparian states sharing international river basins are confronted with what seems like a simple choice: either to engage in protracted and costly conflicts with their neighbors over the rights of ownership and use of water resources, or to cooperate with their neighbors to develop and share the bounty that water in its multiple uses can help produce. In practice, of course, the choice is never so straightforward, for a multitude of factors and forces greatly complexify each situation. As the cases studied here have shown, the choices that are and can be made by states in conducting hydropolitics with their neighbors depend on the *unique* combinations of the geographical features of a given basin with a multiplicity of historical, political, economic, social, strategic, and cultural factors and circumstances specific to that basin.

Although this uniqueness of hydropolitics in each international river basin does not allow for rigorous analytical generalizations or universal policy prescriptions, the comparative case study approach adopted here has produced some general findings and "contingent generalizations" that should help policymakers and concerned citizens to better understand the complex and often contentious nature of hydropolitics between states.[1] Such enhanced understanding and knowledge, it is to be hoped, may in turn help spur the development of more effective means of preventing acute conflicts and facilitating hydropolitical cooperation in the Third World.

This chapter begins by underlining the complexity of hydropolitics and summarizing key findings regarding its relationships to geography, conflict, and cooperation. We then look to the future by assessing, first, those factors that can impede cooperation, and second, those that may promote it. The first group includes a broad range of political, economic, and technical impediments. More encouraging is the second group, which interestingly includes a number of factors generated by the complex interdependencies that hydropolitics inevitably produces.

THE COMPLEXITY OF HYDROPOLITICS

> *Hydropolitics is characterized by great complexity; it is, indeed, one of the most complex arenas of interaction between states that share international river basins. Furthermore, the level of complexity increases with the level of interdependency among the riparians, and interdependency increases as the demand for water grows.*

As the case studies have underscored, transboundary water resources tie up all the riparian states sharing an international basin into a highly complex web of environmental, economic, political, and security interdependencies. These interdependencies, which only grow with time as the need for and competition over the shared water resources rise, compel riparian states to interact with one another indefinitely, making them vulnerable to the vagaries of geopolitics, interstate relations, and domestic politics in an anarchic international system.

In the Third World particularly, colonial-era legacies of contested national borders and divided ethnic spaces; imperatives of state building and national integration; growing competition for transboundary water resources to satisfy multiple societal needs; and lack of financial, technical, and organizational resources and capabilities combine to make hydropolitics a highly complex arena of interstate relations. The inherent uncertainties in all estimations of future water supplies and demand, together with the unpredictability of interstate relations and domestic politics, confront Third World states with complex issues, dilemmas, and trade-offs in conducting hydropolitics with their neighbors. The intricacy of hydropolitics is multiplied in those basins where various sets of riparian states share more than one major river basin, as is the case in the Paraná–La Plata, the Euphrates-Tigris, and the Ganges-Brahmaputra-Barak basins.

Some scholars have suggested that interstate cooperation on such low-politics issues as water sharing may enhance the possibility of reconciliation, compromise, and cooperation in the arena of high politics. Others have argued that the resolution of interstate water conflicts must wait until states have resolved their disputes in the realm of high politics. However, the cases studied here clearly show that in a situation of growing competition and contestation over transboundary water resources, hydropolitics inevitably becomes inextricably intertwined with a multiplicity of issues involving both low and high politics among the riparian states, and it becomes very difficult to clearly demarcate one political domain from the other.

GEOGRAPHY AND HYDROPOLITICS

> *Geography sets the stage and largely defines the overall parameters for the nature and conduct of hydropolitics among states that share international basins. Geography also helps to define the relative bargaining powers of the riparian states and to dictate where and when interstate conflicts may arise, which riparian states may be involved, and what kind of cooperation may emerge among and between which states.*

The *physical* geography of a basin—including its topography, hydrology, geology, and meteorology—defines the overall parameters for the spatial and temporal availability and scarcity of water in the basin as a whole and in each of the riparian states; the degree of dependence of each riparian on the transboundary water resources; and the kind of water projects—whether for navigation, generation of hydroelectric power, irrigation, or so forth—

that can be constructed within the basin. The *economic* geography of the basin defines the locational and quantitative parameters of the changing demand for water for different needs, as well as the nature and amount of resources that different actors can invest to deal with their water deficits. And it is in the realm of *political* geography that conflict and cooperation among riparian states sharing an international basin are played out. Thus, geography defines both the constraints on and the possibilities for conflict and cooperation over the transboundary water resources.

A comparison of hydropolitics in the Ganges-Brahmaputra-Barak and Mekong basins highlights the way that specific geographical features, individually or collectively, shape the nature and conduct of hydropolitics. The Brahmaputra and the Mekong both originate in Tibet, and both traverse a long course through Chinese territory before entering the downstream riparian states. This could have made China, the uppermost and militarily most powerful riparian state, a potential hegemon in hydropolitics in both basins. However, the insurmountable Himalayas on the northern borders of South Asia and the rapids on the Laos-Burma border have so far denied China access to the lower reaches of the two rivers. The spatio-temporal pattern of precipitation in both basins also denies China the opportunity to alter drastically the flow of the two rivers before they enter the downstream states. Thus, physical geography has moderated the potentially hegemonic role China could otherwise have played in each basin's hydropolitics.

Yet, changes in the economic geography of southeast China and Southeast Asia as a whole, and the consequent growing demands for hydropower and an integrated regionwide transportation infrastructure, including riverine navigation, are impelling the riparian states in the Mekong basin to explore new ways of cooperating with their neighbors. In the Ganges-Brahmaputra-Barak basin, in contrast, China is unlikely to push for basinwide cooperation any time soon, in part because of the controversial status of Tibet in its polity, and in part because the economic geography of southwest China and South Asia does not yet require such cooperation. Thus, in the Mekong basin the prospects for basinwide hydropolitical cooperation are improving, whereas in the Ganges-Brahmaputra-Barak basin they remain poor.

In both basins, China has been involved in wars over contested borders and territories with other potential regional powers, namely, India and Vietnam. Consequently, both India and Vietnam have been suspicious of any moves by China to develop close economic and military ties to other regional states or to play a substantial role in the hydropolitics of the shared river basins. Access to the Indian Ocean and the South China Sea—perhaps via a combination of surface transportation and riverine navigation on the shared waterways—would greatly benefit China, but India and Vietnam are not likely to facilitate such access until their own relations with China have reached an unprecedented level of trust. Thus, the changing political geography of South Asia and Southeast Asia will continue to have substantial impacts on hydropolitics in the respective basins.

Although geography plays the leading role in defining the range of hydropolitical constraints and possibilities, geography alone is insufficient to determine the nature, conduct, and outcome of hydropolitics in an international basin.

The case studies show that the nature, conduct, and outcome of hydropolitics in an international basin depend not merely on how the geographical features of the basin combine with one another but also on how they combine with other factors and circumstances. For example, physical geography has endowed Ethiopia—the source of 85 percent of the Nile's water—with a tremendous potential for hydropower generation, water storage, and irrigation. Not only impoverished Ethiopia but also the two large downstream riparians, Sudan and Egypt, would benefit substantially if the multiple-use potential of these water resources could be fully and cooperatively developed. However, as we have seen, this has not happened for a variety of reasons: certain legacies of the colonial era and the Cold War, the contentious nature of Ethiopia's relations with its downstream but more powerful neighbors, the aftermath of the long civil war that led to the independence of Eritrea, and, most importantly, Egyptian warnings against any upstream alteration of the flow of the Nile without its consent.

Another illustration of the way in which specific combinations of geographical features and other factors impact hydropolitics is provided by differences in the relative bargaining powers of some landlocked riparian states in international basins. In the Paraná–La Plata basin, Paraguay, because of its strategic location and the historic rivalry between Brazil and Argentina for regional domination, has been able to play a form of pendular diplomacy between its two powerful neighbors in the hydropolitics of the basin and reap substantial economic rewards by cooperating with both. In the Mekong basin, Laos may be able to pursue much the same strategy vis-à-vis China, Thailand, and Vietnam. In the Ganges-Brahmaputra-Barak basin, however, the opportunity for Nepal to exert similar strategic leverage is likely to be limited by the physical geography of the basin, as well as by the possibility of a growing rapprochement between India and China. Even so, Nepal does have considerable leverage in hydropolitics because geography dictates that India must seek cooperation with Nepal if it wants to significantly improve the water and energy situation within its own territory in the shared basin.

WATER AND CONFLICT

> *The potential for acute interstate conflict over transboundary water resources in international basins arises primarily because rivers flowing and meandering across and along international borders make it problematic for the riparian states to defend core interests and pursue prized goals: sovereignty, territorial integrity, national security, economic development, and social welfare.*

As John Waterbury has pointed out, there is an inherent conflict between, on the one hand, the imperatives of nation building and national self-interest that a sovereign state is expected and driven to pursue and, on the other hand, the multinational rights relating to the ownership, control, and use of river waters that transgress international borders. The problems associated with this kind of conflict are likely to be especially acute in the Third World, where the newly emergent states are often reluctant to accept any dilution of their sovereignty, including that necessitated by bilateral and multilateral treaties and accords governing the use of river water.[2] In a situation of growing water scarcity, the highly complex and multidimensional interdependencies created by transboundary water resources constrain states from asserting their sovereignty and unilaterally pursuing the goals of national security, economic development, and social welfare.

Although national security has traditionally been viewed as comprising the physical and military-strategic security of a state and its citizens, the cases studied here have clearly shown that water security is now an essential component of national security in the arid and semiarid regions of the Third World. This is because all the new constituents of the expanded definition of national security—human security, food security, economic security, and environmental security—can be seriously undermined by water scarcity.[3]

The security dimension of transboundary water resources is most apparent in the case of some downstream states such as Egypt and Iraq, whose very survival depends on assured access to water resources that originate outside their borders. The water-security linkage is also evident in those basins where a river forms the border between two or more riparian states. In such cases, not only do meandering rivers threaten the borders and territorial integrity of the riparian states, but any major activity by one state on the banks or in the mainstream of the shared rivers can be perceived as threatening the security of the co-riparians.

Among the cases examined in this study, the Jordan, Euphrates-Tigris, and Nile basins highlight the potential of hydropolitics to ignite and fuel acute interstate conflicts. Hydropolitics has already played an important role in instigating armed hostilities in the Jordan basin, and on several occasions the Euphrates-Tigris basin has been brought to the brink of war by a conflict over water. Repeated warnings by Egyptian leaders that they would declare war on any upstream state that attempts to reduce the flow of the Nile are clear reminders of how far some Third World states may be prepared to go to protect their water security.

There is little doubt that in the absence of multilateral agreements for the cooperative development and sharing of transboundary water resources, the potential for acute interstate conflicts will keep escalating in all the international basins in the Third World. However, whether or not states will actually go to war with their neighbors over water will depend on the interplay of a broad range of factors and circumstances specific to each basin.

> *While states may not be inclined or able to go to war with their neighbors over shared water resources, unresolved conflicts over transboundary water resources will continue to undermine interstate relations in international river basins.*

As long as disputes over water persist, they will obstruct the development of amicable relations among the riparian states sharing an international river basin. In the absence of hydropolitical cooperation, heightened competition for water will necessarily lead to a downward spiral of deteriorating interstate relations in a shared basin. In the case of Bangladesh, India, and Nepal, for example, it is difficult to imagine these states making a substantial improvement in their contentious bilateral and multilateral relations until the problems associated with the development and sharing of water resources in the Ganges-Brahmaputra-Barak basin are resolved to the satisfaction of *all* the parties. The progress that Bangladesh and India made by negotiating the 1996 Ganges Water Treaty is certainly encouraging but it is not sufficient to radically transform the character of interstate relations in the basin.

Interstate relations are similarly strained in the Nile basin, where Egypt, Ethiopia, and Sudan have each blamed the others from time to time of fomenting unrest and supporting rebellions within their neighbors' territories. In the Euphrates-Tigris, Jordan, and Mekong basins, relations of Turkey, Israel, and Vietnam with their neighbors are also closely linked to the vicissitudes in the hydropolitics of the respective basins.

Even if water wars do not take place, water scarcity can lead to acute interstate conflicts. The economic, environmental, political, and security problems engendered by rising water scarcity, by the lack of cooperation among riparian states, and by real or perceived threats to water security can create serious domestic instability and conflicts in one or more riparian states, the effects of which are likely to spill over into neighboring states.

Water is not only an essential biological need and an increasingly valuable economic good; it is also *the* most politicized natural resource. In ancient civilizations, those who controlled a society's access to water resources received enormous political and economic benefits and enjoyed almost godlike status as the givers and sustainers of life. In the modern world, in developed and developing countries alike, the allocation of available water supplies across different societal groups, economic sectors, and geographical areas remains a highly politicized issue. When water becomes scarce, its political salience inevitably rises and the likelihood of domestic unrest increases.

New and antagonistic group identities can be constructed or imposed around changes in the allocations of scarce water supplies between and within states. As Ted Hopf has pointed out, "Identities become real in the face of some kind of resource scarcity. Or . . . identities become possible given the possession of some level of resources."[4] The economic benefits and costs that every water-related policy or project creates bring into existence new interest groups and constituencies that can seriously undermine or threaten the power and privileges of other stakeholders. Consequently, disputes over water allocations can become intertwined with and aggravate other sources of societal friction—such as those rooted in economic disparities, ethnic tensions, religious rivalries, or linguistic discrimination. In some cases—for instance, the "Kurdish problem" in the Euphrates-Tigris basin and the rebellion in Southern Sudan in the Nile basin—domestic strife can also be exploited by antagonistic riparian states to serve their own hydropolitical interests. At the very least, a continuing state of domestic upheaval in one or more of the riparian states that share an international basin can make it very difficult to develop basinwide cooperation, as has been the case in the Nile basin and until recently in the Mekong basin.

WATER AND COOPERATION

> *In nearly all international river basins, interstate hydropolitical cooperation can be shown to be a "win-win" game in the long run for all the riparian states, especially when the full costs of noncooperation and lost opportunities are factored into cost-benefit analyses.*

In a situation of growing water scarcity, states that share river basins are naturally inclined to view hydropolitics as a "zero-sum" game where one player's gain is seen as another's loss. However, although this simple algebra may appear valid in the short term, it is deeply flawed when applied over the long term. Short-term calculations of gains and losses fail to take into account the economic, political, social, and environmental costs that a lack of hydropolitical cooperation continues to extract from *all* the players. Short-term calculations also fail to factor in the substantial opportunity costs that all the players continue to incur by not cooperating with their neighbors. From a long-term perspective, lack of cooperation in international basins turns out to be a "lose-lose" or "beggar-thy-neighbor" game for all the players.

A case in point is the Ganges-Brahmaputra-Barak basin, one of the most resource-rich basins in the Third World, but also one of the most impoverished. In the absence of an integrated basinwide development initiative, India has benefited substantially by exploiting the potential of the shared rivers within its own territory, but millions of its citizens living in the basin continue to suffer from abject poverty. A persisting state of underdevelopment in the neighboring countries, as well as the political and societal tensions engendered in the border regions of India by the influx of a large number of economically deprived Bangladeshi and Nepalese citizens, continue to pose serious political and security problems for India. By objecting strongly to India's proposals for developing the shared rivers, by raising the issue of water sharing in international forums, and by blaming India and Nepal for floods and ecological degradation downstream, Bangladesh too has paid a heavy price in the past. Recent efforts by the three countries to reconcile their differences and search for ways to cooperatively develop the vast potential of their shared water resources indicate a turn toward a win-win approach.

It is also interesting to note that the advantages of hydropolitical cooperation are such that even states that are hostile to each other in other issue-areas sometimes have explicit agreements or implicit ("covert") understandings for sharing and managing their common transboundary water resources. The covert hydropolitical cooperation between Israel and Jordan, which coexisted with and then outlasted a state of war between the two countries, is a case in point. Even without a formal peace agreement or an explicit water-sharing agreement, Israel and Jordan were reported to hold informal meetings on a regular basis (the Picnic Table Talks on the banks of the Jordan River), to share data and technological know-how to enhance the efficiency of water use in different sectors, and to permit their scholars, technical experts, and concerned citizens to meet and exchange views. The continuing, though intermittent and as-yet unsuccessful, attempts by Iraq, Turkey, and Syria to find ways to share the water resources of the Euphrates-Tigris basin, testify to hydropolitics' ability to encourage cooperation.

> *Although sovereign states are inherently inclined to exploit "their" water resources unilaterally, in the end even the strongest riparian states sharing international basins are compelled to seek some form of cooperation with their weaker neighbors.*

This remarkable finding testifies to the power of hydropolitics to create inescapable interdependencies among riparian states. As a general rule, states first turn to unilateral means to deal with their growing needs for water, but when these means have been exhausted and shortages persist or new demands develop, states are forced to recognize their hydrological interdependencies and the "common pool" nature of their transboundary water resources. Even the most reluctant states are ultimately compelled to seek cooperation with their neighbors because, in a situation of growing water scarcity, hydrological interdependencies restrict the unilateral options available to the riparian states while inflating the environmental, economic, political, and social costs of noncooperation or hydropolitical procrastination.

In several of the cases studied here, a move from unilateralism to bilateralism to multilateralism in hydropolitics is apparent. In the Paraná–La Plata basin, Brazil had historically preferred to construct water projects within its own territory to deal with its growing needs for water and energy. However, having exhausted the more easily available and cost-effective solutions, Brazil was impelled to seek cooperation with its neighbors, resulting in the

Itaipu project with Paraguay. In recent years, as Brazil's need for a regionally integrated market in Latin America has grown, so has her propensity to explore multilateral cooperation in the arena of hydropolitics. A similar pattern can be discerned in India's conduct of hydropolitics in the Ganges-Brahmaputra-Barak basin. In the Middle East, after building the National Water Carrier and cooperating with Jordan on some water projects, Israel has been pushing for multilateral talks to resolve water disputes in the Jordan basin.

Hydropolitical cooperation may take a very long time to develop, may not necessarily lead to the optimal development and allocation of the shared water resources, may not satisfy or benefit all parties equally, and may not be possible without sustained third-party mediation and support; however, once achieved, such cooperation tends to endure.

Although states may take more than a decade, on average, to negotiate water accords, and although there can never be any long-term guarantees about their sustainability, once states enter into such accords they find it very difficult to ignore or abrogate them. The specific provisions of some water agreements and accords may be questioned over time by one or more riparian states, and some terms and provisions may have to be renegotiated, but on the whole such treaties and accords tend to have a high survival rate, despite the vagaries of domestic and international politics.

The 1960 Indus Water Treaty between India and Pakistan is one of the best examples of a water-sharing agreement that has stood the test of time despite serious threats to its survival. Brokered and supported by a neutral third party, the World Bank, as well as by many friendly governments, the treaty continues to be honored despite two wars in the basin, in 1965 and 1971, as well as a continuing state of hostility between the two countries over the contested status of Kashmir—the region where some of the shared rivers that form the Indus basin originate or pass through. Although certain provisions of the Indus Water Treaty have been called into question by one or the other party from time to time, such problems continue to be resolved according to the understandings and mechanisms laid out in the treaty itself.

It is also interesting to note that although the legitimacy of some earlier water accords in the Third World is increasingly being questioned by some states, such agreements continue to form the basis for negotiating new agreements. Thus, for example, several provisions of the 1959 treaty between Egypt and Sudan—and indeed the treaty itself—have been called into question by the upstream riparian states in the Nile basin, but it is difficult to imagine a multilateral agreement in the basin that does not somehow build upon the 1959 treaty. In other cases, proposals put forward by third parties for integrated basinwide development, although not formally accepted by the riparian states, continue to serve as the blueprints against which new proposals are often evaluated. The Johnston Plan for the Jordan basin and the integrated plans proposed for the Mekong basin in the past continue to have important implications for hydropolitics in the two basins. In the Nile basin, the Century Storage Scheme continues to be evoked from time to time.

* * *

Given that hydropolitical cooperation is almost invariably a win-win option, that it is indeed all but inevitable in the long run, and that it tends to endure, why do some Third World states that are facing or will soon face severe water scarcity not cooperate with their neighbors? We try to answer this perplexing question in the next section, which, drawing on the contingent generalizations the case studies have produced, explores the range of impediments that stand in the way of cooperation. Thereafter, we turn to those factors that can promote cooperation.

GROUNDS FOR DESPAIR: NONCOOPERATION

Because of the inherent complexity of hydropolitics, a dismaying array of political, economic, and technical obstacles stands in the way of cooperation among Third World states sharing international basins. The nature and salience of the specific impediments may vary from basin to basin but, alone and in combination, such impediments constrain the willingness and ability of states to enter into cooperative agreements with their neighbors over transboundary water resources.

> *The notion of state sovereignty, although increasingly challenged, continues to be a major impediment to interstate cooperation over transboundary water resources.*

In general, a state does not like to share with other states what it considers to be *its* natural resources. This disinclination, compounded by the inherent uncertainties in all quantitative estimations of future water supplies and demands, and by the unpredictability of interstate relations in an anarchic international system, makes states reluctant to enter into long-term and binding water-sharing agreements with their neighbors. The recognition of water security as a national security concern can further impede cooperation in an international basin, especially if the basin has a history of acrimonious interstate relations.

Furthermore, a state is likely to forgo the benefits to be obtained from cooperation with other states from fear that it may become dependent on those states, and thus vulnerable to their threats to cut off supplies of a critical resource. This is especially true of states located downstream in international river basins, which often fear that their upstream neighbors may "turn off the tap" during crises. Fear of such vulnerability certainly played its part in Egypt's decision to construct the Aswân High Dam rather than to pursue the basinwide Century Storage Scheme; similar concerns underlie the suspicions that Syria and Iraq continue to harbor about the proposed peace pipelines that could carry water from Turkey to other states in the Middle East In short, water is sometimes seen as a weapon that may be used to enhance the foreign policy goals and relative powers of some states vis-à-vis other states in a shared basin.[5]

In some cases, states cite sovereignty and national security considerations to justify classifying water-related data as state secrets and refusing to share them with their neighbors or the international community. On several occasions, Brazil, India, and Israel have been accused by their neighbors and third parties of denying them access to the data that are needed to begin and sustain bilateral or multilateral negotiations for water sharing in the respective basins.

Domestic political support for hydropolitical cooperation is often hard to generate and sustain, and is vulnerable to appeals both to nationalism and to group interests.

The nature and articulation of domestic politics within the riparian states have a major role in defining the nature, conduct, and outcome of hydropolitics in international basins. In democratic or federalist states, the conflicting interests of different interest groups have to be taken into consideration and reconciled before such states can enter into cooperative agreements with other states. Because water can be used for so many different activities, several state agencies or ministries often have jurisdictions over water allocations for different sectors. Bureaucratic competition and rivalries between such agencies within a democratic polity can make it difficult to develop the needed domestic consensus for interstate cooperation, as has been India's experience in the Ganges-Brahmaputra-Barak basin. Thus, democratization and decentralization in the Third World can also complicate the problem of forging interstate cooperation for water sharing.

What the case studies also show is that often water agreements have been signed in the Third World when strong leaders have been in power in one or more riparian states. This was the case with the Itaipu and Yacyreta agreements in the Paraná–La Plata basin, as well as the 1959 agreement between Egypt and Sudan in the Nile basin. However, the case studies also show that pluralistic societies and representative polities are often the best guarantors of the long-term sustainability of international treaties and accords, whereas agreements entered into by authoritarian regimes are more likely to encounter serious problems because the domestic groups most affected by those agreements are typically not involved in the negotiations and may have no desire to see them implemented. In some cases, transitions from authoritarian rule to democratic polity can lead to the renegotiation or cancellation of earlier water-related accords or collaborative projects, as is happening with the Yacyreta project in the Paraná–La Plata basin.

In some states, the ruling elite or regime often exaggerates and exacerbates the unresolved conflicts over water with the state's neighbors to shore up its domestic support. At the same time, groups opposing the ruling elite try to portray interstate cooperation or compromise in hydropolitics as a "sell out" of the national interest, as has often been the case in Bangladesh and Nepal in regard to cooperation with India in the Ganges-Brahmaputra-Barak basin. Weak Third World states that lack domestic legitimacy or popular support are particularly susceptible to such accusations and often find it difficult to cooperate with their neighbors over transboundary water resources.

Cooperation may be further impeded by the fact that water scarcity is often a subnational problem—that is, only certain parts of a country may suffer from water scarcity whereas others may enjoy a surplus of water. In such cases, national leaders are hard pressed to persuade the entire population to accept that cooperation with the neighbors is necessary or beneficial for everyone, especially if such cooperation requires a substantial diversion of national resources, as it often does. Interstate cooperation may also benefit only certain areas and groups within a state, even though the entire country may have to shoulder the burden of paying for the cooperative venture. Further, the new institutions and legal arrangements that need to be created as a consequence of cooperation with neighboring states may conflict with existing institutions and laws in one or more riparian states.

Although water is increasingly being recognized as a valuable economic commodity, the complex calculations required to determine its economic value for multiple uses, across the basin and within each riparian state, impede hydropolitical cooperation in international basins.

Because no economic activity, from low-tech agriculture to high-tech industry, can be started or sustained without direct and/or indirect (embedded) inputs of water, and because of the great economic returns it can help to produce in its multiple uses, water is increasingly being recognized as a highly valuable economic commodity, especially in the semiarid and arid regions of the Third World. Even countries that currently enjoy water surpluses are beginning to recognize the future scarcity value of this valuable resource. Some small countries, such as Bhutan, Ethiopia, Nepal, Laos, and Paraguay, have come to see the hitherto unexploited or underdeveloped multiple-use potential of transboundary water resources as the most valuable asset they have to barter or trade with their neighbors or to attract international investment.

From an economist's perspective, the growing recognition of water as a valuable economic commodity may be good news indeed, because, according to economic theory, this may provide the means for rationalizing the use of scarce water supplies and resolving intrastate and interstate conflicts in the international basins. However, the growing commodification of water also raises very complicated and contentious issues relating to the rights of ownership over the shared water supplies; the existence and nature of domestic and international water markets; and calculations of correct market prices to be charged for water, even within just one sector of the national economy of just one riparian state. For example, in the agricultural sector alone, water can be used for growing a multiplicity of crops, by different groups of farmers, at different locations and times, and with different economic yields. This makes it very difficult to calculate all the economic trade-offs that may result from different water-related policies and rules of allocation. These complexities are greatly compounded by the potential uses of water across a wide range of economic sectors.

Unlike oil, the scarcity of water cannot be made up by resorting to imports because water per se is not traded in large quantities in the international market, except in the form of an embedded input in the goods and services it helps to produce. There are as yet no cost-effective technologies and infrastructure or institutional and legal mechanisms that might make it possible for countries to import or export large quantities of water at market-determined prices. Furthermore, even if an international market for water were to develop at a future date, many of the Third World states that suffer most from water scarcities would be unable to afford large-scale imports of water.

The lack of an international market for water is reflected at the national level. In no country—whether developed or developing—are there efficient and fully developed markets for the buying and selling of water at prices determined by its scarcity value, best alternative uses, or the balancing of supply and demand. Mainstream economics—based on the neoclassical calculus of marginal utility and costs—provides few guidelines for dealing with the economics of "common pool" resources in a scientific and rational manner.[6] Consequently, political considerations rather than economic calculations chiefly determine the allocations of available water supplies in nearly all the developing countries. As a result, huge direct and indirect subsidies are often given to favored sectors and interest groups, even at the cost of creating substantial macro- and micro-level distortions in the national economies. Even Israeli agriculture, one of the most water-efficient in the world in terms of the physical input of water per unit of produce, would not survive in its present form or be internationally competitive without large subsidies for irrigation. Attempts to withdraw such subsidies and reallocate scarce water supplies to more productive and less wasteful economic sectors are already facing serious political challenge from different interest groups in Israel.

The complexity of making rational economic calculations to allocate scarce water supplies within just one riparian state is multiplied many times over when attempts are made to tackle the economics of interstate water sharing in an international basin. Such economic calculations, if they can be performed at all, may show that it is necessary not only to rationalize established and closely linked patterns and practices of land and water use in the different riparian states—a daunting task in itself given the highly politicized nature of water and land use—but also to restructure and integrate the different economic systems across the basin. The optimal economic solution in some basins, based on the comparative advantages of different riparian states, may be to let one or more states specialize in agriculture while the others are encouraged to produce hydroelectricity and industrial goods for mutual exchange. In other cases, population transfers from water-deficient regions in one or more riparian states to sparsely populated and water-surplus regions in other states may be required to solve the collective water problems, as has been suggested for Egypt and Sudan in the Nile basin. However, these economically rational solutions are not likely to be acceptable to one or more of the riparian states on the grounds of threatening their sovereignty, territorial integrity, national security, and domestic stability. And because of the inherent difficulty of calculating, both in the short term and the long run, the full economic costs and benefits of water projects for different societal groups, interstate cooperation can easily give rise to charges of unfairness and exploitation, as has been the case with the collaboration between Brazil and Paraguay on the Itaipu project, and between India and Nepal on some projects in the Ganges-Brahmaputra-Barak basin.

In nearly all Third World countries, large projects for irrigation, water supply, navigation, and hydropower generation are invariably constructed and maintained by the state or public sector. However, the local and national administrations often lack the ability to collect the revenues or taxes owed to the state by the users who benefit from water projects constructed at huge public expense. This can make the deficit-ridden local and national governments reluctant to commit additional public resources for new water that may be required as part of a water-sharing agreement with the neighbors.

The lack of adequate data, of access to technology, and of needed technical expertise severely impedes hydropolitical cooperation among Third World states.

States seeking to negotiate water-sharing agreements require accurate data that are shared and accepted by all parties. States planning water projects such as dams, reservoirs, hydroelectric plants, and irrigation systems also require accurate historical records of precipitation, runoff, and climatic variations in a river basin. These data are needed to determine the locations, capacity levels, and other physical and technical parameters of the planned projects as well as to calculate the trade-offs associated with different options. As things stand, due to the financial, technical, and administrative difficulties many developing countries face, in only a handful of international basins in the Third World are such data collected on a regular basis. In most cases, the needed data are either not available or, if available, are of questionable quality. The secrecy within which such data are sometimes enveloped because of security considerations only compounds other technical impediments to interstate cooperation.

All but a handful of Third World countries currently lack access to the technologies and hardware, such as remote-sensing satellites, geographical information systems (GIS), and on-line computers, that are essential to planning, constructing, and maintaining large water projects. Many developing countries (Laos is a case in point) also suffer from shortages of trained personnel and institutional mechanisms required to implement and maintain large water projects.

In any case, finding optimal solutions for water-sharing problems under conditions of uncertainty and across multiple uses, locations, and stakeholders is a highly complex analytical and computational problem, requiring great technical expertise and computational capabilities for its solution. Only a handful of developing countries currently possess these technical resources and capabilities. Such analytical and computational problems become even more difficult to solve in those basins where several rivers are shared by two or more riparian states, as is the case in the Ganges-Brahmaputra-Barak basin.

It should be noted that the barriers to cooperation that these technical impediments present are not necessarily insurmountable—especially if external assistance is available—and are certainly not as great as those posed by political, economic, and security-related factors. Even so, working in combination with other factors, technical impediments can severely undercut the willingness and ability of some riparian states to enter into water-sharing agreements with their more technically capable neighbors.

REASONS FOR HOPE: COOPERATION

The impediments to interstate cooperation discussed above may seem so numerous, diverse, and daunting as to rule out the prospects for resolving transboundary water conflicts in the Third World in a peaceful and cooperative manner. Fortunately, however, the case studies also show that there are concrete grounds for hydropolitical optimism. Interestingly, many of the reasons for hope spring from the very same interdependencies that have been shown to impede cooperation under certain circumstances. We begin this discussion by examining how real the prospects for future water wars in the Third World actually are.

Third World states do not and may not go to war over water for many of the same reasons that they do not or cannot go to war over conflicts in the traditional arena of high politics.

Many geographic, military-strategic, political, and economic factors and considerations, as well as the larger geopolitical context within which hydropolitics between states is conducted, can prevent states from going to war with their neighbors over water. Third World states have not gone to war over water per se since World War II, and may not in the future, conscious of the high price that such adventures can exact.

Very few of the Third World states that share international basins currently have the military capabilities and economic resources to engage in full-scale wars. This situation is not likely to change in the foreseeable future. Even the most militarily capable and powerful states in the Third World may not go to war with their neighbors over water because hydropolitical belligerence necessarily imposes very heavy costs and penalties on the aggressor. For example, a militarily strong lower riparian state sharing an international basin may decide to occupy or annex the territory of one or more of the upper riparian states in order to control the transboundary water resources, as some analysts of hydropolitics in the Jordan basin have argued Israel has done since 1967. However, as even Israel has discovered, in addition to the costs in human lives, the economic and political costs—both domestic and international—of such occupation or annexation necessarily escalate with time, thus ensuring that occupation or annexation of territory cannot be a cost-effective or long-term solution for the aggressor's water problems.

At the other end of a river, a geographically favored upper riparian state may threaten to impound or divert the flow of a shared river before it reaches the lower riparian state(s). But, unless the impounded water can be indefinitely stored or fully consumed within the upper riparian's territory, a large part of it will naturally find its way to the downstream states. Building large dams, reservoirs, and canals to store or divert the full flow of a shared river can also impose very heavy environmental, economic, political, and social costs on the upper riparian state. Thus, while the potential for acute conflict over water will certainly keep growing over the next century, it may not be possible for most Third World states to resolve their water problems by going to war with their upstream or downstream neighbors. It is to be hoped that a clear recognition of this hydropolitical reality may encourage states to seek peaceful ways of conducting hydropolitics with their neighbors.

Ongoing changes in the international political and economic systems are creating an environment that is more conducive for hydropolitical cooperation in the Third World.

Many ongoing developments in the international political and economic systems provide solid grounds for hydropolitical optimism. To begin with, the notion of state sovereignty that has often obstructed interstate hydropolitical cooperation is increasingly being challenged by global environmental changes, such as the threat of global warming and of a consequent rise in sea level; by growing interdependence in the global economy; and by increasing flows of goods, services, ideas, and information across increasingly porous international borders. One way in which Third World states are responding to these developments is by becoming parties to a growing number of environmental and economic treaties and agreements, at both the global and the regional levels. And because water resources are central to maintaining the health of all local, national, and regional environmental and economic systems, there is a growing recognition worldwide that interstate cooperation must also now extend to international river basins in the Third World.

The quickening pace of globalization and interdependence in the international economy is leading many Third World states to abandon ideological confrontations and rivalries with their neighbors in favor of regional economic cooperation. Driven by new economic imperatives, and by the examples of Western Europe and North America, many regional organizations and institutions for fostering and sustaining regional economic cooperation have emerged in the Third World. However fragile and problematic these efforts at regional cooperation may be, they do represent an emerging consensus that no developing country can now go it alone in the global competition for resources and markets. Because of the centrality of water for all economic activities, the quest for regional economic cooperation is, of necessity, being extended to the arena of hydropolitics in the Third World. The clearest examples of this are the Paraná–La Plata and Mekong basins, where cooperation over transboundary water resources has become an important component of efforts to develop and sustain regional economic cooperation.

At the same time that the world is becoming more interdependent, it is also becoming more democratic. In the Third World especially, there has been significant progress in the direction of democratization and decentralization since the end of the Cold War. If this movement can be sustained, the prospects for avoiding interstate armed conflict over water may be significantly enhanced—the reason being that empirical evidence strongly suggests that democracies tend not to go to war with one another in the modern international system.[7] As mentioned above, despite the problem of building domestic consensus for international cooperation, democratic polities are also often the best guarantors of the acceptability and longevity of international water accords.

The international community now has the necessary experience and commitment, as well as growing leverage, to facilitate water-sharing agreements between Third World states.

The World Bank and other international organizations, including UN agencies active in the areas of food production, sustainable economic development, environmental protection, public health, and meteorology, have engaged in many efforts over the past half century to facilitate cooperation in several international river basins in the Third World. Some of those efforts have enjoyed notable successes. For instance, sustained international efforts yielded the 1960 Indus Water Treaty, which has survived two subsequent wars between India and Pakistan. The comprehensive environmental agreements signed in the Mekong basin during the 1990s likewise attest to the fact that multilateral action can help to overcome entrenched hostilities and suspicions among states as well as the many impediments they face on the road to cooperation.

To persuade Third World states to replace conflict with cooperation, the international community can also now use powerful economic leverage. Nearly all the Third World states sharing international basins are currently heavily in debt, and are likely to remain so for the foreseeable future; thus, international donors and lenders are well positioned to be able to insist that states resolve their conflicts over water before they receive external aid. A "debt-for-cooperation" swap, similar to the "debt-for-environment" swap currently underway in some parts of the Third World, can provide tangible incentives for the debt-laden developing countries to move toward hydropolitical cooperation. At the same time, the growing economic and political clout of local and international nongovernmental organizations in the broad areas of development, environment, and international peace and security is compelling Third World states as well as international governmental organizations to develop and implement more efficient, equitable, and sustainable water management practices at the local, national, and regional levels.

New technologies and water management practices that can facilitate more efficient allocation and use of scarce water resources, and reduce hydropolitical tensions in international basins, are becoming available.

New technologies that can greatly reduce the water intensity of agricultural and industrial production, as well as the wastage of water in other societal uses, are being developed and becoming globally available. These technologies, which focus both on supply augmentation and demand management, can be and are being transferred to the Third World at minimal costs compared to the huge financial burden of constructing new and large water-supply projects, which are often encumbered by political, economic, social, and environmental problems.

Third World states can also benefit from technical resources and hardware that were originally developed primarily for military purposes, but that now have been untethered from their Cold War missions. High-resolution satellites and other remote-sensing, devices and instruments for monitoring surface and underground water flow, and graphic computer simulations of hydrological, topographical, and other features of large landscapes are but a few examples of the new technologies that are now available from many public and private sources.[8] Such technologies can be particularly valuable for those Third World states that do not possess their own high-tech capabilities for collecting accurate hydrological and meteorological data, detecting untapped underground water resources, and verifying compliance with the provisions of water-sharing agreements. In some basins, one or more riparian states may be persuaded or impelled to share their advanced water technologies with their neighbors in order to reduce the overall pressures on the shared water resources, as Israel is reported to have done with Jordan.

An international convention on laws to guide nonnavigational uses of transboundary water resources is now in place.

In May 1997, following nearly three decades of sustained work by the International Law Commission, the UN General Assembly adopted the Convention on the Law of Non-Navigational Uses of International Water Courses, with 103 votes in favor, only 3 against (Burundi, China, and Turkey), and 27 abstentions.[9] The convention clearly lays out the rights and obligations of states that share international basins, and suggests several principles and mechanisms that such states can and should use, including arbitration and mediation, to settle their water disputes. Notwithstanding the opposition of China and Turkey—two regional water powers—and some general reservations about the rights and obligations of upstream riparians, the convention demonstrates that the international community recognizes the growing danger of water disputes escalating to the level of acute conflicts, as well as the urgent need to find peaceful ways of resolving hydropolitical conflicts in international basins.

* * *

The end of the Cold War has created a radically different global context for the conduct of hydropolitics in the Third World. Freed from the machinations and imperatives of competition and confrontation between the two superpowers, the Third World states now have real opportunities to explore peaceful ways of conducting hydropolitics with their neighbors. But if the promise of a more cooperative future is to be fulfilled, the international community must provide sustained political commitment, as well as considerable economic and technical support. As we have seen, water-sharing agreements can take many years to negotiate, during which numerous formidable obstacles must be overcome; consequently, the mediation and support of third parties may be critical to creating and maintaining momentum, and the judicious use by external actors of both "carrots" and "sticks" may be needed to persuade reluctant states to cooperate with their neighbors. However, while third-party help is often necessary, it is of value only if it is based on a deep understanding of the complexity of interstate negotiations about sharing an essential, increasingly scarce, and mostly nonsubstitutable resource. Third parties must also recognize that each river basin is unique—that the specific combinations of local geography, history, economics, politics, and culture define the nature and conduct of hydropolitics in each international basin in the Third World.

Ultimately, however, no matter how sophisticated the understanding of third parties, and no matter how supportive they are of efforts at hydropolitical cooperation, the peaceful conduct of hydropolitics depends on the willingness, attitudes, efforts, and capabilities of the Third World states themselves. As we have seen, those states face many uncertainties as well as formidable impediments in the arena of hydropolitics, and yet they are in many instances forging ahead with bilateral and multilateral cooperation. When we look toward the future of hydropolitics in the Third World, we should do so with a keen appreciation of the potential dangers of escalating demands on shared water resources, but also with a guarded optimism that those dangers can be averted and cooperation fostered and deepened.

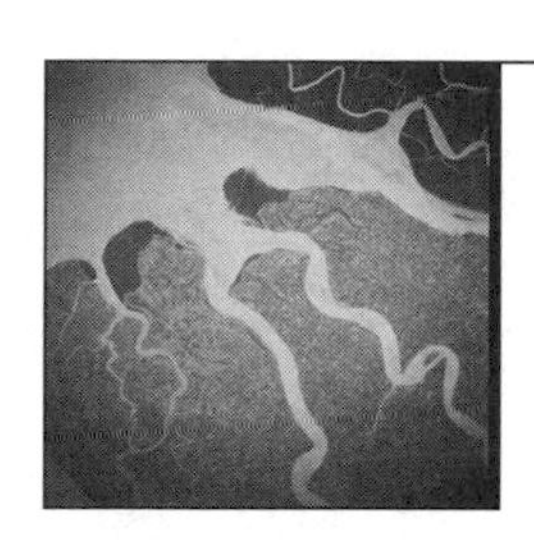

APPENDIX I

Statistical Profiles

Table A.1. Statistical Profiles of the Six River Basins

Watershed	Size of watershed (km^3)*	Average annual flow (km^3/yr)*	Climate	Riparian states (with % of national available water being utilized)	Estimated population of riparian states in 2000 (millions)**	Per capita GNP, 1997 (U.S. Dollars)***
Paraná–La Plata	3,200,000	470	Tropical	Argentina (3.5)	37.0	8,570
				Bolivia (0.7)	8.3	950
				Brazil (0.5)	169.2	4,720
				Paraguay (0.2)	5.5	2,010
				Uruguay (0.6)	3.3	6,020
Nile	2,960,000	30	Dry to Tropical	Burundi (3.1)	7.0	180
				Egypt (111.5)	68.1	1,180
				Eritrea (N/A)	3.8	210
				Ethiopia (7.5)	66.2	110
				Kenya (8.1)	30.3	330
				Rwanda (2.6)	7.7	210
				Sudan (37.3)	29.8	280
				Tanzania (1.3)	33.7	210
				Uganda (0.6)	22.5	320
				Zaire (0.2)	51.7	110
Jordan	11,500	1.4	Dry to Mediterranean	Israel (95.6)		15,810
				Jordan (67.6)	6.3	1,570
				Lebanon (20.6)	3.3	3,350
				Palestine (100.0)		N/A
				Syria (102.0)	16.1	1,150

Euphrates-Tigris	1,050,000	46	Dry to Mediterranean	Iran (N/A)	89.0	1,780
				Iraq (86.3)	23.1	N/A
				Syria (102.0)	16.1	1,150
				Turkey (12.1)	65.7	3,130
Ganges-Brahmaputra-Barak	1,480,000	971	Humid to Tropical	China (19.3)	1276.3	860
				Bangladesh (1.0)	128.3	270
				Bhutan (0.1)	2.0	400
				India (57.1)	1006.8	390
				Nepal (14.8)	24.3	210
Mekong	790,000	470	Humid to Tropical	Cambodia (0.1)	11.2	650
				China (19.3)	1276.3	860
				Laos (0.8)	5.7	406
				Burma (0.4)	49.3	N/A
				Thailand (32.1)	60.5	2,800
				Vietnam (2.8)	80.5	320

Sources:

* Peter Gleick, "Water and Conflict," in *Environmental Change and Acute Conflict* (Washington, D.C.: American Academy of Arts and Sciences, 1992); United Nations, *Register of International Rivers* (Oxford: Pergamon Press, 1978).

** UNDP, *Human Development Report 1997* (New York; Oxford: Oxford University Press, 1997).

*** World Bank, *World Development Report, 1998–1999* (New York: Oxford Univeristy Press, 1999), R190, R191, 232.

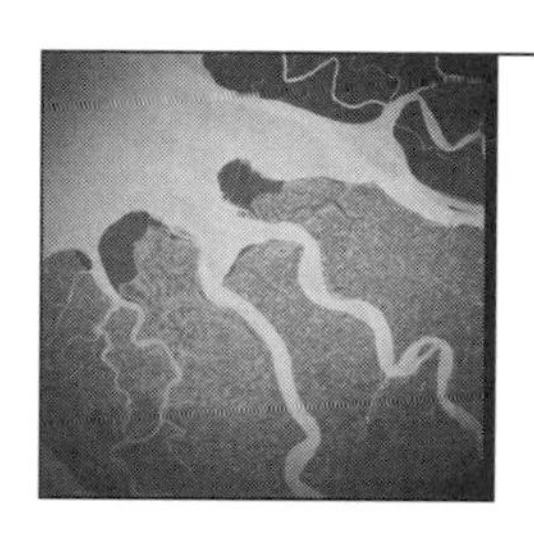

APPENDIX II

Analytical Framework and Methodology

WATER SCARCITY, CONFLICT, AND COOPERATION
An Analytical Framework

The relationship between water scarcity and acute conflict in an international river basin is bound to be highly complex. However, for the sake of analytical tractability, it becomes necessary to focus on the major determinants and consequences of water scarcity to show how these may lead to acute conflict. Figure A.2 is a highly simplified analytical framework showing the relationship of national water scarcity for multiple societal needs with the potential for acute conflict in an international river basin.[1]

In this simple schema, natural processes (A) and basinwide human activities (B) are the two primary instigators of water scarcity (C) in an international basin. Scarcity of water for multiple needs can engender economic and environmental crises (D), diminished quality of life (F), and domestic upheavals (E) within the affected state(s). These consequences of water scarcity, alone and in combination, can generate or reinforce national insecurity (G), which can also be engendered directly by detrimental human activity in other states (B→G). National insecurity, in turn, can create the potential for acute conflict (H). Each of the elements (A to H) as well as each linkage in this simple schema can itself be expanded into a much larger and complex analytical framework.

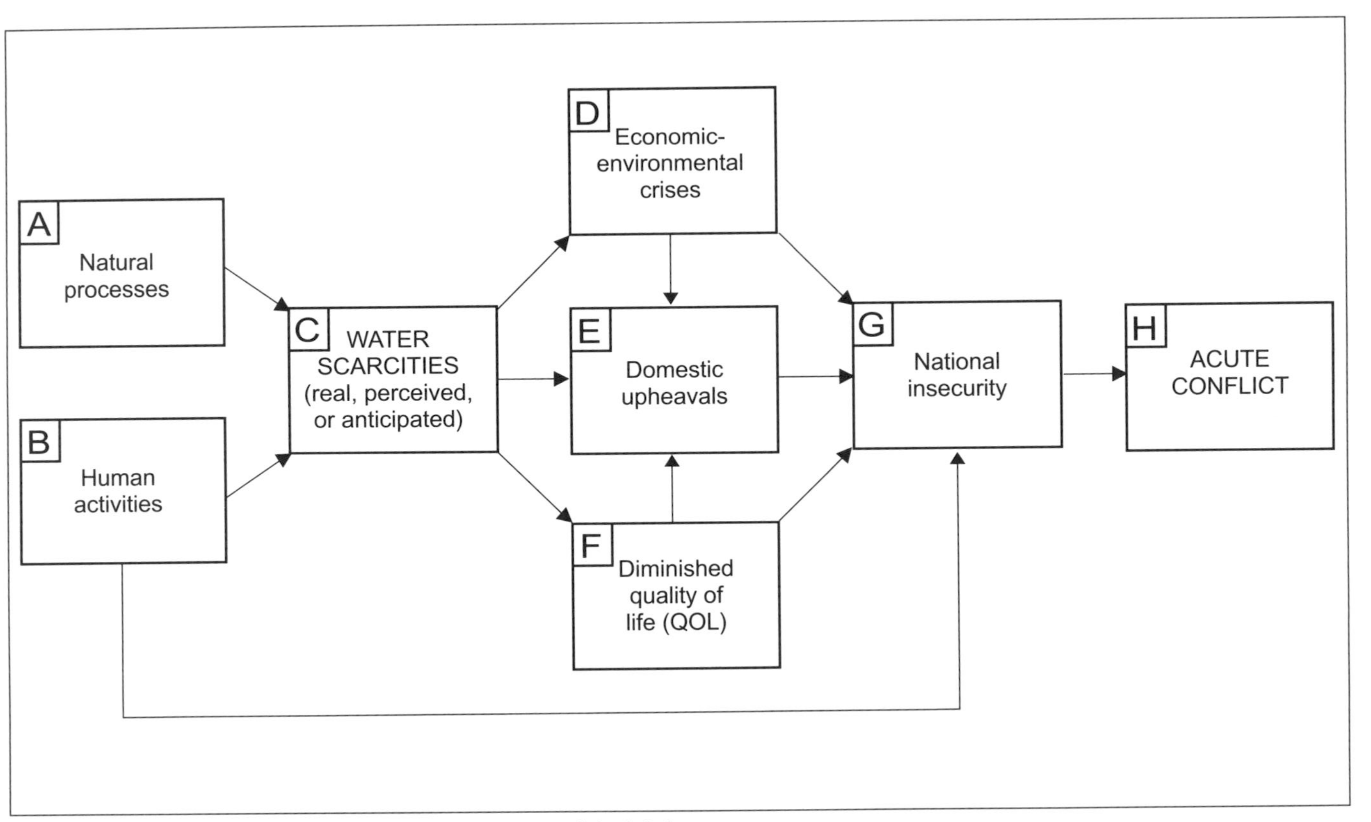

Figure A.2. Water Scarcities and Conflicts: A Simplified Schema

Figure A.3 further specifies the constituents of some elements in figure A.2 as well as some additional causalities and feedbacks that link water scarcity to acute conflict.

In this expanded framework, global climatic changes (A), such as global warming and ozone-layer depletion; other natural phenomena (B), such as droughts and desertification; population growth (C), accompanied by rising demand for water; and a host of human activities in the states sharing a river basin (D) can all lead to severe water shortages, both in terms of quantity and quality, in one or more riparian states. Water scarcity so created can have five major consequences: environmental degradation (F), higher than normal mortality and morbidity rates (G), reduced overall quality of life (H), diminished agricultural production (I), and diminished industrial production (J). Many of these consequences can be mutually reinforcing; for example, the reduced quality of life, engendered by water scarcity, can lead to agricultural and industrial decline (H→I and H→J), which, in turn, can further diminish the quality of life (I→H and J→H).

Another set of mutually reinforcing relationships among the consequences of water scarcity is represented by the feedback loop I↔J↔L↔I. Here, a decline in agricultural production (I) may lead to substantial reduction in industrial production (I→J) by depriving industries of the needed primary and intermediate commodities as well as food for the industrial workforce. This industrial decline may, in turn, further depress agricultural production (J→I) by reducing the flows of capital, machinery, fertilizers, and other inputs from the industrial to the agricultural sectors. Diminished agricultural and industrial production may lead to an overall decline of the national economy (I→L and J→L), which may further depress both agricultural and industrial production (L→I and L→J).

The reduced quality of life (H) can also induce or force a large number of people to migrate within and across international boundaries (M), leading to social unrest (K) and domestic upheaval in the affected riparian state(s), including armed conflict, separatism, and so forth. Once again, there may be reinforcing feedbacks among these direct and indirect effects of water scarcity, represented by H↔M↔K↔H. Large-scale migration across international boundaries can also fuel national insecurity (M→O) in all the adversely affected countries. These insecurities can be further reinforced by domestic insecurity (N→O), engendered by social unrest (K→N) and by a decline of the overall national economy (L→O). National insecurity can also be created directly by basinwide human activities (D→O), including economic, environmental, and military activities in

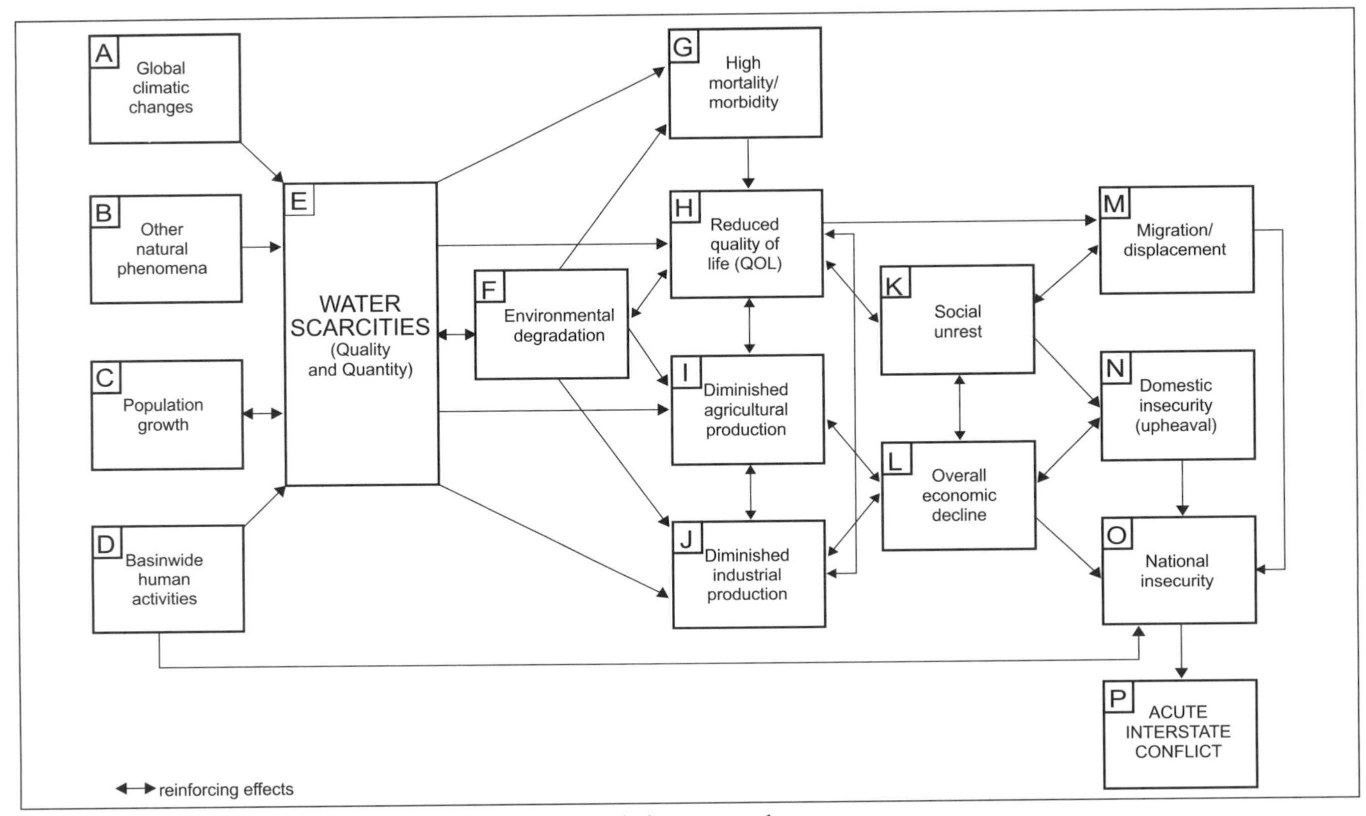

Figure A.3. Water Scarcities and Conflicts: An Expanded Framework

other riparian states. Finally, national insecurity in one or more of the riparian states can create the potential for acute interstate conflict.

It must be emphasized, however, that this abstract analytical framework is a highly simplified version of reality. Many more elements (aspects) of the overall water-environment-economy-politics-society-security system need to be specified and incorporated into the framework, as must many other interlinkages, both causal and reinforcing, to represent the complexity of the water scarcity–acute interstate conflict relationship. It must also be emphasized that there is nothing automatic or inevitable about water scarcity necessarily leading to acute conflict. Given the complexity of the environmental-economic-security interlinkages in the real world, a whole host of intervening variables—historical, geographical, cultural, behavioral, political, and strategic—also need to be considered for a comprehensive analysis of hydropolitics in any international river basin. This is the approach adopted for each of the cases studied in this book.

COMPARATIVE METHODOLOGY

The comparative case methodology guiding this study borrows from, but does not strictly follow, the writings of Alexander L. George and his colleagues who have developed the "structured, focused comparison approach."[2] In the words of Krepon and Caldwell, who have applied this methodology to a critical examination of the domestic politics of arms control treaty ratification in the United States during the twentieth century:

> According to this method, the analyst prepares a set of standardized, general questions that reflect the theory-related objectives of the study at hand. These questions are then asked of each of the cases under investigation. This methodology borrows from both the quantitative and single case study approaches: the analyst treats each case as if it were a unique case—the approach historians normally adopt—in order to examine in what ways it is similar and dissimilar from the other cases under examination. At the same time, posing the same set of questions for each case resembles the statistical or survey research approaches that many social scientists employ. Based on the results of posing the standardized set of questions for each case, the analyst modifies the original questions and hypotheses to account for previously neglected factors. Thus, the process is an iterative one.[3]

The structured, focused comparison approach, when applied to a well-selected set of cases, leads the analyst to formulate context-dependent generalizations about the particular phenomenon under investigation.

Contingent generalizations are generalizations that may or may not be true, according to the contingency, and that specify the contingencies that "activate" or "validate" them. Such generalizations must not only be relevant to actual policy problems; they must also be applicable to the diagnosis of particular situations and to the selection of better strategies by policymakers for the achievement of their desired objective.[4] The proper selection of specific cases to be examined and compared is crucial for a successful outcome of any structured, focused comparative study.

In keeping with the requirements of the above methodology, four structured sets of questions to be addressed in each case study are presented below.

International Context

How and to what extent did decolonization and superpower rivalry in the post–World War II era affect conflict and cooperation over transboundary water resources among the riparian states sharing the international river basin? What roles have international organizations, such as the United Nations and its agencies, the World Bank, and the International Monetary Fund; local and international nongovernmental organizations and epistemic communities; and other international actors played in resolving water conflicts and/or in facilitating interstate cooperation? How effective have these efforts been in terms of the long-term sustainability of cooperation? How amenable is each riparian state to a "carrot-and-stick" approach on the part of the international community?

Regional Context

What was the history of the emergence of sovereign states in the region? What kind of resource-territorial-ethnic legacies did decolonization leave behind? Has there been any fragmentation of a state or states sharing the international river basin since World War II? What is the history and nature of interstate relations in the basin? What is the riparian structure of the basin and how does it affect hydropolitics in the basin? What are the comparative military and economic strengths of the riparian states? What is the current state of the development and use of the basin's waters overall, and in each riparian state? How dependent is each riparian state on the waters of the international basin? Are there other domestic water resources the state can develop unilaterally? What kind of resources—financial, technological, organizational, and human—are available, or likely to be available, to each riparian state for developing and maintaining large water projects? What kind of regional organizations have existed and currently exist for mediating conflict among the riparian states and to what extent is conflict over water explicitly recognized and included in the mandate of these organizations? Are there instances where a regional organization has successfully mediated a bilateral or multilateral water conflict? Are there instances of international and regional organizations working together to solve water conflict and to achieve cooperation in the basin?

Domestic Context

What has been the nature of governments (central administrations) in each of the riparian states since World War II? What constituencies have formed the main support for these administrations? How were the transitions of governments brought about and how stable have they been? Do the riparian states have the kind of control and support needed to enable them to participate in cooperative ventures with other states, without jeopardizing regime survival and domestic security? Have there been, or are there, active rebellions and/or separatist movements that can impede or prevent interstate cooperation? What kind of strategies have the central administrations adopted to facilitate or impede cooperation over water? What domestic circumstances, factors, and actors have enabled the riparian states to adopt these strategies? Are there central agencies for developing, allocating, and managing water supplies? How powerful are these agencies within the respective states?

Intervening Factors

Whereas the international, regional, and domestic contexts provide the background against which conflict and cooperation among states over transboundary resources are played out and dealt with, easily specifiable and deterministic relationships do not and cannot exist between the contextual background and the actual conduct of hydropolitics. A number of intervening factors—historical, geographical, social, political, economic, technical, cultural, and behavioral—inevitably influence the conduct of hydropolitics among riparian states in an international river basin. States retain memories of their experiences of dealing with their neighbors and with the international system. They also have ideal concerns—matters that involve perceptions and desires—that may influence their international behavior as much as, or more than, material concerns. There are also societal customs, values, and beliefs that influence the behavior of states in the international arena. In this study, these noncontextual influences are grouped together as intervening factors. However, rather than specify a large set of questions relating to all the potential intervening factors and their relationships with hydropolitics, the strategy adopted here is to let each case "speak for itself," as it were. Consequently, each case is examined here individually to determine the salience of a variety of intervening factors and to document their contributions to facilitating or frustrating cooperation in international basins.

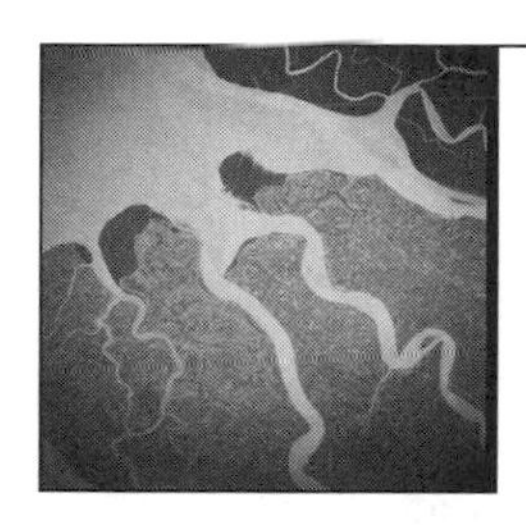

NOTES

INTRODUCTION

1. The author is not at all comfortable with using the term "Third World" to categorize and label vastly disparate sets of states in different regions of the world, at different levels of socioeconomic development. After the breakup of the Soviet Union, especially, the term has lost much of the meaning it may have had. But there are problems also with other labels such as "The South," "Group of 77," "Non-Aligned Nations," and so forth. The strategy adopted here is to use the terms "Third World" and "developing countries" interchangeably. See Lyon, "Emergence of the Third World," in H. Bull and A. Watson, eds., *The Explanation of International Society* (New York: Oxford University Press, 1983); J. Ravenill, "The North-South Balance of Power," *International Affairs* 66, no. 4 (1990): 745–746; and J. Crickshank, "The Rise and Fall of the Third World: A Concept Whose Time Has Passed," *World Review* (February 1991): 28–29.

2. A. K. Biswas, "Water for the Third World," *Foreign Affairs* 26, no. 1 (fall 1981): 148–166.

3. See Sandra Postel, *Last Oasis: Facing Water Scarcity* (New York: W. W. Norton, 1992).

4. For some quantitative data on the existing and projected water scarcities in the Third World, see Peter H. Gleick, "Water and Conflict," in *Environmental Change and Acute Conflict* (Washington, D.C.: American Academy of Arts and Sciences, 1992), 17. Also see, Robert Engelman and Pamela Le Rou, *Sustaining Water: Population and the Future of Renewable Water Supplies* (Washington, D.C.. Population Action International, 1993); and Tom Gardner-Outlaw and Robert Engelman, *Sustaining Water, Easing Scarcity: A Second Update* (Washington, D.C.: Population Action International, 1997).

5. This was clearly demonstrated by the recent war in the Persian Gulf region, which had its origins, among other causes, in Iraqi claims over some oil fields it shares with Kuwait.

Iraq had accused Kuwait of overexploiting these resources to the detriment of Iraqi economy. Also see Ronnie D. Lipschutz, "Strategic Insecurity: Putting the Pieces Back Together in the Middle East," in H. Kriesler, ed., *Confrontation in the Gulf* (Berkeley, Calif.: Institute of International Studies, University of California, 1992), 113–126.

6. United Nations, *Register of International Rivers* (Oxford: Pergamon Press, 1978). It should be pointed out that the numbers and data presented in the *Register* are rather dated. For a critique, see Asit K. Biswas, "Management of International Waters: Problems and Perspective," *Water Resources Development* 9, no. 2 (1993).

7. United Nations, *Register of International Rivers,* 1–56. Also see World Bank, *Water Resources Management* (Washington, D.C.: World Bank, 1993), 38.

8. For a brief but highly organized review of this literature, see T. F. Homer-Dixon, "On the Threshold: Environmental Changes as Causes of Acute Conflict," *International Security* 16, no. 2 (fall 1991): 76–116. Also see Thomas F. Homer-Dixon, Jeffrey H. Boutwell, and George W. Rathjens, "Environmental Change and Violent Conflict," *Scientific American,* February 1993, 38–45; and Thomas F. Homer-Dixon, "Environmental Scarcity and Violent Conflict: Evidence from Cases," *International Security* 19, no. 1 (summer 1994): 5–40. For critical reviews of this literature, see Daniel Deudney, "The Case against Linking Environmental Degradation and National Security," *Millennium* 19, no. 3 (winter 1990): 461–476; Marc A. Levy, "Is the Environment a National Security Issue?" *International Security* 20, no. 2 (fall 1995): 35–62; and Richard A. Matthew, "Environmental Security: Demystifying the Concept, Clarifying the Stakes," *Environmental Change and Security Project Report*, no. 1 (spring 1995): 14–23.

9. Gleick, "Water and Conflict," 3–28; and "The Implications of Global Climatic Changes for International Security," *Climate Change* 15, no. 2 (June 1990): 121–133; M. F. Falkenmark, "Fresh Water as a Factor in Strategic Policy and Action," in Arthur Westing, ed., *Global Resources and International Conflict: Environmental Factors in Strategic Policy and Action* (New York: Oxford University Press, 1986); and Thomas Naff, "Water Security, Resource Management, and Conflict in the Middle East," in *Environmental Dimensions of Security* (Washington, D.C.: American Academy of Arts and Sciences, 1992), 25–30.

10. See Ronnie D. Lipschutz, "Water Resources Will Matter? Environmental Degradation as a Security Issue," in *Environmental Dimensions of Security* (Washington, D.C.: American Academy of Arts and Sciences, 1992). However, Lipschutz also warns against treating water security as a national security issue.

11. Throughout this study the term "international river basin" (or "international basin") represents the whole catchment and drainage basin of a river that is shared by two or more states. For some definitional problems and attempts to resolve them, see James L. Wescoat Jr., "Beyond the River Basin: The Changing Geography of International Water Problems and International Water Law," *Colorado Journal of International Environmental Law and Policy* 3, no. 1 (winter 1992): 301–332.

12. Joyce R. Starr, "Water Wars," *Foreign Policy* 82 (spring 1991): 17–36. For a critique of this view, see Miriam Lowi, "Oil, Water, and Conflict in the Middle East" (paper presented at the Conference on Environmental Change and Security, University of British Columbia, Vancouver, April 29–May 2, 1993); and Lowi, *Water and Power: The Politics of a Scarce Resource in the Jordan Basin* (Cambridge: Cambridge University Press, 1993).

13. On the controversy about global warming, see William K. Stevens, "A Skeptic Asks, Is It Getting Hotter, or Is It Just the Computer Model?" *New York Times*, June 18, 1996, C1, C6.

14. See Myron Weiner, "Security, Stability, and International Migration," *International Security* 17, no. 3 (winter 1992–93): 91–126.

15. See Charles W. Howe, "The Effect of Water Resources Development on Economic Growth: The Conditions for Success," *Natural Resources Journal* 16, no. 4 (October 1976): 939–956.

16. Homer-Dixon, "Environmental Security and Violent Conflict."

17. Also see Arun Elhance, "Central Asia's Looming Water Wars," *Christian Science Monitor*, January 11, 1993, 19.

18. Arthur A. Stein, *Why Nations Cooperate: Circumstance and Choice in International Relations* (Ithaca, N.Y.: Cornell University Press, 1990); and Joseph M. Grieco, "Anarchy and the Limits of Cooperation: A Recent Critique of the Newest Liberal Institutionalism," *International Organization* 42, no. 3 (summer 1988): 485–508.

19. An example of covert cooperation is the Israel-Jordan case in the Jordan basin (see chapter 3). Despite two subsequent wars, India and Pakistan have also been complying with the Indus Water Treaty of 1960 (chapter 5).

20. Peter M. Haas, "Introduction: Epistemic Communities and International Policy Coordination," *International Organization* 46, no. 1 (winter 1992): 1–36; and Emanuel Adler and Peter Haas, "Conclusion: Epistemic Communities, World Order, and the Creation of a Reflective Research Program," *International Organization* 46, no. 1 (winter 1992): 367–390.

21. There are several definitions and characterizations of international regimes. According to one definition, regimes are devices created by self-interested actors to solve or at least ameliorate collective-action problems, including problems about environment and common natural resources. See Russell Hardin, *Collective Action* (Baltimore: Johns Hopkins University Press, 1982); and Friedrich Kratochwil and John G. Ruggie, "International Organization: A State of the Art on an Art of the State," *International Organization* 40 (fall 1986): 753–775. For a survey of the state of regime analysis, see Marc A. Levy, Oran R. Young, and Michael Zuren, "The Study of International Regimes," *European Journal of International Relations* 1 (September 1995): 267–330.

22. See the later sections in this introduction, explaining the choice of cases and time period.

23. M. F. Falkenmark, the Van Te Chow Memorial Lecture, "Environment and Development: Urgent Need for a Water Perspective," *Water International* 16, no. 4 (December 1991): 257.

24. United Nations Water Conference, *Resources and Needs: Assessment of the World Water Situation*, E/CONF. 70/CPBI (New York: United Nations, July 2, 1976), 10.

25. M. F. Falkenmark, "Fresh Water: Time for a Modified Approach," *Ambio* 15, no. 4 (1986): 194–200. These estimates have come under a great deal of criticism lately, mainly because Falkenmark does not include standard of living parameters. See Peter Gleick, "Basic Requirements for Human Activities: Meeting Basic Needs," *Water International* 21, no. 2 (1996): 83–92.

26. G. F. White, "Introduction: World Trends and Need," *Natural Resources Journal* 16, no. 4 (October 1976): 739. One cubic meter of water equals 1,000 kilograms in weight or one metric ton.

27. Projections for water consumption on earth in the year 2000 show a total demand of 9,700 cubic kilometers (cu. km.), comprising 7,000 cu. km. for agriculture, 600 cu. km. for domestic use, 1,700 cu. km. for industries, and 400 cu. km. for all other uses. B. R. Chauhan, *Settlement of International Water Law Disputes in International Drainage Basins* (Berlin: Erich Schmidt Verlag, 1981), 49.

28. United Nations, *Development Hotline*, no. 4, February 1992.

29. A. K. Biswas, "Water for Sustainable Development in the Twenty-First Century: A Global Perspective," *Water International* 16, no. 4 (December 1991): 219–224.

30. The term "entitlement" is derived from Amartya Sen, *Poverty and Famine: An Essay on Entitlement and Deprivation* (Oxford: Oxford University Press, 1981); however, Sen does not specifically deal with water entitlements. As an example of water entitlements, in some parts of India the "untouchables" are barred from drawing water from the same wells as the upper-caste Hindus.

31. Biswas, "Water for the Third World."

32. M. Lipton, *Why People Stay Poor: A Study of Urban Bias in World Development* (London: Temple Smith, 1977). Also see Peter Rogers, "Integrated Urban Water Resources Management," *Natural Resources Forum* (February 1993): 33–42.

33. World Bank, *Water Resources Management*, 31–32. For a report on urban biases in allocating water in Peru, see "Peru's Path: Still Terror-Filled," *New York Times*, April 15, 1992.

34. Biswas, "Water for the Third World," 161.

35. World Bank, *Water Resources Management*, 58.

36. Brian Grove, "Can Everybody Be Served? Water Supply and Sanitation in Developing Countries," *Ecodecision* (September 1993): 76.

37. J. MacNeil, Peter Winsemius, and Taizo Yakushiji, *Beyond Interdependence: The Meshing of the World's Economy and Ecology* (New York: Oxford University Press, 1991); and World Bank, *World Development Report 1996* (Washington, D.C.: World Bank, 1996). A substantial portion of the external debt accumulated by many developing countries has typically been for water-related projects.

38. John Waterbury, *Hydropolitics of the Nile Valley* (Syracuse, N.Y.: Syracuse University Press, 1979), 1.

39. See William K. Stevens, "How Many Species Are Being Lost? Scientists Try New Yardstick," *New York Times*, July 25, 1995, C4. As one example, in the region surrounding the fast disappearing Aral Lake in Central Asia, 20 of the 24 native species of fish have disappeared and the number of wild animal species has fallen from 173 to 38; many of the remaining species are now endangered. See Judith Perera, "The Aral Sea: Approaching Total Disaster," *Ecodecision* (September 1992): 60.

40. Data for this table are from Chauhan, *Settlement of International Water Disputes*, 40. It should be pointed out that these estimates do not take into account recycling and reuse of water for industrial production. In some industrialized countries such recycling has reached a high proportion of the total industrial water use; however, few developing countries are currently able to make substantial use of the technologies for recycling.

41. The World Bank has estimated that tourism worldwide now amounts to a $2 trillion annual industry. In 1988 about 235 million people participated in eco-tourism alone, generating $233 billion in economic activities. About half of all eco-tourism was related to animals. See *Global Biodiversity Assessment: Summary for Policy Makers* (Cambridge: Cambridge University Press, 1995), 16.

42. Biswas, "Water for Sustainable Development."

43. For some problems relating to a "regional" interpretation of an international river basin, see Wescoat, "Beyond the River Basin."

44. See chapter 5.

45. See "The Beautiful and the Damned," *The Economist,* March 28, 1992, 11.

46. Gleick, "Water and Conflict."

47. For a review of literature on interstate cooperation, see Helen Milner, "International Theories of Cooperation among Nations: Strengths and Weaknesses," *World Politics* 44, no. 3 (April 1992): 466–496.

48. This literature is reviewed and referenced in the subsequent chapters.

49. On the role of geography in international affairs, see Saul B. Cohen, *Geography and Politics in a World Divided,* 2d ed. (New York: Oxford University Press, 1975).

50. The former is the case of Bangladesh (chapter 5) and the latter that of Ethiopia (chapter 2).

51. Courtney G. Hauge, "The Nile River: An Analysis of International Law" (paper presented at the Annual Meeting of the Association of American Geographers, Atlanta, Ga., April 1993).

52. United Nations, *Register of International Rivers*. The number is higher since the breakup of the Soviet Union and if the new Central Asian states are counted among the Third World states.

53. Some comparative data on each of the six basins and the respective riparian states are provided in appendix I.

54. Some large and rapidly growing economies, such as Brazil, India, and Israel, have constructed and are capable of implementing large water projects unilaterally. But for most other riparian states in the six basins, external aid is a basic necessity.

55. The author recognizes that the inclusion of other cases where an actual or potential hegemonic riparian state does not exist, as, for example, in the Senegal basin in Africa, may change some of the findings and contingent generalizations of this study.

56. Even the self-imposed isolation of Burma (Myanmar)—a riparian state in the Mekong basin—seems to be ending (chapter 6).

1. THE LA PARANÁ–LA PLATA BASIN

1. "Itaipu Binacional: The Biggest Hydroelectricity Undertaking of the XXth Century," advertisement, *New York Times*, October 30, 1992, A6–A7.

2. Carol Bittig Lutyk, "The Paraná–La Plata: South of the Iguazú," in *Great Rivers of the World* (Washington, D.C.: National Geographic Society, 1984), 333.

3. As a matter of comparison, the Taj Mahal in India is reported to have taken twelve thousand workers about twenty-two years to complete.

4. The quantity of electricity generated per year is given in kilowatt-hours (kwh), and the hourly capacity is given in kilowatts (kw).

5. The basin is also known interchangeably as the Paraná basin or the Paraná del Plata basin.

6. Gerd Kohlhepp, *Itaipu: Socio-economic and Ecological Consequences of the Itaipu Dam* (Brunswick/Wiesbaden, Germany: Friedr. Vieweg & Sohn, 1987), 41.

7. A. A. Bonetto and I. R. Wais, "Powerful Paraná," *Geographical Analysis* (March 1990): 2.

8. United Nations, *The Water Resources of Latin America and the Caribbean and Their Utilization: A Report on Progress in the Application of the Mar del Plata Action Plan* (Santiago, Chile: United Nations, 1985).

9. Bonetto and Wais, "Powerful Paraná," 2–3.

10. See the later section on the Hidrovia Project.

11. United Nations Economic Commission for Latin America and the Caribbean (ECLAC), *The Water Resources of Latin America and the Caribbean: Planning, Hazards, and Pollution* (Santiago, Chile: United Nations, July 1990).

12. See the later section on the Hidrovia Project.

13. Bonetto and Wais, "Powerful Paraná," 2.

14. Paraguay does have alternative access to the Atlantic Ocean through Brazil. However, this is costlier than access provided by the basin's rivers. The same is the case for Bolivia.

15. Bonetto and Wais, "Powerful Paraná," 2.

16. United Nations (ECLAC), *Latin America and the Caribbean: Inventory of Water Resources and Their Use*, vol. 2, *South America* (Santiago, Chile: United Nations, August 23, 1990), 89–126.

17. World Bank, *World Development Report 1996* (New York: Oxford University Press, 1996), 194–195, 204–205.

18. The official capital of Bolivia is Sucre, located near the origins of the Pilcomayo River.

19. The 1950 populations of São Paulo and Buenos Aires were 2.75 million and 5.13 million, respectively. By 1985 these cities had 15.54 million and 10.76 million residents, respectively. By the year 2000, their populations are expected to reach 23.97 million and 13.18 million, respectively. See Stanley D. Brunn and Jack F. Williams, eds., *Cities of the World*, 2d ed. (New York: Harper Collins College Publishers, 1993), 19.

20. Bonetto and Wais, "Powerful Paraná," 2.

21. In monetary terms, whereas energy imports had accounted for only one-ninth ($377 million) of Brazil's total import bill in 1971, the share rose to a quarter ($3.1 billion) by 1975, to over one-third ($6.7 billion) in 1979, and to $10 billion in 1982. In 1990 fuel imports accounted for 23 percent of all merchandise imports and 14 percent of all merchandise exports by Brazil. From 1965 to 1990, Brazilian per capita energy consumption had gone up from 286 to 915 kilograms of oil equivalent. See Simon Collier, Harold Blakemore, and Thomas Skidmore, eds., *The Cambridge Encyclopedia of Latin America and the Caribbean* (Cambridge: Cambridge University Press, 1989).

22. United Nations (ECLAC), *Latin America and the Caribbean: Inventory*.

23. Brazil and Argentina have also been developing their nuclear energy capabilities. According to the UN International Atomic Energy Agency (IAEA), Argentina currently has two nuclear power stations (935 megawatts each) and one 692-megawatt station under construction. Brazil has one station (626 megawatts), and another, 1,245-megawatt station is under construction.

24. World Bank, *World Development Report 1998–1999* (New York: Oxford University Press, 1999), 206–207.

25. World Bank, *World Development Report 1996*, 188–189, 220–221.

26. Brazil renegotiated its debt with the international banks in 1992. Other Latin American countries have been trying to follow Brazil's lead. *The Economist*, "Latin America Cheers Up," April 18–24, 1992.

27. The borrowings of Brazil's electrical utilities in the past accounted for nearly 40 percent of its total external debt. "Brazilian Energy Policy: Pass the Rum," *The Economist*, July 4, 1992, 62.

28. Pope G. Atkins, *Latin America in the International System*, 2d ed. (Boulder, Colo.: Westview, 1989), 78.

29. See *Encyclopedia of Public International Law*, no. 6, *Regional Cooperation, Organizations and Problems* (Amsterdam, New York, Oxford: North Holland, 1983), 61. See also Collier, Blakemore, and Skidmore, *Cambridge Encyclopedia of Latin America and the Caribbean*.

30. Gary Goertz and Paul F. Diehl, *Territorial Changes and International Conflict* (New York: Routledge, 1992), 141–142.

31. See the later section "Hydropolitics."

32. The dates for the latest transitions to representative democracy in the basin are Brazil, 1989; Paraguay, 1989; Uruguay, 1984; and Argentina; 1983.

33. Collier, Blakemore, and Skidmore, *Cambridge Encyclopedia of Latin America and the Caribbean.*

34. See the later section "The Hidrovia Project."

35. There are some indications that the ongoing economic reforms in these countries are likely to worsen income distribution across different strata of society and across regions.

36. Outside the Paraná–La Plata basin, Brazil shares four other international basins, including the Amazon; Argentina shares sixteen basins; and Bolivia shares three. All the international river basins shared by Bolivia and Uruguay together cover more than 90 percent of their respective territories. On Brazil's riparian dilemma, see Jorge Trevin and J. C. Day, "Risk Perception in International River Basin Management: The Plata Basin Example," *Natural Resources Journal* 30, no. 1 (winter 1990): 97.

37. See Luigi Manzetti, "Argentine-Brazilian Economic Integration: An Early Appraisal," *Latin American Research Review* 25, no. 3 (1990); Geri Smith and John Pearson, "The New World's Newest Trading Block," *Business Week*, May 4, 1992; and *Encyclopedia of Public International Law*, 241–249.

38. Alan J. Day, ed., *Border and Territorial Disputes* (Essex, U.K.: Longman House, 1982).

39. Guillermo J. Cano, "Argentina, Brazil, and the de la Plata River Basin: A Summary Review of Their Legal Relationship," *Natural Resources Journal* 16, no. 4 (October 1976): 886.

40. For a detailed description and discussion, see ibid., 863–882.

41. *Encyclopedia of Public International Law*, 238.

42. Ibid., 239. As we shall see in chapter 5, the positions taken by the large and small riparian states in the Paraná–La Plata basin are very similar to those taken by the large and small riparian states in South Asia.

43. Ibid., 238.

44. Ibid., 240.

45. Cano, "Argentina, Brazil, and the de la Plata River Basin," 878.

46. J. Eliseo Da Rosa, "Economics, Politics, and Hydroelectric Power: The Paraná River Basin," *Latin American Research Review* 18, no. 3 (1983): 81.

47. Ibid., 85.

48. Irene Murphy and Eleonora Sabadell, "International River Basins: A Policy Model for Conflict Resolution," *Resources Policy* 12, no. 1 (March 1986).

49. Kohlhepp, *Itaipu.*

50. Murphy and Sabadell, "International River Basins," 140.

51. Beverly Y. Nagel, "Socioeconomic Differentiation among Small Cultivators on Paraguay's Eastern Frontier," *Latin American Research Review* 26, no. 2 (1991): 103–132.

52. Kohlhepp, *Itaipu,* 28.

53. Ibid., 36.

54. For a detailed account of land appropriation, compensation, and settlement problems, and case studies of the socioeconomic and ecological impacts of the project, see ibid.

55. In 1992 Paraguay was reported to be studying a proposal by the Japanese International Development Organization for the construction of a $1 billion aluminum processing plant some twenty miles from Asunción. The facility would be powered by the Itaipu hydroelectric plant. *North South: The Magazine of the Americas,* June–July 1992, 66.

56. Da Rosa, "Economics, Politics, and Hydroelectric Power," 93. Da Rosa also quotes a report in the *Latin American Political Report* of November 25, 1977, that indicates that Paraguay's stand may also have been directed by greed. Paraguay hoped that Brazil would accept to pay $300 million rather than the $130 million and some developmental assistance Brazil offered if Paraguay changed its electric frequency.

57. See chapter 5 for similar issues between Nepal and India in the Ganges-Brahmaputra-Barak basin.

58. See Da Rosa, "Economics, Politics, and Hydroelectric Power," 83.

59. Ibid., 94.

60. Ibid., 95.

61. *The Economist,* August 10, 1991, 34.

62. Ibid.

63. The conduct and contents of the Itaipu negotiations were kept secret until the agreement was signed. In Paraguay especially, there was no public debate on the negotiations being conducted by the foreign minister, the head of ANDE, and only two other official representatives. Kohlhepp, *Itaipu,* 21.

64. Da Rosa, "Economics, Politics, and Hydroelectric Power," 90–91.

65. Ibid., 89.

66. For a short bibliography of Paraguayan opinions against the Itaipu Treaty, see Trevin and Day, "Risk Perception in International River Basin Management," 91 n 11.

67. Da Rosa, "Economics, Politics, and Hydroelectric Power," 84.

68. Cano, "Argentina, Brazil, and the de la Plata River Basin," 880.

69. Da Rosa, "Economics, Politics, and Hydroelectric Power," 105.

70. Cano, "Argentina, Brazil, and the de la Plata River Basin," 864–865.

71. United Nations, *Water Resources of Latin America and the Caribbean and Their Utilization.*

72. Owen Lammers, Deborah Moore, and Kay Preakle, *Considering the Hidrovia: A Preliminary Report on the Status of the Proposed Paraguay/Paraná Waterway Project,* Working Paper 3 (Berkeley, Calif.: International Rivers Network, July 1994).

73. Ibid., 16–18.

2. THE NILE BASIN

1. Cited by Joyce R. Starr, "Water Wars," *Foreign Policy*, no. 82 (spring 1991): 17–36. Also see "Water Wars: The Wave Builds in the Middle East," *Defense and Foreign Affairs Strategic Policy* (September 1990).

2. Over the past two decades Egypt has been diverting Nile water to a huge land reclamation project in the North Sinai desert west of the Suez Canal. For details of the North Sinai Agricultural Development Project (NSADP) and the controversies and tensions engendered by this unilateral project, see Ronald Bleier, "Will Nile Water Go to Israel?: North Sinai Pipeline and the Politics of Scarcity," *Middle East Policy* 5, no. 3 (September 1997): 113–124. (A reviewer of an earlier draft of this book has pointed out that some Egyptian Barraka bottled water is exported to and sold in Israel.) Sudan has from time to time also entertained the idea of supplying the Nile's water to countries outside the basin, for example, to Saudi Arabia. See Joyce R. Starr and D. Stoll, eds., *The Politics of Scarcity* (Boulder, Colo.: Westview Press, 1988).

3. A region of Ethiopia, Eritrea, became an independent nation in May 1993. However, the analysis here mostly excludes Eritrea because it is not yet clear what position it can or would take in the basin's hydropolitics given the distance of its territory from the main rivers.

4. Among other sources, this chapter relies heavily on John Waterbury, *Hydropolitics of the Nile Valley* (Syracuse, N.Y.: Syracuse University Press, 1979); Bonaya A. Godana, *Africa's Shared Water Resources: Legal and Institutional Aspects of the Nile, Niger, and Senegal River Systems* (London: Frances Pinter, 1985); Natasha Beschorner, *Water and Instability in the Middle East*, Adelphi Paper 273 (London: IISS, 1992); and Thomas Naff and Ruth C. Matson, *Water in the Middle East: Conflict or Cooperation?* (Boulder, Colo.: Westview Press, 1984).

5. See Waterbury, *Hydropolitics of the Nile Valley*, 13–14.

6. For an interesting account of the many historical explorations to discover the source of the Nile, see Allen Moorehead, *The White Nile* (New York: Harpers and Brothers, 1960).

7. Some of the water contributed by this lagoon to the Nile may originate in the Central African Republic; however, it is not regarded as belonging to the Nile basin proper.

8. Estimates for the evaporation losses over Lake Nasser differ widely, covering a range from 10 billion to 21 billion cubic meters every year. See, Waterbury, *Hydropolitics of the Nile Valley*, 123–125.

9. A Libyan scheme to pump water out of this aquifer has already engendered much tension between Egypt and Libya. However, this conflict may be resolved if it can be shown that the shared aquifer is independent of the Nile basin hydrology.

10. Mahmoud Abu-Zeid, "Water Challenges and Prospects" (paper presented at the First International Israeli-Palestinian Academic Conference on Water, Zurich, December 10–13, 1992).

11. Peter H.Gleik, "Climatic Changes, International Rivers, and International Security: The Nile and the Colorado," in R. Redford and T. J. Minger, eds., *Greenhouse Glasnost*

(New York: Eco Press, 1990), 147–165; and "Environment and Security: Clear Connections," *Bulletin of Atomic Scientists* 47, no. 3 (1991): 17–21.

12. World Bank, *World Development Report 1998–1999* (New York: Oxford University Press, 1999), 190–191.

13. Peter H. Gleick, "Water and Conflict," in *Environmental Change and Acute Conflict* (Washington, D.C.: American Academy of Arts and Sciences, 1992), 17.

14. World Bank, *World Development Report 1998–1999*, 208–209.

15. Ibid., 222–223.

16. The United States is reported to have forgiven a $7 billion debt owed by Egypt after the latter's participation in the Gulf War in 1991.

17. David Wishart, "An Economic Approach to Understanding Jordan Valley Water Dispute," *Middle East Review* (summer 1989): 45–53.

18. Asit K. Biswas, "The Aswân High Dam Revisited," *Ecodecision* (September 1992): 67–69.

19. Abu-Zeid, "Water Challenges and Prospects," 7–11.

20. Ibid., 11.

21. Herve Plusquellec, *The Gezira Irrigation Scheme in Sudan*, World Bank Technical Paper no. 120 (Washington, D.C.: World Bank, 1990).

22. The Secretariat, "Brief of the Organization for the Management and Development of the Kagera River Basin: Present Status," in Evan Vlachos, Anne C. Webb, and Irene L. Murphy, eds., *The Management of International River Basin Conflicts* (Washington, D.C.: George Washington University, 1986).

23. Two other basins in Africa, the Niger and the Zaire basins, are reported to be shared by ten and nine countries, respectively. However, the shares of some countries in the total catchment and drainage areas of these basins are minuscule. See the United Nations, *Register of International Rivers* (Oxford: Pergamon Press, 1978), 5.

24. The new government of Ethiopia is trying to democratize the domestic polity and to develop friendly relations with all its neighbors, with mixed results, as demonstrated by the border clashes with Eritrea in 1998 and 1999.

25. Christopher Clapham, "The Political Economy of Conflict in the Horn of Africa," *Survival* (September–October 1990): 403–419.

26. "Let Them Eat Cash?" *The Economist*, April 10, 1993, 42–48.

27. For a brief comment on Egypt-Sudan-Ethiopia relations, see Beschorner, *Water and Instability*, 58–61.

28. John Waterbury, "Ethiopie, la grande inconnue," *Bulletin du CEDEJ* (September 1987): 37.

29. Waterbury, *Hydropolitics of the Nile Valley*, 240.

30. See the later section "Other Projects."

31. For the main water-related agreements in the basin during the colonial era, see Beschorner, *Water and Instability*, 76.

32. Godana, *Africa's Shared Water Resources*, 117.

33. Naff and Matson, *Water in the Middle East*, 144–147.

34. Godana, *Africa's Shared Water Resources*, 117.

35. In this respect, Egypt's situation was very similar to Bangladesh's current situation in the Ganges-Brahmaputra-Barak basin, since the latter also needs projects in the upstream countries—India and Nepal—to solve its own water-related problems. Bangladesh has also put forward comprehensive plans for the development of multiple projects within the upper riparians' territories. However, unlike Egypt, Bangladesh lacks the potential to coerce or persuade its neighbors to construct water projects according to its specifications (see chapter 5).

36. Egypt was actively involved in the Owen Falls Dam agreement of 1949 and agreed to compensate Kenya and Tanzania for any adverse consequences they might suffer from the project. See Beschorner, *Water and Instability*, 57.

37. Waterbury, *Hydropolitics of the Nile Valley*, 42.

38. M. Lock Howell and S. Cobb, eds., *The Jonglei Canal: Impacts and Opportunities* (Cambridge: Cambridge University Press, 1988).

39. Inter Press Service, "The Nile Is at the Center of New Egyptian Overtures," October 25, 1989.

40. British Broadcasting Corporation, "Egyptian Minister Comments on Nile Water Projects," March, 26, 1990, BBC World Service.

41. C. O. Okidi, "Legal and Political Regime of Lake Victoria and Nile Basins," *Indian Journal of International Law* 20 (1980).

42. The Soviet Union and India also signed a Friendship Treaty in 1971 (see chapter 5).

43. Waterbury, *Hydropolitics of the Nile Valley*, 117.

44. Ibid., 30.

45. Nasser, along with Nehru in India and Tito in Yugoslavia, was also a leading figure in the Non-Aligned Movement, which sought to keep the newly independent states in the Third World free from superpower rivalry and machinations.

46. Godana, *Africa's Shared Water Resources*, 184.

47. Waterbury, *Hydropolitics of the Nile Valley*, 116–153.

48. Biswas, "The Aswan High Dam Revisited," 67–69.

49. Ibid.

50. Reuters North European Service, "Rosetta Gets Facelift to Bring Tourists to Historic Sites," September 18, 1985.

51. Beschorner, *Water and Instability*, 45–61.

52. Gleick, "Water and Conflict," 5–9.

53. Waterbury, *Hydropolitics of the Nile Valley*, 153.

54. Ibid., 101.

55. Beschorner, *Water and Instability*, 58.

56. The other newly independent state is Bangladesh in the Ganges-Brahmaputra-Barak basin in South Asia (see chapter 5).

3. THE JORDAN BASIN

1. For a historic account of third-party negotiating experience in the Middle East, see Kenneth W. Stein and Samuel W. Lewis, with Sheryl J. Brown, *Making Peace Among Arabs and Israel: Lessons from Fifty Years of Negotiating Experience* (Washington, D.C.: United States Institute of Peace, October 1991).

2. According to a *New York Times* report (July 26, 1994, A8), the walnut table on which King Hussein and Prime Minister Yitzhak Rabin signed the agreement was the same one that had been used by Anwar Sadat and Menachem Begin in 1979, and by Yassir Arafat and Yitzhak Rabin in 1993 to sign peace accords. It was bought in 1869 during the administration of President Grant for the signing of a peace protocol that ended hostilities between the United States and Spain. Ironically, one of the main architects of these peace overtures, Rabin, was murdered by an Israeli extremist in 1995, while Arafat was elected the president of a nonexistent Palestinian state in early 1996.

3. Thomas Naff and Ruth C. Matson, eds., *Water in the Middle East: Conflict or Cooperation?* (Boulder, Colo.: Westview Press, 1984), 182.

4. Although Lebanon is a minor riparian state in the Jordan basin, because only some springs in Lebanon feed into one of the three streams that later make up the Jordan River, it has other rivers within its territory, including the Litani. A hydrological connection between the waters of the Litani and Jordan Rivers is not fully established.

5. Thomas Naff, "Water Scarcity, Resource Management, and Conflict in the Middle East," in *Environmental Dimensions of Security* (Washington, D.C.: American Association for the Advancement of Science, 1992), 26.

6. Hillel I. Shuval, "Approaches to Resolving the Water Conflicts between Israel and Her Neighbors: A Regional Water-for-Peace Plan," *Water International* 17 (1992): 134.

7. M. J. Falkenmark, J. Lunkqvist, and A. Widstrand, *Water Scarcity: An Ultimate Constraint in Third World Development*, Tema V, Report 14 (Linkoping, Sweden: University of Linkoping, Department of Water and Environmental Studies, 1990).

8. See, for example, F. Pearce, "Water Wars on the West Bank," *New Scientist* 30, no. 1771 (June 1, 1991).

9. J. K. Cooley, "War over Water," *Foreign Policy*, no. 54 (1984): 3–26, and Joyce R. Starr, "Water Wars," *Foreign Policy*, no. 82 (spring 1991). For a nonalarmist view, see Natasha Beschorner, *Water and Instability in the Middle East*, Adelphi Paper no. 273 (London: IISS, 1992).

10. The following sections borrow heavily from the writings of Beschorner, Cooley, Gruen, Kolars, Lowi, Naff, Naff and Matson, Savage, Shuval, Stevens, Wishart, and Wolf, among others. I have attempted to reference all borrowings of statistical data, information, and language; however, I apologize to these authors if some references are less comprehensive than they should be.

11. Wadis are small seasonal streams.

12. Naff and Matson, *Water in the Middle East*, 18–19.

13. Beschorner, *Water and Instability*, 9.

14. Naff and Matson, *Water in the Middle East*, 21.

15. This is strictly not true since a wadi does link the Dead Sea to the Red Sea. However, this wadi does not carry any water.

16. United Nations, *The Unified Development of the Water Resources of the Jordan Valley Region* (Beirut, Lebanon: United Nations Relief and Works Agency for Refugees in the Near East, August 1953), 13.

17. Ibid., 25.

18. This aquifer may also be linked to another aquifer underneath the Gaza strip.

19. J. Schwarz, "Water Resources in Judea, Samaria, and the Gaza Strip," in Daniel Elazar, ed., *Judea, Samaria, and Gaza: Views on the Present and the Future* (Washington, D.C.: American Enterprise Institute for Public Policy Research, 1982), 88–91.

20. Radwan Al-Mubarak Al-Weshah, "Jordan's Water Resources: Technical Perspective," *Water International* 17, no. 3 (1992): 125.

21. On the conflict between the two countries about exploitation of this aquifer, see the later section "Hydropolitics."

22. David B. Brooks, "Economics, Ecology, and Equity: Lessons from the Energy Crisis in Managing Water Shared by Israelis and Palestinians" (keynote address at the First Israeli-Palestinian International Academic Conference on Water, Zurich, Switzerland, December 10, 1992), 7.

23. World Bank, *World Development Report, 1998–1999* (New York: Oxford University Press, 1999), 190–194, 232. Lebanon is one of the few countries in the world that has not conducted a population census since World War II.

24. Naff, "Water Scarcity, Resource Management, and Conflict in the Middle East," 27–28.

25. World Bank, *World Development Report 1998–1999*.

26. Ibid.

27. Ibid., 190–191.

28. Ibid., 200–201.

29. Central Intelligence Agency, *The World Fact Book 1991* (Washington, D.C.: U.S. Government Printing Office, n.d.), 153, 177.

30. Al-Weshah, "Jordan's Water Resources," 129.

31. Ibid.

32. See the later section "Hydropolitics" for some details of the 1994 water agreement between Israel and Jordan.

33. Itzhak Galnoor, "Water Planning: Who Gets the Last Drop," in Bilski, ed., *Can Planning Replace Politics? The Israeli Experience* (The Hague: Martinus Nijhoff Publishers, 1980), 215.

34. Beschorner, *Water and Instability*, 11.

35. Ibid., 12.

36. Ibid., 11.

37. *New York Times*, "Week in Review," July 31, 1994.

38. High State Planning Commission, *Statistical Abstracts* (Damascus, 1970, 1979, 1980, 1989, and 1990), cited in Mikhail Wakil, "Analysis of Future Water Needs for Different Sectors in Syria," *Water International* 18, no. 1 (1993).

39. See the following section, "Political Geography," for the ideology of the Ba'th regime.

40. Raymond A. Hinnebusch, *Peasant and Bureaucracy in Ba'thist Syria: The Political Economy of Rural Development* (Boulder, Colo.: Westview Press, 1989), 215–222.

41. CIA, *World Fact Book 1991*, 303.

42. See chapter 4 for a discussion of hydropolitics in the Euphrates-Tigris basin.

43. Also see John Kolars, "Is There Enough Water in the Litani River?" (paper presented at the 1989 Annual Meeting of the Middle East Studies Association, Toronto, Canada, November 1989).

44. Ibrahim Dakkak, "Water Policy on the Occupied West Bank" (al-Siyaasa al-Ma'iya f'il Difa al-Gharbiya al-Muhtala). Also see Miriam R. Lowi, *Water and Power: The Politics of a Scarce Resource in the Jordan River Basin* (Cambridge: Cambridge University Press, 1993).

45. Yaroslav Trofimov, "Thai Option: Israel Finds Alternative to Palestinian Workers," *Far Eastern Economic Review*, July 28, 1994, 79.

46. Tony Allan and Massoud Karshenas, "Managing Environmental Capital: The Case of Water in Israel, Jordan, the West Bank, and Gaza, 1947 to 1995," *Middle East and African Water Review*, abstracts from a conference on water in the Jordan catchment countries held at the School of Oriental and African Studies, London, May 15, 1995.

47. The borders of Jordan, for example, are said to have been drawn by Winston Churchill in one afternoon. The straight-line borders separating Iraq from Jordan, Saudi Arabia, and Syria were mostly drawn on the assumption that nobody lived in that desert region.

48. Peter Beaumont, Gerald H. Blake, and J. Malcom Wagstaff, *The Middle East: A Geographical Study*, 2d ed. (New York: Halsted Press, 1988), 317.

49. Ibid., 319.

50. For a historical account of state creation and water conflicts in the Jordan Valley, see Aaron T. Wolf, "The Impact of Water Resources on the Arab-Israeli Conflict: An

Interdisciplinary Study of Water Conflict Analysis and Proposals for Conflict Resolution" (Ph.D. diss., University of Wisconsin-Madison, 1992), 19–143; and *Hydropolitics along the Jordan River: Scarce Water and Its Impacts on the Arab-Israeli Conflict* (Tokyo; New York: United Nations University Press, 1995).

51. Beaumont, Blake, and Wagstaff, *The Middle East*, 455.

52. Beschorner, *Water and Instability*, 14, 78.

53. According to one report, an engineer working for the Israeli water authority, Mekorot, found a sack of explosives in the Beit Netopha Canal and alerted the police, who removed it only hours before it was set to go off. See Janet Wallach and John Wallach, *Arafat* (New York: Lyle Stuart, Carol Publishing Group, 1990), 121.

54. Beaumont, Blake, and Wagstaff, *The Middle East*, 453.

55. Zaour H. and J. Isaac, "The Water Crisis in the Occupied Territories" (paper presented at the Seventh World Congress on Water Resources, Rabat, Morocco, May 1991).

56. State Comptroller, Government of Israel, *Report on Water Management in Israel*, summarized in *Israel Environmental Bulletin* (Jerusalem: Ministry of the Environment, spring 1991), 4–7.

57. See chapter 4.

58. See Don Peretz, "Perceptions: How the Israelis and Arabs See Each Other," *The World and I* (April 1992): 1–18.

59. A 1964 agreement between Jordan and Saudi Arabia resulted in an exchange of some desert territory between the two nations to give Jordan better access to its only seaport at Aqaba. See Beaumont, Blake, and Wagstaff, *The Middle East*, 310.

60. Beschorner, *Water and Instability*, 16.

61. Gaza is already suffering from severe water deficiency. Its water problems are not discussed here only because Gaza is physically not a part of the Jordan basin. However, a solution for Gaza's water problems will have to be part of any regional water accord.

62. See H. J. Skutel, "Water in the Arab-Israel Conflict," *International Perspectives* (July–August 1986): 22.

63. David Wishart, "An Economic Approach to Understanding Jordan Valley Water Disputes," *Middle East Review* (summer 1984): 45–52.

64. David Wishart, "The Political Economy of Conflict over Water Rights in the Jordan Valley from 1890 to the Present" (Ph.D. diss., University of Illinois, 1985), 66–67.

65. Ibid., 92.

66. Ibid., fn. 82.

67. Phillipe W. Zgheib and Herbert H. Fullerton, "International Protocol for the Integrated Development of Water in the Litani and Jordan River Basins," in *The Proceedings of the International Symposium on Water Resources in the Middle East: Policy and Institutional Aspects* (Urbana, Ill.: International Water Resources Association, 1993), 76. For a discussion of the Johnston Plan, see the later section "Hydropolitics and the Great Powers."

68. It can be argued that India and China have also improved their water supply and riparian positions in the Indus and Ganges-Brahmaputra basins by incorporating parts of Kashmir and Sikkim (India) and Tibet (China) into their territory. However, as the discussion of hydropolitics in these two basins makes clear (in chapter 5), the situation and circumstances in South Asia were and are quite different from those in the Middle East.

69. Wishart, "The Political Economy of Conflict," fn. 83, 84, 85.

70. Ibid., 92.

71. Clyde Haberman, "Water and Concessions Can Mix, Israeli Study Says," *New York Times*, October 10, 1993, 6.

72. Alan Cowell, "Hurdle to Peace: Parting the Mideast's Waters," *New York Times*, October 10, 1993, 6.

73. "Israel and Jordan Sign Draft of Wide-Ranging Peace Treaty: Will Share Water," *New York Times*, October 18, 1994, A1.

74. *Foreign Relations of the United States: The Paris Conference, 1919*, vol. 4 (Washington: Government Printing Office, 1947), 194–195.

75. Samir N. Saliba, *The Jordan River Dispute* (The Hague: Martinus Nijhoff, 1968), 9.

76. Also see David M. Wishart, "The Breakdown of the Johnston Negotiations over the Jordan Waters," *Middle Eastern Studies* 26, no. 4 (October 1990): 536–546.

77. United Nations, *The Unified Development of the Water Resources of the Jordan Valley Region* (1953; reprint, Boston: Chas. T. Main, 1961).

78. George Gruen, *The Next Middle East Conflict: The Water Crisis* (Los Angeles, Calif.: Simon Wiesenthal Center, 1991), 25.

79. It is important to note that at about the same time a similar attempt was being made in the Lower Mekong basin (see chapter 6), and the World Bank was attempting to resolve a water conflict between the newly created states of India and Pakistan in the Indus Valley (see chapter 5). In the event, whereas the World Bank attempt succeeded in resolving the conflict by developing a nonoptimal solution for sharing the river waters between India and Pakistan, the U.S. government's attempts in both the Mekong and Jordan basins failed for different sets of reasons.

80. Georgiana G. Stevens, *Jordan Water Partition* (Stanford, Calif.: Hoover Institution Studies, 1965), 29.

81. However, Israel had already begun to divert water to areas outside the basin using its National Water Carrier.

82. Wishart, "The Breakdown of the Johnston Negotiations," 544.

83. Jonathan C. Randal, "Low-Key Talks Bring Opposing Parties Together," *Washington Post*, May 13, 1992, A29.

84. Aaron T. Wolf, "Guidelines for a Water-for-Peace Plan for the Jordan River Watershed" (paper submitted to the International Symposium on Water Resources Management in the Middle East, University of Illinois at Urbana-Champaign, October 25–28, 1993), 5;

and "International Water Conflict Resolution: Lessons from Comparative Analysis," *International Journal of Water Resources Development* 13, no. 3 (December 1997).

85. L. Strauss, "Dwight Eisenhower's 'Proposal for Our Times,'" *National Review* 37 (1967): 1008.

86. See Wolf, "Guidelines for a Water-for-Peace Plan," 40.

87. Joyce R. Starr and Daniel C. Stoll, *U.S. Foreign Policy on Water Resources in the Middle East* (Washington, D.C.: Center for Strategic and International Studies, 1987), 25–35.

88. Ibid., 27–28, 30.

89. A. Venter, "The Oldest Threat: Water in the Middle East," *Middle East Policy* 6, no. 1 (June 1998).

90. Also see Wolf, "The Impact of Water Resources on the Arab-Israeli Conflict."

91. Joseph L. Dees, "Jordan's East Ghor Canal Project," *Middle East Journal* 13, no. 4 (fall 1959): 357–371.

92. Gruen, *The Next Middle East Conflict*, 23.

93. Beschorner, *Water and Instability*, 8.

94. U.S. Army Corps of Engineers, *Water in the Sand: A Survey of Middle East Water Issues* (Washington, D.C.: G. P. O., 1991), sec. 2, 3.

95. S. Gur, *The Jordan Rift Valley: A Challenge for Development* (Tel Aviv: Prime Minister's Office, 1991).

96. Gary Hoch, "The Politics of Water in the Middle East: The Fast Dwindling Resource Remains the Region's Most Dangerous Problem," *Middle East Insight* 9, no. 3 (March–April 1993): 21.

97. "Rift Valley: Big Ambition in the Vision for the South," *Middle East Economic Digest*, October 27, 1995, 9.

98. Alwyn R. Rouyer, "The Water Issue in the Palestinian-Israeli Peace Process," *Survival* (summer 1997): 57–81.

99. Naff and Matson, *Water in the Middle East*, 181–197.

4. THE EUPHRATES-TIGRIS BASIN

1. Zohurul Bari, "Syrian-Iraqi Dispute over the Euphrates Waters," *International Studies* 16, no. 2 (April–June 1977): 227–244.

2. John F. Kolars and William A. Mitchell, *The Euphrates River and the Southeast Anatolia Project* (Carbondale, Ill.: Southern Illinois University Press, 1991), 6

3. Thomas Naff and Ruth C. Matson, eds., *Water in the Middle East: Conflict or Cooperation?* (Boulder, Colo.: Westview Press, 1984), 87.

4. There are also controversies about the overall size of the basin and about how much of the basin lies within the territory of each riparian state. For example, according to UN estimates, the combined area of the Euphrates-Tigris basin is 884,000 square kilometers (344,760 square miles), of which 41 percent is in Iraq, 27 percent in Iran, 18.4 percent in

Turkey, and 13.6 percent in Syria. However, according to some data provided to the United Nations by Baghdad, Iraq claims 58 percent of the whole Tigris basin and 60 percent of the total area of the Euphrates basin. In a strict hydrological sense, a small portion of the basin also lies within the Saudi Arabian borders. However, the water resources in this area, mainly wadis, are minuscule and highly seasonal. See United Nations, *Register of International Rivers* (Oxford: Pergamon Press, 1978), 14, 20 n. c.

5. Kolars and Mitchell, *Euphrates River*, 104 -105.

6. There is a bilateral agreement between Iraq and Iran, dating back to 1975, concerning frontier commissions, that includes a provision for settlement of disputes over navigation violations over the Shatt al-Arab. Another agreement dating back to 1937 had attempted to regulate navigation of warships on the Shatt. The agreement was later denounced in 1969 by Iran. See George E. Radosevich, James W. Schmehl, Stefanie A. Johnson, and Kristi M. Radosevich, *Middle East Water Resources: International Agreements and Domestic Water Laws* (Washington, D.C.: Middle East Research Institute, 1991).

7. U.S. Army Corps of Engineers, *Water in the Sand: A Survey of Middle East Water Issues* (Washington, D.C.: G. P. O., 1991), sec. 9, pp. 5–11.

8. Radosevich, Schmehl, Johnson, and Radosevich, *Middle East Water Resources*, 24.

9. World Bank, *World Development Report 1998–1999* (New York: Oxford University Press, 1999), 190–191.

10. For more on Iraq's waterworks, see the later section "Hydropolitics."

11. See United Nations, *Report of the Mission of Prince Saddrudin Agha Khan, July 1991* (New York: United Nations, 1991); and *World Water and Environmental Engineering* (September 1991): 9.

12. Natasha Beschorner, *Water and Instability in the Middle East*, Adelphi Paper 273 (London: IISS, 1992), 35.

13. Bari, "Syrian-Iraqi Dispute," 228.

14. Beschorner, *Water and Instability*, 49–50.

15. Ibid., 32.

16. J. Kolars, "The Hydro-Imperative of Turkey's Search for Energy," *Middle East Journal* 40, no. 1 (winter 1986): 53–67.

17. All available estimates for the size and growth rate of population and for current and future water availability and consumption in the basin are highly controversial. These projections are the best estimates based on the assumptions that water use practices in the basin do not change, the total availability of water remains the same, and the national populations continue to grow at their current growth rates.

18. See Kolars and Mitchell, *Euphrates River*, chap. 10.

19. World Bank, *World Development Report 1998*, 230–231.

20. Ibid., 190–191.

21. To take just one example, in 1980 there were major crackdowns by Baghdad against some Shia, Turkish, and Kurdish opposition figures in Iraq. Damascus had provided operational facilities for these opposition groups. See Beschorner, *Water and Instability*, 39.

22. In 1955 the Iraqi government had joined the Western-supported security treaty known as the Baghdad Pact. This pact was strongly opposed by the Arab nationalists within Iraq and by other Arab nations who harshly criticized it as a pro-Western, hence anti-Arab, alliance extending from Turkey to Pakistan. See Christine Moss Helms, *Iraq: Eastern Flank of the Arab World* (Washington, D.C.: Brookings Institution, 1984), 137.

23. Ibid., 7–56.

24. Georges Roux, *Ancient Iraq* (London: Penguin, 1992), 152.

25. Helms, *Iraq,* 18.

26. Iraqi Embassy Press Office, "Qaddasiyat Saddam" (press release, issued in Washington, D.C., May 4, 1981).

27. See D. McDowall, *The Kurds: A Nation Denied* (London: Minority Rights Group, 1992), 12.

28. In October 1984, Turkey and Iraq signed a "Hot Pursuit" agreement whereby both sides could pursue subversive groups within the territory of the other up to a distance of five kilometers. However, Iraq-based PKK activity resumed in 1988, and the same year, following Iraq's brutal suppression of Kurdish dissent, more than sixty thousand Kurds fled into Turkey. This time, Ankara did not allow Iraqi forces to pursue the Kurds within Turkish territory.

29. United Nations, *United Nations Treaty Series*, vol. 37, *1949* (New York: United Nations, 1949), 291.

30. Robert A. Hager, "The Euphrates Basin: In Search of a Legal Regime," *Georgetown International Environmental Law Review* 3, no. 1 (summer 1990): 215.

31. Bari, "Syrian-Iraqi Dispute," n. 30. Also see Stephen Kinzer, "Where Kurds Seek a Land, Turks Want the Water," *New York Times*, February 8, 1999, wk3.

32. Ibid., 239.

33. In November 1970, shortly after Assad came to power in Syria, Egypt and Syria agreed to form a federation that included Libya, with the major aim to formulate a unified policy toward Israel. The federation also reflected Syria's historical fear of its neighbor Iraq. The federation lasted until the end of the 1973 war with Israel when Egypt was forced to adopt a peaceful posture toward Israel. See Bari, ibid., 240.

34. Ibid., 243.

35. *Protocol on Matters Pertaining to Economic Cooperation between Republic of Turkey and the Syrian Arab Republic*, published in the Turkish government's *Official Gazette*, 1987.

36. "The Euphrates Fracas: Damascus Woos (and) Warns Ankara," *Mideast Mirror*, July 30, 1992.

37. As mentioned earlier, the Orontes originates in Lebanon.

38. Ewan Anderson, "Water Resources and Boundaries in the Middle East," in G. Blake and R. Schofield, eds., *Boundaries and State Territory in the Middle East* (The Cottons, Cambridgeshire, England: Middle East and North African Studies Press, 1987).

39. See Wilfred Thesiger, *The Marsh Arabs* (New York: Dutton, 1964).

40. Bari, "Syrian-Iraqi Dispute," 275.

41. Kolars and Mitchell, *Euphrates River,* 222.

42. Ibid., 16.

43. Ibid., 193.

44. Ibid., 220–221.

45. Beschorner, *Water and Instability*, 32.

46. Republic of Turkey, *GAP Master Plan Study* (Ankara: Prime Ministry, April 1989).

47. Olcay Unver and Bruno Voron, "Improvement of Canal Regulation Techniques: The Southeastern Anatolia Project-GAP," *Water International* 18 (1993): 157–165.

48. Kolars and Mitchell, *Euphrates River,* 25. Also see Kinzer, "Where Kurds Seek a Land."

49. Ibid., 260.

50. Ibid., 289.

5. THE GANGES-BRAHMAPUTRA-BARAK BASIN

1. Jagan Mehta, "Opportunity Costs of Delay in Water Resource Management between Nepal, India, and Bangladesh," in David J. Eaton, ed., *The Ganges-Brahmaputra Basin: Water Resource Cooperation between Nepal, India, and Bangladesh* (Austin: University of Texas at Austin, 1992), 2.

2. Among other sources, this chapter relies heavily on B. G. Verghese, *Waters of Hope: Himalaya-Ganga Development and Cooperation for a Billion People* (New Delhi: Oxford and IBH Publishing, 1990); Shaukat Hassan, *Environmental Issues and Security in South Asia*, Adelphi Paper 262 (London: IISS, 1991); and K. L. Rao, *India's Water Wealth: Its Assessment, Uses, and Projections* (New Delhi: Orient Longman, 1975).

3. The rivers and the tributaries of the basin are known by different names in the countries they flow through. For example, the east-flowing river from Tibet is known as Tsangpo or Yalu-Tsangpo until it enters India. Thereafter it takes on the name of Dihang or Siang in the state of Arunachal Pradesh. Farther down in Assam state the river acquires the name Brahmaputra. In Bangladesh the river divides into the Jamuna and the old Brahmaputra. Jamuna, in turn, joins the Ganga to form the Padma river. The old Brahmaputra, which was once the main course but is now a lesser channel, meets Meghna, which originates in India and is known there as Barak. Verghese, *Waters of Hope*, xii–xiii.

4. United Nations, *Register of International Rivers* (New York: Pergamon Press, 1978).

5. For some implications of this physical feature for hydropolitics in the basin, see the later section "Hydropolitics."

6. Verghese, *Waters of Hope*, 11.

7. Access to Tibet from other South Asian countries is only possible through some mountain passes and only during the brief period every year when these are not snowbound.

8. The total number of rivers and rivulets in Nepal is estimated to be close to six thousand, with a combined length of about 45,000 kilometers. B. K. Pradhan and H. M. Shrestha, "A Nepalese Perspective on Himalayan Water Resources Development," in Eaton, ed., *Ganges-Brahmaputra Basin*, 24.

9. There is a total of 230 large and small rivers in Bangladesh. Forty-four of these flow in from India and three from Burma (Myanmar).

10. Peter H. Gleick, "The Implications of Global Climatic Changes for International Security," *Climatic Change* 15 (1989): 309–325.

11. Verghese, *Waters of Hope*, 6.

12. As mentioned earlier, the Himalayas are among the youngest mountains in the world and are still rising in elevation owing to tectonic activity. This leads to a phenomenon known as "mass wasting" whereby the continuous collapse of hill sides and soil erosion on the mountain ranges generate vast amounts of silt, which is then carried down by rivers and tributaries to the plains and to the sea. Accumulated over geological time, these undersea silts may stretch as far south as Sri Lanka.

13. See the later section "Hydropolitics."

14. The Brahmaputra's flow begins to rise in June and reaches a high peak in August, while the Ganges starts rising in June-July to peak in late August or early September. The Meghna usually reaches its annual peak in August-September. All these high flows drain to the sea through the Lower Meghna, causing severe flooding, especially when the peak flows of the three rivers coincide.

15. Verghese, *Waters of Hope*, 5.

16. A substantial amount of water could be stored underground, using a method known as "induced groundwater recharge." What this means is that groundwater could be drawn out during the dry season to create a large capacity in the basin for storing monsoon flows. Special correspondent, "Harnessing Ganga and Brahmaputra," in Sunil Sen Sharma, ed., *Farakka—A Gordian Knot: Problem of Sharing Ganga Water* (Calcutta: ISHIKA, April 1986), 165–168.

17. B. D. Dhavan, "Coping with Floods in the Himalayan Rivers," *Economic and Political Weekly* 28, no. 18 (May 1, 1993): 849–852.

18. Geoffrey C. Ward, "India's Wildlife Dilemma," *National Geographic* 181 (May 1992): 2–29.

19. World Bank, *World Development Report 1998–1999* (New York: Oxford University Press, 1999), 190–191.

20. Bangladesh has had remarkable success in controlling the growth rate of its population over the past two decades. However, it is still expected to have a population of close to 250 million by the year 2030. By the year 2000, the country would require an additional 6 million tons of food. See Task Force on Women and the Environment, "A Brief Study Report on Environmental Degradation of Ganges Basin Area" (paper prepared for presentation in the workshop on Women for Water Sharing, Dhaka, Bangladesh, June 3 1994).

21. Already, nearly 97 percent of those living below the poverty line are concentrated in the hill and mountain regions in the basin.

22. Raghu Singh, "Food for Thought: Too Many People Can Hamper Development," *Far Eastern Economic Review*, September 22, 1994, 26.

23. The government of India has developed a Ganga Action Plan to clean the river. It incorporates 262 schemes for sewers, treatment plants, electric crematoria, public lavatories, riverfront cleanup, and long-term monitoring. However, implementation of the plan has been tardy at best.

24. Amartya Sen, *Poverty and Famines: An Essay on Entitlement and Deprivation* (Oxford: Clarendon Press, 1984).

25. Peter Rogers, Peter Lydon, David Seckler, and G. T. Keith Pitman, *Water and Development in Bangladesh: A Retrospective on the Flood Action Plan* (Arlington, Va.: ISPAN Technical Support Center, 1994), ix.

26. After China, India and Bangladesh are the second- and third-largest producers of inland fish in the world.

27. By comparison, the world's largest hydroelectric project, the Itaipu in the Paraná–La Plata basin, is designed to produce 12,600 megawatts of electricity (see chapter 1).

28. Verghese, *Waters of Hope*, 180.

29. Eric Eckholm, *Losing Ground: Environmental Stress and World Food Prospects* (New York: World Watch), 1976.

30. The overall hydroelectric potential of the Brahmaputra's flow has been estimated as 400,000 megawatts in northeast India and may be more than 50,000 megawatts along the Indo-Tibet bend. Verghese, *Waters of Hope*, preface.

31. Suggestions for electricity generation within Tibet include the construction of a regulation dam about 100 kilometers (62 miles) from Lhasa, which would generate 1,000 megawatts of power and form a lake 200 kilometers (124 miles) up the Tsangpo and Lhasa Rivers. The Chinese have announced plans to augment electricity production in Tibet from 140 megawatts in 1989 to 360 megawatts by the end of the century. Verghese, *Waters of Hope*, 398.

32. Ibid., 283.

33. The Brahmaputra is now navigable by steamers and barges for almost 1,300 kilometers to Dibrugarh in India. Navigation in the river's upper courses has been impeded by the aftereffects of a 1950 earthquake and by disputes between India and Bangladesh. However, Indian vessels are currently cleared to operate on about 1,300 to 1,500 kilometers of the waterways in Bangladesh while moving from Calcutta to the northeast. According to a 1987 protocol signed by the two countries, the navigational potential of the rivers is to be jointly developed and shared. Plans also exist for improving navigation on the Barak River by constructing a dam on the Indian side, which, in turn, will open up a vast hinterland that has hitherto been underdeveloped, primarily because of a lack of transportation and communications infrastructure. Verghese, *Waters of Hope*, 294.

34. Interestingly, despite an ongoing boundary dispute and other tensions between India and China, a 1981 trade treaty between Nepal and China stipulates that trade between them shall be on the basis of costs that would be incurred if the goods were routed through Calcutta or other ports to which both parties have agreed. Verghese, *Waters of Hope*, 303–304.

35. China has constructed a major road through Tibet and through some territory it acquired during the 1962 war with India. This road links Lhasa to the road network in the part of Kashmir under Pakistani control.

36. China is reported to have offered Nepal access to Pakistan through Tibet; however, the cost of constructing the needed road infrastructure is likely to be prohibitive. High transportation costs are also likely to make the price of Nepal's exports highly uncompetitive. Thus, Nepal may have no long-term choice but to seek access to the sea through India. Also see the later section "Hydropolitics."

37. World Bank, *World Development Report 1998–1999*, 200.

38. See "The Bank Pulls the Plug on Nepal Dam," *Far Eastern Economic Review*, August 31, 1995, 62.

39. According to some IMF estimates, the Indian economy now may be the seventh-largest economy in the world. See "Economic Giants," *The Economist*, June 10, 1993, 67.

40. Nepal's modern boundaries were defined in 1816. Burma (Myanmar) became a province of British India in 1886. It was partitioned from India in 1937, but remained part of British India. The country became independent in 1948.

41. Pakistan was allocated two territories with majority Muslim populations. West Pakistan and East Pakistan were separated by Indian territory and located downstream of India in the Indus and Ganges-Brahmaputra-Barak basins, respectively.

42. Bhutan, like Ethiopia in the Nile basin and Thailand in the Mekong basin, has the distinction of never being physically occupied by a colonial power. Until 1971 Bangladesh was the only country since World War II to emerge and be recognized as a sovereign state after a major civil war.

43. See the later section "SAARC and Hydropolitics."

44. This record was tarnished by the imposition of "Emergency" in India during 1975 to 1977, when many fundamental rights guaranteed by the Indian Constitution were temporarily suspended. However, the prime minister at the time, Indira Gandhi, was solidly defeated by a coalition of political parties in the subsequent general election. See the later section "Bangladesh-India Hydropolitics."

45. For example, Assamese rebels have objected to proposals for Indo-Bangladesh cooperation for developing the economic potential of the Brahmaputra's water, claiming that these waters belong to Assam and not to India or Bangladesh.

46. Hassan, *Environmental Issues and Security*, 34.

47. Chetan Kumar, "Beyond Earth Summit '92: Redefining the International Security Agenda," ACDIS Occasional Paper (University of Illinois at Urbana-Champaign, 1993).

48. See John F. Burns, "The Two Women of Bangladesh: At the Top, at Odds," *New York Times*, July 28, 1994, A4; and "A Writer Hides: Her Country Winces," *New York Times*, July 31, 1994, E3.

49. In India, communist parties of different hues have controlled the state governments in Kerala and West Bengal from time to time.

50. See the later section "India-Nepal Hydropolitics" for some more recent developments.

51. Although India is not directly responsible for Bhutan's defense, the Indian army provides training and support to the Royal Bhutanese Army. India has also indicated that any act of aggression against Bhutan would be regarded as an act of aggression against India. After his installation on the throne in 1972, the new king of Bhutan had stated his wish to maintain the Indo-Bhutanese Treaty and to further strengthen friendship with India. However, in 1979, during the Non-Aligned Conference and later at the UN General Assembly, Bhutan voted in opposition to India and in favor of Chinese policy. This notwithstanding, the overall Indo-Bhutanese relations can be characterized as friendly, with the proviso that Bhutan does not step out of the line and be seen to be compromising India's national interests in any way.

52. See *The Bhutan Tragedy: When Will It End? Human Rights and Inhuman Wrongs* (Kathmandu: Sahayogi Press, May 1992).

53. On asymmetrical vulnerabilities, see David J. Singer, *Weak States in a World of Powers* (New York: Free Press, 1972), 376.

54. See the later section "India-Nepal Hydropolitics."

55. See the later section "SAARC and Hydropolitics."

56. Within India itself, there are now more Muslims than in Pakistan. Recently, some right-wing groups and political parties in India have had notable successes in mobilizing the Hindu masses against perceived threats from the growing domestic Muslim minority, and from the spread of Islamic fundamentalism on India's borders. Consequently, Muslims outside India, particularly in Pakistan and Bangladesh, have mobilized to protest against the alleged mistreatment of India's Muslim minority.

57. However, despite India's strengths and advantages, its alleged ambition to become an unchallenged regional power and a potential hegemon in South Asia has been thwarted in the past by a number of domestic and external factors. The continuing conflict with Pakistan over Kashmir since independence; Pakistan's close relationship with the United States and China in the past and currently with some West Asian and Central Asian Islamic countries; India's defeat by China in the 1962 war; ongoing internal movements for separatism, especially in the sensitive northeast and northwest border regions; and the demise of India's "special friend," the Soviet Union, are only some of the factors that have prevented India from emerging and being recognized as a regional power in South Asia. India's domestic vulnerabilities owing to the staggering poverty of its masses have only added to the country's vulnerabilities in the regional security complex. However, the impressive growth registered by the Indian economy in recent years and its growing nuclear and other high-tech capabilities may modify this assessment substantially in the near future.

58. There are estimated to be a total of thirty prospective reservoir sites and eighty-eight attractive sites for hydroelectricity generation in Nepal. Pradhan and Shrestha, "A Nepalese Perspective," 23–35.

59. India has been greatly concerned by the continuing in-migration of a large number of Bangladeshis into its sensitive northeastern states. The mostly Christian and Hindu native residents of these states have felt economically and politically threatened by this large influx of mostly Muslim migrants. In fact, repatriation of these migrants to Bangladesh and/or their dispersion to other parts of India has been one of the main demands of separatist movements in the northeast region of India. Armed clashes between the migrants and indigenous people have already created a bitter legacy of bloody confrontations in the region. The central government in India is also accused of manipulating and exploiting the migrants for votes and for political support, creating further tensions in center-state relations in India. See Sanjoy Hazarika, "Bangladesh and Northeast India: Migration, Land Pressure, and Ethnic Conflict" (paper presented at a workshop on Environmental Change, Population Displacement, and Acute Conflict, Ottawa, Canada, June 18–19, 1991).

60. Aloys Arthur Michel, *The Indus River: A Study of the Effect of Partition* (New Haven, Conn.: Yale University Press, 1967).

61. For a historical and richly documentation account of this project going back to 1861, see Sharma, *Farakka*.

62. Independent India's first proposal to construct this barrage dates back to 1951.

63. Reported in Lincoln Kaye, "Resources and Rights," *Far Eastern Economic Review*, February 2, 1989, 22.

64. See Ben Crow, *Sharing the Ganges: The Politics and Technology of River Development* (New Delhi: Sage, 1995).

65. Indira Gandhi is reported to have been very upset at the assassination of Bangladesh's first leader, Sheikh Mujib, and angry with the new leaders who subsequently took power in Dhaka. To the best of our knowledge, there is no documented account of the extent to which this affected the then ongoing negotiations over water between Bangladesh and India.

66. Amjad Hossain Khan, *Problems of Water Sharing with India* (Dhaka: Approtech Consultants, April 1994), 5.

67. Hassan, *Environmental Issues and Security*, 54.

68. Ershadul Huq, "Flood Plan Stirring Controversy," *India Abroad* (June 4, 1993): 6.

69. Treaty between the Government of the Republic of India and the Government of the People's Republic of Bangladesh on Sharing the Ganga/Ganges Waters at Farakka, December 12, 1996.

70. The party that came to power in Nepal in 1951, the Nepalese Congress, had close ties with the Indian National Congress, which had spearheaded the independence movement in India and formed the central government in independent India. Consequently, the

Indian prime minister, Jawahar Lal Nehru, took a personal interest in developing close ties with the Nepalese government.

71. Nepal could conceivably sell water and electricity to Bangladesh, but both would have to be transported over Indian territory.

72. Lincoln Kaye, "Buyer's Market," *Far Eastern Economic Review*, February 2, 1989, 22.

73. Verghese, *Waters of Hope*, 341.

74. Chandra K. Sharma, *Water and Energy Resources of the Himalayan Block* (Kathmandu: Sangeetha Sharma, 23/282 Bishalnagar, May 1986).

75. China has contributed substantially to the Nepalese economy. For example, the first meeting of a joint committee on economic cooperation took place in 1984, and in 1986 China agreed to increase its imports from Nepal in order to minimize trade imbalances. In 1985 it was agreed that Nepal's border with Tibet should be opened; however, following the outbreak of violence in Tibet in 1989, the border was again closed. In 1991 the interim government of Nepal canceled a visit to the country by the Dalai Lama because of Chinese protests.

76. Kedar Man Singh, "One Less Headache: India, Nepal Resolve a Four-Year Water Dispute," *Far Eastern Economic Review*, February 15, 1996, 53–54.

77. Government of Nepal, *Water Resources Ministry Report* (Kathmandu: Government of Nepal, 1981).

78. Like Nepal, Bhutan is heavily dependent on India economically. In 1986 India accounted for nearly 86 percent of Bhutan's imports as well as 99 percent of its exports, composed mainly of electricity. For 1988–90, grants from the government of India provided 23.3 percent of the country's total budgetary revenue, while direct grants from international agencies amounted to only 8.3 percent. This relationship has not changed much over the past decade.

79. This agreement seems very similar to the Itaipu and Yacyreta Treaties in the Paraná–La Plata basin. The situation of Bhutan—a landlocked and poor country, but rich in hydroelectric potential—seems very similar to Paraguay. In this particular case, India has also acted in a manner similar to Brazil and Argentina in their dealings with a small but potentially resource-rich neighbor.

80. The initiative for a regional organization originated with the then president of Bangladesh.

81. Mohammad Iqbal, "SAARC: Problems and Prospects," *Regional Studies* 9, no. 1 (winter 1992–93): 35–68.

82. Samina Ahmed, "SAARC: Regional Security and National Development," *Regional Studies* 8, no. 2 (spring 1990): 35–45.

6. THE MEKONG BASIN

1. An embargo against North Vietnam had existed since 1964. In 1977 President Jimmy Carter had offered to normalize relations with Vietnam, but the talks stalled over Hanoi's demand for war reparations. See "Vietnam: Lukewarm Welcome," *Far Eastern Economic Review*, February 17, 1994, 15. An embargo against Cambodia was lifted in 1992. Also see the later sections "Political Geography" and "Hydropolitics."

2. The current members of ASEAN are Brunei, Indonesia, Malaysia, Myanmar (Burma), Thailand, the Philippines, Singapore, and Vietnam.

3. Throughout this chapter the names Burma and Myanmar, and Cambodia and Kampuchea are used alternatively for the two riparian states.

4. The growing menace of drug addiction and smuggling originating mainly from the Golden Triangle in the basin is discussed later.

5. Peter T. White, "The Mekong: River of Terror and Hope," *National Geographic* 134, no. 6 (1968).

6. Prachoom Chomchai, "The Mekong Development Plan: Its Problems and Prospects," *Asia Pacific Community*, no. 1 (summer 1978).

7. Mekong Secretariat, *Preparing for New Challenge: The Mekong Interim Committee Annual Report 1991* (Bangkok: Mekong Commission, 1991).

8. For an interesting account of an annual festival on the Tonle Sap, see Murray Hiebert, "The Common Stream," *Far Eastern Economic Review*, February 21, 1991, 24.

9. Thailand banned commercial logging in 1989; however, illegal felling continues.

10. Jeffrey W. Jacobs, "Toward Sustainability in Lower Mekong River Basin Development," *Water International* 19 (1994): 43–51.

11. Murray Hiebert, "Food or Forests?" *Far Eastern Economic Review*, April 7, 1994, 64.

12. U.S. Agency for International Development, *Environmental Assessment of the Lao PDR* (Washington, D.C.: USAID, 1995).

13. Until the economic crisis in Southeast Asia in the later 1990s, the Vietnamese economy was reported to have grown at the rate of 6 to 7 percent per year; however it remains an underdeveloped economy overall.

14. See Paisal Sricharatchanya, "The Mekong Connection," *Far Eastern Economic Review*, September 19, 1985, 2.

15. Hiroshi Hori, "Development of the Mekong River Basin: Its Problems and Future Prospects," *Water International* 18 (1993): 112–113.

16. Owing to the recent slowdown of economic growth in Thailand, the projections have been scaled down considerably.

17. For information on the Mekong Secretariat and the Mekong Committee, see the later section "Hydropolitics."

18. Malcome W. Browne, "Overcrowded Vietnam Is Said to Face Catastrophe," *New York Times*, May 8, 1994, 1.

19. Chomchai, "Mekong Development Plan," 44.

20. Whereas in 1972 only about 2 percent of the cultivated area (amounting to 213,000 hectares) in the Lower Basin was irrigated, by 1980 several irrigation projects were expected to increase irrigated acreage to 750,000 hectares. In 1989 the total acreage irrigated in Kampuchea, Laos, Thailand, and Vietnam, inside and outside the Lower Basin, was estimated at 6,270,000 hectares.

21. Lert Chutanaparb, quoted in Hiebert, "Common Stream," 24.

22. "Thailand: Wet and Dry," *The Economist*, April 10, 1993, 36–37.

23. Hiebert, "Common Stream," 26.

24. See the later section "Hydropolitics."

25. See the later section "International Efforts."

26. Mekong Secretariat, *Preparing for New Challenge*, 119.

27. See Paul Hadley, "River of Promise" and "Seeds of Friendship," *Far Eastern Economic Review*, September 16, 1993, 68–70, 71–72.

28. Murray Hiebert, "The Mekong 1: The Common Stream," *Far Eastern Economic Review*, February 21, 1991.

29. One of these bridges has recently opened.

30. Mekong Secretariat, *Mekong Work Program 1993* (Bangkok: Mekong Commission, 1993), 4.

31. Barbara Crossette, "Echoes for Bosnia and Haiti? Outsiders Gone, Cambodia Unravels," *New York Times*, December 3, 1995, sec. 4, pp. 1, 4.

32. The official names of these countries are the People's Republic of China, Socialist Republic of the Union of Burma, the Lao People's Democratic Republic, the People's Republic of Kampuchea, the Kingdom of Thailand, and the Socialist Republic of Vietnam, respectively.

33. See David P. Chandler and David J. Steinberg, eds., *In Search of Southeast Asia: A Modern History* (Honolulu: University of Hawaii Press, 1987), 1–96.

34. Hari Singh, "Prospects for Regional Stability in Southeast Asia in the Post–Cold War Era," *Millennium: Journal of International Studies* 22, no. 2 (1993): 279–300. Also see David B. H. Denoon and Evelyn Colbert, "Challenges for the Association of Southeast Asian Nations (ASEAN)," *Pacific Affairs* 71, no. 4 (winter 1998–99): 505–523.

35. See chapter 2.

36. M. E. Gettleman et al., *Vietnam and America: A Documented History* (New York: Goove Press, 1985), 461.

37. Frank Chang, "Vietnam Deserves MFN," *Far Eastern Economic Review*, March 3, 1994, 30.

38. At a meeting of donors in 1994, $15.8 million was granted to Cambodia to clear millions of randomly scattered mines. See "Someone to Trust," *Far Eastern Economic Review*, March 24, 1994, 47.

39. Up to two hundred thousand Chinese troops were involved in the invasion of Vietnam's northern border provinces and in occupation of several provincial capitals. The Chinese forces were beaten back and driven out by the Vietnamese within just a month.

40. See Arun P. Elhance and Richard Kendrick, "The Southeast Asian Security Complex and Laos: Trends and Prospects," *Asian Profile* 18, no. 2 (August 1990): 335–352.

41. This invasion and the China-Vietnam border war of 1979 are the first examples of an open military conflict between two communist nations.

42. A point of contention between Vietnam and the Khmer Rouge was the settlement of thousands of Vietnamese in Kampuchea. The government of Vietnam claimed that these people had lived in Kampuchea before 1970 and that they were driven out or fled into exile during that country's civil war. However, the Khmer Rouge charged that this type of resettlement was being used by Vietnam to strengthen its domination over Kampuchea. Consequently, driving out the new Vietnamese settlers as well as others whose families have lived in Kampuchea for generations became a rallying cry for the Khmer Rouge.

43. Rodney Tasker and Chris Pelling, "Trading Charges: Phnom Penh Accuses Thais of Aiding Khmer Rouge," *Far Eastern Economic Review*, April 28, 1994, 20.

44. For unresolved boundary disputes in Southeast Asia, see the sources listed by Singh, "Prospects for Regional Stability," 284.

45. The length of border Laos shares with other countries is Burma, 235 kilometers; Cambodia, 541 kilometers; China, 423 kilometers; Thailand, 1,745 kilometers; and Vietnam, 2,130 kilometers. On a border dispute between Laos and Thailand, see "Mekong, No River of Peace," *Far Eastern Economic Review*, January 16, 1986, 28.

46. China has occupied the Paracel Islands since 1974. Armed clashes between China and Vietnam over the islands took place in 1975 and 1988. Other countries with claims to the islands include the Philippines, Malaysia, Brunei, and Taiwan. All except Brunei occupy some parts of the islands.

47. The bottom of the South China Sea may contain 25 billion cubic meters of natural gas and 105 billion barrels of oil. China is reported to be building permanent observation posts, passing laws on "territorial waters," reserving the right to evict foreign ships, and authorizing the drilling of oil by foreign companies. See John W. Garver, "China's Push through the South China Sea: The Interaction of Bureaucratic and National Interests," *China Quarterly* 132 (December 1992): 999–1028. Also see Michael Vatikiotis, Michael Westlake, and Lincoln Kaye, "Piracy: Gunboat Diplomacy," *Far Eastern Economic Review*, June 16, 1994, 22–23.

48. Mark J. Valencia, "A Spratly Solution," *Far Eastern Economic Review*, March 31, 1994, 30. Also see Michael Vatikiotis, "Sea Worthy: Thai-Malaysian Pact May Be Oil-Exploration Model," *Far Eastern Economic Review*, April 21, 1994, 80.

49. W. Skinner, "Overseas Chinese in Southeast Asia," *Annals of the American Academy of Political and Social Science* 32 (January 1959); and "Overseas Chinese," *The Economist*, July 18, 1997, 21–24.

50. Margot Cohen, "Days of Rage," *Far Eastern Economic Review,* April 28, 1994, 14.

51. Chandler and Steinberg, eds., *In Search of Southeast Asia,* 5.

52. Singh, "Prospects for Regional Stability," 298.

53. Chandler and Steinberg, eds., *In Search of Southeast Asia,* 451.

54. See Muthaiah Alagappa, *Democratic Transition in Asia: The Role of the International Community,* Special Reports no. 3 (Honolulu: East-West Center, October 1994).

55. See B. Buzan, "The Southeast Asian Security Complex," *Contemporary Southeast Asia* 10, no. 1 (June 1988).

56. "Back to the Future," *The Economist,* January 8, 1994, 21–23.

57. Michael Vatikiotis and Brit Lintner, "Pariah No More: ASEAN Edges toward Closer Ties with Rangoon," *Far Eastern Economic Review,* March 3, 1994, 27.

58. See Bruce Cummings, "The Origins and Development of the Northeast Asian Political Economy: Industrial Sectors, Product Cycles, and Political Consequences," in F. Dayo, ed., *The Political Economy of New Asian Industrialism* (Ithaca, N.Y.: Cornell University Press, 1987).

59. Today, Japan's defense expenditure is second only to the United States in the Asia-Pacific region. Also see M. Alagappa, "Japan's Political and Security Role in the Asia-Pacific Region," *Contemporary Southeast Asia* 10, no. 1 (June 1988): 17–54.

60. The Chinese military budget grew by 98 percent between 1988 and 1993 to $7.5 billion, while total military spending was estimated to be around $18 billion ($90 billion in international prices). See Nicholas D. Kristof, "The Rise of China," *Foreign Affairs* 72 (November-December 1993): 59–74.

61. J. N. Mak and B. A. Hamzah, "Navy Blues," *Far Eastern Economic Review,* March 17, 1994, 30.

62. In 1994 Thailand alone was estimated to have as many as six hundred thousand HIV cases. See *Far Eastern Economic Review,* April 7, 1994, 12.

63. See, for example, Ross H. Munroe, "Awakening Dragon," *Policy Review* (fall 1992): 10–16.

64. To take just one example, after establishing full diplomatic relations in 1987, China and Laos signed a defense-cooperation agreement in 1993, following which China is reported to have supplied 1,600 tons of military hardware to Laos. See, Bertil Lintner and Muong Sing, "Ties That Bind," *Far Eastern Economic Review,* February 9, 1995, 18–19.

65. The bridge was opened on April 8, 1994. See Gordon Fairclough, "Spanning the Divide: A Bridge Brings Thailand and Laos Together," *Far Eastern Economic Review,* April 21, 1994, 23.

66. Northern Laos has benefited greatly from its improving relations with China, especially with the thriving Yunnan province. Thailand too has begun to play an important role in the Laotian economy.

67. Agreements between Siam (Thailand) and France pertaining to the water resources of the Lower Basin date back to 1826, and a legal regime to regulate the boundary line and use of the Mekong was established in 1926. However, international efforts in these directions did not begin until the end of World War II.

68. For a discussion of international politics that led to the choice of the Mekong as an area of focus for the bureau, see Lalita Prasad Singh, *The Politics of Economic Cooperation in Asia* (Columbia: University of Missouri Press, 1966).

69. Singh, "Prospects for Regional Stability," 129.

70. Between the 1920s and the 1950s, a number of international commissions were created by the Lower Basin riparian states; however, all had only sporadic operational existence. See *Encyclopedia of International Law* (Amsterdam: North-Holland, 1990), 12:225.

71. For a text of President Johnson's speech at the Johns Hopkins University on April 7, 1965, relating to his vision for the Mekong Basin, see Franklin Huddle, "The Mekong Project: Opportunities and Problems of Regionalism," in *Science, Technology, and American Diplomacy* (Washington, D.C.: U.S. Government Printing Office, 1977).

72. See Jeffery William Jacobs, " International River Basin Development and Climatic Change: The Lower Mekong of Southeast Asia" (Ph.D. diss., University of Colorado, Boulder, 1992), 125.

73. Gilbert F. White et al., "Economic and Social Aspects of Lower Mekong Development" (report to the Committe for Coordination of Investigations of the Lower Mekong Basin, 1962).

74. The proposed Pa Mong dam would have created a lake twice the size of that created by the Hoover Dam in the United States. It would have supplied enough water to irrigate 5 million acres in Thailand and Laos. Its power output would have been 20 billion kilowatt-hours—one and a half times the output of the Grand Coulee Dam, the largest hydroelectric project in the United States.

75. Paul Hadley and Murray Hiebert, "Hostile Undercurrents: Dispute Deepens over Use of Mekong River Water," *Far Eastern Economic Review*, April 2, 1994, 16.

76. China did send a representative to the 1991 plenary session of the Mekong Committee, held in Luang Prabang in Laos. For the first time since 1975, a U.S. representative also attended the session.

77. See Syed Kirmani, "Water, Peace, and Conflict Management: The Experience of the Indus and Mekong River Basins," *Water International*, 15 (1990): 200–205.

78. Larry Lohman, "Remaking the Mekong," *Ecologist* 20, no. 2 (March-April 1990): 61–66. Also see Steve Rothert, *Lessons Unlearned: Damming the Mekong River* (Berkeley, Calif.: International Rivers Network, October 1995).

79. See Rothert, *Lessons Unlearned*.

80. Jacobs, "International River Basin Development," 178.

81. Mekong Secretariat, *Progress Report* (Bangkok: Mekong Commission, 1993).

82. Reuters News Agency, "Six Countries Approve Joint Development Schemes," April 22, 1994.

83. Mekong Commission, *Agreement for Cooperation in the Sustainable Development of the Mekong River Basin* (Bangkok: Mekong Commission, April 1995).

CONCLUSION

1. See appendix II for a definition of *contingent generalization*.

2. John Waterbury, *Hydropolitics of the Nile Valley* (Syracuse, N.Y.: Syracuse University Press, 1979), 1.

3. See, for example, Jessica Tuchman Mathews, "Redefining Security," *Foreign Affairs* 67 (1989): 162–177; Caroline Thomas, *In Search of Security: The Third World in International Relations* (Boulder, Colo.: Lynne Reinner, 1987); Peter H. Gleick, "Environment and Security: Clear Connections," *Bulletin of the Atomic Scientist* 47, no. 3 (April 1991): 17–21; Arthur H. Westing, ed., *Global Resources and International Conflict: Environmental Factors in Strategic Policy and Action* (Oxford: Oxford University Press, 1986); Richard Ullman, "Redefining Security," *International Security* 8, no. 1 (summer 1983): 129–153; Norman Myers, *Ultimate Security: The Environmental Basis of Political Stability* (New York: W. W. Norton, 1993); Niles Peter Gleditsch, ed., *Conflict and Environment* (Dordrecht: Kluwer Academic Publishers, 1997); and Gunther Bachler and Kurt R. Spillman, eds., *Environmental Degradation as Cause of War: Regional and Country Studies*, vols. 2 and 3 (Berne: Swiss Peace Foundation and Swiss Federal Institute of Technology, 1996). For an extensive bibliography of literature linking environment, resources, and security, see Woodrow Wilson Center, *Environmental Change and Security Project Report*, issue 4 (spring 1998), 141–179.

4. Ted Hopf, "Identity and Security: Construction, Imposition, and Choice" (paper presented at the International Studies Association meeting, Washington, D.C., March 1994), 30.

5. During the 1991 war to evict Iraqi forces from Kuwait, even the United Nations is reported to have discussed using Turkish dams on the Euphrates to deprive Iraq of a significant portion of its freshwater supply. Gleick, "Environmental Security," 8.

6. See Daniel W. Bromley and Michael M. Cernea, *The Management of Common Property Resources: Some Conceptual and Operational Fallacies* (Washington, D.C.: World Bank, 1989.

7. Bruce Russett, *Grasping the Democratic Peace: Principles for a Post–Cold War World* (Princeton, N. J.: Princeton University Press, 1993). For a critical analysis of the idea of "democratic peace," see Ido Oren, "The Subjectivity of the 'Democratic' Peace: Changing U.S. Perceptions of Imperial Germany," *International Security* 20, no. 2 (fall 1995): 147–184.

8. For an interesting use of spy satellites for environmental causes, see Verne G. Kopytoff, "Tortoises Get Some Unusual Help from the Military's Spy Satellites," *New York Times*, May 14, 1996, C4. The Cooperative Monitoring Center (CSM) at the Sandia National Laboratory of the U.S. Department of Energy in Albuquerque, New Mexico, is pioneering a major effort to apply military technologies to environmental and resource problems, including problems of water sharing in international river basins. Information on CSM's programs is available from Cooperative Monitoring Center, Sandia National Laboratory, P.O. Box 5800, Albuquerque, NM 87185-1373.

9. United Nations General Assembly, *Convention on the Law of the Non-navigational Uses of International Water Courses*, A/RES/51/229 (New York: United Nations, July 8, 1997).

APPENDIX II

1. Based on Thomas Homer-Dixon, "On the Threshold: Environmental Changes as Causes of Acute Conflict," *International Security* 16, no. 2 (1991): 76–116.

2. Alexander L. George and Richard Smoke, "Appendix: Theory for Policy in International Relations," in *Deterrence in American Foreign Policy: Theory and Practice* (New York: Columbia University Press, 1974), 636.

3. M. Krepon and Dan Caldwell, eds., *The Politics of Arms Control Treaty Ratification* (New York: St. Martin's Press, 1991), 6.

4. Ibid.

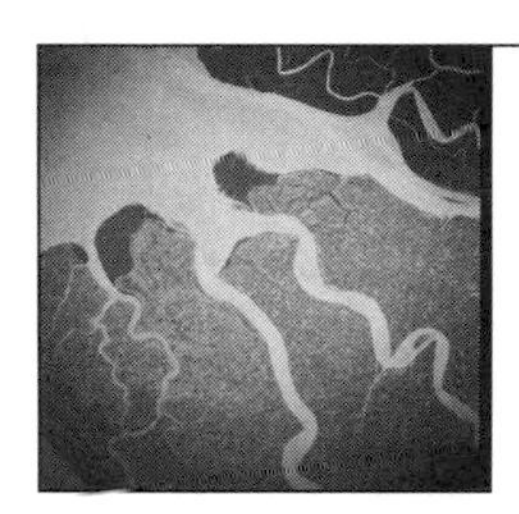

INDEX

Arun P. Elhance has been an assistant professor of geography at the University of Illinois at Urbana-Champaign; co-director of the Program on International Peace and Security and director of the Program on Global Environmental Change at the Social Science Research Council in New York; and senior fellow at the International Peace Academy in New York. He has published extensively on issues related to environment, development, and security.

UNITED STATES INSTITUTE OF PEACE

The United States Institute of Peace is an independent, nonpartisan federal institution created by Congress to promote research, education, and training on the peaceful resolution of international conflicts. Established in 1984, the Institute meets its congressional mandate through an array of programs, including research grants, fellowships, professional training programs, conferences and workshops, library services, publications, and other educational activities. The Institute's Board of Directors is appointed by the President of the United States and confirmed by the Senate.

Jennings Randolph Program for International Peace

This book is a fine example of the work produced by senior fellows in the Jennings Randolph fellowship program of the United States Institute of Peace. As part of the statute establishing the Institute, Congress envisioned a program that would appoint "scholars and leaders of peace from the United States and abroad to pursue scholarly inquiry and other appropriate forms of communication on international peace and conflict resolution." The program was named after Senator Jennings Randolph of West Virginia, whose efforts over four decades helped to establish the Institute.

Since 1987, the Jennings Randolph Program has played a key role in the Institute's efforts to build a national center of research, dialogue, and education on critical problems of conflict and peace. More than a hundred senior fellows from some thirty nations have carried out projects on the sources and nature of violent international conflict and the ways such conflict can be peacefully managed or resolved. Fellows come from a wide variety of academic and other professional backgrounds. They conduct research at the Institute and participate in the Institute's outreach activities to policymakers, the academic community, and the American public.

Each year approximately fifteen senior fellows are in residence at the Institute. Fellowship recipients are selected by the Institute's board of directors in a competitive process. For further information on the program, or to receive an application form, please contact the program staff at (202) 457-1700.

Joseph Klaits
Director

HYDROPOLITICS IN THE THIRD WORLD

This book is set in Goudy; the display type is Rotis Sans Serif. Marie Marr designed the book's cover, and Joan Engelhardt and Day Dosch designed the interior. Pages were made up by Day Dosch. David Sweet copyedited the text, which was proofread by M. Kate St. Clair. The index was prepared by Frances Bowles. The book's editor was Nigel Quinney.